IRON MAIDEN

RUN TO THE HILLS

THE AUTHORISED BIOGRAPHY ◆ 3RD EDITION

Visit the Iron Maiden website at: www.ironmaiden.com

Contact the Iron Maiden Fan Club via e-mail at:
fanclub@ironmaiden.co.uk

Or by post at:
Iron Maiden Fan Club
PO Box 3803
Harlow
Essex CM20 2BW
UK

Tel/fax: +44 (0)1279 442 666

Printed in the United Kingdom by MPG Books Ltd, Bodmin

Distributed in the US by Publishers Group West

Published by Sanctuary Publishing Limited, Sanctuary House, 45–53
Sinclair Road, London W14 0NS, United Kingdom

Chapter 16 written by Dave Ling
Chapters 17–22 written by Chris Ingham

Cover artwork by Peacock Design

Photographs: Ross Halfin, Simon Fowler, George Chin, Robert Ellis,
Denis O'Regan, Tony Mottram, Mark Weiss, Masa Itah, Dimo Safari
and Lawrence Watson. Illustrations of Eddie by Derek Riggs, used
courtesy of Iron Maiden.

ISBN: 1-86074-542-3

RUN TO THE HILLS

THE AUTHORISED BIOGRAPHY ◆ 3RD EDITION

MICK WALL

Sanctuary

This book could simply not have been written without the help, patience, love and understanding of the three most important Maidens in my life: Linda, Annie and Diana. And the Iron men behind the scenes: Gerry and Colin.

Thanks also to Dave Ling, who went to a great deal of effort to see the band in practically every part of the world over an 18-month period.

Thank you all.

Contents

Foreword

This book was written by Mick Wall, someone respected enough by the band for us to want him to take on the task. A fan and friend of Maiden for many years, Mick decided to approach not just the current members but also past members of the band, plus management, agents and past and present members of the crew for the material for this book. It makes interesting reading, even for me, because everybody has a different view of how things have happened over the years!

I hope you enjoy this book as much as I did. It hasn't been edited in any way, which is how it should be.

Cheers.

Steve Harris,
Essex

Introduction

The book you now hold in your hands is the result of an imperfect attempt by one man to tell the full, unexpurgated story of Iron Maiden. I say "imperfect" because it would take several volumes to go into absolutely every single little detail, occurrence or memory that I eventually managed to unearth from my extensive travels into the past and present lives of the extraordinary group of individuals that have made the Maiden story what it is. And anyone expecting a blow-by-blow, who-played-what-instrument-on-which-track account of their music is going to be sorely disappointed.

The same goes, really, for the endless parade of "party stories" I compiled along the way. It will hardly come as news to discover that Maiden and their crew spent a good deal of their "offstage" time on their earliest tours bingeing on booze and groupies. Instead, I wanted to write a book about the really big events in the story of Iron Maiden. So, when it comes to the rock 'n' roll, yes, each album gets re-examined and discussed, but it is the historical worth of these releases that I was most concerned with establishing more than the mere technical details. All Maiden fans have their favourite songs and albums; we don't need to agree on all of them. What this book tries to do is put them into some overall picture that makes sense and perhaps explains why and how these records got to be made in the way they did in the first place.

As for the sex and the drugs, instead of racking up a list of "and then we got the fire extinguishers out"-type anecdotes – the kind that, admittedly, liberally sprinkled the features I wrote on the band for *Kerrang!* in the '80s – this book concentrates more on the behind-the-scenes side-effects of the so-called "good times", how they cost at least two members of the band their jobs and how – paradoxically, in the case of original singer, Paul Di'Anno –

his failure to keep it together actually allowed Maiden to become even more successful when they surprisingly replaced him, two albums into their career, with the more ambitious Bruce Dickinson, an enforced move that would prove crucial in transforming them from the promising New Wave Of British Heavy Metal band they were with Paul into the enormodome-eating, mega-monster US rock stars they became with Bruce.

But that's just one part of the story I wanted to investigate. I also wanted to go behind the scenes in the boardroom and find out how and what prompted the decisions made by their management and their record-company chiefs that would have their own irreversible impact on their story. No matter how talented you are, someone still has to push the buttons somewhere. For the first time, this book talks to the button-pushers: major-league players like Capitol's A&R chief in the early '80s and later EMI president, Rupert Perry, and of course the band's own long-serving and charismatic Sanctuary management team, led by ex-Cambridge drop-out Rod Smallwood. Between them, they were able to raise the necessary level of both funds and enthusiasm to keep the band going until the band's third album, *Number Of The Beast*, took their financial position out of the red for the first time in their careers. I wanted to know just what it took to turn a backstreet East End pub band with talent and ambition into a multi-million-dollar industry.

And of course I wanted to talk to the band themselves, both the current line-up and as many of their previous members as I could track down. This I found hugely enlightening, from ex-singer Paul Di'Anno's cheerfully philosophical confession that "I know you've probably heard a lot of naughty things about me, mate, but the thing is, they're all true!" to Dennis Stratton's lengthy, earnest reasons why, frankly, he blew it, even though he still insists to this day that it wasn't really his fault. And, of course, most powerfully of all, the recollections of both Steve Harris and Bruce Dickinson, embodying perhaps the most volatile, creative and ultimately self-destructive relationship the band has ever endured. From a distance, in the '80s, it looked like Maiden had it all sewn up. However, as you'll discover from reading this book, nothing could have been further from the truth.

And while here in the post-Bruce years the band have shed some of their cachet with the critics in Britain, it's interesting to note that, with former Wolfsbane singer Blaze Bayley now fronting them, Maiden have begun to make some of their most challenging and brutally honest material ever. So, too, in this book, you'll find the band and everyone else I spoke to at their most brutally honest, and as far as possible I have allowed everyone to have their say, both pro and con, so that as many sides of the various stories are represented as possible. The picture that emerges is both hilarious in parts and deeply unsettling in others, the magnificent highs and bottom-of-the-well lows faithfully recorded for all to enjoy from a safe distance.

In looking at their past, most of all I hope to be able not just to explain the whys and the wherefores of Maiden's present but also to try and map out a vision of what the future now holds in store for both the band and their fans. For a band that has never been played on daytime radio, a band that refused to do *Top Of The Pops* for 15 years and whose single 'Angel And The Gambler' is over ten minutes long, I'd say that this is an achievement that speaks for itself.

The original late-'70s punks always talked about never selling out. How ironic, then, that it was a heavy-metal band from the same era that actually put that philosophy into practice to such devastating effect. Fifty million record sales later, Maiden have yet to write their first real love song, or indeed have the word "baby" inscribed in the lyrics of any of their 40-plus hit singles. That fact alone would be enough for me to want to write about them. The fact that they have also been largely ignored by the mainstream rock media merely adds piquancy to the dish. Here's a band deserving of everybody's respect and attention whose story has never been told properly before. This book is my honest attempt to try and do something about that. Whether I've succeeded or not is something that you'll have to decide for me. But, like the band itself, a lot of blood and guts and love went into this book, and I hope it rocks your socks off.

From one fan to another, with all the respect you deserve.

Mick Wall,
Oxfordshire

1 *Steve*

The story of Iron Maiden is not one that can be properly told by any one person, which is why, in this book, you'll find myriad voices from the band's past and present all doing their best to tell their sides of this complex and fascinating tale as honestly and as accurately as they can. Sometimes the various accounts are contradictory, an inevitable and no less rewarding result of the different personalities, opinions and backgrounds that have been involved in the making of this historic rock band.

And yes, it may be that some of the deeper truths of the Maiden story will only reveal themselves – both to the band and to its followers – after carefully reading between the lines, balancing the various accounts and deciding for ourselves what the *real* story is. As the old Chinese proverb goes, the more that is revealed, the less you see clearly. Or, as guitarist Dave Murray – who, along with founding member Steve Harris, is one of the only survivors of the band that originally signed to EMI Records back in 1979 – said at one stage while he was being interviewed for this book, "I can't wait to read it and find out what it is we've actually been up to all these years."

That said, the real story of Iron Maiden begins and ends with the dreams and ambitions of one man, Steve Harris. It was he who came up with the name, the songs, the idea and the attitude, and it is he that's been making sure that Maiden stick to their chosen task, come hell or high water, ever since. Indeed, there wouldn't be any story to tell if it hadn't been for 'Arry, as the band affectionately know him, and the intense vision he had for "a rock band that would make great albums, put on superb live concerts and never, ever sell out", as he puts it.

Team captain, sergeant major, leader of the gang – Steve Harris is all of those things to Iron Maiden. Tough, tattooed and uncompromising, he's only about five feet eight inches tall, but he's not the sort of bloke you'd want to have a fight with. Not unless you were prepared for a fight to the death. And that's how he's approached his career in Iron Maiden, as a fight to the death, first against the prevailing late-'70s conformity of punk and then, in the '80s, against mainstream, MTV-orientated corporate rock. These days, the fight is against time, the need to prove that Maiden is as vital, as interesting and as exciting as ever, despite the changes in line-up, the trend swings and the general feeling that maybe, yes, this time hard rock and heavy metal really are dead.

Not so, says Steve Harris, strapping on his bass guitar. Fuck you, says Iron Maiden. "We will prevail" – it's been Maiden's message from the very beginning, and now, as the pendulum begins to swing back in the direction of senses-shattering, arena-sized rock with a capital R, the 21st century is gonna have to start getting used to it, too. That is, if Steve Harris has got anything to do with it. And, as you'll discover from reading this book, he usually has…

Born in Leytonstone, east London, "in my nan's back room" on 12 March 1956, Steve Harris grew up the eldest of four children but the only boy. "I've got three sisters, all younger than me," he says. "My dad was a truck driver and my mum was a full-time mum. She did a couple of sideline jobs, but most of the time she was looking after the four of us. My dad also had four younger sisters who were always about the place, plus my nan on my mum's side, so I grew up in a house surrounded by women.

"Looking back, I suppose it might be one of the reasons why I got into music as well, because there was always music on in the house. My sisters and their friends were always dancing about to records – The Beatles, Simon And Garfunkel, all that kind of stuff. I don't know whether I liked it or not at first; it was just always on in the background. Then, as I started to grow up, I decided I *did* like it. I can remember all the words to some of those songs, even now, so I obviously took it all in."

Before music, however, there was sport. A keen footballer, cricketer and tennis player, as a schoolboy Steve dreamed of becoming a professional footballer, preferably for his beloved West Ham United, a local east London club which at that time featured England World Cup winners Bobby Moore, Geoff Hurst and Martin Peters in their first team. "I used to play football in the street, either with mates or just kicking a ball against a wall. If I didn't have a ball, a tin can down the alley would do. I was always out playing with my mates, and music didn't really come into it, then. In fact, I should think football was the first thing I probably felt strongly about."

Steve's first speculative visit to a football match came when he was nine years old and an older pal took him to see West Ham play at their home ground, nearby Upton Park. "You could just jump on a bus and get over there," he recalls, "so we did, on our own – no grown-ups – and then saw them beat Newcastle four-three. And that was it. I was hit. A Hammers fan, totally! My dad and grandad were Leyton Orient supporters [another local East End team], and they were well pissed off when they found out. But my dad was always away driving, and they never actually took me to a game, so it was their own fault I turned out a West Ham fan. I had the replica shirt and everything."

Football was to become the focus of Steve's life for the next seven years, as he strived to make his dream of actually becoming a West Ham player come true. Passionate in everything he did, the dream consumed his every thought as a child. "I played football for the school team, as well as tennis. I liked music and drawing, but football was always number one for me, as a kid. I remember watching the World Cup final between England and West Germany, in 1966. I was 'round a mate's house, and I distinctly remember the first German goal going in and writhing about the floor, thinking, 'Oh my God, it's all over! The end of the world!' I can still see it: black-and-white TV in the corner of the room and a goldfish tank beside it. That was annoying, 'cause it was in colour! I remember that as if it was yesterday."

By the time he had begun his secondary education at Leyton High, Steve was playing for the school football team every Saturday and for a private local amateur club, Beaumont Youth, every Sunday. "I suppose I was about twelve or 13 by then. I played in every single position, except for centre-half and goalkeeper, and that was only because I was too small, but usually I would play on the wing, 'cause I could run really fast with the ball. We had a good side at Beaumont. Of the eleven lads who regularly turned out for the first team, about seven or eight of us ended up on different professional clubs' books. We actually played against Orient Youth once and beat them five-one. My dad and uncle came over to watch and Orient scored after about 30 seconds and we went, 'Bloody hell, they're shit hot.' And then we won five-one! I scored two of the goals, so Dad was really pleased. At that point, we started saying to ourselves, 'Hold on a minute, we're beating professional youth-club sides,' and I started to think about the possibility of maybe turning professional myself."

Soon the talented teenager had caught the attention of a little-known but locally legendary old East End footie scout by the name of Wally St Pier. This was no mean feat, according to Steve: "He was, like, this mythical figure lurking about the place. No one ever knew if he was there or not, but apparently he watched me play two or three times, or whatever, and then I got a request, via Beaumont, to go down and train for West Ham. I was 14 and I couldn't believe it! The bloke who used to run the club just came over and told me. I was, as they say, completely over the moon, Brian. When I first went to West Ham, though, I was shitting myself, to be honest. But luckily enough, there was another bloke I knew from the club, Keith Taylor, who was chosen to go down as well. I still see him sometimes. Even my dad was over the moon. He made a joke about it, being West Ham, but he was well pleased. It was exciting stuff, at the time."

But the reality of training twice a week at Upton Park forced Steve to open his eyes to what making it as a pro footballer actually entailed. He was also developing tastes for new things that were entirely detrimental to the fitness-first pursuit of a would-be professional sportsman. "The thing about becoming a professional footballer is, you have to be incredibly dedicated. It's a bit like becoming a monk, and that's hard when you're just 14 or 15. You're just at that age when all your mates are starting to go out and enjoy themselves and you know you can't. I wanted to start going out and meeting birds and having a drink and a laugh with my mates, but I was training every day of the week – twice a week at West Ham, once for the school team, then with the Sunday side. The only day I wasn't actually training, it was the Games period at school, and that was football as well. On top of that, I was playing three games every weekend. It was unbelievable. I was so fit, it was incredible, but you don't realise that at the time.

"What I did realise was that it wasn't really what I wanted to do, which was a bit of a shock, in a way. Ever since I was eight or nine, from the first

West Ham game I went to, I thought, 'This is what I want to be.' My little son now, he's only seven, but he's, like, 'I wanna be a footballer when I grow up.' And I was the same. And then, when you get down there, you find you've got to be really dedicated, or it's just a waste of time. There were a lot of very talented players that didn't stick at it. I didn't think I was any worse or any better than any of the other players at the time. I just thought, 'I can't do this. I can't be dedicated to this.' And I thought, 'If I can't be dedicated to something I love, what is it I really want to do, then?'

"But my parents didn't push me too hard. Some parents really push you, but mine didn't do that at all. I tried to push myself, but I just thought, 'I don't really want to do this.' It was such a shock to realise that. I completely gave up football for about a year after that, and it freaked me out. Like, "What *am* I gonna do?"

Steve would eventually return to playing football after a year or so and really enjoy it again. "I was playing just for the enjoyment of it. I started playing again for a club I used to play for, Melbourne Sports, and I've been playing for them, off and on, right up till this season."

By now, though, he knew what he wanted to do, now that he'd given up his dream of being the next Geoff Hurst. He'd decided that he was going to be a rock star. He'd already started growing his hair. "At the football, people used to call me Georgie Best, because of my hair being so long, but it was nothing to do with George Best. It was more to do with Chris Squire, out of Yes. My hair was never an issue until I went to join a tennis club when I was about 16 and straight away this bloke said to me, 'Oh, your hair's a bit long, isn't it?' And I went, 'Listen, before we start, my dad doesn't even tell me to get my hair cut, so I'm not taking it from you.' He said, 'Well, there's no need to be like that.' And I said, 'Well, don't be telling me about my hair,' and I got up and walked out and that was it. I didn't play tennis for quite a while after that. I don't know whether that would have happened in football, with the dress codes they impose on you when you sign professionally, but I did have this big thing, at that time, about not getting my hair cut. It was just the principle."

Music, the one occupation that would allow Steve to express himself *and* keep his hair long, was the obvious answer. "I didn't actually start playing guitar till I was 17, but I'd been buying records on and off since I was 14 or 15. The very first record I ever had was bought for me. I was only about five at the time and I asked my mum and dad to buy the theme from *Exodus*. I just loved that piece of music. I think I've actually still got the record somewhere. It's a real epic, the sort of thing I've always got off on. So really, from that time onwards, once in a while I used to go out getting records. But I was 14 when I actually bought my first album, a compilation album of all these reggae hits, 'Monkey Spanner' by Dave And Ansel Collins and 'Big Five' by Judge Dread, all that kind of stuff."

It was 1970, a time when reggae, bizarrely, had become the music of preference for the first generation of British skinheads. Reggae music and Ben Sherman shirts, Doctor Marten boots and tartan-lined black Harrington jackets were the order of the day down Steve's way. "Most of us were what you'd call skinheads, I suppose," he admits. "I wasn't necessarily a great fan of all that. I only really bought the album because you had to learn a few of the steps, you know, to throw the shapes at parties. If you didn't know the shapes, you didn't get the birds. None of us were really, totally into it. It was just that that was what was going on. I didn't actually have the haircut, of course. No, I never had the number-one crew-cut, but I used to have all the gear – the Doc Martens, the two-tone tonic trousers with turn-ups and the braces, all that stuff. And then you graduated into the round-collar shirts with the tank-tops and the flares and that sort of stuff, and then it went from that to grandad shirts and getting the loon pants and the wooden crosses and getting into Free and Black Sabbath."

Steve got friendly with a pal called Pete Dayle and they used to spend hours at Pete's house, playing chess or Subbuteo "and listening to all these weird fucking albums that he had, stuff I'd never heard of before, and I'd be thinking, 'What's this?'" Mainly, "this" was albums by progressive rock artists such as Jethro Tull, King Crimson and Genesis. "He'd just put them on in the background. Everyone used to spend all their money on football gear, and he used to spend his money on albums and really good hi-fi stuff. At first, I thought, 'This bloke's weird.' But then, I'd start hearing some of these albums again and again and some of it would start to interest me and I'd ask him all about them, and he'd be, like, 'Well, this is a bit of Jethro Tull and that was a bit of Yes.' It was all early Genesis, Black Sabbath, Deep Purple, Led Zeppelin. Some of it I sort of thought, 'Yeah, that's interesting,' and other stuff, I thought, 'That's fucking weird.'"

The turning point came when Pete allowed Steve to borrow a couple of albums and have a listen to them properly at home. "I borrowed a Jethro Tull album, *Stand Up*, and I think an early Genesis album and a Deep Purple album. They blew me away. I was, like, 'I've seen the light, man!' Especially the Tull and the Genesis stuff. I just couldn't believe how good it was. Pete had said to me, 'You've got to listen to it two or three times. The first time you listen, you won't take it all in.' So I listened to it a few times and I couldn't believe how good it was. Stuff like 'Musical Box' [from the 1971 Genesis album *Nursery Cryme*]. I mean, even now it still gives me goosebumps, listening to it."

To this day, press Steve Harris on what his all-time favourite albums are – besides the Iron Maiden collection – and he'll come straight back at you with *Foxtrot* by Genesis, probably *Recycled* by Nektar and "I don't know, probably a Jethro Tull album". He admits that, when he tells Iron Maiden fans this ("They always ask what your favourite album is"), he is usually met with blank looks. "I got a letter back from a couple once that I'd met in Winterthur, Switzerland, and they said they'd bought all those albums and given them a try but that it all sounds so dated now, and so I wrote back saying, 'Perhaps you had to be there, you know,' because it just completely changed my life, really. I thought it was fucking amazing. And the next step was I immediately wanted to have a go at trying to play this stuff myself."

What he originally had in mind was a crash course in drums, "but I thought, 'Well, I can't get drums, 'cause I ain't got room for 'em and it's just too noisy.'" In the end, he settled for a cheap, old, acoustic guitar. "I thought I'd do the next best thing to drums and get a bass guitar and start playing along with the drums, but someone said to me, 'No, you've really got to learn to play acoustic guitar first,' and I didn't know any different so I went and bought myself an acoustic guitar and learned a few chords, which is when I realised that this had nothing to do with bass. So I traded it in and got myself a Fender copy bass – 40 quid – and that was it."

Another school pal, Dave Smith, showed him the four basic guitar chords that he would need to play rock – E, A, D and G – and Steve began to practise on his bass every day. "Once I got my hands on the bass, something just clicked and I knew I could do it. It was, like, 'Fuck learning chords. Just hit the strings,' you know? And it was wonderful. I just immediately got into making these really weird sounds, way down low. And I think bass is just easier to pick up than guitar, which is quite hard to play properly, really. You can learn to play a bass line like 'Smoke On The Water' a lot quicker than you can learn the chord changes, and those are the simplest chord changes of all. I just loved it. I thought, 'This is for me.' I did get a few books – I got a few songbooks – but, of course, at that time, none of them had anything in there for bass. It was all just for guitar, and even the ones that did have bass notes in were usually wrong."

Sensible enough to steer clear of the overly-technical neo-classical musical marathons in which Yes and Genesis then specialised, he began by trying to play along to easier-to-follow rock hits of the day, such as Purple's aforementioned 'Smoke On The Water' and 'All Right Now' by Free. "Just simple bass lines," he admits. "Well, I say simple, but some of Andy Fraser's bass lines for Free were never simple at all, but to begin with I stuck to the more basic ones, the blues-based stuff. I distinctly remember trying to play along to 'Paranoid' by Black Sabbath. I just could not get it. I threw the guitar on my bed and walked out in a huff, but then the next day I came back, picked it up and played it all the way through, note for note. Once I got going, I started getting into bass lines with a bit more subtlety to them, and I started trying to be a bit clever and trying to learn stuff by Chris Squire and people like that, which I didn't get too far with for quite a while."

Steve had been plucking away at his Fender copy for just ten months when he persuaded Dave Smith to form a band with him. "We were called Influence," says Steve. "Dave was a year older than me and played the guitar. The vocalist was a bloke called Bob Verschoyle, who I used to play football with, and he just thought he'd have a try at vocals. And he weren't bad, as it goes. Then this other bloke called Tim – I can't remember his second name – played rhythm guitar and the drummer was a guy called Paul Sears, who was shit hot. He was a really good drummer. He was better than the rest of us put together. He'd been around, played a few club tours and this and that, and he was a couple of years older than the rest of us. He'd started at quite an early age, and he was really good. He used to play really like Simon Kirk, out of Free and Bad Company. He used to thrash the fuck out of the drums, and I loved it."

There were, of course, precious few gigs to be had at that stage, but a great deal of time was spent practising around Steve's nan's house, bashing out favoured hits of the day of which they thought they might be able to muster passable imitations.

Steve: "We did a couple of Who numbers and 'I'm A Mover' by Free. Then, later on, I did Free's 'Mr Big', because then I could do a bass solo. We'd do a couple of originals with stupid titles, like 'Heat-Crazed Vole', which Paul, the singer, wrote, and one called 'Endless Pit', which I came up with the riff for and which actually ended up being the riff to 'Innocent Exile', which eventually ended up on the second Maiden album. I think Bob wrote the lyrics to one of the other songs. I can't think what it was, though.

"We used to rehearse in my nan's back room, and it was quite funny, really, because I used to worry that we'd disturb the woman next door with all the noise, but my nan was hard as nails and she was always, like, 'I don't give a shit what she thinks. If she comes 'round to moan about it, tell her to fuck off!' Tough as old boots, my nan. Then, one day, she came back from the pub and said she'd just seen the woman from next door and said she asked her about the noise, whether it disturbed her, and the old girl went, 'Oh, no, I don't hear a thing. I'm a bit mutton [deaf], dear.'"

Their one and only gig as Influence was at a local talent contest in nearby Poplar, where "we only had to play for about 15 minutes, which was great, because we only really had about four songs we could play, and we did the only three originals we had. It was just like an old little village church hall, and we came second! The band that won it were a sort of Osmonds-style thing – you know, terrible. Mind you, we weren't much better. I was so nervous that I fucked up this long intro we'd worked out for the opening number, and Bob, the singer, thought I was tuning up and didn't come in when he was supposed to, so I had to start again. This time, we all came in at the right time, and everyone thought it was part of the song anyway, so we got away with it. But it was terrible, really. We didn't get paid or anything. We were cheap in them days! I think there were about five or six entries, so it wasn't a major thing or anything, and there weren't that many people lurking."

Influence may not have come first, but they did make one important new friend that night, the promoter of the contest, David Beazley, soon to be known under the more Maiden-friendly soubriquet Dave Lights. "I lived in a church vicarage called the Bridgehouse, which was also a community centre," says Dave, "and I'd been putting on, like, youth-club nights since I was 15. This particular night – it must have been in about 1973 – I'd decided I was going to do a talent contest, and Steve and his band entered. They came in second. The winners were some band whose parents had put loads of money into them – two girls and boys, a sort of family-orientated Abba-type thing – but of course, being a bit of a rocker myself, I thought Steve's lot were easily the best thing that night, and so we got talking."

As luck would have it, Steve's girlfriend at that time, Lorraine, had been to school with Dave's girlfriend, Kim, and soon they were all going out together, often to a pub Steve was very fond of on the Barking Road, beneath the Canning Town flyover – also, ironically, called the Bridgehouse – which nearly always featured a live band. Indeed, Lorraine's first date with Steve, whom she had known since their school days, involved a night out at the Bridgehouse to see some friends of his play in a band.

By the time they were offered their second gig, some weeks later, at a pub called the Cart and Horses in Maryland Point, Stratford, Steve had changed his mind about the name of his new band, ditching the Influence moniker in favour of something "a bit more entertaining, a bit more up, 'cause we were trying to get some gigs and Influence sounded a bit frowny. It didn't sound like a good time, you know?" So they changed the name in time for their next gig to Gypsy's Kiss, which in Cockney rhyming slang means "piss", as in "I'm going for a Gypsy's". Whatever the name, this first band was destined to last just a handful of gigs before juddering to a halt. "We did three gigs at the Cart and Horses pub," Steve recalls, "and two at the Bridgehouse in Canning Town, and then we split up! Musical differences." He laughs about it now, but he admits that he didn't find the demise of Gypsy's Kiss so funny at the time: "The truth is, I can't remember what the real reason was we never stayed together, but we folded up, basically. It just sort of petered out after that. I suppose the others lost interest, or whatever. A lot of these things do, at that age. You do five gigs at 18 and it's like you've done the lot, for some people. They're happy then. That's all they want, a taste. But a taste wasn't enough for me. I really enjoyed doing gigs and I wanted it to last forever."

The idea of finding another four musicians was, at the time, a daunting prospect for the novice bassist. "Basically, they were the only ones I knew, and they'd all sort of vanished," Steve admits. Ever resourceful, he decided that the best way forward was to try and join up with an already established band. Nothing too fancy (yet), just someone that took the idea of playing gigs on a regular basis as seriously as he did. He thought that he'd found what he was looking for when he teamed up with an older bunch of guys in a band called Smiler.

Led by two twin brothers called Tony and Mick Clee, both guitarists, Steve auditioned for them at a pub called the White Hart in Enfield in February 1974. "The idea was to try and get into a band with people who were already a bit further down the line than me, because I wanted to start learning things, I wanted to get on, and Smiler were fairly well established on the pub scene. They'd done a few gigs, they had a set together and I was shitting myself going for the audition. This was the first audition I'd ever been to, so of course I said to them, 'Well, I've done a lot of work already with various bands,' you know, giving it the big 'un, as we say. I was still only 18 and they were all, like, 26, which I thought was really old at the time.

"I asked what sort of stuff they were doing, and one of them said, 'Well, we do a bit of Wishbone Ash and we do a Free song and something by Savoy Brown.' It was a bit more boogie sort of stuff than I was used to, but that was good, because I had to go home and learn stuff, and I actually got on quite well with it. They were playing lots with twin-neck guitars. They were very into that whole Wishbone Ash thing.

"So I thought, 'Yeah, this is all right,' and I got the job with them, and I had to learn a whole hour-and-a-quarter set. It was all covers – there was one original, I think, but again it was a boogie-based sort of thing, straight twelve-bar. And so that was a really good experience, plunging in and having to actually learn a whole set, and we were literally gigging within a few weeks. I was really thrown in at the deep end, but I liked it. No messing. And we went down well. That sort of stuff goes down really well in pubs, anyway. It's easy to tap your foot to."

However, a problem occurred when, within a few weeks of Steve playing his first pub dates with the band, "the drummer wanted to leave, because the band were getting offered more and more gigs and he simply couldn't give them the time". So Smiler began looking around for a new drummer, and that's when Steve first met a young drummer by the name of Doug Sampson, who would later be among Iron Maiden's earliest recruits.

Born in Hackney on 30 June 1957, Doug Sampson auditioned for Smiler in 1975 at the age of 18. The audition took place in a room behind a pub somewhere near Chingford, north London. "We did have other drummers," says Steve, "and, if I'm totally honest, the others were technically better than Doug. But Doug was a herbert, a bit of a geezer, a bit of a laugh – you knew it as soon as he walked in – so we took to him more. He was a good drummer, don't get me wrong, but his attitude and his persona fitted in better. The band was called Smiler, after all, and that was Doug – always smiling."

"The band played bluesy, boogie-derived stuff," Doug recalls, "mainly covers of Savoy Brown, Wishbone Ash and ZZ Top. The twins were in charge, but Steve obviously had some ideas of his own, too. It was my first proper band. Before Smiler, I'd played in small bands with mates from school. No one that would have stuck out. Just doing mainly rock stuff – Cream, Hendrix, that sort of thing."

With Doug safely on board, Smiler struck out once again on the east London pub circuit. They were starting to include occasional snatches of the twins' original material into the set, and Steve began experimenting for the first time with "maybe writing something of my own". Up until then, the band had relied on one brother or the other to provide the lead vocals. At that time, however, it was decided that a "real" singer should be brought in to do justice to the new songs that they were hoping to include in the set.

Placing an ad in *Melody Maker*, they ended up recruiting one Dennis Wilcock, another future member of Iron Maiden, albeit a short-lived one. Steve remembers the changes: "We started to pull a few people in and I started to write a couple of songs here and there, trying to pull in some more hard rock. I got them to do 'Rock Candy' by Montrose and stuff like that, and we did do an early version of 'Innocent Exile' – which was now called 'Innocent Exile' – and there was 'Burning Ambition', another version of which ended up being the first B-side of the first Maiden single, 'Running Free'.

"Then, when I started writing a couple of other things that were a bit more like what I'd eventually get into with Maiden, they said, 'Ah, no. There's too many time changes in it.' They didn't say, 'We're not going to do it.' They just didn't show enough enthusiasm for it, and I just thought, 'I'm gonna have to leave. I'm gonna have to form my own band, 'cause I think these songs are pretty good.'"

When Steve jumped ship, Doug was invited to join him in his new band, but the drummer was hesitant. "Doug Sampson left Smiler with me, but it was a while before we played together again," says Steve. "We were getting on well together, and we were a great rhythm section, and I thought I owed it to him to let him know what was on my mind. I didn't ask him to leave with me; I just said to him, 'Look, this is what I'm gonna do. I'm telling you because you're my mate, but you do whatever you want,' because the band had got stuff going on, they had gigs happening, and all they had to do was replace me and carry on. I don't know why, but he just said, 'Oh, fuck it. I've had enough and I'm leaving as well.'

"So, basically, that was it, and I left to form my own band. But I didn't have any other musicians or anybody involved at that time. I thought I was just going to write some songs and try and get some people together, so I couldn't offer Doug a job or anything, you know? It was just, basically, 'I'll call you up sometime in the future if anything happens,' or whatever. But then he joined another band, and I think I actually got the Maiden thing together and he wasn't actually available, so I ended up getting Ron Matthews."

Doug Sampson recalls being asked to join Steve in his new band, but says now that he declined, as "it wasn't just Smiler I'd had enough of, really. I was just a bit fed up with the whole rock band thing, at that point. I was completely skint and I had to get some money in, so I decided to get a job." He got one making vending machines, but before long "the bug bit again, as it always does, sooner or later" and he joined a band called Janski, "which specialised in playing covers of The Eagles and Latin rock type stuff".

Starting again from scratch but using the East End contacts he had built up in Smiler to help him, Steve spent the latter weeks of 1975 putting together what would become the first-ever line-up of Iron Maiden. Formed on Christmas Day 1975, the original band was in fact

Steve (bass), Dave Sullivan (guitar), Ron "Rebel" Matthews (drums), Paul Day (vocals) and Terry Rance (guitar).

Steve: "Well, Ron and Dave... I can't remember if it was an ad in the paper or a friend of a friend or what. I can't remember now how they came into it. I know Terry used to play in a poppy sort of band, and he found out about us through word of mouth or an ad in the paper – everything was based around the *Melody Maker*, in those days; it was the one for all the phone numbers for the gigs and the ads there for the musos in the back – and Paul Day was, basically, just another local herbert who fancied having a go at singing. He was pretty good, actually. He ended up being in a band called More, who funnily enough supported Maiden on a European tour a bit later on."

Dave Sullivan and Terry Rance were Walthamstow boys, East End born and bred, who'd known each other for years. For a while, before joining forces with Steve Harris, they were briefly in a band together called The Tinted Aspects, which Dave now characterises as "one of those bands, the biggest gig they play is in the bedroom. Terry was a bit older than me, and he'd played in a couple of different bands, I think. Then we started writing together, just stuff that never really got played live. The Tinted Aspects didn't last long. Then Terry answered an ad in the *Melody Maker* and I just sort of tagged along. I suppose I was about 21 at the time. I was a bit of a late starter, actually. I only started playing the guitar when I was 17, and it all went rather quickly.

"I was into heavy rock, maybe not quite so hard-edged as the way Maiden was starting to go. To begin with, we did a lot of covers – Wishbone Ash, Thin Lizzy, anything that you could work a sort of dual lead guitar thing into it – and it was developing reasonably well. It was still quite raw, but the makings was all there."

Sullivan recalls that their audition for the band involved a run-through of 'Smoke On The Water'. "It was, like, one take, and they went, 'Yeah, good enough. You're in.' There was Steve and Ron first, then there was me and Terry, and almost at the same time Steve said he had a singer in mind. I can't remember whether Paul [Day] was there when we auditioned, but Steve already had Paul in mind... I think we were good. The fact that some of the numbers are still in the show says a lot. It needed work, but that would come."

Steve came up with the name of the new band, Iron Maiden (named after a medieval torture device that could be described as a coffin lined with long, sharp spikes), simply because "it just sounded right for the music. I was sitting around at my mum's place, talking about names for the band, and that was the name that was bandied about, and I said, 'Yeah, that's great. I like that.' I don't remember if I thought of it or my mum did or someone else in my family. I can't remember. But I do remember saying it to my mum, and she went, 'Oh, that's good.' I think I had a short-list of four or five names and she said, 'Oh, yeah. That's the best one.'

"The film *The Man In The Iron Mask* was about at the time and I'd seen that, and I think it probably came from there, although there wasn't actually an iron maiden in the film. I just thought it was a good name for a band. Iron Butterfly were known before that, and funnily enough, when we did our first couple of gigs at the Cart and Horses, we had a phone call behind the bar one night, and still to this day I don't know whether it was a fucking wind-up or what, but someone phoned up and said, 'We're called Iron Maiden and you can't use the name,' and all this, but I just said, 'That's tough shit, because we're called Iron Maiden, so bollocks!' I must admit, I was all bravado on the phone, but when I came away I thought, 'Oh shit,' 'cause if they *had* registered it – you know, even though we were only playing pubs – then we wouldn't have been able to use it, and by then I was really set on it. But we never actually heard any more, so it might have been one of my mates winding me up, doing a northern accent. I don't know."

When Steve complained that he didn't have anywhere decent to rehearse his new band, Dave Lights said that they could come and rehearse at his house, in Folly Street, just behind a pub called the Sir John Franklin, not far from the Blackwall Tunnel. "They rehearsed there for nearly a year," remembers Dave, "usually about three or four times a week. I was in my own band, too, as a singer, at the time. But, I mean, we never even had a name, and we couldn't get through the first few bars of 'Smoke On The Water' without collapsing. But Steve was up to good stuff, I thought, the real thing, you know? Plus I had to like it, really, seeing as they were at my house rehearsing three times a week for hours on end. You could say that, by the time they actually did their first gig, I knew the songs quite well!"

"Where he lived, it was, like, this old house that used to be owned by nuns or something," says Steve, "only they weren't there any more and

Davey Lights was living in there. He offered us some space to rehearse in, in this little bit under the stairs. Like Doctor Who's TARDIS, it was, and he had this place in there where he said we could rehearse. And then he said, 'I know a lot about doing the lights, you know,' and all this sort of stuff, and we sort of went from there."

"We used to practise in Dave Lights' place," confirms Dave Sullivan. "It was an old convent, or something. I know some nuns used to live over the back. We actually played live in Dave's back garden, once, and I always remember about three nuns turned up! It was funny, 'cause it turned into a sort of mini Beatles on the top of Abbey Road type of thing. Eventually, the police turned up and we had to stop."

Maiden took up semi-residency in the Cart and Horses. Dave drove the van while Steve used his contacts from Smiler to conjure up gigs. By this time, there was another new face on hand who had recently volunteered his services, former Smiler stagehand Vic Vella. "He was a good few years older than us," Steve recalls, "and he had this sort of unflappable quality, which you need around you when you're doing a gig." These days, Vic works for Steve personally, helping build the tennis courts, football pitch and "my very own pub" that now adorn the countryside mansion Steve owns in Essex. Back then, he was "our driver, our gear-shifter and our sort of older head. Vic was a good bloke to have on your side, and you needed a bit of that, the places we were playing then. If someone needed to speak to our manager, we used to point at Vic."

From the outset, Steve made it clear that he wanted the new band to concentrate on playing original material. "I knew we'd have to start off doing some covers, just to get a few gigs," he says, "but I already had a few songs written, and that was what it was really all about, as far as I was concerned, getting the others to learn the songs first and getting everything else to fit around them."

Essentially, Steve formed Iron Maiden to play the songs he was then starting to write. But his new band-mates weren't discouraged from coming up with their own ideas as well. "Generally, if we had an idea, Steve would listen to it, and if he liked it, it was in," remembers Dave Sullivan. "Me and Terry would go 'round to Steve's with a couple of acoustics and he would plug his bass into an old tape recorder, I seem to remember, so that he was amped up but not too loud. He lived at his nan's, in those days. To begin with, it was just some carry-over ideas from his previous band – stuff like the 'Innocent Exile' riff, which came from Steve's days in Smiler – and me and Terry would suggest a few things, too. I particularly remember that the starting riff to 'Iron Maiden' was mine. We tossed it in and sort of threw it around between us. Then Steve would slightly mould it and come up with something else, which became the song."

"I played some of the songs and I told them the sort of stuff I wanted to do," Steve explains. "They were into Wishbone Ash and all that. Dave Sullivan, in particular, was well into Wishbone Ash. I won't say I knew totally what I wanted to do, 'cause I don't think you ever really know that, but I did have a direction that I knew that I wanted it to go in. I wanted to play hard rock, heavy stuff with a lot of aggression to it, but I also wanted to play stuff with lots of melody and lots of twin guitar in it. It could have been anybody's songs, but it just happened to be that I'd been writing some stuff and trying to get stuff together, anyway, 'cause I thought, 'Well, I can't get people in if I've got nothing to play 'em, so I'm gonna have to write more stuff than I've written already.'"

Freed from the responsibility of having to play somebody else's tunes, Steve let his imagination run riot, and it was during this intense period of creativity and searching for identity that killer new songs like 'Iron Maiden', 'Wrathchild', 'Prowler' and 'Transylvania' – all numbers that were destined to become tracks on the first two Maiden albums – began to emerge. "They were very early incarnations, if you like. Also, 'Purgatory' comes from that time, only then it was called 'Floating'. It was quite a different version of it, actually. They were impressed with the stuff, you know, but the rest of the set was made up of covers. The idea was always, though, that, if we did a cover, try and make it one that people wouldn't necessarily know. In Smiler, some of the stuff we covered was pretty unpredictable. It wasn't what people in a pub would necessarily know, and often they'd think it was an original. So I decided I'd rather go that route, rather than playing stuff that's too well known. So instead of 'All Right Now' by Free we'd do something like 'I'm A Mover'.

"We did do a couple of songs which became a bit more known later on but weren't at the time. 'Jailbreak' by Thin Lizzy was one like that. And we did a song called 'Striker' – which was nothing to do with football – by this band called Tucky Buzzard. They were a band on the Deep Purple label, and I got into them through the twins in Smiler, 'cause they used to like them. We weren't trying to pull the wool over people's eyes. We weren't lying about things. We just thought, 'There's much more of an appeal than just going in and playing covers,' because every other band back then was playing The Doobie Brothers and 'All Right Now'. I thought, 'Sod that. I really want to get into doing our own set.' So, as soon as an original came in, a cover would go out."

Even then, the Harris penchant for an unexpected time change, which would become the hallmark of all of Iron Maiden's most respected work, was already much in evidence. "At that stage, the most technical stuff we'd do was something like 'Transylvania', or probably 'Iron Maiden', which I suppose was a bit off the wall for some people," he admits. "At the time, the others did think it was a bit strange, but I was heavily influenced by progressive rock, and to me these time changes didn't seem strange at all. I thought they fitted perfectly. Bands that were really progressive, to me, were bands like Genesis, Jethro Tull, ELP, Yes, King Crimson – I used to really love *In The Court Of The Crimson King* – So I used to love off-the-wall changes coming in out of nowhere, like, 'Where the fuck did *that* come from? Where's his head at?' You know?"

However, Steve admits that, in those early days, "It wasn't always easy, because, although Dave and Terry were really excellent rhythm players and they managed the twin guitar very well, neither of them could really play lead guitar the way I wanted. I wanted a band that was gonna play some fast stuff and some stuff that was a bit more complicated but that would rip your head off with some leads as well, and neither Dave nor Terry could really do that. I was starting to think I'd need another guitarist to do that."

The first casualty of the original Maiden line-up, however, was neither of the two guitarists but singer Paul Day. Dave remembers the occasion: "I went off to Florida for a holiday, and I think, when I came back, Paul was already gone and Denny was in. I was reasonably happy, but I wasn't sure of his vocal ability. But Denny had the image that Steve was angling for. Den had been in a few bands, and he was a bit older than us lot and he liked to lay down certain rules. I always remember him swinging the mic 'round at the Cart and Horses and he nearly knocked me out. I thought, 'Yeah, that's different.'"

"We felt that Paul was an all right singer but that he didn't really have enough energy or charisma onstage," says Steve. "We did our first 25-odd gigs with him, I think all along hoping he would get better, 'cause he had a great voice, but onstage he just wasn't confident at all. Not then, anyway. He was really nervous, and it just wasn't happening, so we decided to change him, and that was when Dennis Wilcock joined."

The singer's own post-Smiler venture having foundered almost before it had begun, Wilcock, "a massive Kiss freak", was more than happy to indulge his passion for what he saw as onstage theatrics but what Steve now laughingly describes as "a lot of poncy face make-up". It was Wilcock's idea to introduce an element of showmanship into proceedings, and he would take to the stage with a large red star painted across his right eye. During 'Prowler', he'd don a flasher's mask – an idea he'd filched from an early Genesis show – and grubby mac, and then, as one of the guitarists launched into a solo, Dennis would pretend to be a vampire and creep up on him from behind and pretend to bite his neck. The highlight of the new show came, of course, during 'Iron Maiden', when the singer would run a (blunt) sword across his mouth and spew out gobfuls of fake blood. Steve and the rest of the band thought it hilarious when two girls fainted at the sight of it all during a gig in Margate.

Steve: "Den wasn't technically as good a singer as Paul, but he really had the charisma and the fun side down to a T. I must admit, I thought he looked a bit of a prat when he used to go out there with this big red heart painted over one eye – just like Paul Stanley out of Kiss, you know? Dave might have had a bit of eyeliner on too, sometimes – when he was pissed his bird put it on him to do a gig, but I used to give him a bollocking for it!

"With Dennis, it was make-up in a different way. At least he had a stage persona, which was an improvement on Paul. And whatever you thought about the way he looked, at least he really threw himself into it, and that was important. I wanted to play these pubs and dives we were doing as though we were onstage at the Hammersmith Odeon or something, and Den was really good at that."

However, Wilcock brought with him news of a guitarist mate of his that, he said, would blow them away. His name was Dave Murray. "I said, 'Well, if he's that good, get him down here,'" recalls Steve. "So he did. And that's when everything really changed…"

To begin with, Steve had it in mind to actually add a third guitarist to the existing Sullivan/Rance/Matthews/Wilcock line-up. "I knew not many bands had done that, but the ones that had – like Lynyrd Skynyrd – had done something really good with it," he explains now, "and at first I thought it might be good to try something similar. Dave and Terry were good twin guitar players, and I thought, 'If this bloke Den is bringing along is as good as he says he is, maybe he can sort of blister away over the top.' But as it turned out, it wasn't to be."

Dave Sullivan: "The lead sound was a bit lacking in maybe the quality of what Steve and Den might be looking for at the time, and there were a few discussions about that, yeah. At first, Steve just wanted to get a third guitarist in. I wasn't too bothered, but Terry wasn't too keen. He didn't think a third guitarist was required. But people take things a bit personally, sometimes, as a slight on their ability, and that's how Terry took it. But I was quite open to it, at the time. Dave Murray was already on the sidelines, I think. I wasn't there when he auditioned. I think he auditioned just with Steve and Den."

"I wanted to get Davey Murray in the band," says Steve. "I've always thought he was a great guitarist, and he could play lead better than anybody else I knew, so I thought, 'Well, fuck it,' you know? 'Lynyrd Skynyrd have three guitar players. Why can't we?' I didn't have a problem with having three of them in there, but the others weren't into it. They were just not into having another guitar player. I don't know whether it was because they had this partnership and they thought it was happening or whatever – and it *was* happening; they just weren't particularly good lead players. So that was it, really. I just said, 'Well, if you're not gonna have someone come in the band then you have to go,' because by now I'd decided this is what I wanted to do."

Dave Sullivan remembers the time well. "It was just before Christmas 1976. We'd just played Walthamstow Assembly Hall, and it was the first time we'd had a poster up for a gig. It was the first-ever Iron Maiden poster, which Steve drew himself. I've still got one, actually. But myself and Terry must have left just after that. We had a meeting in the pub and Steve more or less said, 'We're gonna split the band and give it a rest.' I'm not sure if it was mentioned about Dave Murray joining. I think there were a few things that people weren't happy with and discussions got a bit clouded at the time. There were a few things said about saving up some money to get a better PA and just sort of stepping the whole thing up a bit. We were a bit gutted about it, yeah, but they were so determined. They said, like, 'For the time being, we're gonna split the band and maybe work something out later on,' but I think Dave was already in the shadows."

"There was a bit of a thing with both [Rance and Sullivan], at the time," says Steve. "It wasn't just their playing. Sometimes they weren't sure about their commitment, as far as, like, doing certain gigs or whatever, 'cause they both had pretty good day jobs, I think, and they were a bit concerned about that. I wasn't interested in that. I was, like, 'Fuck the job! I don't care how well you do in your job. The band's got to come first.' I said to all of them, 'Anybody that comes into the band, that's got to be the attitude.' It was, like, 'I don't care whether your brother or sister's getting married, or whatever. If we've got a gig that night, we're doing the gig.' That was always my attitude: Maiden comes first."

Sullivan says it wasn't until about six months later that he and Terry Rance discovered that Maiden was back in business with Dave Murray installed on guitar. "I must have spoken to Ron [Rebel] and he told me things were carrying on, but I wasn't terribly bothered by then. I remember I was trying to buy a flat, 'cause I was getting married at the time and I had a lot more important things on my mind."

It was a decision, Sullivan admits, that would be the cause of much regret, as the years passed and he watched the name Iron Maiden became famous around the world, but one about which he is now cheerfully philosophical. "Obviously, I think I'll always regret not being part of it, 'cause we were there at the start. I'm not really sure I'd be there now, though, because I think maybe it just wasn't to be. Good luck to them, I say. I'm a self-employed contract designer for oil companies now, but I'm still in contact with Terry. We still write together and do a few bits and pieces, but just for fun, you know? Very different from Maiden. Steve was always deadly serious about that, right from the start."

The last word has to come from Steve: "When the others made it plain that it was either them or Dave Murray, there was no choice. There was no way I was gonna let Dave go. Not only was he a nice bloke, he was just the best guitarist I'd ever worked with. He still is."

2 Dave

You wouldn't know it from looking at him onstage with Iron Maiden, where he spins around and throws exuberant shapes while effortlessly cranking out those breakneck lead-guitar lines, but Dave Murray is actually the shyest, most endearing rock star you could ever hope to meet. At 41, he still has the cherubic good looks that made him the main target of affection from members of the opposite sex during the band's earliest days, his down-to-earth manner and gentle charm still intact despite the years on the road and the multitude of gold and platinum discs accrued along the way.

Warm and generous with his time but never over-friendly in that showy rock-star way that a lot of guitarists and singers have when they're talking to a journalist, Dave Murray has never been pushy about anything, least of all his songs (of which he's written, on average, one for every other album) or his place in the inter-band hierarchy (second only to Steve Harris). One to keep his cool in a crisis just as much as Steve, but in an entirely different, more benign way, Dave sums up the true, ever-so-'eavy, ever-so-'umble spirit of Iron Maiden. These days, he lives on the exotic island of Maui with his California-born wife, Tamar, and their beautiful ten-year-old daughter, Tasha, but back when he first met Steve Harris and joined Iron Maiden, in 1976, Dave Murray was just another East End geezer with some flash ideas.

David Michael Murray was born in London, at the Royal Middlesex hospital in Edmonton, on 23 December 1956. He has two sisters: Pauline, who is six years older; and Janet, who is three years younger. The Murray suffix comes from the mixed Scots and Irish blood on his father's side. Like 'Arry, football was the young Dave Murray's first love. He was a handy midfield goal-getter, he says, before music took over everything in his teens. "I grew up in the Tottenham area of London, so I was always a

Tottenham Hotspur supporter, though I must admit I've never actually been to a game. I just used to watch them on TV, you know? It was kind of handed down to me – my mother and father were both Spurs supporters – but it all kind of tailed off for me, the football thing, once I got to be about 15 and started following bands and buying albums and stuff."

These days, sister Pauline has teenaged sons and daughters of her own, who all come to the Maiden shows whenever they play in London. "My younger sister, Janet, has got a daughter, Zoe, and apparently her teacher's got an Iron Maiden poster up in the classroom! And it's sweet, you know? It's cool, but a bit weird, too, 'cause it's hard to believe we've come that far. Even though I've probably forgotten a lot of it, the stuff I do remember, most of it still feels like yesterday to me."

Dave's mother held down a number of part-time cleaning jobs while his father drew disability payments after being pensioned out of work at an early age due to illness. "It was a slow, debilitating kind of thing, where he couldn't physically do stuff," says Dave. As a result, the family was constantly being moved around by the local council and, by Dave's reckoning, "I must have gone to about ten different schools by the time I was 14. We lived all over the East End of London – some right dodgy areas, some of them, too – basically because we were so poor. We'd be housed in one place for a while and then moved on to another housing estate somewhere else a few months later."

Frustration and poverty caused Dave's parents to fight a great deal. When that happened, Mum would take Dave and his sisters to the local Salvation Army depot, where they would often spend weeks at a time sheltered from their father's bitter moods. "But we'd always go back, sooner or later." These were the formative early experiences that shaped the character of the future Maiden guitarist, events that would force him to turn in upon himself and teach him how to keep his mouth shut and "just get on with things" during times of trouble. "I grew this sort of protective shell around myself," he says. "You had to know how to keep your head down just to survive." These were habits that would hold him in good stead during the trials and tribulations that eventually ousted so many other members of the band in later years.

"It was a very hard upbringing. Being given anything new was a rarity. It was very hard, and in a way it still affects me now, but at the time, looking around at other families we knew, it wasn't much different. We were all poor. The first thing I did when I made some money with the band was I bought my parents a house [a pretty, semi-detached place in Woodford]. I'd always wanted to do that, because of all the poverty they were used to, just to give them back something solid so they wouldn't have to move around any more. It was something I'd always dreamed of doing, if I ever made it with my music, and after that part of the dream had come true I thought that was it. Like, if everything fell apart tomorrow, at least I'd have done that, and that made me feel good. My father has since passed away, but mum still lives in the house."

Having to move around so much as a child and constantly being the new kid on the block meant that Dave got picked on a lot. He had to toughen up quickly in order to survive. His father – who had once been part of the circle of "friends" that congregated around notorious '60s East End villains like the infamous Kray twins, Ronnie and Reggie – encouraged his son to fend for himself. "My father used to drink with the Krays at a pub called the Blind Beggar, in Whitechapel. I don't know if he ever got up to any shenanigans with them or what, but funnily enough Nicko's father used to hang out with them as well, and when he and my dad met up years later, at a Maiden gig, they sat there talking about the old days for hours. It was really weird. And I think that sort of background meant I grew up a lot more streetwise than I probably realised. It's only now, looking back, that it seems funny.

"I was always the new kid in class, and it got to be that you had to fight your way in to get accepted, sometimes. And then, as soon as you'd made friends, you were moving on again, and it would start all over again. And so I had a lot of fights, yeah. In fact, my dad taught me to box from an early age. He bought me a pair of boxing gloves, you know, little ones – I've still got them around somewhere – and he was teaching me constantly to look out for myself."

One of the Murray family's brief residences was a flat over a club in Clapton that used to book acts that had been successful in the '60s, "groups like The Hollies, The Searchers and The Dave Clark Five. I used to wake up in the middle of the night and I could hear all this going on below, so I would wander downstairs and see all the people dancing and my sister Pauline would catch me and take me back upstairs. And I used to go down there when the bands were setting up in the afternoon, and I found it all really interesting. The guitars and everything looked very flash, you know? It was the era of The Beatles, and my sister was always playing Beatles records. She was a member of The Beatles' fan club. I was always surrounded by music when I was growing up, and that was kind of a good thing. With all the trauma of constantly moving around, the music was always something that was consistent. There was a piano in this club as well, and I used to have a tinkle around on that. That was when I was about five or six."

Prophetically, considering the hundreds of cardboard-guitar-wielding fans that used to turn up at the earliest Maiden shows, Dave's first guitar was, he confesses, "one I made myself out of cardboard. So, of course, I thought it was great, years later, when kids used to turn up at Maiden gigs with their cardboard guitars and pretend to start playing them. I could really relate to that! I used to cut out the shapes and sort of stuff 'em with paper to pad it out and taped it all up. It was great. I used to play along to all my sister's Beatles records and pretend I was John Lennon."

Cricket was the other big thing in Murray's childhood, cricket and football and boxing. Music was different; music was great, but it was "mainly something my sisters did" and something that he wouldn't come back to in earnest until his was in his mid teens. "I was always in the school cricket team, because I was a good bowler. My big claim to fame was that I once bowled six guys out in one over and I got carried off the pitch. And football, as well. I used to play in the school football team a lot. I was always Bobby Charlton, you know? The midfield genius who scored a few goals as well. And whatever school I went to, if I could, I always used to do a bit of boxing. I started doing that, getting in the ring for real, when I was about eleven. I think, being from east London, there was a lot of gangs and stuff like that, and you had to know how to defend yourself on the street. We were all in rival gangs, and so even if you were just standing there, minding your own business, there was always a chance another gang would just turn up and suddenly you'd have to sort of fight your way out."

The Murray family finally settled in a house in Clapton in 1970. Like Steve Harris and a great many other East End teenaged boys at the time, for a while Dave was a skinhead. Unlike Steve, however, Dave had the haircut, too. "Yep, number-one crop, Doc Marten boots and braces," he grins sheepishly. "The full monty." He even took up with a local skinhead gang and regularly found himself "getting into a bit of bother – street fights and the like. You had to be light on your feet." It's not a part of his past that he's particularly proud of now. It was just something "that all the kids 'round our way were into. Lots of times, gangs would come tooled up, but you couldn't afford to run away or your life really would have been hell. They'd never have let you be, you know?

"I had the Crombie coat and the Levi Sta-Prest trousers and I was in a skinhead gang, and I had a violent couple of years of being out on the street. Then I went completely to the other extreme and became a hippy. I decided that I preferred the more sort of peaceful attitude to life. What happened was, I did actually go to one football match – it was an Arsenal game – and there was serious fighting going on, and I thought, 'I've had enough of this,' you know? It was horrible. Looking back, I see it as all part of growing up and having a bit of an identity crisis, trying to find out who you are, sort of thing. So I let my hair grow long, got an Afghan and decided to become a hippy, man!"

Again just like Steve Harris, until he could find his way around the rack marked "Rock" at his local record shop, Dave was also into the reggae hits of the time that were largely associated with being a skinhead. "I used to buy all those *Tighten Up* albums that used to come out," he says. "They were, like, reggae compilation albums, and they'd have on all that stuff that I was into at the time – Dave And Ansel Collins, Jimmy Cliff, Prince Buster, all those guys. It was just the music that would be playing in these clubs or parties we went to. It had a great rhythm and you could dance to it. I was just like any teenager, trying new paths until you find something you're really comfortable with. The music thing was always there for me, but because of the east London background there was always the violence mixed in there as well. It was a case of finding out more about the music and getting away from the violence."

The moment that changed Dave's musical tastes forever, and would eventually lead him to a life he would never have thought possible back in his boots-and-braces days, occurred when he was 15. He'd just heard Jimi Hendrix's 'Voodoo Chile' on the radio for the first time and "everything changed, just like that. Getting into rock music wasn't like a gradual process for me; it was completely sort of extreme, totally black and white. I heard 'Voodoo Chile' by Jimi Hendrix for the first time on the radio and I thought, 'Fucking hell! What is *that*? How do you do that?' And I turned into, like, this detective, trying to track down and discover who this was and what was going on here. And that's when I started really hanging 'round record stores and buying albums. I was about 15 or 16 and I got quite a few Hendrix albums to begin with, then some blues albums, and then I started to think about playing, wondering what that would be like."

A love of rock music led quickly to "a complete engrossment with everything to do with it – the clothes and the whole sort of rock culture". Dave started to grow his hair long, much to the derision of his former skinhead mates; he took to wearing an Afghan coat and reading the *Melody Maker* every week; and he started to go to gigs and hang out with a new set of friends, "the ones that were into playing", chief of whom was a guy called Adrian Smith. "We lived a few streets away from each other," Dave recalls, "and we were both into the guitar, so we started hanging out and playing."

"Meeting Dave and getting to know him was great for me, because he was a little bit further down the road than I was, in terms of playing," says Smith. "I was still bashing about on an old acoustic which Dave had sold me for a fiver, or something. Meanwhile, he was already onto his first Gibson copy, or whatever. I think I was a bit jealous, actually, but we used to go 'round each other's houses and play and it was great. I think we both really learned a lot."

By the time he had left school at 15, Dave had already discarded the idea of finding "a proper job" in favour of a career playing electric guitar, dreaming of the big time. Adrian Smith says that, by then, "Dave Murray was already very much the sort of local rock star. He'd been playing for about eight months, he'd mastered a few chords and everybody was dead impressed. He had really long hair, quite far-out clothes and a proper electric guitar, you know? We'd never seen one before in real life. Just on the telly."

"The idea for me wasn't so much to do with being a star as just having a job that allowed me to play the guitar," says Dave. "I wasn't too choosy about what sort of music I played. Not to begin with, anyway. I just loved music and started to get off on the whole sort of lifestyle. But it was the guitar that really drew me in. It had been there in me, right from when I was six or seven and I made my own cardboard guitar. It was like it was there somewhere, but I just left it alone and came back to it eight or nine years later. But once I did, I really took to it quite seriously. Suddenly I couldn't get to know enough about it, first with albums and then with playing the guitar for myself."

His first group was an unlikely trio called Stone Free, which he and Adrian formed with another schoolmate. "We were about 16," he says, "and it was me and Adrian on guitars and this other mate of ours called Dave McCloughlin on bongos, and we only ever did one gig and that was in our local church hall one Saturday afternoon. There were about six people there to see it, and I think we did about four or five songs, mainly T Rex and Jimi Hendrix covers. And afterwards, one of these old women who was running the thing gave us a can of Coke and a Mars bar each as payment."

Dave and Adrian would continue to play together in little impromptu outfits throughout the rest of their teens, writing together sometimes and talking often of what they would do (and who they would do it to) if they ever made it. "But it was always clear that Dave would be off the moment a proper band came along and asked him to play," says Adrian. "He was always looking to jump onto the next rung. I don't mean that in a negative way. He was a really good guitarist, and it was the natural progression for Davey to look for the best band he could find to play in, which he eventually did with Maiden. But back then he was always the one leafing through the ads in *Melody Maker* and ringing up to go to auditions, whereas I hardly ever did anything like that. I was already writing my own songs by then and didn't really want to join anybody else's band. Dave was the exact opposite. He couldn't wait."

Dave: "I wanted to experience what it was like to actually get up and play guitar in front of a roomful of complete strangers. I really thought it would be good practice for going onstage later. My thoughts were just that I wanted to keep playing with lots of different people, the more diverse the better, just so that I could get some experience. So I used to get *Melody Maker* every week and run through the ads, and it became, like, a regular thing. I was always going to auditions on a Saturday or Sunday morning."

It was the result of one such audition which brought him the invitation to join "this sort of soft-rock, American-type band" called Electric Gas. "This was in about 1973," he recalls. "It wasn't totally what I was into, but it was different, so I liked it. I would play with anybody in those days, just for the experience. I was with them for just under a year in the end, but we never really got beyond rehearsing and playing very occasionally at some pub or youth club somewhere. No one really came."

Then there had been "this sort of mad punk band" called The Secret. "The Secret was more of a proper set-up," says Dave. "They had a manager and a record deal and they seemed to get quite a few gigs, you know, so I got stuck in there. I didn't have to cut my hair or anything. It was, like, a mixture of styles. This was still in the very early days of punk, when it was still a bit glam as well, I suppose. But it was great, because I ended up recording a single with them. It was called 'Café De Dance', and it was released on some indie label so obscure I can't even remember what it was called now, but it came out in about 1975. So I'll always remember The Secret. It was the first time I'd had a chance to go into a proper recording studio, and I really enjoyed it."

Nevertheless, Dave left The Secret almost as soon as the single was released, "because by then I had met Steve Harris and Dennis Wilcock and a few other faces as well and was thinking about getting back into a more sort of heavy rock-type vibe. I mean, as soon as I hooked up with Steve, that was it, really. I'd actually found a band that played music I really loved, so there was no turning back."

"The first time I met Dave Murray was when he came to audition," remembers Steve. "He'd been in a band with Dennis Wilcock called Warlock – not the Warlock that later came from Germany, just another local East End mob – and Dennis had been really impressed by Dave's guitar playing, so he got him to come down to audition for us, and he was amazing. I mean, Davey just blew us away!"

Steve's sister, Linda, had just started going out with a lad called Nick Lideye, who also happened to be a bass player, and his band used to rehearse in a large, abandoned truck trailer that sat in the back of the Essex farm that his parents owned. "They had this trailer in the back of the field and Nick said, 'Oh, you can use it for your auditions, if you like,'" remembers Steve. "So Davey came out for this audition and we dragged him all the way out into this big, muddy field and into the back of this big bloody trailer thing. But after he'd finished playing, we told him straight away, 'You've got the job.' I remember we got him to play on 'Prowler' and he just blew us away, totally, and we said, 'Right, you're in!'"

"I remember going across this cow field to get to this sort of caravan where they had all the gear set up," says Dave. "It was all a bit strange, really. I wasn't at all used to the countryside, but I dragged my guitar case over these muddy fields and I remember turning up covered in shit, you know? But they all seemed really friendly, so I plugged in and away we went."

As the new band embarked on 1977 together, the line-up was now Dennis Wilcock on vocals, Steve Harris on bass, Dave Murray on guitar and Ron Rebel on drums. "Davey came in and he was that good he could do it on his own," says Steve. "He was one of those guys who really could play the guitar with his teeth, you know? And that became part of his thing – playing the guitar with his teeth, throwing it behind his back, playing it upside-down. He could do the lot! We thought we'd eventually get another guitarist, just for the harmonies and stuff, but we were able to do it as a three-piece with a vocalist for quite some time, and a lot of the harmonies I used to play on the bass. But the more new songs started to come through, the more it became obvious that, while we could manage on our own, where we were actually going with our own original music was always towards a more twin lead guitar sound, so we started looking around for another guitarist."

Bob Sawyer was another regular face at places like the Bridgehouse and the Cart and Horses and, although he wasn't as good a lead player as Dave Murray, if you showed Bob what to do he could pick it up quickly, and so the band began drafting him for their gigs. Taking the stage name Bob Angelo, he was "a nice enough bloke", remembers Dave Murray, whose says that his only fault was that "he probably tried a bit too hard".

"Bob worked out quite well, for a while," recalls Steve. "He was a couple of years older than us, but he was a good guitar player. The problem was, instead of trying to complement what Davey was doing, he started battling with Davey, which was a big mistake, 'cause he was never gonna win that one. I used to like Bob. He was a character, without a doubt, and I'm not knocking him, but I remember a gig we did in Barking

– we had a residency down there, on a Friday and Saturday night – and I remember Davey doing his guitar piece – you know, with his teeth. And then Bob, when he did his solo thing, he was trying to make out he could play it with his teeth, too, only he was cheating. He'd sort of turn his back to the audience and use his hands. And I could see it, 'cause I was standing beside him, and the people right at the front would have seen it, too. So afterwards we had this massive fucking row, 'cause I said, 'What the fuck are you doing? You're pulling the wool over people's eyes!' It wasn't like he was even getting away with it. So we had this massive row, and then he went, anyway, not that night but soon afterwards."

One of the strangest gigs the band almost played in those days was when they were bizarrely booked into a slot at the Roxy in Covent Garden in 1977. Then a well-known punk club catering exclusively for a new-wave audience, the engagement came via a well-meaning if ultimately misguided attempt to try and "mould the image of the band" by an independent label who had taken an interest in them. Another well-known East Ender, Garry Bushell, an early supporter of both Maiden and punk rock who was then writing for the weekly magazine *Sounds*, explains the mix-up and the unexpected repercussions it would have: "The cock-up came about through the involvement of a certain Suzanne Black of the reggae label Klick Records, who then had a distribution deal with RCA. She was interested in the band, and they were flattered by her attention, but it seems they had very different things in mind. The band wanted a recording deal but were a mite bemused to arouse the interest of a reggae label. Ms Black assured them that the label wanted to branch out into rock, although later it became clear that what she was really keen on was moving into management. Anyway, they auditioned for her and she was impressed. A couple of days later, however, she was issuing plans for the band's development of a very unusual nature."

First, Black suggested that they incorporate a few "commercial" covers into their set. Her own bizarre suggestion was a cover of Todd Rundgren's 'I Saw The Light'. Secondly, she said that they should drop all their pyro and their stage props. And finally, and most ludicrously of all, she recommended that they cut their hair short and spiky and try to adopt a more punk-orientated image. "Safety pins and all!" cries Steve, still aghast at the thought 20 years later. But when the band politely told her where to go, Black wailed that it was too late, that she'd already booked them onto the bill at the Roxy for a special showcase gig to which she had invited several major record-company A&R men.

Dismissing out of hand the unthinkable notion of turning punk, Steve felt duty-bound to at least go and check out the venue for himself first before deciding whether or not to actually do the gig. After all, "It wasn't every day we got A&R people from the majors coming down to see us. Not in east London!" But on the night that he and Den Wilcock showed up, Gene October was leading his band, Chelsea, through their punk-by-numbers paces and the place was awash with what Steve laughingly later described as "all these weirdos diving about spitting all over each other and soaking the singer in spew. I said, 'Fuck this. If we play down here, there's gonna be a riot!' Imagine if our fans had gone down there and the punks had started gobbing on them. There would have been a right knuckle. So there was no way we'd play there and no way we'd go along with the rest of her ideas. She freaked out, but that was the end of her."

It wouldn't be the last time that Iron Maiden would be told that, if only they'd cut their hair and ditch their overtly "heavy" image, they would stand a better chance of landing a record deal. It was the summer of 1977, the height of punk, and ever since Johnny Rotten had complained that he'd fallen asleep while watching Led Zeppelin's admittedly hugely over-indulgent film biopic, *The Song Remains The Same*, and dubbed them "boring old farts", the whole genre of heavy rock music became so devoutly uncool that no one in the British music press was prepared to take seriously the idea of a new heavy rock band coming along. Not right then, anyway.

But the band had already set their sights and made up their minds and, although it would be another two years before even their first live performances were reviewed in the music papers, they remained implacable on the subject of their image, their music and their meaning. Even though they actually had more in common with punk mythology – working-class kids playing provocative, high-energy music – than 90 per cent of the predominantly middle-class poseurs then writing for the music press, Maiden rejected punk. Not because they didn't believe in The Sex Pistols – vocalist Paul Di'Anno, who later replaced Dennis Wilcock, was a huge Pistols and Clash fan – but because they didn't believe in jumping on the bandwagon, which is what every other new band in Britain appeared to be doing in 1977. "As soon as someone else said, 'You're good but you should go more commercial,' or, 'You're good but you should cut your hair,' we just said, 'Oh, all right,' and walked out," recalls Steve Harris.

In the meantime, encroaching new attitudes didn't prevent the band from packing them in back home in reliable Maiden strongholds like the Harrow in Barking and the Plough in Leytonstone. Their immediate problems centred yet again around their increasingly unsettled line-up. Indeed, there were to be a further half-dozen changes to the fledgling Maiden team over the next two years. Amazingly, however, the first person to be fired from the existing Harris/Wilcock/Murray/Matthews/Sawyer line-up was actually Dave Murray, after a gig at the Bridgehouse in 1976 which ended badly when Bob Sawyer caused a rift between Dave and Dennis. "I'd only been in the band a few months," remembers Dave. "Bob took some things I'd said totally out of context and went to Dennis and said, 'Oh, Dave's just said this about you.' Like, totally misquoted me! And there was no animosity there between me and Dennis, but Bob's gone over and given him all this and it's pissed Dennis off. So then Dennis came over and had a few words with me. I can't even remember what it was about – something pathetic, something you say after a few beers that's really silly, you know? But Bob made it from a molehill into a mountain.

"Then I remember getting a call a few days later to go and meet at Steve's house. I used to drive around in an old Mini in those days, this broken-down old thing that was a health hazard, really. No windscreen wipers. If it rained, you'd reach out with your hand and wipe it. But on the way over to Steve's, it actually caught fire! Luckily, I had a little fire extinguisher that I carried in the car, 'cause you knew something was gonna happen sooner or later. So I'm spraying this stuff all over the trunk – we're talking serious flames here – and getting covered in smoke and oil. And then I turn up at Steve's like this, covered in shit, you know? And the first thing he says is, 'Well, I'm sorry to have to tell you this, but you're fired.' I was, like, 'Oh.' But it wasn't really Steve this was coming from. It was Dennis.

"So I got back into the burned-out Mini and drove off. It was a terrible moment, really. I mean, obviously I was quite upset about being sacked from the band, and then I'd nearly, like, died in this car, and I thought, 'Well, what else can go wrong now?' I think I went home and got completely drunk. Getting the sack from anything is pretty horrible, but because I believed in it and I loved it so much, getting sacked from the band was quite painful. I didn't know what to do."

What he did was join another East End rock band then beginning to make a small reputation for themselves locally, Urchin. Fronted by his old mate Adrian Smith, Urchin "wasn't as heavy as Maiden," says Dave, "but they definitely rocked and were, like, the next best thing to Maiden at the time." Urchin's music was set in a "more mainstream sort of vein than Maiden," says Adrian. "We were into the more catchy sort of rock songs, and being the singer as well I was more into playing rhythm guitar. But with Davey playing his lead over the top, it gave it an added edge. So, yeah, we were pretty pleased to have him back."

"Adrian was singing and playing guitar, and they were looking for another guitar player," confirms Dave, "so it just happened to fall together at the right time. It was less than a week after I'd been given the sack from Maiden and I went straight into doing the same sort of pubs that I'd been doing with them, and that was when we did that single."

Urchin had signed a small deal with DJM, which provided for two singles with an option on an album. Their first single, 'Black Leather Fantasy', had already been recorded but remained unreleased. Undeterred, the band returned to the studio – this time with Dave Murray – to record the ostensible follow-up, which was entitled 'She's A Roller' and would belatedly see the light of day in 1980. "It's not the greatest record you've ever heard, put it that way," says Adrian Smith now, "but I'm still quite proud of it. You can really hear me and Davey rocking out on it."

"At that time, Urchin were in a similar position as Maiden," says Dave. "They had some original songs, but they also did some covers, stuff like Free and Thin Lizzy, but it was actually Urchin who were the first to make a record, which was quite a big thing then. Personally, I tried not to make any comparisons between the two bands. I was, like, 'Maiden was good, but it's gone, so I'm just gonna have to carry on.' And I mean, Adrian's not just a good guitarist; he writes good songs, too. So it was pretty exciting, what with the record and stuff. I felt like, 'Well, at least I'm going forward, you know?'

"But, to be honest, I don't really remember a lot about it. I remember being really pleased that we were going to make a record, because I'd never really done anything like that before. Not properly. But I can't even remember what the song was called now. What I do remember, of course, is that the session was produced by Vic Maile, who had just had a hit with '2-4-6-8 Motorway', by Tom Robinson, which we all thought was great."

With both Dave Murray and Bob Sawyer now out of the picture, and temporarily disillusioned with the twin lead guitar concept, Steve Harris decided to take a gamble and, for the first (and only) time in the band's career, advertised for a keyboardist. The ad which appeared in *Melody Maker* read, "Iron Maiden want rock KEYBOARDS/SYNTH player. No pros or poseurs." The result: the recruitment to the band of one Tony Moore. Sadly, Moore was destined to play just the one gig with the band before Steve decided that it wasn't working out and scrapped the whole idea of having a keyboardist anywhere near them, a position that he would steadfastly maintain for the next ten years.

But then, the one gig they played with Moore – at the Bridgehouse, in November 1977 – turned out to be such a disaster that Steve ended up scrapping the entire band. On guitar that night, they had installed another old mate of Den's called Terry Wrapram, who until then had been plying his trade in a local outfit called Hooker, and on drums, stepping in as an eleventh-hour replacement for Ron Matthews – who had decided to rebel no more and jacked it in just days before the gig – was one Barry Purkis, who would later find temporary fame as Thunderstick, the ludicrously masked drummer in fellow early-'80s rockers Samson. "I can't really remember exactly what happened with Ron," confesses Steve Harris. "It was, like, one minute he was there, the next he was gone. It was all to do with commitment, I think. The band was taking up more and more time and we were doing more and more of our own songs, and I think he just couldn't keep up, you know?

"So we tried Thunderstick for one gig. He was great in rehearsals, but when we played the Bridgehouse, he was completely out of it. He said he'd had a row with his missus or something. That was his excuse afterwards, anyway. He'd dropped a couple of downers or something like that and he was just terrible, all over the fucking place, and he did a drum-solo thing, and it was *that* bad. There was people talking all the way through it at the bar, 'cause the bar was literally right in front of him, and he stopped in the middle of the drum solo and he yelled, 'Stop talking, you cunts, and listen to the maestro!' We were so embarrassed. It was just a nightmare! I used to say Thunderstick did two gigs in one for us that night: his first and his last."

As chance would have it, watching in the audience that night was Doug Sampson. Currently occupying the drum stool in what he now describes as "a sort of Latin pop band" called Janski, he'd heard about Steve's new band and decided "to have a gander, 'cause they were becoming quite well known, locally, by then. They'd been off the road for a while, putting a new line-up together, and I decided to check them out. I'd seen them play a few times before, with the old drummer, Ron Rebel, usually playing the Cart and Horses, and it was definitely more my cup of tea than what I was playing with Janski, put it that way. I went to this gig at the Bridgehouse, and it was packed. They always drew a good crowd, right from the beginning. One of my main memories of that night, actually, is the guv'nor of the Bridgehouse telling me they'd broken the record for the amount of people they'd had in there. It was amazing, if you think about it. I mean, they didn't have any records out, they were completely unknown outside the East End, probably, yet they always had a few hundred people down at their gigs. It was very impressive, compared to what you usually saw down in places like that.

"And I remember Thunderstick wore this very heavy make-up, sort of like the full-face Kiss make-up type thing. And I remember the guitarist had like a black band of make-up across his eyes, kind of like a mask painted on. Denny was the singer, and they had keyboards. I didn't know him, and I didn't think it really suited the band, but it still sounded like Iron Maiden. With or without keyboards, you could still always hear what they had."

Spotting Doug in the crowd afterwards, Steve got chatting and asked him what he was up to. When Doug revealed that he had begun playing again, in Janski, the invitation to "come down and have a jam" was swiftly issued. Doug admits that he was "well chuffed. I remember talking to Steve afterwards and he was saying, like, he wasn't all that happy with the way the keyboards was working out, and he wasn't too happy with the drumming that night, either. I don't think he had a problem with the image as much as the playing. He was just into making sure the band played his music the best it could be played, and I don't think either of us thought Thunderstick could do that then, really. So, when he asked me if I fancied auditioning for the band, I said yes straight away. I mean, I really fancied it."

But before Steve could give Dennis the news, the agitated vocalist had some news of his own to tell Steve that threw the whole situation into disarray once more: Dennis had decided that he, too, would be leaving the band. He had been happy with the additions to the new line-up. They might not have been great players, but all three of the new boys were as heavily influenced by Kiss and Alice Cooper as Wilcock was himself, and the singer was determined to keep what he thought of as a "theatrical dimension" to the band's performances. What's more, he was sick of Steve's domineering attitude.

Doug Sampson: "Denny had decided he'd had enough and was gonna form his own band, which he eventually did. They were called V1. I don't think things had been going well generally between them and Denny. I can't remember exactly, but I think they did another gig and he didn't turn up or something."

"Den let us down in the end," reflects Steve. "He just didn't turn up one night. So we dashed 'round to his house to see if he was all right, and he was fine but he just said, 'I ain't coming down. I'm leaving the band.' I said, 'Well, can't you do the gig tonight first and then leave the band?' I mean, he really left us in the shit. But he was, like, 'No. I've made up my mind.' So I said, 'Fuck it. We'll do the gig without him.' And we did!"

Now without a singer and forced yet again to start from scratch, Steve Harris temporarily gave up on the idea of finding what by now had become a quest for "the perfect frontman" and decided to concentrate on "getting the basics right". He admits to being "well happy" to have Doug Sampson back to play the drums. "He'd always been my first choice." Now what he needed to do was recruit a real first-choice guitarist, and as far as Steve was concerned there was still only one man who could fill those shoes in Iron Maiden.

"About six months after I'd been sacked from the band, I was with Adrian in Urchin," says Dave Murray. "We were playing one Saturday night at a pub venue in north London called the Brechnoch when who should be there but Steve. And I was really pleased to see him. I mean, we'd never had any problems. It was only really Dennis Wilcock that sort of objected to me. And we were talking after the gig and Steve told me that everyone had gone and he wanted to put the band back together with me and a couple of new guys, and so he asked me if I wanted to rejoin the band and I just said yes straight away.

"And the thing is, you know, me and Adrian, there was a friendship thing between us that went back to when we were, like, 15, and there was a loyalty thing as well, because of the band, but I just said yeah straight away. I mean, I didn't even have to think about it. I just said, 'Sure, yeah!' It was just my immediate reaction. At the same time, I knew I was letting Adrian down and everything, but this was how strongly I felt about Steve and Maiden. I just felt that, out of any band that I'd ever been in, this was the one that was really going to do it, because of the songs and Steve's attitude and the direction and whole focus of the thing, even then. So, although I obviously felt very loyal to Adrian, I thought the most important thing was to join the band that I really believed in."

Breaking the news to Adrian was, he admits with a smile, "pretty awkward, actually". He deliberately told another member of the band first, "because I didn't really have the guts to tell Adrian myself straight off. Because I didn't want to hurt our friendship, I subtly dropped a hint to the bass player, Alan Levitt, that I was gonna leave, and he was really unhappy about it. And then he told Adrian and that was it, really.

"There was another guy, a guitarist Adrian knew called Andy Barnett, who was kind of on the sidelines, and I think he just stepped right in. He'd already been playing with Urchin off and on for a while, so it wasn't too bad for them. It wasn't like they couldn't carry on or anything. I mean, we stayed friends and that, and it wasn't like we fell out or anything."

"I think his heart was always with Maiden, even after they fired him, but we didn't take it all that well to begin with," Adrian recalls ruefully. "We all went 'round to his house, the whole band and crew, and we all stood around trying to make him feel really guilty, but it didn't work – or, at least, not enough to make him change his mind. I think he did feel terrible about it, but that was Dave, you know? He wasn't doing it for mercenary reasons; he just genuinely preferred the sort of thing Maiden were into. So you have to say to him, fair play, you know? You're following your heart."

With Dave Murray back in the band, the new trio began to rehearse regularly, working exclusively on the songs that Steve had been stockpiling all the while. "A lot of the songs that finished up on the first two Maiden albums were being worked on by then," says Steve. "'Prowler', 'Iron Maiden', 'Wrathchild', 'Another Life', 'Innocent Exile', 'Sanctuary', 'Transylvania', 'Purgatory', 'Drifter'. They didn't all sound like the way they ended up, but the lyrics and most of the riffs were all there. And because the songs kept coming, I just felt that, if we could only find the right singer, we'd definitely be in with a shout of making something out of it, you know? And unlike before, when I was just in a hurry to get someone in to sing my songs, I was prepared to wait for the right person, this time, and so were Dougie and Dave."

"To begin with, it was just the three of us – Steve, Davey and me," explains Doug. "We started rehearsing, but we had a bit of trouble getting a proper singer for a while. Singers are always the hardest part of any band to find. They've got to sound right, they've got to look right and they've got to be good onstage. There's lots of things you have to take into account, when it comes to choosing a singer. Most people reckon they can sing, but the truth is that very few people can get in front of a rock band and sing and make it look convincing. There's always one bloke who can really sing but is useless onstage, or one who jumps around and is brilliant, really looks the part, but can't sing for shit. And it held us up for a good while, because we were determined to find the right person. We didn't just want to go out with anyone just for the sake of it. We'd all already done that, so this was our attempt to get it right this time and do things properly."

Iron Maiden continued to rehearse as a three-piece outfit throughout the summer and autumn of 1978, turning up three times a week at Star Studios, in Bow. "One or two blokes had been suggested to us," says Steve, "but no one we thought was particularly special."

"Then we all went down to this pub called the Red Lion, in Leytonstone," says Doug, "to see the Radio Caroline Roadshow, which featured a lot of heavy rock music in them days, with all the DJs looning about and stuff. It was strange, because it was like everybody in the pub knew we were on the look-out for a singer, because the band was quite well known, locally, and we got recognised in places like that. Anyway, purely by chance, Steve got chatting to this bloke at the bar whose name was Trevor, who said he'd got a friend who was a singer."

"It was a mate of mine, Trevor Searle," confirms Steve, "who said, 'Oi, you're looking for a singer, ain'tcha?' I was, like, 'Yeah. What about it?'

He said, 'Well, I got this mate of mine. He's a bit of a singer, like.' I said, 'Oh yeah? We're all a bit of a singer, mate.' He says, 'No, this bloke's really good.' I said, 'What's he look like, then? I bet he looks like shit, don't he?' He said, 'No, he looks good.' I said, 'Oh, fuck it. Get him down, then.'

"By this time we were a bit despondent. We'd had a few people down and stuff like that, but nobody that really clicked. Anyway, we set a date and a couple of weeks later Paul walks in and it was, like, 'Well, he looks all right.' He had a bit of an attitude on him, and all that, but he seemed all right. He said, 'Do you know "Dealer" by Deep Purple?' As it happens, I didn't know that particular one, but Davey knew it and he showed me the chords and away we went. And fucking hell, did he sound good or what? I mean, there's sort of a quality in Paul's voice, a raspiness in his voice, or whatever you want to call it, that just gave it this great edge. And he was obviously a bit of a character.

"So the next step was, OK, it sounds great on that, but what's it gonna sound like on one of our own songs? So we started trying 'Iron Maiden' and 'Prowler', and he sounded brilliant on those, too. So then I think we sent him away and told him we had some other people to see, which was a lie. I just wanted to hear what the other two thought first before I said anything. But they thought he was brilliant as well, so I thought, 'Right, this is the boy.'"

3 Paul

Wide boy. Jack the lad. A bit of a geezer, as they say down Leyton way. That's Paul Di'Anno. Or at least, that's the legend of Paul Di'Anno. With his gruff vocal style, short punk-length hair, leather jacket, tattoos and come-and-have-a-go-if-you-think-you're-hard-enough rapport with the audience, Paul Di'Anno would become "the perfect frontman" for which Iron Maiden had been searching when he joined the band, in November 1978.

But how much of the legend actually resembles the truth? "All of it," says his lifelong friend and fellow musician Lee Hart. "Every last scrap of it. There's absolutely nothing about Paul that is put on or fake. He couldn't really be anything but a rock 'n' roll singer. Either that or a gypsy. In fact, he's a bit of both, I suppose."

An accomplished singer and guitarist in his own right, these days Lee acts as Paul's manager, but the pair have known each other since they were both kids. Lee and Paul and another mate of theirs, Phil Collen (who would later join Def Leppard), all lived three roads apart in the East End, and they all started out "playing the same pubs in different bands at about the same time".

"This was in the late '70s, I suppose," says Lee. "Phil was in a band called The Dumb Blondes, and Paul was in any number of different local pub outfits. He used to get up and sing with anybody that would have him. I was in a band called The Roll Ups, and we all used to go to each other's gigs and watch each other play. We used to joke about which one of us would make it first. Of course, Phil went on to have tremendous success later on with Def Leppard, but in my heart of hearts I always assumed that Paul would be the one to make it, because he was mad, such a character. He just used to take over the room when he walked in. And he had this brilliant voice, absolutely brilliant, full of personality. I mean, love him or loathe him, Paul was so completely out there, you just kind of knew he would end up doing something."

Unlike Dennis Wilcock, whose preference for onstage props like fake-blood capsules, duelling swords and face make-up distanced as many potential fans as it attracted to the group, Lee remembers that, with Paul, "It really was a case of what you see is what you get. There was no act involved, or very little. Paul never used to dress up for gigs. He just turned up and went straight on, and what you saw onstage, that was really him. Paul is just a born natural, made for the stage. And the frightening thing is, he hasn't changed one bit as the years have gone by. If anything, he's even madder than before. He's, like, an older version of what he was like back then, but multiplied by ten. In the nicest possible way, too. I mean, he's a really good bloke. He's just...mad!"

After many letters, phone calls, faxed messages sent through intermediaries and several hastily rearranged last-minute appointments, I finally caught up with Paul Di'Anno on a mobile phone lent to him by a mate while he was trudging down Wandsworth High Road on his way to the off licence at about 9.30 one evening in the late summer of 1997. He was back in the country briefly, he explained, sorting out a place to live for the next few months until he could get a proper British immigration visa sorted out for his newly-wed Bulgarian wife. He cheerfully acknowledged that his life was, as always, a hectic mess of contradictions that failed to please anyone but himself. He was just about to release a solo album, he said, but had already decided that, even though "it's the best thing I've done for ages", rather than spend time promoting it he was going to reform his original post-Maiden band, Battlezone. "We've been offered some tasty gigs in Europe and America and, well, I can't say no, can I?"

As for Iron Maiden, "To be honest with you, mate, I don't remember too much about all them Maiden antics and shenanigans. Got a head like a sieve, me. I never remember anything. It's all so long ago now, isn't it?" He's never been one to keep records. "That way, you don't bear no grudges. I've never kept a record of anything I've ever done. Every time I do a new album, I never listen to what I did last time. Every time I step up in front of a new band, I never think about the last band I was with.

It's just not in my nature. I'm the same in life. Never look back, that's my motto."

The eldest of ten children from his mother's two marriages, Paul comes from what he describes now as "a whole tribe of family members", including five sisters and four brothers. "My dad died and my mum remarried. Di'Anno was my dad's name. They say the first born are always the mad ones. Even my mum will tell you that." He says he was always aware of his "larger-than-life" image, even as a child – "I used to put it about a bit at school, when I could be bothered to go," he says – but claims that it was "just a natural reaction to being brought up in a boring place like Chingford", where the family resided when he was growing up.

"I know what people say about me," says Paul, "but the thing is, most of it's true, so I can't complain, really. I know people have said it's been my undoing, and perhaps it has in some ways, especially back in the Maiden days, but I can't be anything else but myself, can I? And at least I can get up in the morning and look myself in the face. Besides, what I want to know is, wasn't rock 'n' roll *supposed* to be all about people getting up and doing mad things? Things they were told they couldn't do or weren't supposed to do? It's *supposed* to be about breaking a few rules, ain't it? And I mean you've gotta do it while you can, ain'tcha? I don't want to be sitting there at 60 thinking I'd never had a bit of fun, you know what I mean?"

However, the suggestion that he never really put on an act onstage, that he was always just playing himself, is one that he refutes: "Yeah, well, people who say that, they weren't there to see me just before I went onstage, on my knees, shaking and praying. It's the same now. Don't matter whether it's big shows or small shows, I'm always shitting myself just before I go on. Then, once I'm out there on the stage, I'm a different person, I really am. Onstage... I know you've heard it all before, but it's that Jekyll and Hyde thing that rock singers always talk about. It's all true! I don't know. The excitement, it grabs me, even now, and I just can't control myself. And it's the best feeling ever, actually. Better than sex, better than drugs...better than the best!"

Paul says that he first heard of Iron Maiden "in about 1977. I had a mate that knew Steve, too, Loopy, who later became our drum tech in Maiden. The family had moved closer into the East End after my dad

died, and we were all at the same school, only I think Steve was a couple
of years ahead of us, and we knew he had a band and we thought we'd
go along and check 'em out. We went to see 'em in a pub in Stratford –
I think the singer then was the other Paul [Day], the bloke who didn't
use the blood capsules. I wasn't at all impressed, actually. We walked out
after about two numbers. I thought it was horrible! I remember they had
this one song that I think was called 'Striker', which I thought was a
scream! It was so appalling, I couldn't get it out of my head for days."

As a teenager, Paul was into "The Sex Pistols, The Clash, The Damned,
Led Zeppelin, the Stones. I was into a lot of stuff, and as I got older it
started to broaden out. I mean, you ask me today who my favourite singer
is in the whole world and I'll say, 'Pavarotti.' Well, you've got to, ain'tcha?
I mean, who's better? Who's even near him? I suppose the closest in heavy
metal would have been Rob Halford, when he was in Judas Priest," he
says, tongue firmly in cheek.

Rock music, according to the gospel of Paul, "is about attitude as much
as it is about songs. And for it all to work, you've got to have both." Which
is why, in retrospect, he thinks he was so suited to the task of fronting Iron
Maiden. "Me and Steve were perfect opposites, so it fitted. The songs were
all pretty serious, but my approach to them – at least, onstage – wasn't. And
I do like having a laugh. There are so many miserable gits in the world. I
don't want to be another. I mean, I hate to say it, but – especially here in
the UK – it's just fucking miserable, sometimes. I love the people, but so
many of them are such hopeless, miserable gits. They give up without even
trying, then spend the rest of their lives moaning about what everybody else
is doing. We've all got troubles, and God knows I've had my fair share over
the years, but you can't let it rule you, can you? I get out and try and do
something about it, even if it's just to help me forget."

When Paul first went to audition with Maiden, in November 1978, in
an effort to impress them he boasted that he'd already been the singer in
several notable touring bands, none of which, remarkably, the others had
actually heard of. "But that was Paul, never one to let the truth spoil a
good story," chuckles Steve Harris knowingly.

"By the time I came to audition for Iron Maiden, I'd only really sung
in a couple of dodgy punk bands that never got beyond the rehearsing
stage, really," the singer admits. "We might have done a few pub gigs. I

can't remember." In fact, he was then occupying the microphone in a pub rock band called Rock Candy, a name lifted from the title of an old Montrose song that, coincidentally, Maiden had played live during some of their earliest incarnations. "I can't remember how I got talked into it, but I heard that Maiden were looking for a new singer, so I went down to have this little jam with them. I think we did a couple of Deep Purple numbers or something. That seemed to go all right, but at the end they were, like, 'We'll be in touch. We've got a lot of other people to see, too.' And I was, like, 'Fair enough. Whatever you say,' you know? Then Steve came 'round to my parents' place – the next day, I think it was – and said, 'If you want it, you've got the job.' I thought, 'Yeah, all right.' I was pleased, like, because otherwise it would have been a waste of time, but I wasn't over-the-top excited or anything. You've got to remember, they were just another pub band to me then."

Doug Sampson: "Paul came down to audition and my first impression of him was that he was very friendly, very jack the lad, you know, but a very likeable bloke, in fact. Then Steve played him a tape of Denny singing the songs we wanted him to sing, so he got the melody line and the words and he took it from there. And he was good. Really good. The sound of his voice, which was sort of gravelly and loud, suited the way we played really well, I thought. So, straight away, I knew. But he left and we discussed it and within about five minutes we'd agreed – 'Yes, he's the bloke for the job.'"

"I didn't care how long or short his hair was," says Steve. "I thought he looked great and sounded great. A bit later on, he started wearing silly, frilly, Tom Jones-style vests, because he was into Adam Ant. Half the time, though, I think he was doing it to wind us up, 'cause he knew we'd go mental at him. But Paul was into all sorts of stuff. It didn't matter; it didn't really affect us. Later on, he started wearing pork-pie hats and things like that, again to wind us up, 'cause he knew we weren't into that sort of stuff. But it didn't bother me. He pissed me off when he wore the frilly shirt onstage, I must admit, 'cause I thought he looked fucking stupid. But Paul was great, the genuine article, you know? He was a bit nervy onstage, but the nervous energy came across in a good way. He was very different, more down to earth than Dennis Wilcock, that's for sure. Di'Anno was all black leather, onstage and off. He was a real geezer."

It wasn't until Steve started showing Paul some of his lyrics and explaining what he had in mind for the band, however, that Paul started to realise that, as he says, "I thought there might be more to this lot than meets the eye. When Steve started playing me some of the songs they had been working on all this time, it made sense, suddenly. I could see where he was going with it, and I thought they had something. That's when I started to get into the idea of what we were doing and realised that this had the potential to actually be a bit more than just another pub band with a few daydreams."

With the new Harris/Murray/Sampson/Di'Anno line-up in place, Steve confidently began to book gigs for the new band. Paul actually made his live debut with Maiden at the Ruskin Arms, on High Street North, Manor Park, east London, a venue that – along with the Bridgehouse and the Cart and Horses – would prove to be a stronghold for Maiden over the next two years. As Dave Murray says, "From the moment we walked onstage that first time at the Ruskin Arms, I think we all knew we'd got it right this time. It couldn't have gone better, really. The place was packed, the songs sounded great and we went down a storm. It was amazing!"

"Every time we played, it was like we picked up more fans, and I suppose the word went out," says Steve. "People started telling each other about it and bringing their friends along, and it just seemed to build really quickly. And 'cause we could guarantee an audience, we didn't have to rely so much on doing covers to keep the pub owners happy. In fact, the more original material we started to do, the better it seemed to go."

"We started to build up a little following, to where we were actually packing the places out," agrees Dave. "We used to do mainly original stuff with a few covers thrown in, fairly obscure things like 'I Got The Fire' by Montrose, 'Doctor Doctor' by UFO and a couple of early Van Halen ones, like 'Ain't Talking 'Bout Love'. But we were already playing most of the material that went on the first *Iron Maiden* album, in one form or another."

By the middle of 1979, Maiden were holding down residencies in familiar strongholds all over east London, and other bands then ploughing the same furrow of clubs and pubs began to look on in envy as Steve Harris' new line-up began breaking house records wherever they played. But little local jealousies broke out into open hostility in some cases, when the band began adding a series of tongue-in-cheek one-liners to the small ads Steve used to place in the Gig Guide section of *Melody Maker*. These varied from the not-unreasonable boast of "YOU AIN'T SEEN NOTHING YET" to more colourful snippets like "THE ONE AND ONLY RED HOT, VISUAL, ENERGY ROCK BAND", or, better still, "WE BREAK, SHAKE, SHOCK AND ROCK, WE MAKE THE REST LOOK AVERAGE STOCK!"

"There were so many old farts banging 'round the pubs in them days – probably still are – and they really thought they knew it all, some of them," explains Steve. "They played nothing but covers, and I think they hated us because we thought we were better than that. So you'd get a few snide comments from one or two of 'em, sometimes, but we just used to laugh it off, most of the time. Sticking stupid things in the ads was basically done to wind them all up, because we knew they read every word and took it to heart, so we really used to lay it on."

Best of all, though, had to be the small box ad that Steve placed in the *Melody Maker* announcing Maiden's comeback after their six-month lay-off in 1978. It read simply, "Iron Maiden are not only the *best* visual, high-energy, *original*, loud but talented, good-looking, tasteful, heart-breaking, hard-hitting, bloodsucking, mind-blowing, *hard rock band in London!* We're also very nice blokes, kind to our fans and our families, hostile to other bands, but above all we're brilliant, ace superstars and we're honest! And we're BACK!!! SO FANS, RECORD COMPANIES, A&R MEN, AGENTS, PROMOTERS, FINANCIERS AND ABLE YOUNG LADIES, WATCH THIS SPACE FOR DETAILS!" It was shortly after the appearance of this last bit of harmless nonsense that the band found one of their gigs at the Cart and Horses disrupted when members of various rival East End combos invaded the stage and poured beer all over Maiden's monitors. A "massive barney" ensued, according to Steve Harris, "but we didn't mind a ruck in them days. We could all look after ourselves. It never happened again, put it that way," he grins mischievously.

After leaving school at 16, Steve had worked for 18 months as a trainee draughtsman and soon he had begun designing his own posters for some of the gigs. "If we had half a dozen gigs in a row, I'd try and do a poster for it, just to stick up here and there in pubs and record shops, places where our fans might see 'em." And he came up with the distinctive Iron Maiden logo, which is still used on their albums and official merchandise today, a marvellously angular and solid design that fitted the muscularity and boldness of the band's raw sound. "It was amazing, the reactions we got right from the start," he says. "We put a few posters around, but it was all very cheap and cheerful. I did all the drawing for the posters myself, 'cause I was quite good at art at school. I remember one I did really early on of this hooded character that kind of floated about and that type of thing. But it wasn't just the posters or the daft ads; it was the vibe we started to build up at the shows. Our thing was, we would always try and treat going onstage at the Ruskin Arms or wherever as though we were playing Madison Square Garden or somewhere. We always tried to put on a show as well. We thought we'd go into the pub and try to completely blow them away!"

Their secret weapon in this department was Dave Lights. Having procured "a home-made dry-ice machine from Vic Vella", he had soon added a bubble-making device and an array of colourful lights and "controlled explosions" to his arsenal of "show-stoppers".

"The band started playing live again, and Steve asked if I was interested in doing some roadie work," Dave recalls, "so I said, 'I'll tell you what. I'll make you up some light boxes.' I was always handy at that sort of thing, taking things apart and putting them back together again. I used actual window-boxes from the vicarage. Steve still has them, I think. I took the flowers out and put normal light fitments in with bell-cable wire, on/off light-switches, so they'd flash on and off, with different-coloured gels, and just sort of made it up as I went along, really."

Unfortunately, not all of the explosions Dave came up with were as controlled as the band would have liked, and on one memorable occasion he nearly burned the Tramshed in Woolwich down to the ground when one of his "little explosions" went too far. "[Dave] used to pile on the powder like nobody's business," Vic Vella recalls.

"I did actually blow Steve up once, onstage," Dave admits. "He was wearing these PVC trousers, and I ended up setting fire to them! If I couldn't get proper pyro, I'd just buy boxes and boxes of fireworks and empty them into containers. You never really knew quite what concoction you'd get. And I used to make the boxes out of old Swan Vesta tins, tobacco tins, stuffed with gunpowder siphoned from fireworks and ignited by tiny fuses. Well, this particular night, it was a special occasion, one of the first big gigs outside the East End, and so I decided to pile it on bigger than usual. We thought, 'Well, it's a bigger gig than usual, so we'll make a bigger bang than usual.' But, of course, when it went off, everything just exploded! And it was right where Steve was standing, and I remember his PVC trousers caught fire. Well, they just sort of melted, actually. He had to peel them off bit by bit, along with all the hairs on his legs."

After the first few gigs, "they got a bit more sophisticated," says Dave, and he designed the first-ever Iron Maiden backdrop, "which was basically a string of light-bulbs which would flash and rotate around the name. It was a bit like a cheap hotel sign, I suppose, but the punters loved it!" What Dave is less willing to discuss, however, is the fact that he had broken into a closed-down LED factory in nearby Poplar and made off with a pair of theatre stage lights, a disreputable act that did, however, bring new meaning to the phrase "light-fingered".

"Vic Vella sold me the first ever primitive sort of lighting rig we used, which he'd made himself," says Dave, "and then he came up with our very first dry-ice machine. He'd put a kettle element into the bowl of an old vacuum cleaner and we'd drop the ice in there and the evaporated ice would come out of the tube that used to lead to the broom-handle attachment. I would get up really early and go down to the old Billingsgate fish market and ask for a few slabs of ice. They got to know me, and it became a regular thing. They started keeping big slabs of it aside for me."

Ever inventive, the centrepiece of the show that Dave would put together for the band was an ominous-looking *papier-mâché* mask, which he placed in the middle of the backdrop and through the mouth of which he would funnel what was left of the dry ice. Then, later, the smoke was replaced by "blood", which would spurt out as from a severed vein during the band's end-of-set anthem, 'Iron Maiden'.

"A friend of mine was doing Art at college and he took a mould of my face and we used that at the back of a stage," says Dave. "This big, scary face! And of course we gave him this nickname, Eddie the 'Ead, from this joke that was doing the rounds at the time."

For the record, Dave Murray recounts the original joke for us: "A wife had a baby, but it was born with only a head and no body. 'Don't worry,' says the doctor. 'Bring him back in five years' time and we'll probably have a body for him.' So five years go by, and there's Eddie the 'Ead, as his parents have called him, sitting on the mantelpiece, when in walks his dad. 'Son,' he says, 'today's a very special day. It's your fifth birthday and we've got a very special surprise for you.' 'Oh, no,' says Eddie. 'Not another fucking hat!'"

Dave Lights: "The biggest moment was always during 'Iron Maiden'. We'd get to the line in the song which goes, 'See the blood flow...' and I'd have fake blood, which would spurt out of the mask's mouth. I'd made this thing up from fish-tank tubing using an old fish-tank pump, which ran into a tin of fake blood, so we'd get to that bit in the song and it used to spurt fake blood everywhere and the bulbs would come on and start to flash and rotate. It was pretty daft, I suppose, looking back, but no one else was doing stuff like that in the pubs where we played, so we thought it was fantastic."

"I can't remember whose face he moulded it from now," says Steve Harris. "Some ugly bastard, anyway, whoever it was. Dave Lights made this thing around the lettering to the band's name. They were just underwater bulbs, and the lights used to come on or chase around. It was quite small, really, but there was just something up there to show who we were. We wanted everyone to know who we were and not forget us. And then we used to have this fish-pump thing in the back of the mask that fake blood used to come out of. Dougie used to get covered in fake blood every night! And he had blond hair, so he could never get the bloody stain out! I used to say, 'Are you sure you don't mind about this?' But I used to be thinking, you know, 'Too bad if you do,' because it was a great part of the show. And he'd go, 'No, it's all right. Fuck it. It's all part of the show,' and we used to have a right lark with it."

The second version of the 'ead, which followed soon after, was again constructed by Dave Lights, only this time the mask was made of fibreglass and was slightly bigger, and was now equipped with eyes that lit up at appropriate junctures in the show while huge clouds of red smoke issued from its contorted mouth at every opportunity. But if their stage show was already evolving into the arena-filling spectacle it later became, musically there was still one vital piece of the jigsaw missing: a second guitarist. For a time, the band battled on with a succession of partners for Dave Murray, none of whom quite fitted the bill.

"First, we gave it a go with this guitarist we tried called Paul Cairns, who we used to call Mad Mac," says Doug Sampson. "but it was like... I don't know. It just wasn't meant to be. We thought he'd work out OK, 'cause he could play all right; but the minute we got onstage, we knew it wasn't happening. Our first gig was at the Bridgehouse again. It was in the middle of winter and there was about five inches of snow on the ground that night. It really was a bad night, and I couldn't blame anyone for staying home, but I got there and Paul hadn't turned up yet. He was off buying a leather belt or something, and he eventually turned up really late, which didn't exactly do him any favours, turning up late for your first gig."

But at least Cairns managed to stay the course for more than three months. His successor, Paul Todd, never even got as far as playing his first gig. "His girlfriend wouldn't let him," Steve Harris recalls dismissively. Then there would be Tony Parsons, who joined the band briefly in September 1979 and would last a little over two months. "He was a good guitarist, but not good enough that Davey couldn't do everything he did ten times better," recalls Steve. "A lot of gigs, we just played as a four-piece, 'cause Davey was so good he could do a lot of it on his own. The plan was always to get a second guitarist in, but finding one that could match Davey was just really difficult."

Once they were playing live and drawing in the crowds, though, no matter who was occupying the other side of the stage from Dave Murray, Paul Di'Anno, for one, was convinced that the band would land a record deal sooner rather than later. "I thought we would definitely get a record deal," says Paul, "just on the mad reaction we were getting from the shows. And the shows were really good. It was always a phenomenal live band. I don't think we really realised it at the time, but we were. The shows ran on pure adrenaline and aggression. And we were the same age as most of the kids in the audience, too, so that made it like a real gang. And wherever we went, whenever we played, they were there to cheer us on."

One young fan from the very earliest days was Keith Wilfort, who later ran the band's official fan club for many years. Catching Maiden's first ever Cart and Horses performance purely by chance (he claims that he was giving the barmaid's boyfriend the slip at the time after getting caught taking her out for a drink), the generously proportioned pundit was "converted on the spot" after witnessing the band blasting out 'Transylvania' at top volume. One night, not long after, Keith walked into the Bridgehouse wearing a T-shirt he'd made himself which proudly proclaimed the legend "CHARLOTTE RULES OK" across the front in honour of Dave Murray's popular contribution to the set, 'Charlotte The Harlot'. He soon followed this with a more elaborate "INVASION" T-shirt, adorned with battling Vikings and thunderbolts. Thus Keith became the first person to design an Iron Maiden T-shirt, even preceding the first official T-shirts, which were simple red-and-black items.

"We'd go over and do a gig in Barking," says Steve, "and the fans from Hackney would all come over to see you. Most of 'em didn't have transport or anything, so we used to give a few of them a lift back in the old Green Goddess, as we used to call the old van we used to pile around in. But sometimes there was just too many of them and we couldn't get them all in there, so we just used to get them to sit on the back and give them a lift to the station and drop them off there. They were a right gang of herberts, most of 'em, but they just loved the band and we loved them."

Appearing at free open-air festivals in such salubrious surroundings as the Teviot estate in Poplar and Wapping Park also ensured that Maiden continued to add to their growing number of regular fans. Nevertheless, even before Paul Di'Anno had joined the band, it had become apparent that what the band needed now was something to draw attention to themselves outside east London. Being big in their own back yard wasn't enough to entice the A&R men at the west London-based record companies down to their gigs. Used to frequenting better-known London rock spots like the Marquee, the Rock Garden, Dingwalls and the like, most major record-company scouts had never even heard of the Bridgehouse, let alone the Plough in Leytonstone or the Harrow in Barking, all venues that Maiden were regularly able to pack out, now that they had a new singer.

Steve Harris: "The trouble was, we tried to get gigs closer in to town, but it was practically impossible. The punk thing was still really happening then, and places like the Marquee just didn't want to know about any long-haired band they'd never heard of. Also, we wanted to start branching out and playing gigs outside London, and there was no way people would just take us on spec, so that was when the idea of doing our first proper demo tape came up. Basically, we did it to help us conjure up a few gigs. We had no idea of the impact it would have. I mean, the minute we'd done the tape, from that point on, everything just went off like a rocket!"

Impressed by a demo of Dennis Wilcock's and Terry Wrapram's new band, V1, which had been recorded out in Cambridge at a small but professionally run studio called Spaceward, "We could do worse than follow suit," says Steve. It was more expensive than most of the East End studios with which they were acquainted but, as Steve says, "We decided that doing it on the cheap was a false economy. We knew we'd only probably get one go at it, and we wanted it to sound the best we could." And so it was that time was booked for Maiden to go into Spaceward, one 24-hour session that would begin on the morning of 31 December 1978 and carry on right through to the following morning. It was New Year's Eve, a time when the studio would normally be empty, and Steve managed to haggle the price down to just £200 "plus an engineer prepared to work on New Year's Eve". For their money, Maiden would return home with four Steve Harris compositions – 'Iron Maiden', 'Invasion', 'Prowler' and 'Strange World' – all properly recorded for the first time and ready to be made available on cassette to prospective club-bookers and anyone else who might be interested. They went for it.

"We didn't know what to expect, going into the studio for the first time," says Steve. "We just hoped the engineer was gonna be good enough to record us, and that was it, really. We just went in there with a naïve attitude and, as it happens, it was pretty good. The songs were very together already. We didn't have to arrange much. They were very tight, 'cause we were doing them live all the time. We knew exactly what we needed to do. It was just a question of whether we could record it all in time. But we went in and the tracks went down really quick. I think we did most of them in the first take."

Dave Murray: "We were actually supposed to go back for a second session a couple of weeks later to polish off a few mixes and add a few bits here and there, maybe, once we'd had a chance to listen to it for a couple of weeks. The thing is, though, they wanted an extra £50 off us for the master tape and we just didn't have it on us at the time. And when we went back, two weeks later, they'd already wiped the master and put something else over it! We couldn't believe it. So, in the end, we just had to put it out as it was, which was all from that one mad session down in Cambridge on New Year's Eve."

"We spent all the money we had on the studio and there was nowhere to stay," says Steve. "We were just, like, kipping in the back of the van. I'll never forget it – New Year's Eve and it was snowing like anything, and we were all in the back of the van, freezing our nuts off in the night. But luckily enough Paul Di'Anno pulled this nurse in the pub and, oh, she was a life-saver! She invited us all to this party and we crashed out at this party for a while and then we went back to her place. She had a one-room bedsit, and there was all the band there, and we all crashed out in the corner. And of course Paul's, you know, sorting this bird out in the bed in the other corner. They waited till they reckoned that we were asleep, but of course we weren't. We were listening to everything that's going off. Everything! That was so funny."

However, the fun and games really started when the band handed a copy of the original four-track Spaceward demo to a London DJ called Neal Kay, then just making a name for himself on the burgeoning heavy-metal club scene. Kay ran regular "heavy metal nights" at a venue he had dubbed the Bandwagon Heavy Metal Soundhouse, which in reality was a sweatbox attached to the side of the Prince of Wales pub in Kingsbury Circle, northwest London.

What made Kay's nights unique was not just that they appeared to go completely against the grain of the prevailing trend for all things punk, but that they did so with such aplomb, such humour and such skill. For starters, they had the largest club PA then in existence, a 2K affair piled up to the rafters, the kind of rig a big band would normally use. And they had quasi-psychedelic lights which would flash and zigzag across the walls, as if in tune with the music, which most nights was a headbanging mix of established crowd-pleasers, like 'Doctor Doctor' by UFO, or almost anything by Judas Priest, but with the emphasis firmly on the new. Rock was no museum piece, as far as Kay was concerned, and he refused to play tracks that were more than ten years old, going out of his way to dig up the latest rock sounds from wherever he could find them, sometimes on import, sometimes brought in by Bandwagon regulars, a committed group of HM devotees who later took to bringing down crudely fashioned cardboard guitars, which they would wield intently during the most cataclysmic guitar solos, eyes closed, backs arched, fingers a blur of frenzied fantasising.

As a result, the Bandwagon used to be packed every time it opened its doors. But what really gave the place its reputation as the *numero uno* metal night out in London was the larger-than-life personality of Kay himself. A self-styled "godfather of metal" who refused to give up wearing flared trousers at a time when even Dave Murray was forced to admit that, *après* punk, flares just looked plain silly, Kay's Heavy Metal Soundhouse wasn't just a disco; it was a crusade. With a beard as long as his hair and hair as long as his legs, Kay was once mockingly (but accurately) described by Garry Bushell as looking "like a sawn-off Catweazle". That impression – coupled with his insistence on referring to everyone, including his wife, as "man" – made Kay an easy target for the holier-than-thou music press, who delighted in poking fun at him and his self-proclaimed "followers". But this just turned the maniacal DJ into an even bigger martyr to the Soundhouse regulars and more people than ever came down to the club to find out for themselves what all the fuss was about. Encouraged by his messianic zeal, as time went by more people started bringing down their own selections for Kay to play, some of them actual demos of new bands that the regulars either knew about or had formed themselves. One of these came from a group he had heard of but had never seen play: Iron Maiden.

Kay recalls very well the evening Steve Harris, Paul Di'Anno and Dave Murray all turned up at the Soundhouse and handed him a copy of their recently completed Spaceward demo. "We weren't asking him to play it at the Soundhouse, though we wouldn't have minded. It was more about just trying to get a gig down there, maybe," recalls Dave Murray. Kay, then still basking in his new-found glory, was imperious. "I said, 'Oh, yeah. You and five million others,'" he recalls with a wince now. "I told them to leave it with me and maybe I'd get a chance to hear it a couple of weeks later. I really hate myself for that now!" Then, when he did finally get around to playing it, "I nearly fell over!" he chortles. "I was running and screaming 'round the lounge like a lunatic. I just couldn't stop playing it. The next day, I phoned Steve Harris up at work and said to him, 'You've got something here that could make you a lot of money,' and he laughed at me. He thought I was kidding!"

In fact, Kay was never more serious or more right. The four tracks on the original Spaceward demo still practically leap out of the speakers when you play them nearly 20 years later. Refreshingly shorn of what Steve Harris once called "the kitchen-sink production values" of stately '70s monoliths like Led Zeppelin and Deep Purple, this was rock music made raw and alive again, played for kids by kids, fast and furious and barbed-wire catchy.

"For a start, it was a pretty together demo," says Kay. "There were a few bum notes, but Steve and the band had realised that you need to use a decent studio. They hadn't wasted time. They'd gone in and worked hard, and the whole package was put together amazingly well. They'd obviously thought it out to the best of their ability at the time, and musically it was staggering. It was the melody plus the power that impressed me. Aggressive bands have been a dime a dozen ever since, but no one since has had the tunes, too. The combination of speed, power, the key changes and Dave Murray's melody lines bowled me over. It was very unique and very impressive. Definitely the most impressive demo I'd ever had delivered to me."

Overnight, Kay was transformed into an Iron Maiden zealot, impatient to begin spreading the word to the faithful down at the Soundhouse, where he immediately set about playing tracks from the tape at regular 15-minute intervals. But no one was more surprised than the band themselves when 'Prowler' turned up at Number 20 in the Bandwagon's own Heavy Metal chart, published then every week in *Sounds*. (Kay had begun to contribute a weekly chart to the magazine in 1978 and, like everything else he did at the Bandwagon, he took this task very seriously, basing the charts strictly on requests received from his regulars down at the Soundhouse.) By the issue of *Sounds* dated 21 April 1979, 'Prowler' had reached Number One, where it would stay for another three months. A week later, Maiden played their first gig at the Bandwagon and the result was instant pandemonium.

Steve Harris: "I left the tape with [Neal Kay] and that was that. There were kids giving him tapes all night. I didn't know if he was even gonna listen to it, let alone start playing it at the club. I just went down there to get a gig there, 'cause I'd heard a couple of bands had done gigs there, but he started playing the tracks, and suddenly there were all these requests going on. They had this Soundhouse Bandwagon chart in *Sounds*, and that's when 'Prowler' got to Number One. It was amazing! We went down there one night, me and Paul, just to check it out. We thought, 'No one knows us from Adam,' you know? 'We'll be all right.' Then they put 'Prowler' on, and the next thing there's all these nutters giving it loads down the front, throwing themselves about, headbanging and playing air-guitar and all this business. I couldn't believe it, that one of our songs could do that. It was weird! Me and Paul were just looking at each other, like, grinning from ear to ear, thinking, 'Fucking hell! This is a bit of all right!'

"So, after that, we just went up there and said, 'What about a gig, then?' And he went, 'Yeah. We wanted to get in contact with you, anyway, because I love the tape, man.' So we did the gig and it just went down a storm. It was absolutely packed, and we just went down incredible. And of course Neal loved it. He absolutely *loved* it! And really that was the start of the band getting some recognition outside the East End, the fact that Neal loved the tape so much, and then the fact that the punters who went to the Soundhouse – which was really the heavy metal hardcore – loved it so much, too. It was just the spur we needed."

The Spaceward demo also helped to procure them even more shows. "Mainly US air force bases," recalls Paul Di'Anno. "That was the first time we ever played to Americans, and they went berserk! We used to play a longer set, there. They'd make us play for four hours, and we only had about an hour and a quarter of our own original material, so we used to have to do loads of covers by Montrose, UFO and Van Halen, loads of stuff American rock fans would know, and they loved it!"

But the magic that the Spaceward demo appeared to work for Maiden didn't stop there. An even more influential figure – who had been given a copy of the tape and had also decided there was something going on here that deserved closer inspection – was now looming on the horizon, someone who admittedly knew nothing about east London but who appeared to know a great deal about every other place in the world to which the band could wish to go. His name was Rod Smallwood and, as Steve Harris has always freely acknowledged, "If Rod hadn't have come along when he did, I honestly don't know if any of this would have happened. We'd have probably got signed in the end and made a few albums, but somehow I just don't think it would have happened for us in the way it did, if it hadn't been for Rod."

Acting as both business manager and personal mentor, Rod Smallwood was to become the other key personality – besides Steve Harris – in the Iron Maiden story. Until Rod appeared on the scene, in the latter half of 1979, Steve had always carried the burden of the band's responsibilities and commitments, the decision-making and the organising. Now, in this burly Yorkshireman, he had found someone he trusted enough to carry out most of those duties, someone who understood both the music and the business and who the band could trust not to try and sell them down the river at the first available opportunity. In close consultation with Steve, Rod would act as the driving force behind Maiden's inexorable rise to the top over the next ten years. He fulfilled many roles: the experienced music-business pro who would steer them through the (for the band) murky and unmapped waters of publishing contracts and multiple-album record deals; the extrovert backstage raconteur with an endless stream of amusing stories about his days working as a booking agent and the different characters he had encountered on his many adventures around the world; and the fatherly figure who was always there on the road with them, not just for the media-blitzed major-city shows but also through the thick and thin of the more usual bread-and-butter outposts many other managers would have gladly left the band to get on with on their own.

Ironically, Rod had made the decision to retire from rock management soon after a messy and unpleasant split from his previous clients, Steve Harley And Cockney Rebel, and was actually considering sitting some exams to get started in a career as a lawyer when he was first given a copy of the Spaceward demo. "I had no intention of getting back into management," he smiles now, "but a mate asked me to listen to a tape he had that he thought was pretty good. As a favour, I did, and it just blew me away! I couldn't stop playing it. So that's when I got in touch with Steve."

Steve remembers the contact well: "Andy Waller was a bloke I used to work with for a while in this architect's office, a draughtsman I knew who was a bit of a music fan. I gave him a copy of the tape and he really loved it. He was a rugby lad as well, which is how he knew Rod – they played for the same rugby team – and, 'cause he knew Rod was in the music business, he told him about the tape, and Rod said, 'Look, let me have a copy and I'll tell you what I think.' And, well, he's basically been telling us what he thinks ever since..."

4 Rod

Roderick Charles Smallwood was born in Huddersfield, Yorkshire, on 17 February 1950. The son of a policeman, Rod is – on the surface, at least – a near-perfect example of what's recognised in Britain as the archetypal Yorkshireman, a hard-working, hard-playing, cricket-loving, rugby-worshipping, ale-quaffing, spade-calling, indomitable spirit that fills any room he walks into with his larger-than-life personality and back-slapping bonhomie. But underneath the party-hearty exterior, Rod is also a very serious and knowledgeable music businessman, dedicated to his work and as passionate now about all things Iron Maiden as he was in 1979, when his rugby chum Andy Waller first passed him a cassette of the band's Spaceward demo.

"The great thing, for me, about getting involved with Maiden was that I actually really liked the music," he explains. "It wasn't one of those usual music-business situations where a manager gets involved with an act because he simply sees the potential to make some money. In fact, I had no intention of becoming anybody's manager, at that point, but they kept on at me to come down to a gig, and I thought I'd go just to offer them a bit of advice, maybe, just to be polite, really. I really liked the tape, the first time I heard it. It was right up my street – big, loud, fuck-off rock music! And it was unusual at that time to hear a new band from London even attempting something like that. Don't forget, this was at a time when the punk thing was all that was new in the A&R departments of the record companies in the UK, and I was never that into punk."

Growing up in northern industrial Huddersfield in the '60s, the closest Rod ever got to Swinging London, he says, was "listening to The Beatles and the Stones on the radio. That was what music was to me then, something you listened to on the radio. Playing rugby and cricket were always much higher up on my list of priorities. Probably still are!" As a result, Rod didn't really get into buying albums and reading the music papers until he went to college and "a pal played me some Frank Zappa". By the end of his first year, he found himself "very, very heavily into Deep Purple, Grateful Dead, Pink Floyd, The Doors. Anything album-oriented, I was probably into it. It never occurred to any of us to buy singles. It was the late '60s/early '70s and the idea was, get the album, get home and get fucked up, basically." He shakes his head and smiles before adding, "Things don't change much, do they?"

Arriving at Trinity College, Cambridge, in the autumn of 1968, ostensibly to read architecture, Rod now claims that the majority of his time at Cambridge was spent "playing rugby and going to parties". The fact that he would also – however unwittingly – busy himself with laying the foundations for all that came later by becoming Trinity's unofficial social sec was purely accidental, he insists. "There isn't really one social union at Cambridge. Each college has its own thing. But generally speaking, in those days there was the occasional college disco and the May Ball. The Trinity May Ball was the biggest annual social occasion, and I got involved the first year I was there, not organising it as such but helping out on the day. It was one of those things where you have lots of different areas with different sorts of entertainment going on. I remember the main attraction that first year was John Hiseman's Colosseum."

Colosseum was a proto-'60s jazz-rock/fusion outfit featuring Hiseman on percussion, Dave Greenslade on keyboards, Tony Reeves on bass and, at the time that Rod met them in 1969, one Dave "Clem" Clempson on guitar. The only member of an earnest bunch that aspired to bring something of a more "rock 'n' roll" spirit to proceedings, typically Clempson didn't actually turn up for the show until just minutes before the band was due to go onstage, and Rod got his first taste of what it was like to have to shepherd a wilfully errant musician about his business.

"Clem was regarded as a shit-hot guitarist at the time," says Rod, "and I just thought he was a lovely guy. I was responsible for meeting him at the gate, taking him to the stage and then taking him to the bar afterwards and getting him pissed. I thought, 'What a great job!' Afterwards, I was told that he could be hard to handle, but I thought he was great. I got him a drink and a smoke and he was fine, so I thought, 'This is great.' Then, the second year, I got more involved, this time in booking the various acts."

In a move that was to prove charmingly prophetic in a way that neither man could have guessed at the time, Rod enlisted the help of fellow Trinity undergraduate Andy Taylor, a Geordie who came from a similar northern, working-class background and who remains his partner and best friend to this day, some 30 years later. "Me and Andy are the same age," Rod reveals. "He's actually six days younger than me, although he's never looked it!"

Indeed, while Rod has always favoured the standard rock manager's kit of jeans, sneakers, band T-shirt and leather jacket, his shoulder-length hair only receiving its first serious snip when he reached his 40s, Andy Taylor is a strict suit-and-tie man. Balding, bespectacled and with all the rock 'n' roll attitude of a pinstriped City banker, Andy's strict, businesslike demeanour would prove the perfect number-crunching foil to Rod's streetwise, ideas-first, front-of-shop persona. At least, that's how they've always played their parts in public. Behind closed boardroom doors, however, their perceived roles blur more efficiently into one. Rod is just as likely to huff and puff over the figures while Andy enjoys, as he cheerfully admits, "very old brandy and very large cigars".

Someone who has known both Rod and Andy for nearly 20 years and has seen the partnership at close hand is Howard Jones, lawyer for Iron Maiden, Paul McCartney, Pink Floyd and Kate Bush. "They're a magnificent double act," he says. "Of that there's no doubt. But it's not as simplistic as the old good-cop/bad-cop routine. They're both extremely charming and very knowledgeable in what they do. Rod understands the music and the industry intimately and Andy understands the intricacies of contracts and finance as only someone with his qualifications can. But it's the way their minds work together to solve problems or come up with new ideas which is really astonishing. They may look quite different on the surface, but when they go into meetings they speak as one. They're just a tremendously good team. Unstoppable, really."

And so it would prove. Building on the back of their successes first with Iron Maiden and then with a string of new rock artists over the years, including at various times WASP, Helloween, Skin, Poison and, latterly, Bruce Dickinson, Rod and Andy would turn their Sanctuary Group of companies into a massively successful organisation which now includes record labels, a publishing company, recording studios and rehearsal complex, travel agency and numerous entertainment-industry spin-offs, such as a children's TV production company and music-book publishing wing. Teaming up with the established investment firm Burlington (already listed in the City), the Sanctuary Group plc was floated for the first time on the London Stock Exchange in January 1998. Valued at more than £20 million when trading began on 23 January, the company's shares have since soared and Rod and Andy's personal stake in the venture is now comfortably estimated to be worth around £10.5 million each. Not bad for a pair of northern grammar-school boys.

"I'm from Newcastle and Rod's from Huddersfield," says Andy Taylor, "but we've got a lot in common, in terms of our outlook on things. We were both grammar-school boys who somehow managed to get to Cambridge, so we both had a bit of go about us, and funnily enough both our fathers were policemen as well. I don't know if that was significant, but we always had a lot more in common than people sometimes assume when they first see us together."

At Cambridge, Andy had started to study for a degree in what was then known as natural sciences. "In those days, it wasn't easy being a grammar-school boy going to Cambridge," he explains. "You had to pick something you stood the best chance of finding a place you could get in on. I mean, in those days, you didn't do Economics in grammar school, so there was no way I had any business A-levels, because nobody did any. They might have done it in private schools, I don't know, but the thought of doing an Economics degree wouldn't have crossed my mind, because I didn't have any qualifications in it. My best subjects were Science, which is logic orientated rather than artistic. I preferred the scientific side, which is what Business and Economics and everything else is. That was where my skills were, so that's what I did my degree in."

They had met, typically, at a party not long after Andy had arrived at Cambridge, in 1969. "We were both invited to a party at the Graduate Society," recalls Andy, "and I was going along with a nurse. Rod happened to be behind me with that nurse's friend, and he overheard me say that I was a graduate at Trinity College, Cambridge. Although it was my first year, it was his second, and so we started to chat. We went back with these nurses to the nurses' home and, of course, it's been a standing joke between us ever since over what happened next. Basically, one of us slept in the bed and one of us slept on the floor, and the truth is I honestly can't remember who got what, but I always swear it was me who got the bed and Rod always swears that it was him. But that was probably within a few weeks of me starting at Cambridge, 30 years ago, and we've been friends ever since."

"Andy's a great guy," says Rod. "Always has been. Brilliant mind and full of surprises. The 1970 Cambridge Trinity May Ball was the first thing we ever did together, booking all the acts and organising everything. It wasn't until the following year that we got it right, though. The first time we did it, we made the classic mistake of booking the stage times for all the bands without allowing time to take down and set up all their gear in between. It never occurred to me they would need a change-over time. I just had them all coming on straight after each other! I thought I knew it all, as you do at that age. The next year we did it, though, we had two stages with everything timed to go off as one stage ended and a DJ in the middle. We were well slick by then."

Andy also "got roped into doing all the college Student Union things, as well" and brought Rod with him. "We organised the May Balls, the Rag Balls, we did discos and dances, and just ended up doing all these sort of things together," Andy remembers. By Rod's third year at Cambridge, he and Andy had built up a sizeable reputation at the venerable old university for knowing how to show end-of-term students a good time. A working routine was quickly established: Rod, in jeans, would organise and have all of the personal contact with the bands while Andy, in a dinner jacket, would arrange and attend the various dinners.

"We ended up putting on all sorts of different acts," says Rod. "Graham Bond, Chris Farlowe, Bridgett St John, John Martyn, a few different reggae-type bands, or blue-beat bands, as they were called then. The gigs would all start at about ten in the evening and go on until six the following morning. I remember we once got offered Led Zeppelin for £1,000, and Yes for about the same. Whether they'd have done it or not, I don't know, but a thousand quid was quite a lot of cash in those days, practically the entire year's budget, so we never went for it in the end.

Contrary to popular belief, we never made any money ourselves out of these things. Whatever you made you just ploughed back into having an even bigger do next time. But suddenly there I was dealing with the booking agents for all these bands, some of them quite well established, and I suppose that was where I got a taste for working in that area. It seemed like the music business was all about being paid to put on a party. I thought, 'Bloody hell! If that's all there is to it, I'm laughing!'"

Rod would get most of the musical acts he booked from Horus Arts, a locally based agency that provided the talent for most of the universities around the country. "I was friendly with the boss, Barry Hawkins," he recalls. "He was a good bloke who realised I didn't know much about it at first, and so he used to offer me some good advice on what was available and the sort of prices and facilities we would need to have to get them on the bill." In retrospect, he says, it was "almost inevitable, I suppose" that Rod should eventually end up working as a booking agent when he left Cambridge.

Andy, too, was keen to explore further the idea of perhaps making some sort of career out of what he now describes as "the wider entertainment business. I always conceived that I would be going into business, but what sort of business it would be, exactly, I didn't rightly know, to begin with. But before coming to university I'd run dances and things in my local town. From about the age of 15, I used to do dance halls – get in a band, or get in a discotheque, or usually just put them on together, put on soft drinks and things and sell tickets. You know, make money from running things. Being a sort of small-time promoter, I suppose. And I did a lot of work in restaurants and pubs and things. So, even before I met Rod, the whole sort of entertainment area was what I was into. If somebody had said, 'What do you think you'll want to go into when you leave university?' I think I would have said, 'Entertainment,' in the wider sense. It's a funny thing. It's not like I picked it, more like it picked me. I was just always involved, somehow. Maybe it was just the age I grew up in, the '60s. It was the first time young people had wanted to be really entertained in that way, and it was up to other young blokes like me and Rod to try and meet that sort of demand, because we wanted to enjoy ourselves, too."

Andy thinks of himself as "someone who likes and enjoys music but isn't fanatical about it". With obvious exceptions, like "The Beatles,

Elvis Presley, Frank Sinatra, Johnny Cash, people like that", he's the kind of CD buyer who never remembers the names of the artists, just the titles of the songs or pieces of music that he wants to hear. Therefore, it comes as no surprise to learn that "I'm always happy to leave any musical decisions that need to be made to Rod. I have very funny taste in music. I like country music and folk music and much more melodic-type music than most of the acts I've been involved in... I like music as a means to relax, to have on in the background. I like music while I'm driving, and I listen to mainly that sort of nice, relaxing music, rather than unnecessarily intense music, whereas of course Rod's the complete opposite. He loves rock music and going to gigs and the whole lifestyle aspect of it, and it works quite well that way.

"But you can be much more objective about everything when you don't have a strong opinion about the music. Rather than having any bias, which can go either way, I can get on with things sensibly, because, if you're really into the music and you happen to dislike a certain record, it's impossible to sell it, and if you love it too much, you might blind yourself into believing it's a lot better than it is. When you actually have no real view about it at all, other than knowing that certain people you respect believe in it, then it allows you to be very objective, which a lot of people find very hard to be in this business, I've found."

The most memorable booking Rod and Andy made while they were at Cambridge was almost certainly when Rod somehow managed to persuade legendary Detroit rockers The MC5 to appear at the Trinity May Ball in 1971. The MC5 had first come to prominence in 1968 as the "house band" for American activist John Sinclair's White Panther Party, presenting their own vicious brand of hard rock as an uncompromisingly violent strain of revolutionary socio-political ideology. Their first album, the enormously influential *Kick Out The Jams*, had been recorded live in Detroit and released in 1969 to much critical acclaim and no little controversy. The follow-up, *Back In The USA*, released in 1970 and produced by then-prominent US rock critic Jon Landau (who later went on to manage Bruce Springsteen, after making his memorable claim of having "seen the future of rock 'n' roll" at an early Springsteen show), was regarded as one of the hardest-hitting rock records of its time by the time Rod booked them. However, it hadn't sold well, as most of the tracks had consistently been denied mainstream radio airplay. Meanwhile, the band's anti-everything notoriety had become troublesome in the extreme, as they now found themselves the target of regular raids and personal harassment from the police and right-wing groups at home in America. It was the era of the Kent State riots, when the National Guard was called in by President Nixon to break up an anti-Vietnam demonstration at Kent State University, which resulted in the guardsmen shooting dead more than 20 unarmed student peace demonstrators, and political student paranoia was rife. When John Sinclair was arrested on what the band regarded as trumped-up drugs charges and looked to be going to jail for some time, the band wondered – perhaps not unreasonably – which of them might be next. As a result, The MC5 were seriously considering a permanent move to England, where they were fêted by the critics and unknown to the authorities, when Rod made his bid to book them for the 1971 Trinity May Ball. As usual, it seemed that Rod had both luck and timing on his side, the two most important ingredients for success in the music business, as with anything else.

"Booking The MC5 was the best deal I ever did as a student," Rod reflects. "I remember it very clearly. The deal was done with a London agency called Gemini, which I also later worked for. But the deal was £200 plus six bottles of champagne and two ounces of grass. That was the deal! And for that we got The MC5, this self-styled anarchic, American 'revolutionary' group playing the Trinity May Ball! I must admit, I thought it was quite funny, watching them walking around after the gig amidst all this finery, straight from the streets of Detroit. I mean, the Trinity May Ball is very much part of the upper-class English summer season, like Henley and Ascot. It's part of the real old English establishment. And I'll never forget it, this long-haired group of so-called anarchists swanning around, drinking champagne, all out of their heads. I think they loved it, actually."

While Andy stayed on for another year to finish his degree, Rod dropped out of Cambridge "on a whim" just after the 1971 May Ball, sold all of his possessions ("books and records – I didn't have much else") and moved to Paris with his girlfriend. He didn't even stick around for long enough to take his final exams. "It just seemed like the cool thing to do," he shrugs now. The idea of having any sort of career path mapped out "was unheard of, as far as I was concerned".

"Rod's probably one of about ten people in a hundred years that haven't come out of Cambridge with a degree," guffaws Andy Taylor. "As usual, I just think he was in a hurry, though I don't think he quite knew what for, really, at the time. But you can't exactly say it's held him back, now, can you?"

"I returned from Paris after three months and decided to make the trek to Morocco," says Rod. "That was the pre-requisite, in those days of the utopian hippy lifestyle, and again it was just the cool thing to do. It was either Morocco or India, one of those places. I didn't mind. I just wanted to go. This was the late '60s/early '70s, and you just didn't think about things like jobs. You thought about travel, you thought about having fun, you thought about getting laid and getting stoned and everything else. A lot of people I knew then didn't have a clue what they were going to do. You just thought about the present and experiencing as much as possible in life. It was about keeping things very, very informal and doing things for the short term. I mean, you did actually think, if you ever got to 35, you'd be very lucky. But then, 35 when you're 20 is ancient! Of course, we know now it's not…"

In order to save up the cash for his proposed trek down the well-trodden hippy trail that led "from north Africa down through India and the Himalayas and on into the South Seas – I think that was the plan", in the late summer of 1971 Rod talked his way into a temporary job at the same booking agency, Gemini, that he'd used to book The MC5. He spent most of the few weeks that he was there arranging dates for folksy English progressive rock outfit Barclay James Harvest. When Lindsay Brown managed to lure the band away from Gemini and over to MAM, the rival booking agency for whom he was working at the time, he also offered Rod a full-time role booking with the company. "I went from £12 a week plus a small share of commission to £35 a week plus proper commission, and suddenly I was loaded," Rod recalls gleefully. "£35 a week! I was, like, 'Whoa! Here you go!'" The trip to Morocco would have to wait.

Andy Taylor: "I was studying, and when I left Cambridge I went on and eventually qualified as a chartered accountant, but I always stayed in touch with Rod. I remember, the last year I was at Cambridge, he still hung around. He used to stay over and sleep on the floor a lot, I seem to recall."

Rod was at MAM for 18 months before he left to work for the management company of a new MAM act then just making the headlines for the first time: Steve Harley And Cockney Rebel. Formed by vocalist and former journalist Steve Harley in 1972, Cockney Rebel arrived in the slipstream of glam rock – a genre then dominating the British music scene – with their quirky 1974 hit single 'Judy Teen' and the accompanying Top Ten album *The Psychomodo*. Further hits – most memorably their January 1975 Number One 'Come Up And See Me (Make Me Smile)' – allied to Harley's arch-English charm, surreal Dylan-esque lyrics and studiously theatrical stage image meant that Cockney Rebel were soon held by critics in the same high regard as David Bowie, Roxy Music, T Rex and Mott The Hoople. Within a few years, however, the group had split, their efforts to break America having left them no better off in the US and virtually forgotten back home in the UK.

For Rod, working with Harley and Cockney Rebel would prove an invaluable lesson in what he now jokingly refers to as "the dark arts of rock management". While working with a chart act like Cockney Rebel was obviously "a tremendous introduction" to his career in management, he confesses that he found dealing with the egocentric Harley "very difficult indeed". Nearly 25 years down the line, Rod is loath to go into the details of his eventual fall-out with the self-absorbed Cockney Rebel singer, except to say, "It was the main reason I didn't immediately offer my services to Maiden as a manager. I had been Cockney Rebel's agent early on, and then I went into management with Trevor Beeton at Trigram, their manager. I had a reasonable salary for the time and a small profit share, which unfortunately never realised anything, and Trevor was a very decent person, but Steve Harley was never that big. And he was a pain – selfish, egotistical, obsessed. He completely put me off management. The guy was a real pain in the arse. He got convinced by EMI that we weren't the right management company for him, particularly in America, which may or may not have been true. I was 23, I think I was learning pretty fast and I think I did a lot of good things for his career. If you look at how his career went after we stopped looking after him, I think that bears me out.

"But that experience put me right off management. Despite all the work I'd put in on his behalf, after he told Trevor that Trigram was fired, he didn't even call me. Not a word of thanks. I haven't seen him since, but a couple of people recently have said, 'Harley sends his regards.' He can keep them."

However fraught his first foray into management may have been, nothing prepared Rod for the shock he got when he realised "how few real friends I had when I wasn't the happening young manager of a hit band any more. You walked into pubs and places where you used to be surrounded by people ready to talk to you and have a drink and suddenly, when you walked in, it was all 'Oh, is that the time?' and a lot of turned backs. I suppose I was naïve, but I was really shocked and disillusioned. I'd always been quite sincere in my dealings with people, or at least tried to be. It never occurred to me that they only wanted to know me 'cause they wanted to get near the band, or whatever. Without that band behind you, you really found out who the real people were, and there weren't that many, I can tell you that."

For a while, Rod accepted a freelance commission to manage an RCA signing called Gloria Mundi – "kind of punk meets glam rock. Good band, but there wasn't much of a vibe going on for them" – and he was, by his own admission, "getting bored by then. I was completely disillusioned by the whole business." He decided to pack it in.

One friend who did remain true, however, was Howard Jones, who worked for the firm of Bernard Sheridan, who were then lawyers for Cockney Rebel, among others. Rod had got to know Howard – then completing his Articles – as his day-to-day contact there, and the two had soon become firm friends. Looking for something else to do now that he'd made up his mind to quit rock management, Rod talked to Howard early in 1979 about maybe going back to university and doing a law degree.

"He came to see me and said he'd decided that he was going to be a lawyer," recalls Howard, "and he wanted me to obtain some forms for him. Then we played tennis one evening – I remember it vividly – at Lincoln's Inn Fields, and he said thanks for the forms but he was going to hold on for a while because he'd found this band and he was going to see if it worked, and if it didn't he would be back in touch. And, well, he hasn't come back to me about it yet…"

"God knows what gave me that idea," Rod wonders now. "I'd never fancied it before, or since! But I was getting older. I was in my late 20s by then and thinking, 'Well, maybe I should get something sorted,' and Howard was very, very helpful. He went to the Law Society and started getting things together for me."

What saved the world from the implausible sight of a bewigged Rod Smallwood holding forth before m'learned friends was a modestly packaged four-track cassette that his rugby pal Andy Waller had pressed on him some days earlier. "It was four tracks," he says. "The original Spaceward demo, basically. And because of my background – which is basically heavy rock – I was, like, 'Yeah, this is really happening.' And it was pretty different from what most new bands I knew were doing at that time, which was mainly punk stuff. I'd never really liked punk. Gloria Mundi had a very musical side, too, but punk never really appealed to me. I just never got off on it. I suppose the fashion aspect put me off. I've always been very anti-fashion."

Rod liked the tape, all right, but that was as far as his interest lay, to begin with. Still intent on leaving the music business behind, the turning point came when the long-term relationship that he was in at the time ended abruptly. "About 20 of us went off on a rugby tour of California," he says, "in a team from Rosslyn Park and London Welsh called the Muppets, after a West End night club. We played at this tournament in Santa Barbara in April 1979, and it was great – out every night, beautiful weather, completely blitzed the whole time, hanging out with brilliant people and still getting up in the morning ready to play a game of rugby."

To economise, the group had purchased last-minute standby tickets from Freddie Laker's now defunct airline, then the cheapest transatlantic service in Britain. When five of the party, including Rod, arrived late for their check-in time ("We were still pissed from the night before!") and missed their flight home, they were forced to wait another four days before their tickets would allow them to travel again. When Rod finally got back to London, his long-suffering girlfriend announced that she was leaving. "She was sick, she said, of being a rugby widow," he sighs. "She was unhappy, because I was playing rugby all the time. I used to play Saturday, Sunday and most Wednesdays, with training on Tuesdays and Thursdays. I played for Rosslyn Park and I took it all very seriously, never missed a game, never missed training. It did sort of take over my life for a while, but that was probably as much to do with the fact that there wasn't really anything going on in my life then that I could really relate to. Not until Maiden came along."

Not knowing what to do next, his mind turned back to the tape he'd been playing before he left for America. Playing it again and again, he became convinced that there was something better than average going on here. He reached for the phone.

"It was like one thing ended and you have to have something going for you," he explains, "so I started thinking about the tape. Andy Waller put me in touch and I spoke to Steve on the phone and arranged to see a gig. They were playing in the East End most nights, but I wasn't going there. You must be joking! I said, 'Why can't you do the Marquee?' But they just couldn't get into places like that, then."

Instead, they compromised, and Rod used some of his old booking-agent connections to get them a couple of gigs in west London, one at a well-known pub venue called the Windsor Castle, on the Harrow Road, and one at an equally well-populated pub called the Swan, in Hammersmith. Neither occasion, however, would go exactly to plan.

"I didn't introduce myself at first, in case they were crap," Rod admits, "but I was quite impressed by the set-up. They had their own little PA and lights and smoke coming out of the Eddie death's-head thing at the back of the stage. The only trouble was that they wouldn't go on until all their mates from the East End arrived. The pub management wanted them on time and a dispute developed in which Steve eventually told them to stuff it and they packed up their gear and left without playing a note. Steve wanted the guy to give them 15 minutes, because they had mates coming a long way, but it was one of those ego things where the manager wouldn't give in. But you just don't play Steve like that. He's always going to tell you to fuck off, which of course is what he ended up doing, as he still would. But it was quite funny, actually. I remember this guy saying he'd have them banned from playing every venue in northwest London. Wonderful, really, when you think they were playing Wembley Arena, down the road, just a few years later. But I watched all this and then eventually spoke to Steve and the others briefly, and I liked them straight away. They had a lot of charm and a lot of innocence and a lot of heart."

Steve apologised to Rod for the no-show and both men parted agreeing that the next gig, a few days later at the Swan, would go better. But there was trouble again when Paul Di'Anno got himself arrested for carrying a knife less than 30 minutes before the band was about to go on. "Steve sort of sidled up to me about five minutes before they were due to go," Rod recalls wryly, "and said, 'I don't know how to tell you this, but...'" Paul had been mingling with fans and friends outside the venue when two passing policeman decided to conduct a spontaneous stop and search and frisked the hapless frontman for drugs. Paul wasn't carrying any drugs in those days, but what they did find was the flickknife that he'd taken to carrying around with him. He was immediately arrested, taken into custody and whisked, handcuffed, to nearby Hammersmith police station.

"I explained that I was just about to go onstage, but they weren't having any of it," Paul remembers sheepishly. "I even offered to come straight over to the nick after the gig but they just didn't wanna know. It would have spoiled their fun, giving me a break, wouldn't it?" Paul was eventually fined for possession of an offensive weapon, but by the time he got back to the Swan, the gig was over.

Rod: "Steve said, 'I don't know how to tell you this, but we're not playing.' So I said, 'Why not?' He said, 'Paul's been arrested.' So I said, 'Well, look, I'll call the cops.' So I did, but all they said was that Paul had been 'detained' and that they wouldn't be releasing him for at least an hour. So I said to Steve, 'Look, why don't you play without him, at least to give me an idea? Do you know the words?' He said, 'Yeah, I wrote them.' So I said, 'Look, why not just give it a shot?' And they did it, and they were great! I'd never seen anything like Steve and Davey onstage. It was clear they obviously loved playing, really loved being onstage, looking the audience right in the eye with total attitude and total self-belief. The charisma onstage just from Steve and Davey was very, very powerful and I was blown away. I just thought they were going to be major from the word go, and that was before I'd even seen them with the singer!"

Rod was still unsure, though, whether he actually wanted to take the plunge and become their contracted manager. "I said, 'Look, I'll help you all I can. I'll get you a deal. But will I manage you? At the end of the day, I don't know. Let's see how it goes.'" In fact, it wasn't until after he arranged their signing to EMI and publishers Zomba that Rod and Iron Maiden actually put anything down on paper between them.

"It was all down to trust," says Steve Harris. "I don't know why but I just felt the first time I met him that Rod was someone who wouldn't let you down. We'd met a few people from the biz by then and most of 'em were so full of bullshit you didn't know what they were going on about, half the time. But with Rod, he just cut through the crap and immediately started lending a hand. And the more he got involved, the more it was just obvious he knew what he was doing. And, I mean, he's a laugh, too, isn't he? You work hard with Rod, but you always have a laugh, too. And that's important, I think. I mean, we're a band. We're not, like, rocket scientists or anything. You're meant to have a laugh, aren't you?"

Now, of course, the fun could really begin...

5 NWOBHM

While there's no doubt that the recruitment of Rod Smallwood as manager was to prove crucial in the band's long-term development, by hastening the arrival of the sort of major record deal they'd only dreamed about until then and being an invaluable navigator of the stormy seas that lay ahead, it's also worth remembering that, by the time Rod arrived on the scene, in the late summer of 1979, Iron Maiden was a band already beginning to ride the crest of a wave. As ever, Rod's timing was impeccable. Following on from their surprise topping of Neal Kay's Heavy Metal Soundhouse chart in *Sounds*, the magazine had run its first live review of the band at a show at the Music Machine in Camden Town (now better known as the Camden Palace), which Kay had organised for them in May under the guise of his burgeoning success. Deciding that the time was right to take his Bandwagon on the road, Kay had booked the Soundhouse's three most requested new bands onto the same bill, which meant that Maiden were sandwiched between Black Sabbath copyists Angel Witch and the more bluesy, old-style boogie of Samson, with Kay himself installed as both MC and DJ for the evening.

Sounds journalist Geoff Barton, who was there that night, would later write, "I do definitely recall Maiden being the best band of the evening, infinitely preferable to the Sabs-worshipping Angel Witch and way ahead of Samson." However, the most intriguing aspect of the event, Barton says now, "is that a band like Iron Maiden or Angel Witch could even exist at a time like that." They were the first new, young, overtly "heavy" rock bands that had sprung from the streets of London since the early '70s, and Barton – as the recognised in-house metal writer on *Sounds*, at that time – was intrigued enough by what he saw that night to talk his editor, Alan Lewis, into letting him pen much larger subsequent features, not just on Iron Maiden but also on the whole new British rock scene that Barton felt sure was bubbling underground and of which he believed Maiden merely represented the tip. He even had a name for it: NWOBHM (the New Wave Of British Heavy Metal).

"The phrase New Wave Of British Heavy Metal was this slightly tongue-in-cheek thing that first cropped up in a subheading," he says, "and we just expanded it a bit to give the feature some sort of slant. To be honest, I didn't really feel that any of these bands were particularly linked in a musical way, but it was interesting that so many of them should then be emerging at more or less the same time. It was a good thing for the genuine rock fans who had really gone to ground, hiding in their wardrobes, waiting for punk to go away so that they could emerge, blinking into the light, like one of those hairy cave-dwellers in a Michael Moorcock book. We began by doing a feature on Def Leppard, who had just released their first, independently produced EP, 'Getcha Rocks Off'. Then Maiden came along, just as we were really starting to take notice of Neal Kay's Bandwagon, and so we did a feature on them. And then suddenly here was Samson and Angel Witch, then Tygers Of Pan Tang and Praying Mantis, and so we did features on them, too, and it just kept going from there."

The cornerstone of the burgeoning NWOBHM scene was a twelve-page colour feature that Barton eventually put together for the magazine, at the tail end of 1979, under the humorous headline "KERRANG!" These days, of course, *Kerrang!* is a weekly magazine in its own right, one recognised around the world as the leader in its field. Like a lot of great ideas, however, it would never have got past the drawing-board stage if it hadn't been for one man's own genuine passion for the idea.

Geoff Barton: "Because of the phenomenal response we got from this NWOBHM thing we were running with originally, the *Sounds* editor, Alan Lewis, had come up with the idea of putting out an entire magazine devoted to not just the NWOBHM bands but the wider rock scene itself. By then, there was also a lot of American kind of new-wavey metal bands coming along, too. I was starting to receive tapes and records from all over the world, all purporting to somehow be connected or influenced by the

NWOBHM scene, and so the idea was to put them all together in this one-off colour mag."

Barton had been given a week at home to come up with all the articles and reviews while Lewis oversaw the design and choice of pictures from his office. But when Barton returned to the *Sounds* office seven days later, he was informed by a disgruntled Lewis that the publishers had changed their minds at the last minute about risking the expense of a magazine devoted entirely to heavy metal. "They just binned it without a second thought," Barton recalls. "I thought, 'Right. That's that, then.'" After they got over their initial disappointment, however, the pair decided that, rather than waste an entire week's work, they would simply run the magazine as a free, one-shot colour gift inside the following issue of *Sounds*. It was to prove a masterstroke, giving the widest possible exposure to a newly emerging music and culture deliberately disdained or, at best, ignored by the rest of the weekly music press.

"I remember we had a picture of the Samson drummer, Thunderstick, on the cover," says Barton. "He was wearing this S&M bondage mask with a zip over the mouth, and the response we got was just overwhelming. I think it became one of our biggest-selling issues that year. So then the idea resurfaced of actually putting out a colour metal one-shot in its own right, so we did what amounted to a sequel, which is how the very first issue of *Kerrang!* went on sale, in 1980. It was actually listed as issue 'Number One B', and it had Angus Young, the guitarist from AC/DC, on the cover. Again, it was just meant to be a one-off, but it completely sold out, literally, within days of going on the newsstands. So then we did another and another until it became obvious that this was really a monthly magazine in its own right, which was quite extraordinary, really, for that time, because you have to remember there were only four big music papers in those days: *Sounds*, *NME*, the *Melody Maker* and *Record Mirror*. Magazines like *Smash Hits* and *Q* and *The Face* simply hadn't been invented yet, and to suddenly have another music title – albeit a monthly – and to have it devoted to heavy metal... I mean, no one would have predicted that, even just a few months before. It was weird, to say the least."

What Barton could not have foreseen, however, was the grip that the frankly scatty phrase NWOBHM would have on the imagination of the rest of the music and media world. However unwittingly, Geoff Barton and *Sounds* had begun a process that would help define the parameters of a whole new genre in rock music and, whatever the level of their respective success in the years that followed, the names Iron Maiden, Def Leppard, Diamond Head, Praying Mantis, Samson, Angel Witch, Tygers Of Pan Tang and the myriad others that swiftly followed (Ethel The Frog, anyone?) would forever after be linked in the minds of rock historians with an era summed up, for better or worse, by that one careless phrase that Barton had half-jokingly come up with one rainy afternoon in the *Sounds* office. "We ran the feature, and the response we got from both the readers and other bands themselves was just phenomenal," he says. "It was obvious that, whatever you called it, there was definitely something going on out there. Suddenly there were new heavy metal bands springing up everywhere, it seemed. Of course, not all of them were as competent or as interesting as bands like Iron Maiden and Def Leppard, but the fact that they were even trying was news back then, and we just ran with it. For about two years, in the end."

Ironically, considering the short shrift most of the post-punk music critics could be expected to give any band called Praying Mantis or Angel Witch, the motivation behind this apparent resurgence of interest in a genre long since proclaimed dead by the likes of the *NME* came from a dissatisfaction similar to that levelled at punk, with what a new generation of kids saw as the self-indulgent, album-orientated monoliths that had preceded them. By 1979, bands like Led Zeppelin, Pink Floyd, ELP and Yes – all prominent members of the ruling rock royalty of the day – were rarely seen in Britain, and when they did deign to make fleeting appearances they invariably spurned the idea of actual touring in favour of more languorous (not to mention lucrative) strings of dates at large, impersonal arenas like London's Earl's Court. Rock bands had become grandiose and pompous, the music they played old before its time. As a result, the gap between those on the stage and those not had never been greater.

Punk wanted to wipe the past out and start again, but in its hurry to tear down the edifice, it had overlooked the obvious – that, at its foundations, hard rock and heavy metal weren't so different from what the best punk rock imagined itself to be: raw, alive, unafraid to offend, unafraid to be ridiculed and spat on for the clothes it wore and the life it chose to lead. The now-famous Sun columnist Garry Bushell, another *Sounds* writer and early Maiden follower, later identified "the real need of rock fans to find bands they could relate to again, and the real need for the metal genre to produce a young, dynamic alternative to lazy, geriatric metal monoliths well past their abdication time. Bloated by excess, castrated by indulgence, pampered by sycophants and hangers-on, the old rock stars had become like lumbering dinosaurs, out of touch with their fans and unable to deliver the basic promise of good hard rock – to deliver excitement and escapism, to violate with volume and erect rock dreams against the world. The old guard had outlived their function, which is why the new breed is so readily received."

The "new breed", as Bushell calls them, had also absorbed some of the more practical lessons of punk. For instance, you could release limited editions of your own records on small, independently run labels that didn't offer you any big cash advances, like the majors, but also didn't dick you around over the artwork of the album sleeve or what the A-side of the single should be (which is what Def Leppard – a teenaged five-piece from Sheffield who would go on to become one of the biggest bands in the world – did, releasing the four-track EP 'Getcha Rocks Off' on their own Bludgeon Riffola label, original copies of which are now worth a small fortune). Also, like punk, the NWOBHM fans even started their own fanzines, and by 1981 titles like *Metal Fury* (edited by your red-faced author), *Metal Forces*, *Metal Mania* and countless similar titles had all made the leap from the back-room press onto the shelves of WH Smith as the demand for articles on the new, revitalised UK rock scene rapidly increased.

Malcolm Dome, a life-long hard rock and heavy metal devotee, who at that time was a deputy editor at Dominion Press, publishers of educational scientific journals such as *Laboratory News*, had begun contributing articles on the NWOBHM scene to *Record Mirror* in 1980 and later became a leading writer for *Kerrang!*, where he remains a senior editor to this day. He has no hesitation in describing the years between 1979 and 1981 – the apotheosis of the NWOBHM – as being "some of the most exciting for new rock music this country has ever witnessed. It was always more of a scene than a genre," he reckons. "I went to the Bandwagon quite a few times, when Neal Kay was there, and it had a great vibe. There wasn't anywhere else like it then. People criticised Neal for his arrogance later on, but he was playing stuff that you simply wouldn't have been able to hear anywhere else, and in that respect I think his involvement in spreading the word about new British bands like Iron Maiden and Praying Mantis was crucial in bringing the attention of magazines like *Sounds*, and then *Record Mirror*, to an evolving scene that they otherwise would probably never have known about."

Dome recalls attending a typical NWOBHM night at the London Lyceum in 1980, when the bill featured Tygers Of Pan Tang opening, followed by Praying Mantis and topped by Iron Maiden. "It was a stupendous show," he says. "The Tygers were clearly still feeling their way, but Praying Mantis were really good, really solid. Then Maiden came on and blew the lot of them away!" Of all the new bands then emerging, however, "Maiden were clearly identified, pretty much from the word go, as being at the vanguard of the new movement," says Dome. It became a self-perpetuating phenomenon. "The more exposure in the media the Bandwagon got, the bigger the NWOBHM thing appeared, and the bigger the NWOBHM thing appeared, the more important Iron Maiden appeared.

"Maiden were regarded as at the top of the pile of the NWOBHM, and rightly so, in terms of where they stood musically. With the possible exception of Def Leppard, they were obviously streets ahead of everyone else, but it was also clearly because of the amazing exposure Neal Kay's Bandwagon had given them. It's one thing to be this great new band but another to be this great new band at the forefront of a whole new wave in rock music. That's news! But of course, like any scene, it completely fed upon itself. I remember Neal was particularly fond of Praying Mantis, too, who always got a lot of plays down at the Soundhouse. Probably even more than Maiden, some nights. Well, Praying Mantis was another band, like Maiden, that Neal could – perhaps not unjustly – claim he had discovered. But then he hardly played the first Def Leppard EP at all! He would play a track from it occasionally, perhaps, but not half as often as he would play something by Maiden or Praying Mantis, and you couldn't help but suspect that that had to be partly due to the fact that he hadn't had anything to do with bringing Def Leppard to the world's attention. It became an ego thing."

In time, however, the influence of the NWOBHM scene would be felt in every corner of the world where rock music was played. "It just gave a new spin, a different kind of edge to traditional long-haired rock music," says Lars Ulrich, drummer and founding member of '90s metal megastars Metallica. A self-proclaimed "fanatical Diamond Head fan" who had followed the group around on tour in Britain in the summer of 1980, Ulrich was also in enthusiastic attendance at several early Iron Maiden shows. "I mean, I was a teenage Deep Purple fan from Denmark who thought it didn't get any better than that, you know, who was then suddenly thrown into this whole NWOBHM thing. And it sounds weird, but basically it changed my life." He had returned to America that year with the avowed intention of "forming my own NWOBHM band. Obviously, we weren't British, but we saw Metallica, musically and attitude-wise, as being in that same sort of vein. In America at that time, the only rock music that you heard on the radio or saw on the TV was from bands like REO Speedwagon and Journey. There was nothing with any real edge going on outside maybe AC/DC. And they weren't American, either. We were much more influenced, early on, by bands like Diamond Head, Iron Maiden, Motörhead... We wanted that really rough, aggressive sound that you just didn't get anywhere else."

For their part, Steve Harris claims that Iron Maiden were only "vaguely aware of any real scene outside the Bandwagon and our own gigs. We just read about this whole NWOBHM thing in *Sounds*, like everybody else." Nevertheless, as a direct result of Barton's endeavours in *Sounds*, Maiden were quickly identified as being at the forefront of the NWOBHM and were soon included in their own feature-length article in the mag. This was when the errant guitarist Paul Todd was still (albeit briefly) in the line-up, staying with the band just long enough to participate in their first proper photo session, shots from which accompanied that first *Sounds* feature. While his replacement – the woe-faced Potters Bar lad Tony Parsons – was also destined to last just a few short weeks, Maiden spent the late summer and early autumn of 1979 belting up and down the country in their Green Goddess with Vic Vella at the wheel, Dave Lights and his box of tricks in tow and, more often than not, Paul Di'Anno's old mate "Loopy" Newhouse, who acted as Doug Sampson's drum technician, and another all-round helper pal of

Steve's called Pete Bryant, who later became a London fireman, a career for which he says that he felt eminently suited after his experience of helping Dave Lights "trying to put his fireworks out every night".

The Green Goddess, a three-ton truck that Steve had bought with £3,000 borrowed from his saintly Aunt Janet (almost her entire life-savings), was large enough to accommodate the whole band, their equipment and crew members and remain just under the official HGV limit, which meant that they could all be insured to drive it. A much-needed improvement on its predecessor, a clapped-out old Transit van of dubious insurance status, Vic Vella had spent two days on the Goddess, converting the interior into a scaled-down but very serviceable tour bus. "Vic kitted it out really good," Steve recalls fondly. "It was lined with teak on the inside and there was an intercom fitted so we could tell the driver when we wanted to stop for a slash. The back half held all the gear. Vic put a shutter on the side and nine bunks on the front half, just enough for the band and the crew." Unable to afford the luxury of hotels, they would book their out-of-town gigs around long weekends away, sleeping in the Goddess as Vic or, more often than not, 'Arry himself took turns at the wheel. "We used to park the van outside my nan's place and we used to load the gear into her back room. It used to go right up to the ceiling. It was the same room we used to rehearse in with my first band, so she didn't mind." Dave Murray remembers playing at a gig in Birkenhead at a small venue called the Gallery Club, "and it was so cold that when we woke up we were covered in a thin layer of frost! It was horrible, but we had to laugh," he adds, still smiling 20 years later. "And the way the gigs went down so well always made up for it. We never thought about the hardships. We just thought about the gigs."

However, the band had only been in possession of their beloved Green Goddess for a few weeks when a gang of thieves made off with the vehicle from a road in Clapton, along with over £12,000 worth of equipment. "We nearly died when we discovered it was gone," Steve recalls. "We thought, 'Well, that's it, then. We're fucked.'" They half-heartedly placed an ad in the following week's *Melody Maker*, appealing for the return of at least their instruments and amps, in return for a "no questions asked" guarantee, adding, "Due to the above event, it seems unlikely we will be able to play for some time." "We thought we'd stick the ad in, just in case," says Steve, "but basically we never thought we'd see any of it again."

Then their luck changed, and a few days later the police rang Steve at home to tell him that they'd found the truck and apprehended the villains, four local youths from nearby Homerton, led by a 26-year-old train guard from Stratford named Ilkay Bayram, who were all later charged at Old Street Court.

"It was very, very lucky," says Steve. "I think the only thing we didn't get back was two amps, which they'd already flogged. The police said they found it on the Kingsmead estate, in Hackney, which is a notoriously rough area, well known for that sort of thing. I think the police actually caught them knocking off some other job and then followed them back to Hackney and found the old Green Goddess at the same time."

Back on the road again and full of good intentions, the band introduced a strict "no women" code aboard the bus, a rule which, it almost goes without saying, was broken on their first day out on the road. Vic Vella tells of getting "stuck with two birds", who actually turned out to be so helpful that they were eventually rewarded with jobs in tour catering years later, when the band could afford such conveniences.

Inevitably, the tales revolving around the extra-curricular activities of various band members and their touring entourage from this period are manifold. Typical of any young band winging its way around the country for the first time, most of their adventures involved copious amounts of alcohol and ranged from the fairly standard sort of item, like the time the band got so pissed off by the way in which they were treated when they actually got to stay in a proper hotel that Paul Di'Anno felt it necessary to make his feelings felt by literally pissing off the hotel (ie leaving his calling card splashed all over the plant pots in the lobby while Doug Sampson thoughtfully redecorated the walls by applying a fresh layer of green gob), and the nefarious exploits of another as-yet unnamed travelling companion from those days called Ken Jenkins, a friend of Dave Murray's whose chief ambition appeared to be to keep the party going, no matter what. As Garry Bushell dryly puts it, "Ken was never, ever seen sober. Suffice to say that, if the man is still alive today, it is a moving testimony to medical science and/or the indestructibility of the Cockney liver."

Dave Murray: "We used to hurtle all around the country in the Green

Goddess, four of us asleep in the back of it and one in the passenger seat next to the driver, Vic. We couldn't ever afford to stay in hotels, so we ended up kipping in some funny places. Paul was good at pulling birds that would let some of us crash at their places while the rest of us slept in the van. They were truly the good old days. We had a lot of fun."

Vic Vella took to jotting down his own private thoughts in ballpoint pen on the itineraries, including such acute observations as "This man is so tight he wouldn't give his own shit away" with an arrow next to the name of one pub owner the band encountered on their travels, while another scrawled entry recounts the time when they parked the Goddess for the night in what they thought was a conveniently open yard, only to discover, on waking the next day, that they had in fact spent the night in a car park and were now surrounded by hundreds of other vehicles. It took them two hours to squeeze their way out.

Then there was the time that Doug Sampson persuaded Vic to "do a Dennis Weaver" with the green machine (as in the early Steven Spielberg classic, *Duel*), tailing some hapless motorist for miles through the lonely Scottish countryside, or the time that Paul Di'Anno fell drunk into somebody's back garden and made off with a washing line of women's lingerie wrapped around his head.

"Paul was the worst," says Doug Sampson. "He could never stay out of trouble for long." Vic recalls how Paul used to while away the hours on the motorway by terrorising the rest of the occupants of the bus with his astonishingly accurate pea-shooter, a fairly tame habit that grew more dangerous by the hour in the confined space of the bus as the members of the band took it in turns to threaten to kill their errant frontman if he didn't stop zinging peas at them while they tried to sleep. At this point, says Doug, "He'd give you this all innocent look, like, 'But I'm only having a laugh!' But he didn't enjoy it unless it really annoyed you, which, after a while, it would."

"Paul was one of them blokes who used to love starting trouble but didn't like to stay around and finish it," says Dave. "I remember he was in this row with two blokes down the Rock Garden one time and I stepped in to try and calm things down, and when I looked around Paul had gone and the next thing I know I'd been bottled. But you couldn't hate him for it. Or not for long, anyway. He was such a charming sort of

Smiler, October 1974.
L-r: Mick Clee, Steve Harris, Dennis Wilcock,
Doug Sampson and Tony Clee

Gypsy's Kiss, November 1973.
L-r: Paul Sears, Bob Verschoyle,
Dave Smith and Steve Harris

Iron Maiden
outside the East
End's famous Blind
Beggar pub, 1976

Iron Maiden from
November 1976.
L-r: Dave Murray, Dennis
Wilcock, Steve Harris, Bob
Sawyer and Ron Matthews

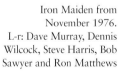

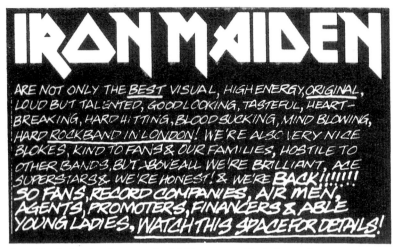

Steve Harris' handmade posters for Maiden attracted both fans and controversy

The first incarnation of Eddie the 'Ead

This October 1979 Maiden line-up lasted
two weeks. L-r: Steve, Doug Sampson, new
singer Paul Di'Anno, Dave and Paul Todd

Kiss fan Dennis Wilcock

Dave and Steve in full flight at the Music Machine, 1979

The free-flowing Dave Murray at Neal Kay's Bandwagon, 1979

Dave and Paul at the Music Machine, 1979

Heavy Metal Chart

1	1	**PROWLER**, Iron Maiden, **Demo Tape**
2	7	**XANADU**, Rush, from **'Farewell To Kings'**, Phonogram
3	6	**D.O.A.**, Van Halen, from **'Van Halen II'**, WEA
4	2	**QUEEN OF SPADES**, Styx, from **'Pieces Of Eight'**, A&M
5	4	**OVERKILL**, Motorhead, from **'Overkill'**, **Bronze**
6	5	**TYRANT**, Judas Priest, from **'Sad Wings Of Destiny'**, Gull
7	9	**IRON MAIDEN**, Iron Maiden, **Demo Tape**
8	13	**SPEEDY'S COMING**, Scorpions, from **'Fly To The Rainbow'**, **RCA**
9	10	**BLUE COLLAR MAN (LONG NIGHTS)**, Styx, from **'Pieces Of Eight'**, A&M
10	14	**GREEN MANALISHI (THE TWO PRONGED CROWN)**, Judas Priest, **CBS 12'' Ltd Edition 45**
11	8	**DOCTOR DOCTOR**, UFO, from **'Strangers In The Night'**, **Chrysalis**
12	19	**CATCH YOUR TRAIN**, Scorpions, from **'Virgin Killers'**, RCA
13	3	**HOMEBOUND**, Ted Nugent, from **'Cat Scratch Fever'**, Epic
14	17	**SUITE MADAME BLUE**, Styx, from **'Equinoxe'**, A&M
15	11	**CRAZY ON YOU**, Heart, from **'Dreamboat Annie'**, Arista
16	15	**SUPERNAUGHT**, Black Sabbath, from **'Volume IV'**, NEMS
17	—	**ANTHEM**, Rush, from **'Archives'**, Mercury
18	12	**RIFF RAFF**, AC/DC, from **'Powerage'**, WEA
19	16	**NOBODY'S FAULT BUT MINE**, Led Zeppelin, from **'Presence'**, Swansong
20	—	**SYMPTON OF THE UNIVERSE**, Black Sabbath, from **'Sabotage'**, NEMS

Compiled from record requests at The Bandwagon Heavy Metal Soundhouse, Kingsbury Circle, London NW9.

Maiden's first Number One – top of *Sounds*' Heavy Metal chart, compiled from audience requests at the Bandwagon

Paul and Loonhouse at the Music
Machine, October 1979

Headlining in the East End was one
thing: now it was the Marquee

The "more in hope than
anything" ad for their stolen gear

Maiden's first recording: 'The
Soundhouse Tapes'

Maiden's first photo session for *Sounds*, October 1979. L-r: Doug Sampson, Paul, Tony Parsons, Dave and Steve

Rod's notes for tour expenses

December 1979 ad

Paul Di'Anno on the Judas Priest tour, 1980

I WOULD just like to warn Dave Murray the lead guitarist of Iron Maiden that if he steps foot inside Manchester again I will personally pummell his brains in, cos he's ruined what I thought was an ace relationship with my girlfriend. And may I point out that no matter how much she rubs his name in my face I still think Deb Brown of Wythenshawe is the best yet.
— Jealous Dave

Typical Dave Murray fan mail, printed in *Sounds*

TERRY DRAPER FOR ENGIN-EAR PRODUCTIONS LTD PRESENTS

ALL NIGHT
HEAVY METAL BASH
at the
GLOBAL VILLAGE
VILLIERS STREET, CHARING CROSS
FRI. 10th AUG.
IRON MAIDEN
+
URCHIN
Support + Surprise appearance + DJ Joe Lurig. Entrance £2 from 9pm.
Lic. Bar till 3am. Hot Food + Soft Drinks till 6am.

A landmark night for Urchin founder Adrian Smith, who would go on to join the night's headliners. August 1979

Dennis Stratton

Maiden's first *Sounds* cover

Another first – the band's debut at the Rainbow, 1 April 1980

The band signs to EMI. L-r: (standing) Martin Haxby, Brian Shepherd, Steve Cook, John Darnley, Ashley Goodall, (seated) Paul, Doug, Rod, Dave and Steve

Iron Maiden's first single, 'Running Free', with cover by Derek Riggs

The band's first ever sales award – a UK silver record for *Iron Maiden*, plus Japan's *Music Life* award for best band, April 1980

bloke, and very funny, you knew he didn't mean any harm. It's just that he couldn't help himself. That's just the way he was."

While Maiden were making their presence felt for the first time around the rest of the country, the band also managed to slot in a gig every other week at increasingly familiar London strongholds like the Soundhouse and, closer to home, the Bridgehouse or the Ruskin Arms. Dave Murray recalls both Maiden and Motörhead being asked to judge an air-guitar competition down at the Soundhouse one night. "I always got to know the cardboard-wielding regulars, because I'd done just the same when I was a kid, although I was a good bit younger when I did it than most of the hairy monsters down the Soundhouse," he adds with a cackle.

It was soon after that, though, that Motörhead's singer, Lemmy, asked Steve if Maiden would like to support them at a special charity benefit gig they had planned at the Music Machine on 3 September. Motörhead were billed that night as Iron Fist And The Hordes From Hell, and the gig sold out immediately. Even better, from Maiden's point of view, they went down a storm before the notoriously partisan Motörhead audience, further proof that the band were finally beginning to build a plausible rep for themselves outside the East End.

"The *Sounds* articles got us really noticed for the first time," says Steve, "and because of that we started getting gigs a bit further afield than the old East End. I remember going up to do a gig in Aberdeen, at a club called Ruffles, where we pulled over 300 people, which we thought was brilliant for that time. And they were all up on the tables, shouting and cheering! We'd never seen anything like it, and that was all because of the tape being in the Soundhouse charts in *Sounds* and the general sort of vibe that was going on around this new wave of metal thing. It did lead to getting our first reviews in the music papers, but even more importantly than that it led to the fact that we were able to go to other places and say that we'd been in *Sounds* and we'd been in the Heavy Metal chart and blah blah blah. One weekend, we did a gig in Blackpool on the Friday night and we went across country. Then we stayed in Berwick that night and then we went up to Aberdeen and did a gig on the Sunday night, then back home the next day. It was knackering, but it was all building work, just to keep the whole thing going."

Playing before new and appreciative crowds around the country for the first time, it became more apparent than ever that what the band urgently required in order to keep their momentum going was the release of a record. But their latest brush with "the um and ah brigade", as they quickly became known in the Maiden camp, had not been promising. A rep from Chrysalis Records had come down to see the band play a couple of free nights at the Swan, in Hammersmith (Rod remembers sitting up all night making the posters by hand), but despite several follow-up phone calls he wouldn't say yes and wouldn't say no. (Just "um" and "ah", presumably.)

So far, however, Rod had deliberately avoided approaching any of the major London record companies directly. "We wanted to make sure the fire was really burning bright before we started dragging A&R men down to the gigs," he explains. Now, with *Sounds* deciding that the time was right to run their first major interview with the band, which they would splash across the front page of their 27 October issue, Rod seized the moment and began to exert serious pressure on the top A&R (artist and repertoire) men he knew, urging them to "get their asses down to see this incredible band I'd found".

His first move was to "pull in a few favours I was owed" and get Maiden their first booking at London's prestigious Marquee Club, in Wardour Street, spiritual home and oft-shared starting point of the careers of many a future Brit-rock legend, from The Who and David Bowie to Jimi Hendrix, Pink Floyd, The Sex Pistols and countless others. Having decided to pull out all the stops, including leaning on some of his old Cockney Rebel contacts at EMI, Rod was determined "to show the majors what they'd been missing all this time".

The gig was scheduled for Friday 19 October, and Rod set about persuading A&R reps from both EMI and CBS, as well as A&M and Warner Bros, to come along to the show. He recalls having a £5 bet with Uli, who used to book the bands for the club, that Maiden would actually sell out the show. In those days, you could cram nearly 800 people into the Marquee on a good night, and the idea that an unsigned band that had never played there before could sell it out was so outlandish that Uli was convinced that Rod was either being hopelessly optimistic "or had completely lost his marbles". By seven o'clock that evening, however, the last ticket had been sold and the kids were still crowding around the tiny doors of the Marquee trying to blag their way in. Uli handed over his fiver to Maiden's beaming manager "with a look of utter astonishment on his face," Rod recalls gleefully.

Interestingly, Steve remembers having his own £5 bet with Rod, not over whether the show would sell out or not – both men felt confident of that – but by what time. "The bet was that the place would be sold out by seven o'clock. Rod said it would and I said, 'No way,'" Steve smiles. "He made me give it to him and all."

"It surprised everybody except me," says Rod. "Every step with Maiden, you could just feel what was going to happen. It really was just one of those seemingly unstoppable things. The band were just pure reality. They're a great band playing live, and Steve has always written fantastic songs, but they have a certain heart and soul that I don't think many other bands have got, I really don't. What makes Maiden different, in terms of their attitude and their honesty and their integrity, is it's all genuine. A lot of people in that situation try to be that or pretend they're that, but Maiden *are* it. Maiden *stinks* of it! Maiden are what their fans think they are, and that's part of why they took off in the first place and why, also, they're still around today."

But not everybody at that time shared Rod's vision, and although scouts from both CBS and Warners came to the Marquee that night, they both later turned down the band's request for a record contract, while the A&M scout didn't even bother to show up. Fortunately, however, EMI was prepared to take a different view. Brian "Shep" Shepherd, who later went on to become managing director of A&M Records, was the head of A&R at EMI in 1979, although it was his assistant, John Darnley – whom Rod already knew well from his days with Cockney Rebel – whom Rod actually persuaded to accompany him personally to the Marquee that night. Still smarting from his clash with the powers that be at EMI over Steve Harley, Rod had set his sights on a deal with CBS.

"It's funny how these things turn out," he says. "At the time, I said, 'Right, that's it. I'll never fucking work with EMI ever again!' But I knew John. I liked him and trusted him. And it's ironic, because Sanctuary Management artists have sold well over 55 million albums now for EMI, which, if you average it out over 18 years, is more than three million a year. So we've done all right, haven't we? The fact is, I did still know a lot of people at EMI, and at the end of the day I knew they'd be able to do the job, and so I thought, 'I've just got to put my own personal reservations behind me and do what's right for Maiden.' And this was a totally different situation, anyway. Steve Harris is a very different personality to Steve Harley, much more reasonable, and as a manager I was much more in control of the situation. And so I thought, 'Why not? Let's just go for it and see what happens.'"

Knowing that they might not get a second chance to impress, Maiden had gone out of their way to make the Marquee their biggest show to date. Apart from alerting the hundreds of fans that they had in the East End to the need to turn up for this one, and making sure that Dave Lights' box of tricks was brimful of fiery show-stoppers, Rod had also spent several nights in the bar of the club, "oiling the gears" with its owner, Jack Barry. He eventually persuaded Barry to let the band use their own backdrop for the show, a practice unheard of in those days, when the Marquee's own, now-famous logo had become an integral part of the visual landscape for any band, however big or small, wishing to tread its hallowed, beer-sticky boards. He also persuaded Barry to allow the band to sell their own T-shirts in the foyer. "It was a plain red T-shirt with 'IRON MAIDEN' written in black on the front," recalls Dave Murray. "It was probably, like, the cheapest thing we could get, but we thought they were fantastic!"

"We always wanted to do things right, even when we were starting out," says Rod, "and we got them to let us dress the Marquee window up with this death's-head mask, with horns and whatnot, and we got black-and-white photographs of the band stapled up all over the place. And, of course, we got them to let us use our own backdrop, with the Maiden logo and Eddie head, anything to make it seem that bit special. So many bands in that position don't bother with any of this stuff at all, but we always did a number, right from the word go."

John Darnley, who had always liked Rod, despite the falling out over Cockney Rebel, stood by Rod's side throughout the 90-minute show and could hardly fail to be impressed. His report back to EMI was enthusiastic enough to persuade his boss, Brian Shepherd, to check out the band personally, which he did ten days later, venturing into the wilds of Kingsbury and the hidden kingdom of Neal Kay's Bandwagon Soundhouse, where Maiden had returned for yet another roof-lifting appearance. Shep actually got lost on the way, and by the time he'd finally made it through the doors of the club Maiden were already halfway through a scorching set, the bodies down at the front of the stage literally being heaved through the air. Sensibly repairing to the bar at the back of the room, Shep admits years later that "I couldn't really see a thing", although the glimpses he caught in between the home-made banners, the cartwheeling, shirtless bodies and "the sheer atmosphere they generated" (as usual, the place was packed) left the veteran A&R chief in little doubt that here was a band that would certainly sell records. You only had to be there at the Soundhouse when they played to see that they already had their own fans. He decided there and then to offer them a deal.

"Brian came along, and he's not exactly tall, but he stood right at the back, and I doubt whether he could really see a thing, because the place was heaving, but the atmosphere was electric," says Rod. "It was obvious there was something happening, so he said, 'Yeah, you've got a deal.' I told the band afterwards and they were ecstatic. But I told them to calm down and that nothing was signed yet and that the real hard work would start when we did sign. But I don't think they were listening. Not at that particular moment, anyway. All they heard was the word 'deal', and that was it. It was drinks all round!"

Inevitably, there would be a time lag between Brian Shepherd telling Rod he'd got a deal and EMI actually issuing a contract for the band to sign. In Maiden's case, the detailed negotiations that Rod entered into with EMI on their behalf took two months to complete. Ever astute, he knew that the worst thing the band could do at this point was sit back on their laurels and wait for EMI to call. As Rod says, "There are all kinds of deals, and we wanted to make sure that the deal we did with EMI was a long-term one and not just one of those where they can opt out if the first album isn't an immediate hit." Aware of the notoriously short memories that record-company A&R men can have, Rod knew that the best way forward at this point was to keep the name Iron Maiden as much in the public eye as possible. The fact that *Sounds* chose just that moment to put the band on its front cover for the first time was "an incredible bonus", he admits now, but what really made the band's commercial potential apparent to EMI was the release of their first and now legendary EP, 5,000 copies of which they scrimped and saved to have pressed and released –

with their own, aptly-named Rock Hard Records label stuck on the vinyl – on 9 November 1979. The idea for the name came from a concept that Rod intended to filch from a notorious Stiff Records T-shirt which was then doing the rounds bearing the legend "If It Ain't Stiff – It Ain't Worth A Fuck". "Credit where credit's due," he smiles. "I was going to nick it and have these T-shirts made with 'If It Ain't Rock Hard – It Ain't Worth A Fuck', but in the end we never got around to making the T-shirts."

In the face of what, until that point, seemed to be total apathy from the majors, the idea of releasing their own independently produced record had been a subject much discussed over the latter months of 1979. Sheffield's Def Leppard had just done something similar with their own EP, 'Getcha Rocks Off', a shrewd move that had eventually landed them a record deal with Phonogram Records. Now, with Rod onboard to encourage them and show them how, the decision was taken to release three of the four tracks that had been featured on the original Spaceward demo: 'Prowler', 'Invasion' and 'Iron Maiden'. 'Strange World', the fourth track, was left off because the band felt that the quality of the recording didn't really do justice to what was, at that point, one of their more epic live numbers. (Although a new, re-recorded version of the song would appear on the first Maiden album some months later, the Spaceward demo version would not resurface until 1995, when it was included on the band's comprehensive compilation album, *Best Of The Beast*.) Steve had already come up with a name for the EP: 'The Soundhouse Tapes'.

"It was very frustrating," he says, "because everywhere we'd go we'd do really well at the gigs, and then afterwards there'd be, like, all these fans asking where they could buy one of our records, and when we told 'em there wasn't any yet they couldn't believe it. They'd seen the charts in *Sounds* and a lot of 'em just assumed we must already have a record deal of some kind, but we didn't. Not then. So then, they'd be, like, 'Well, where can we get a copy of the tape?' And I think that's when we really got the idea of putting the Spaceward demo out as an actual record. It had never really occurred to us before that we could do that. We were that amazed ourselves to see tracks from it, like 'Prowler', turning up in Neal Kay's *Sounds* chart that we'd never thought, 'Well, what if we made the tape available to the public somehow?' But now we actually had people asking us for it, offering us money straight out of their pockets for a copy of the cassette. So that's when we started to think, you know, 'Maybe this is a good idea,' so that at least those Maiden fans that were now coming to the gigs regularly could take some of our music home with them to listen to."

"We called it 'The Soundhouse Tapes', 'cause that's how we felt about them at that time," explains Paul Di'Anno, "that this was a tape that the regulars at the Soundhouse had made famous, through requesting tracks off it enough times to put 'Prowler' to the top of the Soundhouse charts in *Sounds*. And we wanted to make clear that this was something we were doing that was strictly for the sort of mob you got down at places like the Bandwagon, the real hardcore, the hardest of the hard. This was something for them, you know?"

For the front cover, they used a colour photograph of a shirtless, fist-raised Di'Anno addressing the audience, taken by one of the Soundhouse regulars, a pioneer cardboard-guitar hero who bore a remarkable resemblance to Shaggy from *Scooby Doo* and who was cheerfully known to everybody except his mother as Rob Loonhouse. For the back cover, they cheekily filched ten smaller black-and-white shots from a contact sheet given to them by a photographer "to look at". Steve designed the sleeve himself and hand-wrote the lettering, including some suitably "messianic" sleeve-notes from the Prophet Kay, who preached, "Every so often a special band emerges from the mass of untried and unknown hopefuls which fill the streets of the rock world. Iron Maiden is just one such band, bringing with their emergence a style of rock music so hard, gritty and honest in its delivery that only success can justify their hard toil! The tracks on this EP were the first ever recorded by the band and are the authentic, un-remixed cuts taken from the demo tape recorded at Spaceward Studios in Cambridge on 30 December 1978 and subsequently presented to the Soundhouse a week later. After one hearing, it was obvious that Iron Maiden would become one of the leaders of present-day heavy metal, combining the sort of talent and hard drive that the music world must not ever ignore!" It may read now like the sort of fifth-form tosh you'd expect to find in the lowliest of fanzines, but it was heartfelt, nonetheless, and certainly prophetic. From this moment on, Iron Maiden really did become, as Kay predicted, the leaders of present-day metal, the seven studio albums that they would eventually release throughout the '80s the benchmark up to which every subsequent generation of would-be heavy metal greats has had to measure. And it was all there on that first, artfully produced EP: the out-of-control riffing of 'Prowler'; the manic, unexpected time changes and dynamism of 'Invasion'; the dizzying speed and power of 'Iron Maiden'.

Never intended for retail but more, as Steve Harris says, "as a memento for the Maiden fans who were there right from the start," the 5,000 seven-inch vinyl copies of 'The Soundhouse Tapes' were made available by mail order only (price: £1.20, including postage and packing) and were distributed by Keith Wilfort and his mum from the family home in Beaconsfield Road, East Ham. Miraculously, they managed to send out over 3,000 copies within the first week, demand for the record far exceeding the band's wildest expectations. "To be honest, I thought we might be pushing it a bit, doing as many as 5,000 to begin with," remembers Paul Di'Anno. "Then, when we sold the lot out within the first couple of weeks, I really could not believe it. I just couldn't get my head around that many people sitting at home playing our record." But it didn't stop there. Rod remembers taking calls from both HMV and Virgin during the third week, both trying to order enormous quantities of the record because so many kids had come into their stores asking if they could get them a copy.

"We did 5,000 pressings and we'd sold them all in no time at all on mail order," says Rod. "Then what happened was you got all these kids going in the record shops asking for 'The Soundhouse Tapes', which of course the shops had never heard of. At that time, the Soundhouse charts were really important, and so they soon found out what was happening and we got orders in from both Virgin and I think it was HMV for, like, 20,000 copies each of the EP! There's no doubt, we could have really cashed in at that point. It was our record, not EMI's, and we could have made enough to clear our debts, if we'd wanted to, maybe got it in the charts, even. But there was just no way. It really was something special for the true die-hard Maiden fans, and we'd already made that quite clear. If we'd then changed our minds, just to get our hands on a bit of cash, it would have been selling out the kids who'd gone to all the trouble to send in for one of the original 5,000 copies. We thought, 'No, we'll wait until we can do it properly with EMI.'"

Steve Harris agrees: "It would have totally destroyed the magic of having one of the original 5,000 copies, so we said, 'Bollocks to that!'"
The deal that Rod finally thrashed out with EMI was an extremely clever and unusual one for the time. As Rod says, "There are all kinds of deals – deals driven creatively, deals driven by cash, various option deals..." The one struck between EMI and Iron Maiden was a five-album deal, plus a £50,000 advance and recording costs, to be spread over three albums. But it wasn't the cash up front that Rod was going for; it was the long-term commitment of the record company to the band, and the clause that Rod insisted on inserting which altered the entire complexion of the deal was that EMI should not have an option to drop the band until after the third album had been released. Until then, major record companies always had the option to drop any new signing after just one album, sometimes even after just a couple of singles. Rod was determined that that should not be the case with Iron Maiden.

Howard Jones, who had agreed to act as Rod's and Maiden's lawyer in the negotiations, recalls Rod spelling out the basic strategy he wanted him to employ. "Rod's aim was that, whatever the level of advance, just to make sure we got a contract that committed the record company to at least three albums from the band," he says. "Rod was always in it for the long haul. He knew what he was doing."

"It was a five-album deal, but with the first three albums absolutely firm," explains Rod. "We didn't care about the big advances, but it was a very conscious thing to get them to absolutely commit to making and releasing three albums, come hell or high water. It was an enormous help, not just at home in Britain but, most important of all, for all those other territories in the world where we wanted to go and where we thought the band would do well. So, with a firm commitment to make three albums, all their other companies around the world knew we'd be back time and again. The metal market around the world was not good at that time and we needed to get everybody taking it seriously and working on it."

Steve Harris points out the logic in the strategy: "OK, you get the money up front for the record deal, you go in and make the album and you might make the best album that's ever fucking been made, but what happens if they don't promote it? What happens if they don't market it? No bugger's gonna buy it, 'cause no one's gonna know about it in the first place. Then, if they don't buy it, you're dropped. What's the point of that? You've got to look to the third album, not the first album. That's the way I always looked at it, even then. So, when Rod signed us to EMI, I said to him at the time, you know, 'I don't want you getting no one-album, no-option deal.' He said, 'Eee...fucking get off!' and he went in and beat them up and got a three-album deal. A guaranteed three albums, you know? So I was pleased, 'cause I didn't trust no bastard in them days, you know? I trusted Rod, but I didn't trust them, you know? Not then. And I knew we had something. We just had a certain something. I don't know what it was, I can't put it into words, but I just knew we had something...from the songs, mainly, but also from the following that we were getting. I thought, 'People don't follow bands like this unless they're real.' They just don't. Not where I come from, anyway."

"It was quite a small advance," says Rod, "and we decided to take most of it for the first album, with the idea that continued revenue from record sales would provide the money to cover the future running costs. This wasn't a big signing for EMI. This was just another run-of-the-mill signing, done with no fanfare whatsoever, because metal didn't mean much at that point. So I went there knowing there would be low expectations to begin with. No one really expected us to do anything outside the UK, because they didn't perceive there to be a really thriving market for rock music back then. There were bands like UFO, Judas Priest and The Scorpions, who all still did OK, but they'd all been going since the early '70s. Now there was punk, and no one saw anyone new coming through on the rock side. Not internationally, anyway."

Martin Haxby, who was the business-affairs executive at EMI with whom Rod and Howard were thrashing out the deal, recalls how the contract EMI eventually agreed with Maiden was "an unusual one. Ahead of its time, really, at least as far as signing a brand new artist was concerned. Signing any rock band always requires a lot of investment from the record company, because, without mainstream radio and TV support – which rock has always lacked, even more so back then in those pre-MTV days – it was important to keep the band on the road touring, and that costs money. So, knowing that he would be coming back to us fairly frequently to help finance the various tours they had planned, I think Rod knew the only deal we would agree to would have to be one where the level of up-front cash advances was kept quite low. So, in terms of asking for money up front, his demands were quite modest, really. But where he really scored was in getting the company to agree to making a three-album commitment. That was not something we would have normally agreed to with a new artist."

The inevitably question that arises from this is, would EMI have signed Iron Maiden at all if it hadn't been Rod managing them, or someone equally well known to the company? Haxby, who later went on to take a place on the board of EMI and these days is the Director of Business Affairs on the board of Sanctuary Group plc, clings tightly to his diplomatic-immunity badge. "Well, let's just say Rod had enormous drive and energy, and that's always hard to ignore," he comments wryly. "I'll be honest and admit that we did think committing to three albums was risky, and for a while the deal sort of hovered over the precipice because of Rod's stubbornness on this point, but at the end of the day we just believed in Rod. He was just so enthusiastic about this band. He was like a sort of Panzer tank – he just rolled right over you! And after seeing the band play live and the general euphoria that surrounded them, it wasn't hard to come to the decision in the end to take a punt."

"We had a lot more ambition and potential than EMI realised," says Rod, "but we knew that. The idea was, if they know they're gonna have to keep dealing with this, that we're gonna be coming back to them again and again, they would be forced to get off their bums and do a job, or at least help us do our jobs better by giving us the cash we were going to need. First off, we had a few debts – people who had lent Steve money early on, things like that – and we badly needed to get some new equipment, so I said, 'I'll take £35,000 for the first album, £15,000 for the second and nothing for the third.'"

The band would survive beyond the first album thanks to Rod carefully monitoring their pipeline royalties (money accrued from foreign record sales that usually take six to nine months to be paid over to the artist). Every time they built up a small surfeit, Rod would go in to see EMI and ask them to allow him to dip into the funds in advance of actually receiving the full amount later in the year. "I'd go in to Martin or speak to Phil Roley, who was the Finance Director in the

Business department at EMI at that time and who, again, went on to become one of the major heads of the company," he explains, "and I'd have the figures all worked out, exactly what we needed the money for. I'd say, 'Look, we've got a ten-grand pipeline. Can I have some of it?' And we'd get five grand maybe, and we'd run things like that."

It was a carefully-worked-out, high-risk strategy that depended entirely on the band breaking through to other markets besides the UK, and quickly. But such was Rod's confidence in the commercial potential of Iron Maiden that he felt sure it was a gamble that would pay off in spades. So it was, then, that the band was finally called in to the famous old EMI building in London's Manchester Square during the first week of December 1979 to sign their contract. Pictures of the band holding up the contract and quaffing free EMI beer were published alongside a story announcing the deal in the trade weekly *Music Week* in the following week. Temporary guitarist Tony Parsons had been given his marching orders some weeks previously, and Maiden actually signed to EMI as a four-piece, comprising Steve, Davey, Paul and Dougie.

"It was weird," recalls Paul Di'Anno. "We signed the deal, got pissed, then left the building and went down the pub and got more pissed, then home and...nothing. I don't know what I expected to happen, once we got a deal – a big limo pulling up outside the door or something – but there I was the next night, watching telly, thinking, 'Well, this is it, then, I suppose.'"

Dave Murray: "It was like climbing little mountains. You'd get to the top and put your flag in and then begin the next climb. I remember doing the Marquee for the first time and we were amazed because it was filled to the brim! I mean, at the time, I thought that was tops. I didn't think you could really get any bigger than that. But we just kept on going, and next we had 'The Soundhouse Tapes', then we had the deal with EMI... I mean, it was blinding. I kept thinking, 'This is it, now. It'll stop now and we'll just sort of carry on gently.' [Laughs] No chance, mate!"

6 Dennis And Clive

With the release of 'The Soundhouse Tapes' in November 1979, Maiden set out on their first lengthy club tour of Britain, a string of steamy one-night stands in such salubrious rock clubs as the Middlesbrough Rock Garden, the Retford Porterhouse and the Brunel Rooms in Swindon. Back on the road, "the old antics" recalled by Paul Di'Anno continued unabated, and Dave Murray became the target of several outraged letters from disgruntled boyfriends printed in the pages of *Sounds*, including one particularly worrying missive from someone calling himself "Jealous Dave", who wrote, "I would just like to warn Dave Murray, the lead guitarist of Iron Maiden, that if he steps foot inside Manchester again [the band had played at UMIST on 13 October] I will personally pummel his brains in, 'cause he's ruined what I thought was an ace relationship with my girlfriend. And may I point out that no matter how much she rubs his name in my face I still think Deb Brown of Wythenshawe is the best yet."

"Yes, I do remember there being one or two letters like that," Dave grins. "I don't know what that was all about. As you know, I always like to retire early after a show and go to bed with a good book."

Two dates from that tour stick out most in the collective memory, the first being Aberavon Nine Volts Club, which they played on 9 November, the day that 'The Soundhouse Tapes' went on sale for the first time. In a state of suitable post-gig inebriation, they'd visited a closed-down ghost train nearby that some local fans had told them about and spent half an hour running around, trying to spook each other. But when Vic Vella accidentally trod on a concealed power-button, which activated the equipment, the result, as Garry Bushell recalls, "was several white-faced, brown-trousered herberts legging it as if Dracula himself had just offered 'em a quick bite." But the most memorable night of the tour was undoubtedly Maiden's first headline appearance at the Music Machine, in London, on 5 November, Guy Fawkes' night in Britain and the one night of the year when Dave Lights could reasonably expect a bit of competition, as most of the country lit up the night with their own fireworks and bonfires. Never one to duck a challenge, however, Dave just built up his stockpile of pyro to even more ridiculous dimensions than usual. However, come the fateful moment in the set, as his arsenal of lights and explosives went off, so did all the power, as he'd blown every fuse in the house. "Talk about a show-stopper!" he jokes feebly now, but the delay nearly cost Maiden the gig and there were stern words for the hapless technician in the dressing room afterwards. "They were pissed off," Lights remembers, but the gig had gone so well that "it almost sort of added to the atmosphere. I think some of the kids even thought it was part of the show."

Suddenly, it seemed, all eyes were swivelling their way. When *Sounds* splashed a full-colour picture of Paul onstage across the cover of their 27 October issue under the headline "Not Just A Pretty Face", their fate was sealed. In what was a gem of descriptive writing – likening Dave Murray onstage, with his long, flailing blond hair, to "a charlady who's fallen over and is waving her mop frantically trying to signal for assistance" and drawing the readers' attention to Paul Di'Anno's "roughly hewn stable-boy charm" ("He made me sound like I smelled of horse manure!" Paul later complained) – Geoff Barton managed to convey both the serious musical intent and the down-to-earth, no-bullshit sense of humour that would come to characterise the band's public profile over the years. "I'd hate for us to become too earnest or intense," Di'Anno was quoted as saying. "I fall over on my arse, make cock-ups, and that's what it's all about, innit? When we get time off, we go and see West Ham play and I act like an 'ooligan, and I can't see that ever changing..."

Elsewhere in that first feature, Steve Harris, as ever, had a more serious point to make, taking Barton to task over the true validity of his NWOBHM invention, insisting that, far from anything new, the old rock scene had never really died out in Britain, that it had merely gone underground while the media remained seduced by punk. "There were still thousands of kids into the music," he insisted. "It was just that the press didn't write about it." With bands like Maiden getting a major record deal and finding themselves on the cover of a magazine, all that would change, said Steve.

He was right. Even before Rod had thrashed out their recording contract with EMI, he had already managed to land them a lucrative publishing deal with Zomba Music, for which they received a cash advance of £40,000. (A publishing company establishes a copyright for an artist on all of the original material that he or she comes up with and actively chases up royalties accrued from a variety of sources around the world, including record sales, radio and television performances, cover versions by other artists, film-soundtrack usage and any other media where someone is likely to want to perform or broadcast one of the artist's original songs.)

Rod Smallwood: "In terms of money up front, it wasn't an extravagant deal, but again it was all about commitment and getting the company to focus on the long term. Clive Calder and, at that time, Ralph Simon, the heads of Zomba, were very intelligent and could see the potential of the band, too. We knew we wouldn't make tons of royalties from radio play, because we knew from day one that Maiden were never going to be a rock band like Dire Straits or The Police, where you heard them on the radio all the time. But we knew that, with a band like this, because of their integrity, they would never lose their fans, and that what you missed out on in terms of mainstream airplay would be more than made up for by the fact that they wouldn't be here today, gone tomorrow, that they would have a career that outlasted most pop careers by an enormous ratio. We weren't pinning our hopes on any one particular song; we were gambling on their whole sort of musical outlook and the general character of the band to build up a loyal audience."

Another important personality who volunteered to climb aboard the Maiden tour bus at this point was booking agent John Jackson. Now the head of the enormously successful ICM/Fair Warning agency, back in 1979, when Rod first began sounding him out about Maiden, John was just another rock enthusiast working as a booker for the Cowbell agency.

"I started out in 1972 as a booker at what was originally the Chrysalis agency and then got renamed Cowbell a few months after I joined, looking after acts like Procol Harum, Ten Years After, Roxy Music and Wild

Turkey," he recalls. "I was always into rock, and my favourite band was Free. By the late '70s, however, we were doing quite a lot of punk bands, like The Stranglers, for example, and AC/DC, who were perceived as being this sort of half punk, half metal band. For a while, apart from the really well-established rock acts, there just didn't seem to be much else out there that wasn't punk. Then, in 1979, I remember hearing about this heavy metal band called Saxon that was getting a lot of interest. I think that hit they had, '747', was either out or just coming out, and I'd been told they were a bit like The Stranglers of this NWOBHM thing, which was a pretty accurate description, in retrospect. But they were playing at the Music Machine one night and so I thought I'd go along and see them."

What Jackson didn't know until he got there, however, was that Iron Maiden was the support band. "I had no idea who was supporting," he admits. "I wasn't there to see them, and it was only by chance that I got to the Music Machine early that night and just happened to catch their set. And thank God I did, because I was much more impressed with them than Saxon. I just loved the band straight away, and obviously the fact that there were also a lot of punters there didn't hurt, either. So I looked at Maiden and said, 'Yeah, I'll have them.'"

So impressed was Jackson, in fact, that he didn't even stay for the end of the Saxon set. Instead, he got up early the next morning and set about discovering more about the band. He began by finding out if they had a manager. "I thought, 'Whoever it is, I'll number him straight away,'" he smiles. He then adds, "When I found out it was Rod, I wasn't sure what to make of it at first. I already knew Rod, because he'd been a booker with a rival agency in the early '70s. In fact, I'd nicked a band from him in 1975 called Be-Bop Deluxe, and at first I wondered if he'd still have the hump with me. But I really wanted this band, and so I thought, 'It doesn't matter. I'll just ring him up anyway, and if he reacts badly then that's that.' And then, the day I was going to ring him, he actually called me up. He said, 'Oi, you. I've got a group for you. Have you heard of Iron Maiden?'"

At first, Jackson admits, "I didn't let on I'd seen them already and thought they were great, because I wanted to see what he had to say first." But they both went to see Maiden at one of their two free nights in October 1979 at the Swan, in Hammersmith, and afterwards John finally came clean with Rod, explained his interest and offered to represent

Maiden as their personal booking agent, a job he continues to oversee with considerable acumen and aplomb to this day. It was another crucial appointment, as Jackson was now perfectly placed to put Maiden forward for any of the choice support slots, both in Britain and abroad, that would be coming up over the next 18 months.

"A good agent like John Jackson doesn't just do the donkey work of booking venues and arranging tour dates," explains Rod. "He keeps you informed of everything else that's going on in the rock world, letting you know well in advance of all the important festivals and tours that are likely to be of interest to your band, either now or in the future. Getting Maiden on as the support band for the Judas Priest and Kiss tours, which we did the following year, didn't just happen by accident. That was John at Cowbell getting our foot in the door for us first and me persuading EMI to let us have the money to pay for Maiden to do it. Without that kind of support, there's no way we would have been let anywhere near those tours. Every other up-and-coming rock band in Britain would have given their eye teeth for a similar opportunity, but because we had a well-respected agent like John in our corner fighting for us, and because EMI had the foresight to allow us to dip into the pipeline royalties to help pay for it, we were able to make those things happen."

"Of course, once you've got the tour, the band have to go out there every night and prove that they're good enough to deserve a shot like that," says John, "but with Maiden you always felt that they'd never bottle out of anything you put in front of them. Nothing was ever too big. And so you felt confident enough to go for the really juicy tours. Rod obviously had enormous confidence in their capabilities, and I felt it, too, and together we just kept pushing it until we arrived at where we are today, which is with a band that can now headline their own festivals and tours and are used to playing, literally, to millions of people around the world."

Jackson remembers bumping into Chris Wright, who was then head of A&R at Chrysalis Records, at the Swan when Maiden played there in October. Earlier in the evening, both men had also attended a gig at the Fulham Greyhound by Maiden's NWOBHM rivals Praying Mantis. "I remember Chris Wright asking me which ones we were going to sign," he says. "I said, 'Iron Maiden,' and he ended up signing Praying Mantis for

Chrysalis." Not being one to say "I told you so", Jackson allows the rest of his thoughts to remain unsaid, but nearly 20 years and over 50 million records later it's clear which man made the right choice that night. When Maiden returned to the Marquee on 9 December – another tumultuous performance at which Uli had been forced to hang the "All Sold Out" sign on the door and to which Rod had brought "as many heads as I could round up from EMI" – it was, for the first time, as returning champions. As Malcolm Dome prophetically commented in his review for *Record Mirror*, "Maiden received the sort of reception that must send cold shivers down Jimmy Page's fretboard. This lot are going to blast the older generation of heavy rockers clear out of their penthouse suite in the coming months."

However, the most immediate consequence of having both Cowbell and now EMI behind them was that the four band members could now give up their various day jobs. Steve, who had lost his apprenticeship as a draughtsman when the firm he worked for made him redundant, was then employed as a road-sweeper. "In terms of the band, it was the best job I ever had," he reflects. "You had to start really early, but that meant you were finished by lunchtime, most days, and I would be back writing songs or rehearsing by the middle of the afternoon." Dave Murray was flying under a similar flag of convenience as a storeman for Hackney Council. "I used to spend most nights with the band and most of the day sleeping behind some boxes in a corner." Both Doug Sampson and Paul Di'Anno were on the dole, although for some reason Paul was fond of telling people that he'd worked as a North Sea Oil rigger, which he hadn't.

However, there was still one last piece of business to complete, now that the band had secured a major record deal, and that was the official appointment of Rod Smallwood as full-time Iron Maiden manager. It wasn't, Rod insists now, that he wanted to wait until the band had a record deal under their belt before making his appointment official. "Having given up management once before, I wanted to make sure that this time around the people I was dealing with weren't going to become arseholes in two years' time," he says, referring back to his bitter experience with Steve Harley. "I gave it four months with Maiden before I decided that they wouldn't and, as you can see, I wasn't wrong."

Taking up the kindly offer from Ralph Simon of "a free room with a desk and a phone" at the Zomba offices, in Willesden High Road, Rod's decision was imparted to the band with typical Yorkshire brusqueness. Steve Harris remembers sitting in a pub around the corner from Rod's office – where, as usual, they could be overheard enthusiastically making plans for the future – when the bassist suddenly turned to Rod and asked, point blank, "Does this mean you're gonna manage us then?" At this, Rod put down his pint and replied simply, "Fucking right, I am!"

Rod decided to call his new management company after the Maiden song that would actually become the band's second single, 'Sanctuary'. "I just wanted to call it after one of the band's songs, because I really thought, 'Well, if it wasn't for them, I probably wouldn't have even still been a manager,'" he explains, "so I looked through the list of song names and 'Sanctuary' just fitted great. I thought, 'Yeah, sanctuary from all the bullshit of the music business.'"

Nevertheless, there was one member of the band who now admits that he saw the full-time appointment of Rod Smallwood as a mixed blessing: guitarist Dave Murray. "I didn't doubt his ability or his integrity," he says. "It wasn't like I thought he was a bad manager or anything. It was just that…I was kind of scared of Rod, actually, back then. I mean, I love the guy dearly now, but back then I was really kind of frightened of him, because I'm shy as well. I used to just back into the corner in meetings, but whenever he was around I used to go even more into my shell. He was, like, this really powerful man who knew exactly what he was doing and why he was doing it, and he knew how to do it, too. And maybe I was a bit frightened that I was gonna be the next to go. I mean, if I really think back, in my heart of hearts, that's probably how I felt, and so that's probably why I was so quiet and shy and everything and why I didn't want to say anything to get on anyone's bad side, 'cause I was happy being there."

Nevertheless, Dave now claims that he and his manager "never really had a proper conversation until after the first album. Rod and I never really spoke that much for maybe the first year he was the manager. Then, finally, one night we went out together in the middle of the Kiss tour and got really paralytic and just had a good old head to head. I just kind of opened up and we had a good old talk about everything, and that was it. Everything was all right after that. Before that, I think there was always that thing with me, like maybe I could be next. I mean, I was frightened to death of him when I first met him!"

Steve Harris is surprised that Dave should ever have felt like that. "Davey, of all people, has never been in fear of losing his job in Maiden," he says. "He fell out with Dennis Wilcock, yes, but I was sorry about that, and when he rejoined the band I thought he actually showed a lot of faith in me and the songs, which I thought was brilliant, and I've never forgotten that. But then, he'd be the first one to admit it, he's not the sort of person to make decisions. He likes to go with the flow, playing guitar and smiling. That's all he's ever wanted to do, and, you know, that's wonderful, really, if you can do that, but you've got to have someone in the band who's gonna make decisions and someone who's gonna go out and get the gigs and take the bull by the horns, and that was always me, until Rod came along. Then we shared it."

Like Steve, Rod is aghast to learn the news that his principal guitarist should have been so wary of him when they first began working together. "I just thought he was The Quiet One," he says. "You know, there's usually one member of the band who just goes with the flow and nothing seems to bother them, and that's who I thought Davey was. It wasn't until we went out one night on tour and got absolutely legless together that we really started to get to know each other. Now, of course, we're best mates."

As conscientious as ever, Rod advised Steve and the band to take the management contract he'd offered them to an experienced music-business lawyer to look over for them. He even gave them a list of well-known legal firms that specialised in the music business to choose from. Steve remembers how, in the end, "I just closed my eyes and stuck a pin in the list Rod had given us". The name he landed on, Stephan Fischer, proved to be a little too willing to help, advising them that he could get them a better publishing deal with Zomba, for example, than the one that Rod had negotiated for them.

"Although we'd agreed our publishing deal with Zomba, because the band had been busy working on the album and touring, they still hadn't actually signed the Zomba contract yet," explains Rod, "and Stephan Fischer picked up on this and told them he could get them a better deal, which, in truth, he probably could. But then, I could have probably got them a better deal with Zomba, at that point, because by then the first single had come out and been a hit and so we probably could have squeezed a bit of extra cash out of them. But the thing is, I'd already given Zomba my word, and there was no way I was going to go back and break that. I was looking at it from a long-term commitment thing, as well – the royalties were good, and we wanted Zomba to work with us, not against us, so I said, 'Look, if you want me to go back and break my word, I will. But then what happens? Who do I break my word to next? You?' Here we were building a very firm foundation and now someone was going to ruin all that just for a bit of extra cash? Steve, who is a very honest person, who always sticks to his word, grasped the point completely. He was pissed off because all he wanted was someone to steer him through the fine print, and instead, like lawyers do, Stephan Fischer was trying to take over everything, so Steve fired him."

The band switched to the far more understanding legal firm of Gentle Jayes, whose David Gentle still represents the band today "for personal stuff", or whenever there is a clear conflict of interest in the work Howard Jones does for them on behalf of Rod. (This happens most often when they have to extend the management agreement every few years, in which case Howard Jones reverts to being just Rod's lawyer and David Gentle becomes the band's lawyer.) "You have to keep the financial side and the legal side very open, so that everybody knows where they stand," says Rod. "I must say, David Gentle is very good and still looks after the boys for personal stuff today."

With the announcement of the EMI deal came a fortnight of back-to-back club dates, squeezed into the middle of which, on 14 December, Radio 1 broadcast Maiden's first-ever radio session for the station. Recorded at the BBC studios in Maida Vale, west London, in November and broadcast "live" on DJ Tommy Vance's *Friday Rock Show*, the band contributed four tracks to the programme: 'Iron Maiden', 'Transylvania', 'Running Free' and 'Sanctuary', the last two both new numbers that Steve and Paul had cooked up together, the latter with the help of Dave. This was the first time that Steve had shared writing credits with any of the other band members.

"The response we got to the programme was very good, I seem to recall," says the show's former producer, Tony Wilson. "It was a very exciting time again for rock music in this country, and right at the very front of this sort of wave of new bands was Iron Maiden. Groups like Def Leppard and Saxon were obviously tremendously popular and much discussed, too, at that time, but nobody quite matched the response we got to that first Maiden session. I don't know if it was because they were more overtly metal than some of the other bands, or whether it was because they simply had more fans at that stage, but they seemed to strike a chord with our listeners straight away and became sort of instantly popular overnight. After that, of course, Tommy and I had them back on the show whenever we could."

Maiden had recorded the Radio 1 session still as a four-piece. Now, with EMI in a hurry to get the band into the studio to begin recording their first album, the need to fill the vacancy for a second guitarist was more pressing than ever. "We could have easily done the album as a four-piece," says Steve, "but that was never the idea. We were always looking to be a band that had twin lead guitars, so we thought, 'Right, now we've got a deal we've just got to get this sorted.'" At first, they actually offered the job to Dave Murray's old Urchin sparring partner, Adrian Smith, but Urchin had just landed a deal themselves and Adrian was loath to abandon his plans just as it seemed his band might be getting somewhere themselves. Instead, they placed an ad in *Melody Maker*, which read, in part, "Must be HM freak. Twenty-two or under." Dennis Stratton, another long-haired East End musician who was, in truth, neither of these things, applied anyway and was "pleased, but rather surprised" to get offered the job.

Born in Canning Town on 9 October 1952, Dennis was 27 and had been playing in another well-known East End pub band called Remus Down Boulevard – a mouthful that quickly got abbreviated amongst the paying customers to RDB – when a friend first drew his attention to the ad. Dennis had spent the last three years playing guitar and sharing lead vocals in RDB, who had once looked like breaking into the big time themselves, but a familiar combination of inexperience, poor timing and just plain bad luck had meant that they'd never really realised their commercial potential and now, their moment gone, it looked like they never would. Characterised by Stratton himself now as "one of those bands that always used to play the Bridgehouse, Canning

Town", RDB had been picked up by former novelty-hit-maker now turned record-company chief Jonathan King. More familiar to the British public in his role as esoteric TV presenter and chat-show guest, for a time in the late '70s King and his younger brother, Andy, ran their own London-based record label, UK Records. A well-known rock enthusiast, King had originally intended RDB to become one of his first major signings to the label, in 1978. This, in turn, had led to offers of management from a company called Quarry, who also managed the affairs of Status Quo and Rory Gallagher, then two of the biggest-selling rock acts in Britain and Europe.

Dennis Stratton: "We recorded our first album, which was *Live At The Marquee*, and the angle King had come up with was that no one had done a debut album live before. We were well known enough by then to pack out the old Marquee, and so we just went for it. We were pretty pleased with the way the recording went, and then King had the idea of an album sleeve with a picture of a big, flash American car on it – a Chevy, I think it was – taken with a fish-eye lens so it looked like a spaceship, with us sitting in it, with the RDB logo upside-down. I must admit, it looked quite impressive."

But the RDB album was never released. "They pressed up copies of the album but he changed his mind and got into TV or something and did a disappearing act," says Stratton with a shrug. "His brother ended up looking after it, and it all just lost momentum and went downhill, basically. It was like waiting for a bus that never comes." But they still carried on with Quarry and toured Europe with Status Quo. "That was a really eye-opening experience for me," he says. "My first taste, really, of the real thing." Other bands that Stratton had "plugged in with at various times" included No Dice (a sort of poor man's Rolling Stones), whom he "did a couple of gigs at the Marquee with and some demos". Mainly, though, he reverted to doing pub gigs with RDB. With a wife and a child to support, he had to work as often as he could.

A marine engineer by trade, Dennis had passed a City and Guilds exam at the age of 20 but had already started playing with RDB at 18, and so, "when it got to the point where we were touring the north of England, that all went to pieces. So I got into building work and painting and decorating." By 1979, he would often find himself working all day at a string of casual labouring jobs and playing all night in a pub somewhere with RDB, a regime that was slowly "turning me into a zombie. I never got any sleep and just used to end up nodding off whenever I had a spare five minutes. Although it wasn't much money to begin with, getting the Maiden gig when I did was a Godsend, quite frankly."

Dennis actually remembers meeting Steve Harris for the first time at the Bridgehouse some months before the *Melody Maker* ad appeared. "I'd seen Maiden a couple of times down there and thought they were good. They certainly knew how to pull in the punters, that's for sure. Steve was a regular drinker down the Bridgehouse and, because we were both in bands, we sort of got to know each other, just to nod and say hello, but for some reason I never used to equate this Steve bloke at the Bridgehouse with Iron Maiden. He was just a bloke who used to come and watch us play sometimes. Then someone called me and said they were advertising for a guitarist in the *Melody Maker*, a second guitarist cum backing vocalist, which is what I'd been doing in RDB, so I got the paper and I wrote to this address with a photo, which they also wanted. The funny thing is, the photo was from the Bridgehouse, and I was wearing a West Ham scarf in it, so of course Steve spotted that straight away."

Then, on the bus home from Stratford a few days later, he bumped into Lorraine, Steve's girlfriend at the time and future wife, who coincidentally happened to be a friend of Dennis' girlfriend. "She recognised me from the photo," explains Stratton, "and the first thing she said to me was, 'Have you received a telegram yet?' I said, 'No,' and she said, 'Oh. You will.'" Dennis was living in Canning Town at the time. The next day, a telegram arrived. "It just said, 'CALL ROD SMALLWOOD – RE IRON MAIDEN,' so I did, and I don't know if it was Rod I spoke to but he told me that the band were rehearsing at Hollywood Studios in Clapton, east London, and that I should get my arse down there as quick as possible."

When Dennis arrived, he found a full-on audition in progress for both a guitarist and a drummer. "We had a drink and a chat and it was like I'd got the job," he says. "They didn't need to hear me play or sing, 'cause Steve had already seen me down the Bridgehouse and decided. He just wanted to have a natter first. It was, 'Can you learn these songs? 'Cause we signed to EMI and we're gonna be doing an album.' I was, like, 'Yes!

No problem.' I was pleased as punch, you know, because you could tell just by the gear they had and the set-up that they were taking it seriously, and there was a bit of a vibe to 'em. So that was it. I was in."

"Dennis' band, RDB, used to play Friday nights, I think, at the Bridgehouse," recalls Steve. "They were quite an established band down there, so I knew he could play and sing and that he looked the part onstage, and so we just had a brief talk with him first, just to find out what sort of bloke he was and let him know what our situation was and what we were looking for from a second guitarist type of thing. To be honest, looking back, I think we were in such a hurry to get someone in, in time for the album, that we just went ahead and offered him the job without really thinking about it too much, which probably partly explains why we had all the problems we eventually ended up having with Dennis. I mean, he was a nice bloke and all that, but he wasn't really our age and he just wasn't really into the same sort of stuff, musically and in other ways, that we were. He sort of stuck out. But we didn't see that at the time he first came down. We just thought he could do the job and he was local, so that was good, and so we just said, 'Right, you're in.'"

Dennis was immediately put on the payroll and rehearsals for the first album began immediately, with the new guitarist struggling to learn all the material in the shortest time possible. "Everybody was on about £60 a week, I think, which wasn't much, even then," he recalls. "Fortunately for me, I was on about £20 more than the others, 'cause I was married with a kid and that."

As for the music, Dennis admits now that, for a more melodically inclined all-round musician/singer like himself, he found some of the hard-edged, more extreme numbers that Maiden specialised in "very strange. Quite a challenge, in a way. There was nothing predictable about any of them. They tended not to follow what you sort of thought of as the normal rock progressions." The sudden and unexpected time changes that would become such an important feature of the quintessential Maiden sound he found "completely bewildering, at first. Musically, they were a law unto themselves. Because a lot of the stuff like 'Phantom Of The Opera' or 'Iron Maiden' had so many different changes in the songs, it took me a while to get my head around it. I remember I was trying to work my way through 'Prowler' or something, and Paul was, like, 'If you think that's hard, wait until you get to "Phantom Of The Opera"!' But it was definitely different. I'd done a fair bit of session work by then, and it wasn't really like anything I was used to playing, but it had its own edge, its own identity, and I respected that. In some ways, I suppose it was kind of a challenge for me, but as a musician who reckoned he could handle most things, I started getting into it on that level."

Then, just as it seemed that the band had finally found a settled line-up, the decision was taken to replace Doug Sampson on drums. This time, however, it wasn't personality problems that were at the heart of Steve's decision. It was, he says, a far more pragmatic reason. Doug's health simply wasn't holding up to the non-stop touring schedule on which the band had now embarked. Between August and December 1979, Iron Maiden played 47 gigs at various clubs and dives around the country, and the late nights in hot, smoky venues and the long days spent huddled in the back of the Green Goddess on their way to the next gig had begun to take their toll on the inexperienced young drummer. As he now admits, "I don't suppose I really looked after myself. But at that age, you don't know how to, do you? We were doing a lot of touring, just going from gig to gig in the back of a van, and you end up feeding on rubbish, drinking far too much and then trying to sleep in the back of the van, which of course you can't, not really, with four other blokes all trying to do the same thing. You'd come offstage sweating like a pig and then go straight into this draughty old van and on to the next gig, and it was like I was ill all the time. First it was really bad 'flu, and then I had a virus which used to really knock me out and leave me feeling absolutely drained. I wasn't really conscious of it at the time, but I suppose it must have affected my playing. Whatever, it was the beginning of the end for me, really. I think Steve was concerned that the big tours that we knew would be coming up might be put in jeopardy because I was always so ill."

"At that time – and he'd be the first one to admit it – health-wise, he just didn't seem to be up to it," says Steve. "I mean, we were doing gigs all the time now, and I remember him saying, 'Oh, fucking hell, I'm knackered. I just can't keep up with all this work.' He said, 'I can't fucking hack it.' I'd say, 'You're doing well. What's wrong with you? You're still playing all right,' and all that, but he just kept saying it all the time, and that worried me, I've got to be honest, so I thought, 'Bloody hell, this ain't gonna get any easier from now on in.' It was, like, 'We're only doing two or three gigs a week. What happens when we're doing five or six a week and a proper tour for a year?' That was the ultimate aim. So then I just thought, 'Well, it just ain't gonna work with him.' I like to think it was a mutual decision, though I suppose it was a bit of push and a bit of shove, if you like. But he knew, to be honest. We just couldn't take any chances, at that stage. It was a now-or-never sort of thing. So I talked to Rod and I talked to the others and we decided that, sad as it was, you know, Dougie would have to be replaced."

"The thing was," says Sampson today, "you could see Steve's point of view. I never had any doubt that Maiden would be huge one day. It was just a matter of time. And I wasn't the only one that thought like that, even then. It was a good feeling when we got the deal, and a good few drinks passed the lips, but things also got very serious after that. They were making plans and they had to know that everybody was 100 per cent ready to deliver."

Doug Sampson was officially "let go" from Iron Maiden after their final gig of the year at the Tower Club, in Oldham, on 22 December. On the following day, he was called into the office for a meeting, but when he got there, "There was only Rod and Steve there to see me, and I kind of knew straight away. They just said that they were worried I wouldn't be able to fulfil all the commitments they had coming up – really big stuff, like the Judas Priest tour, which they were already in the frame for – and stuff like that. They said they didn't think things were gonna work out at that time, and that they thought it was best to part company. I didn't argue. I could see their point."

Despite his accurate reading of the situation, Doug admits that he was still bitterly disappointed to lose his chance at stardom. "Of course it was a blow," he says, "but I could see what was gonna happen with the record deal and one thing and another, the heavy touring schedule they had coming up. But I had no way of knowing at that point how big the tours would actually be. I mean, when I look at what they actually went out and did after that – they toured non-stop practically for about three years – the truth is, I don't think I could have handled it, so maybe it turned out for the best."

When it ended, Doug decided to "give being a musician a rest for a while and go into something else". He would never play professionally again. For a time, he ran an off-licence, a branch of the now-defunct Peter Dominic's. These days, he's a forklift truck driver for a small London firm. "I eventually formed a band again, because the bug wouldn't leave me alone," he says, "but I never really played professionally again, not like I had with Maiden. Of course, I sometimes see them on the TV or hear them on the radio and think, you know, 'That could have been me,' but seeing the amount of work that's been put in, I appreciate it's not a gift that's come out of the sky. It's not like winning the lottery. Everything they've got you can be sure they've worked bloody hard for, and they deserve everything they've got. Good luck to them, I say."

Finding a replacement for Dougie became even more imperative than their hunt for a second guitarist had been. They could play live and even record as a four-piece, if they had to, but not without a drummer. More ads were hurriedly placed in the music press and the word went out. Within days, there were enough enquiries for the band to think about hosting auditions. Then Dennis Stratton came in and told them about a mate of his who could not only play a bit but was definitely looking for a new situation to get into. His name was Clive Burr.

According to the received wisdom of the time, Clive Burr had been brought to Steve Harris' attention by the all-knowing Neal Kay, who had spotted the future Maiden drummer during his short tenure with their London NWOBHM rivals Samson. Steve, on the other hand, now claims that "we got Clive through auditions. We auditioned a few people. One bloke I'd seen who was really good was John Mylett, who had been in a band called Nutz, who were quite well known for a time in the '70s, before the punk thing came in and blew them away. Then later he joined another band who became quite well known as Rage. And it was between him and Clive, basically. In fact, John may even have been a better drummer, technically, than Clive, but in the end we gave it to Clive because he had this certain feel to his playing that felt right, and he was a nice bloke. Clive just had a certain something about him we liked, you know? And he was also from 'round our area as well, a West Ham supporter, so that sort of helped as well. And John had this kind of attitude about him, like he'd been there, done it and just wasn't all that impressed with starting again, so he was sort of not sure about what he was gonna do, and I thought, 'Well I ain't having none of that. I don't want someone who is gonna come in and then bugger off if they get a better offer.' We wanted someone like us, who was hungry and didn't mind mucking in, so we chose Clive."

"Dennis suggested Clive and we arranged an audition," says Rod Smallwood. "Clive came in and I thought, 'Wow, I hope he can play, because he looks great.' He had this big, cheery face and great clothes. Clive always looked a million dollars in those days. It was obvious he could play, and he seemed like a really nice bloke as well, so we decided to offer it to him. I remember Clive had to leave early from the audition, because he had a job playing in a pub that night, and so, after we'd picked him as our man, we decided to surprise him and all turn up at this pub he was playing and tell him he'd got the job. He was so embarrassed, because he was playing brushes in this geriatric old pub, just as background noise in a boozer for a fiver and a few beers, you know? I seem to remember it was Boxing Day. But it was definitely Dennis that suggested him, yeah."

"It all came from a chance meeting," says Stratton. "Me and Clive had first met years before when we were still both just starting out in bands, and I was walking into this pub called the Golden Fleece, down in Forest Gate, and Clive was just walking out and we bumped into each other. It was strange, because I hadn't seen Clive for about five years, at that point. So, of course, straight away, it was, 'What are you doing now?' I told him I'd got the Maiden gig and he said, 'That's great. They're not looking for a drummer, are they?' And when I said, 'Well, yes, actually they are,' he nearly fell over! It took me a couple of days to work it into the conversation that I might know of someone who could replace Dougie. I mean, it was Steve's band and I'd only just joined, so I didn't want to seem too pushy. So it took time, but I eventually said something and Steve said, 'Well, bring him down, then.' I can't remember if Clive had heard much before he arrived, but I do remember him playing 'Phantom Of The Opera', 'cause he played it really well. Then he left and Steve asked us what we thought, and we all thought he was great. So that was it – Clive was in. We practically snatched him from his drum stool during a local pub gig. I remember it was Boxing Day 1979."

7 Eddie

1980 was year zero for Iron Maiden, the year that their story ceased to be about the simple dreams and ambitions of a gang of doing-our-best, East End innocents and became the saga of an all-conquering, megastar rock band. Like all the best transformations, it had all the outward appearances of having occurred overnight but, as Steve Harris points out, "It had actually taken me, personally, about five years to get Maiden to that point. Once it all started happening, though, even from the inside it felt like things were moving really fast. Maybe a bit too fast, sometimes, I don't know, but we didn't know if we'd last five minutes or five years at that point, so we just went for it while we could."

January 1980 found the band ensconced in Kingsway Studios, west London, recording their first album for EMI. Essentially a run-through of most of the highlights from their existing live set, sessions for the first, eponymously titled Iron Maiden album had nevertheless become fraught with difficulties as the band struggled to capture their live sound convincingly for the first time in a recording environment. "Basically, we just couldn't find a good producer," Steve recalls with a frown. Exploratory work in the studio had already begun while Doug Sampson was still in the band, and the band began recording as a four-piece with engineer Guy Edwards at a small, locally favoured studio in the East End. But they were unhappy with the "muddy" sound of Edwards' recording, and so quickly abandoned the idea. The only track to survive was 'Burning Ambition', a second-rate Steve Harris number that eventually found a home on the B-side of what would soon become their first single, 'Running Free'.

After the aborted effort with Edwards, they had then turned to producer Andy Scott, himself a guitarist in The Sweet, a singles-orientated, ersatz glam-rock band that had enjoyed a string of "rock lite" hits in the early '70s. Once again, however, the experience was not a productive one, and no recordings were ever completed. Scott had tried to insist that Steve use a conventional guitar pick, as opposed to the bassist's preferred full-finger technique. "I told him what he could do with that," Steve deadpans. Then his manager demanded a guarantee that Scott would produce the album before he finished producing the single, "so I told him where he could go". Finally, Brian Shepherd intervened and suggested that they try veteran rock producer Will Malone, who had picked up production credits with both Black Sabbath and Meat Loaf. With tour dates already beginning to fill up their diary, the band was left with little option but to give it their best shot with the venerable knob-twiddler, and time was booked at Kingsway for the sessions to begin immediately. But yet again the band was unhappy at the way in which the producer conducted himself throughout the sessions, relying heavily, as they tell it, on Kingsway's in-house engineer, Martin Levan, to do all the work.

"The way it worked out in the end," says Steve, "we could have taken a complete stranger in off the street and sat them in the producer's chair and it would probably have sounded just the same, 'cause we did it all on our own with the engineer. We knew what we wanted, and thank God the engineer was good, but as for Will Malone... Well, we just bypassed him, worked around him, you know what I mean? We'd go in there, we'd do a tape, then go in and say to him, 'What do you think, Will?' And he'd have his fucking feet up on the mixing desk, reading *Country Life* or whatever, completely mongled out of his head, and he'd look over the top of it and go, 'Oh, I think you can do better.' So we used to bypass him and went to the engineer. And he was good, thank God. We actually got some good sounds down and basically produced it ourselves.

"It was freaky, but the thing was, I've always been pretty headstrong, in that sense. I only respect people when they give me a reason to. Then I respect them because they've proved to me that they deserve respect. I don't go by reputations; I only go by what I see. We were told this guy had done Black Sabbath and Todd Rundgren and all these people, and we found out later all he'd fucking done was a string arrangement or something on one of their songs, you know? But I thought, 'I don't care what he's done. I'm not gonna let him fuck our album up.'"

Paul Di'Anno agrees: "Oh, Will Malone was dreadful, yeah. You could tell he thought he was far too big to be messing around with something like this. He just never put anything into it at all. I don't know why he even bothered showing up, most days."

Not for the first time, however, Dennis Stratton saw things a little differently to the others. But then, as Stratton is only too eager to remind us, "When I went into the band, they'd only really done demos. They'd never recorded seriously and I had, with No Dice and at other sessions, and it was just generally acknowledged that I was more experienced than they were, that's all.

"I listened to the Spaceward demos, and there was so much scope for improvement, production-wise, backing-vocals-wise, harmony-guitars-wise... But it was down to Steve and Rod to choose a producer, and they got Will Malone in. Personally, I really enjoyed the experience. Will may not have been the greatest producer in the world, but it meant that we could get on with it with the engineers, and I like working with engineers. That's where a lot of the real work's done in the studio, having ideas, building a song up with the help of a good engineer."

Confidence in his own abilities and enthusiasm for any band he was involved with was never Dennis' problem. If anything, he was prone to let his enthusiasm get the better of him, and ironically it was on those occasions that it "really pointed up the difference between Den and us," Steve says. There was the way that the guitarist felt things should be done, at heart, and the way Steve knew would work best for Iron Maiden.

A prime example was the controversy that ensued over some "extra bits and pieces to 'Phantom Of The Opera'" that Dennis had cooked up on his own with Martin Levan while the others were away from the studio. Allowing his fondness for the polished pomp of Wishbone Ash and Queen to obscure his vision, Dennis took the title of Steve's blood-and-thunder epic a little too literally and proceeded to remodel the track into something that sounded, in the words of Steve Harris nearly 20 years later, "like 'Bohemian Rhapsody' gone wrong. They played it to me and I went, 'What the fuck's *that*?'"

"By the time we came down to doing 'Phantom'," says Stratton, "I got on really well with Martin, who later went on to work with Mutt Lange and Def Leppard, and so, when it came to doing all the harmony guitar parts and the backing vocals for the choruses, I really went to town to try and produce what I thought was the best possible sound I could to go with the song. I mean, I swear it wasn't anything to do with me trying to push the band in a new direction, or anything like that. I honestly felt what I was adding to the track was perfect Iron Maiden-type stuff. Once they'd said something, though, I did see it, yeah. It sounded too much like Queen. But that's me – I get carried away. Rod heard it and said, 'It sounds just like Queen. Get rid of the voices.' So they did. They took the voices and guitars that I had added off the tape and you were left with the original, raw, live Maiden song, which is exactly what they were after, not anything too polished. But I think that's when Steve and Rod decided I was trying to intentionally change the sound, which I wasn't at all! I thought I was just adding to it, not taking away from it."

It was the start of a rift that would continue to widen over the coming months. "I was disappointed, let's say," Dennis continues, "because I thought it sounded great, but I was a new member of the band, so I had to listen. Ultimately, I didn't mind. It was their band. They'd done all the work to bring it to where it was when I stepped in. And, you know, you put too much on, you can always take it off. That's the way I've always done it, too. But I admit, I was a little bit upset. But if that's not the right direction, if it's not NWOBHM enough, then fair enough. Rod wanted them to stay as this raw, young, new-wave metal band, and he was right. History has proved that, I think."

"I noticed Dennis was so much more into playing stuff like 'Strange World' than he was 'Iron Maiden' or 'Prowler', because it was more slow, melodic, and you could tell when he was playing a solo he just really got into it," says Steve. "But when he was soloing on one of the heavier songs, it wasn't with quite the same passion. You just knew. It just wasn't."

Whatever the nagging worries about their new guitarist's musical direction, it was too late to do anything about it now, as the band plugged gamely away in the studios until, finally, they found that they had eight finished numbers from their live set safely recorded and awaiting one final mix, which they hurriedly completed at nearby Morgan Studios in February. Meanwhile, EMI busied themselves with preparing for the release of the band's first single, 'Running Free', which had been finished especially early and handed over to the record company some weeks previously.

Released in the UK on 15 February 1980, 'Running Free' became not just Iron Maiden's first single but also their first hit, selling more than 10,000 copies in its first week of release and, to everyone's utter astonishment (including Rod Smallwood's), immediately leaping into the UK national charts at Number 44. "Actually, I thought it might go in a bit higher," Rod sniffs theatrically, enjoying every moment before admitting, "No, even I was surprised by that one. I knew it would sell straight away to all the Maiden fans that were already waiting for it, but I was genuinely taken aback to see it shoot so high into the chart. Not that I let on at the time, though!"

"Because all these people had been going into shops asking for 'The Soundhouse Tapes', and because of the vibe surrounding us then, we knew we'd definitely sell a few copies of whatever we put out first," says Steve. "And of course Rod was utterly convinced that we'd go zooming straight into the Top 40, and I suppose we thought, 'Well, we probably will.' But then, when it actually happened and you could go into Woolworth's and see it listed in the official chart... Well, I mean, it just blew us away. And then, the first time they played it on Radio 1, on the Tommy Vance show, amongst ourselves we were, like, 'Bloody hell, listen to that! That's us!'"

"The most surprised of all, of course, were the radio pluggers at EMI," says Rod. "As far as they were concerned, a record simply didn't get into the charts unless it was either played to death on the radio or by a really well-known artist, and we were neither of those yet. But we knew that, whether it got onto the radio or not, there would be a big demand for 'Running Free'. So, when it went into the charts, they were, like, 'How the fuck?' The first radio promotion person we had at EMI was a guy called Paul Watts, and you could tell the attitude right off. He was, like, 'Ho, ho, ho. This will never get played on the radio.' So, to gee them all up, I remember being in a meeting with all the various heads of department the week before the single came out and saying, 'And don't forget, when we get offered *Top Of The Pops*, tell them we won't do it unless we can do it live.' And they were all, like, 'Are you *serious*?' I was, like, 'Yeah, I'm absolutely bloody serious.'"

The longest-running and most widely watched pop show on British television, *Top Of The Pops* is a veritable institution of British broadcasting. A 30-minute weekly reflection of the week's national singles charts, its format has hardly changed since its inception in the mid '60s –

half a dozen records chosen from the week's chart climbers mimed by the artists themselves and topped off with whatever is Number One each week. At that time, actual live performances were almost unheard of. The Beatles had managed it a couple of times in the '60s, and there had been several occasions when the artists were happy to contribute live lead vocals to a pre-recorded backing tape, but a genuine, amped-up performance by a living, breathing rock band hadn't been a feature of the programme since 1972, when The Who tore apart the set at the climax of a live and fearsomely splenetic performance of their hit '5.15'. Besides, in those pre-MTV days, *Top Of The Pops* was still the most influential chart show on TV, a must-do for any artist hoping to impinge their music on the nation's consciousness. As a result, grateful for any kind of exposure they could get, artists literally fought amongst themselves to get a spot on the show. Being an unknown band and laying down conditions for your first appearance, therefore, was considered unthinkable. Nevertheless, that's exactly what a bemused Paul Watts found himself having to do when, sure enough, he received a call from the *Top Of The Pops* production office the day after 'Running Free' entered the charts.

While it's fair to say that the BBC staff were surprised, to say the least, by the response they got (they initially refused point blank to comply with Maiden's wishes, until Watts was forced to make it clear to them that the band simply wouldn't appear under any other circumstances), in the end they did climb down from their lofty broadcasting perch and agreed to allow the band to perform 'Running Free' live on that week's show. A small step for a potential chart climber, perhaps, but a significant victory for a band whose very reputation relied on their ability to perform as a top-notch live band.

"The whole *Top Of The Pops* thing wasn't such a big deal to me, to be honest," says Steve. "I mean, once we realised we were gonna go on it, I phoned 'round people and told my mum, 'We're gonna be on *Top Of The Pops*,' because your family, that's all they know about the music business. You say you're signed to EMI and they just look at you with blank faces. You say, 'We're on the telly tonight,' and they immediately know what you're on about. But personally I had a bit of an anti-*Top Of The Pops* thing, because they never had anyone decent on there, anyway, in those days, and I was really adamant that I wasn't going to do it if they were gonna make us mime to a playback. That was just my attitude, then. It was maybe a young attitude, strong-headed or whatever, I don't know, but that was the attitude. I just thought, 'Bollocks to them! What have they ever done for me?'"

Dennis Stratton: "We wanted to do it live but, because we'd always been used to playing extremely loud, it made it tricky bringing the volume well down. But me and Dave Murray got together and worked it out that, by adjusting the master volume and gain on our amps, we could use them against one another to get the same powerful-sounding guitars but at low volume. Clive had to put pads on his drums, so, although on the programme we had Marshall amps stacked up behind us, there was only one cabinet working. But we still got that heavy-metal sound. I remember on the next stage to us was Shakin' Stevens. When he did his little Elvis dance, I remember his trainers were squeaking louder than what we were actually playing."

"Everyone rang their mums," admits Dave Murray. "Then I remember we were all driving through London, listening to Alan Freeman doing the charts on Radio 1 on the old ghetto blaster, waiting for him to run down the chart so we could tape the bit where he read out 'Running Free'. We had twin cassette decks so we could record it. It came on and we pushed the record button and we made Vic stop the truck in case we got a bad signal. Then they played it and we all started cheering."

A surprisingly catchy collision between Gary Glitter-style drums, razor-edged guitars and Paul's rough-as-sandpaper vocals, 'Running Free' was Iron Maiden at their punk-metal apotheosis. Indeed, were it not for the blisteringly busy guitar break that Davey supplies midway and the sugary, Wishbone Ash-style harmony vocals on the chorus, this could well have been a record of one of the more musically accomplished punk bands. Certainly Paul Di'Anno, who penned the lyrics, thinks so: "I suppose you'd have to call that one a very autobiographical song, though of course I've never spent the night in an LA jail. I've certainly seen the inside of a few London cells in my time, though! It's about being 16 and, like it says, just running wild and running free. It comes from my days as a skinhead, and I think what's great about it is that it really sounds like that on the record – the energy just sizzles off it, even now, all these years later."

Another striking feature of Maiden's first single was the introduction into the scheme of things of one of the most important characters in the entire Maiden story: Eddie, the cartoon creation of self-styled English eccentric and former art-school drop-out Derek Riggs. Taking his name from the infamous mask he would soon replace as their main onstage prop, Eddie was destined to become the mad, mythical human monster cum band mascot that would subsequently adorn all of Maiden's future record sleeves, posters, T-shirts, baseball caps and every other scrap of merchandising that would eventually bear the band's logo over the next 20 years. Not that you actually got to behold the beastly one's countenance on the 'Running Free' sleeve. That was a feast that they were saving for the album cover. Instead, what you got was a lurid cartoon of a rock fan fleeing from a tall, shadowy figure wielding a broken bottle at the end of an alley graffitised with the names of such close-to-home legends as Judas Priest, The Scorpions, Led Zeppelin, AC/DC and, of course, 'Arry's beloved Hammers (underlined twice!).

Now 40, Derek Riggs has spent the last 18 years working exclusively on hundreds of different paintings and drawings of Eddie for Iron Maiden, doing his best to depict the band's monstrous mascot in the increasingly outlandish settings to which their own adventure-filled albums would take him, from a mummified Egyptian god on the *Powerslave* sleeve to the very Devil himself on *Number Of The Beast* and several quantum leaps of the imagination in between. But whether it be as a laser-packing time cop (*Somewhere In Time*), a lobotomised vandal (*Piece Of Mind*) or a figure strapped to an electric chair (*The X Factor*), the one thing that never changes is the thrill that runs through an Iron Maiden audience the moment Eddie bursts forth onto the stage at the climax of every show. If you've never seen Iron Maiden live, you won't know what is so palpably obvious to those of us who have been there to see it for ourselves, that Eddie is the immortal soul of Iron Maiden, the defining symbol of the eternally youthful, blissfully uncompromising spirit of the band's music. No matter what your age (and, after nearly three decades, there are plenty of Maiden fans whose memories are now longer than our hair), Eddie stands for that part of us that will never stop loving loud, live, over-the-top rock music, that will never shrink or hide from adversity and never give up hope that there are still better times to be had...somewhere. That's why

Eddie no longer belongs either to Derek Riggs, Rod Smallwood or Steve Harris. He belongs to us all.

"The thing about Maiden is that onstage they're this big, roaring rock band, but offstage they're just a nice, quiet bunch of people," says Rod. "Even Paul, who was a great ringleader onstage, didn't really have a great deal to say for himself offstage. The band didn't really have a Lemmy figure, if you know what I mean. They didn't have that one figure who utterly stamped his presence and image on the band in a way that was obvious enough to make a good album cover. There wasn't anything extra to give the image that continuity. So I went looking for someone, something, an image that would look good on the record sleeve and say something more about this band than just another photograph of them onstage."

Rod was in John Darnley's office at EMI one afternoon when, of all things, a poster on the wall for trad-jazz star Max Middleton caught his eye. "It's not like I'm a big Max Middleton fan or anything," he says, "but the artwork on this poster was just so striking you couldn't miss it. Your eyes just went to it as soon as you walked in the room. So I immediately asked John, 'Who did that for you?' And it was this guy I'd never heard of called Derek Riggs. I asked to meet him so he could show me some more of his work, and in the middle of a load of drawings for what he thought would be good sci-fi book covers there was the first album sleeve! It was this sort of cartoon of this mad-looking sort of punk monster, but as soon as I saw it, I knew. That was it! The only change we asked Derek to make was to make the hair a bit longer, so it was less obviously like a punk. Derek had been around all the record companies trying to sell it for a punk band – album or single, he didn't mind – but I saw that and thought, 'No, that's for us. That's exactly what we need.' I remember taking his portfolio around to show the band. I just threw it on the table and said, 'See if you can pick out your album sleeve,' and it was the first one they picked out. It was just obvious to everybody from the word go – there was Eddie. It was like he'd been done just for the band."

"People always ask if Eddie was inspired by Maiden's music, but I'd never even heard of Iron Maiden when I drew the first Eddie," Derek admits. "I've never really been into heavy metal. In fact, when I'm drawing, instead of listening to whatever Maiden are up to, I'm much more likely to spend most of my time listening to Beethoven, Stravinsky or even The Spice Girls. In those days, though, I was quite fond of punk, and originally that's what Eddie was supposed to be, this sort of brain-damaged punk. I was very influenced by the punk idea of wasted youth, this whole generation that had just been thrown in the bin, no future and all that, which is funny, because I then included it with some other stuff I'd been sending around to various sort of science-fiction book publishers to see if they could use any of it on one of their book covers, or whatever. I didn't really know what else to do with it. I've never even really been into art, not in the conventional sense, not since they threw me out of art college, in Coventry, when I was 19.

"But no one was interested. I was pretty crap at book covers, actually. I discovered I could paint city streets really well, but that wasn't much help when it came to sci-fi. Then, out of nowhere, Rod and Maiden picked up on this particular image, only they wanted me to make it a bit less like a punk and more like them, so I redrew him with pretty much the same face, the same body and clothes and everything, just with longer hair. It was still spiky, but now it was long and would shoot out in all directions."

"I liked the idea, because it gave you great visual continuity," says Rod, "and it made the Maiden sleeves just stick out a bit more than the average sort of could-be-anything sort of sleeves most rock bands used then. And it became a very important part of Maiden's image, in that way. We've never done a lot of television and we've never really been on the radio, but because Eddie struck such a chord with the Maiden fans, we didn't need to be. Wearing an Eddie T-shirt became like a statement: 'Fuck radio. Fuck TV. We're not into that crap. We're into Iron Maiden.' And of course we've had a lot of fun with Eddie over the years, trying to find new and ever more outrageous things for him to be and do. Sometimes the ideas come from Derek, although usually they either come from me or one of the band. But it can be anybody or anything that inspires us. Like with *Number Of The Beast*, where we had Eddie in hell with the Devil as his puppet, only the Devil's got a puppet Eddie, too, and it was, like, well, who's the really evil one here? Who's manipulating who? The concept was very simple, but the way Derek executed it was fantastic. Originally, he came up with it for the sleeve of the 'Purgatory' single, but we said, 'No, that's much too good,' so we kept it for the album. We had the artwork months before we had the music."

The idea of turning the original Eddie the 'Ead that had adorned the backdrop of every Maiden gig for the last three years into the recognisable face of Riggs' Eddie was a fairly obvious one. Smoke still billowed from its mouth during the usual 'Iron Maiden' finale, only now the ghastly, staring mask had acquired not just long, spiky hair but also a long, spiky personality to match. But the real masterstroke was when they eventually hit on the idea of having a three-dimensional Eddie that didn't just stare from the back of the stage but actually ran about it, terrorising both the band and the astonished audience. Rod credits Rupert Perry, former EMI managing director in the '80s, for the original suggestion that Eddie might become more than just a useful merchandising icon, that he might somehow become an active part of the show.

"Rupert was at a show with us one night," says Rod, "and he just said, 'Smallwood, why don't you get this guy onstage?' And I thought, 'Yeah, he's right. That would be great.' At first, it was just me with an Eddie mask on. I'd just go bounding around the stage like a lunatic during the intro to get the audience worked up, and the place would go mad, so we started doing it every night. Once, in Detroit, a guy from the record company came up when I had the mask on and asked me if I'd seen Rod. I just growled! Then various tour managers did it. One tour manager we had, Tony Wiggins, absolutely refused to do it, so he would always wear cord trousers to the show, because he knew we'd never let Eddie go onstage in cords! It had to be a leather jacket and jeans. So Tony never did Eddie."

"I can't actually take all the credit," insists Rupert Perry. "It's true that it was me who first said to Rod, you know, 'What if the Eddie character could move?' but I was thinking more along the lines of something that would happen at the start of the show, perhaps before the band even came on. But Rod, in his genius, took that and turned it into something much more exciting. And now, of course, Eddie is a very big and important part of every Iron Maiden show. It would be hard to imagine them without him. He's become like the sixth member."

Originally, Eddie's brief but blustery appearances took the form of a leather-jacketed man (usually Rod, he admits, or one of their tour managers) in a specially designed mask. But as the band's international career took off around the world and the arenas they filled grew larger and larger, so too did Eddie. Bigger and more berserk with each new album that rolled around, by 1984's *Powerslave* he was over 14 feet tall and able to launch thunderbolts with the wave of one giant, bandaged hand. Clearly, this was no mere man in a frightmask.

Dave Lights remembers how the idea arose. "I had taken my family to see *Jack And The Beanstalk* in pantomime the previous Christmas," he says, "and I remember how impressed all the kids had been every time the giant walked onstage. It was basically a bloke on stilts but dressed up to look about ten feet tall. It was just such a simple, marvellous effect that I mentioned it to the band and said, 'You know, maybe we could have Eddie as some sort of giant when he comes onstage.' I think, the first time we did it, on the Number Of The Beast world tour, the Eddie we had was about eight feet tall, but he ended up about 14 feet in the end, I think. He just kept growing, getting bigger and more ridiculous with each tour we did, and it's kind of become the best part of the show. It's always right at the end, during 'Iron Maiden', and it's just turned into this big, mad celebration. Just when you think you've seen all the effects there are, had all the best lights and heard all the best numbers, suddenly here comes Eddie and it just sends everybody right over the top."

The band's current tour manager, Dickie Bell, who has worked with Maiden since 1981, says, "The kids fucking love Eddie more than they love the band. And you can see why. It's 'cause he's one of them. In their minds, he's like the Maiden fan from hell! And when he gets up onstage, it's like one of their own getting up there and doing it for them. It's like Eddie is the ultimate headbanger!"

Back in February 1980, however, the world of giant Eddies and world tours was still some distance away. Instead, the band had to make do, for the time being, with touring with a very different kind of stage monster: Neal Kay's *Metal For Muthas*. At the same time that Brian Shepherd had first offered Maiden a deal with EMI, another rock-friendly face in their A&R department was Ashley Goodall, a young gun who had already decided to take his own punt on the burgeoning NWOBHM scene about which *Sounds* was increasingly raving. Rather than plump for any particular band, though, Goodall conceived the idea of gathering up the cream of the crop of the NWOBHM bands and putting tracks by all of them onto one catch-all NWOBHM compilation. Enlisting the aid of the ever-willing Kay to choose the tracks and drum up some publicity for the release, it was the whiskery-minded DJ who suggested the title of the album, *Metal For Muthas*. Hardly subtle, but certainly memorable, and so, in Kay's arcane terminology, the two had begun "recruiting heroes to the cause".

They ended up with nine bands, most of which could, broadly speaking, be conveniently sheltered underneath the NWOBHM umbrella (although how The EF Band – a metal-by-numbers clone from Sweden – qualified, Kay only knows!). Most prominent, of course, was Maiden, who were also, significantly, the only band on the album to have two tracks featured: 'Sanctuary' and 'Wrathchild'. But then, Maiden was also the only band on the album to have Rod Smallwood managing them.

"We were sure it wouldn't be worth us doing it unless we could do it our way," he says, "which meant we insisted on at least a couple of days to do the recording with EMI's in-house guy, Neil Harrison, in their basement studios at Manchester Square. And we insisted on having two tracks included, with one of them as track one, side one. Our attitude was, 'We do it our way or we won't do it at all.'"

Elsewhere, there were tracks by genuine NWOBHM stalwarts Samson ('Tomorrow Or Yesterday'), Angel Witch ('Baphomet') and Sledgehammer ('Sledgehammer'). Inevitably, however, there were some notable exceptions, not least Saxon, Def Leppard, Diamond Head and Tygers Of Pan Tang, all of whom were in varying stages of negotiation with other major labels for deals of their own and therefore unavailable for EMI's project. The rest of the album was padded out by distinctly second-division, bandwagon-jumping guff like Toad The Wet Sprocket's 'Blues In A', which isn't nearly as exciting as it sounds, and Ethel The Frog's game but amateurish 'Fight Back'. They even included a track by former A&M artists Nutz, a band that hardly qualified as new at any stage of its unremarkable career.

Reviewing the album in *Sounds*, Geoff Barton came straight to the point: "For something that's supposed to act as a standard-bearer for the New Wave Of British Heavy Metal, this *Metal For Muthas* disc is a joke. And not a very funny one, either." He then went on to accuse it of being no more than "a low-budget cash-in" that, "far from giving NWOBHM a boost, cannot do it anything other than considerable harm". The album's only saving grace, Barton concluded, was Maiden's contributions, recorded in under a day at EMI's basement studios at Manchester Square before they went in to begin recording their own album. "Out of the nine bands concerned," he wrote, "only Iron Maiden can emerge with their heads held high," and described their music as "raucous heavy metal/punk crossovers and tantalising tasters for their own forthcoming album".

Not everybody felt as harshly, however. Malcolm Dome gave the *Metal For Muthas* album a glowing review in *Record Mirror*, which he says he still stands by today. "I must admit, I found it all very exciting, at the time," he says. "It seemed clear to the cynics that *Metal For Muthas* was being used to promote Iron Maiden, who had two tracks on it, while everyone else had just one. But then, the Maiden tracks were by far the best, no question. It was a shame they couldn't get Def Leppard or Diamond Head as well. But then you looked at who else they had on there – Ethel The Frog, Toad The Wet Sprocket, Angel Witch, Samson, Praying Mantis – and I still think it was actually a fine summation of that period."

The Metal For Muthas tour, which featured Maiden, Praying Mantis, Tygers Of Pan Tang and Raven, as well as the ever-present Neal Kay, presiding as both DJ and "mein host" for the evening, was scheduled to run right through February. This was Dennis Stratton's first experience of playing live with the band, and he admits now that he was "shell-shocked by the response they got from their fans. I mean, I'd already done 30,000-seaters, when RDB supported Status Quo in Germany, and even though we got to play some quite big places on the Metal For Muthas tour, like the Lyceum and Aberdeen University, obviously they were nothing compared to some of the arenas I'd done with Quo. But the atmosphere on that tour – that was unbelievable, like nothing I'd ever experienced before! With Maiden, the crowd were just hysterical. As the lights went down, the sound they started to make was frightening. I mean, they were crazy! Musically, it was bordering on punk rock, like thrash metal is nowadays, and the audience was just fanatical. I'd really never experienced anything like it. And Maiden was definitely going down the best each night. To me, it was all heavy-metal music, but for some reason the fans could pick out that Maiden were different. Maybe it was the riff work rather than the chord work. But whatever they had, they had it before I came along. It was a really dedicated following. And so, the way it went, it couldn't fail. Everybody was so behind Maiden each night on that tour, you just couldn't see anything stopping us."

"We didn't look at it like we were in competition with the other bands," says Steve Harris. "The way we thought of it, when they started calling it the NWOBHM movement, it was as if we were all up there, all trying to do it together. And it was an up yours to all the other kinds of music, like punk, that had got in the way, basically, and an up yours to all the people who had ever told us to cut our hair or try and go punk. I knew that we had a rent-a-crowd, if you like, who would follow us around, but when we were playing places like the Lyceum in London, which was the biggest gig we'd done up till then, it was pretty packed out. But there weren't just Maiden fans there, and we liked that aspect of it. Again, it was just getting through to more people that might not have seen us otherwise."

"Some nights, I'd stand at the side and watch the other bands and you wouldn't see the audience getting so wound up," says Paul Di'Anno. "I reckon it was the punk thing we had. Saxon and Tygers Of Pan Tang, bands like that, they were just like the old rock bands, really. We were more street. The kids could tell the difference. I could tell the difference. I'd go to other shows and the crowd didn't jump around like at one of our shows. It was a completely different atmosphere."

"Everywhere we went, we went down really well," says Dave Murray. "There were people just waiting for the tour to arrive. It felt like the punk thing was kind of coming to an end and there was this gap and that everybody was just waiting for something to happen again. And it was great, because rock was supposed to be dead, you know? But the reality was that there was loads of kids out there who were coming to the shows or forming their own bands. Everybody remembers us and Samson, Angel Witch and Def Leppard, but I thought it was great that there were groups like Toad The Wet Sprocket, too. I can't remember what they sounded like, but I always remember them, 'cause of the brilliant name. It still makes me smile every time I think of it."

However, a hiccup occurred when the final week of dates had to be cancelled when it became apparent that Steve Harris would need time to return to Morgan Studios to complete the final mixes of the first Maiden album. But as their booking agent, John Jackson, explains, "It actually worked out better for them that way, in the end. Initially, the Metal For Muthas tour was only going to be about three weeks long. Then, when Maiden had to leave the tour to finish the album, we decided to make up for it by rescheduling all the dates they had cancelled for the summer. But by then the album had been a big hit and the demand for tickets was suddenly so great that we kept having to add dates on.

"It started out as about seven rescheduled dates from the Metal For Muthas tour in April. We had Praying Mantis on the bill, Neal Kay and then, on some shows, Tygers Of Pan Tang. But by May Maiden were headlining their own tour, playing in some of the places they'd just been supporting Judas Priest in, and they ended up playing something like 55 more shows in Britain that year. We just kept adding and adding and adding as each one sold out. We even sold out the old Rainbow Theatre in Finsbury Park, which is now closed but back then was one of the biggest venues in London. And then we sold out a couple more nights at the Marquee. We were just doing cracking business wherever we went."

With the final mixes of the album now completed and handed over to EMI for imminent release, Maiden got their biggest break yet in March, when they managed to hitch a ride as special guests (read "support act") on the British leg of Judas Priest's world tour, 15 shows in the sort of major concert-hall venues they'd dreamed of playing since they were kids themselves, queuing for tickets to see Priest at the Hammersmith Odeon, where they would make their debut on 15 March.

"Couldn't believe our luck, mate!" Paul Di'Anno cries. "It was weird, too, 'cause I actually remember going to see them play the old Hammy Odeon on their previous tour. If anybody had said to me then, 'Next time Priest play here, you'll be up there, too,' I'd have said they were taking the piss, you know?"

Meanwhile, the members of Judas Priest were left pondering their own fortunes after taking great offence to Di'Anno's comment to Garry Bushell in *Sounds* just prior to the tour that Maiden would "blow the bollocks off Priest". Already concerned with the threat that the onset of the NWOBHM might pose to their own position as newly installed heads of the domestic hard-rock scene, Paul's leery boasts put the Priest camp even more on the defensive. For years, they had struggled for recognition beneath the looming shadows of more eminent '70s rock goliaths like Led Zeppelin and Black Sabbath. Now, in 1980, with both Zeppelin and Sabbath joining Deep Purple in retirement and the success of albums like the live double *Unleashed In The East* (1979) and their new studio offering, *British Steel* (featuring the hit single 'Living After Midnight'), Priest's star at last appeared to be on the ascendancy. Only fellow '70s survivors UFO appeared to offer any real challenge to their position at the top of the tree in Britain in 1980, and even they had begun to falter with the departure of blond *wunderkind* guitarist Michael Schenker. Then along came Iron Maiden and the NWOBHM...

Unaware of the ill feeling about to blow their way, and excited merely by the prospect of touring the country with a band they had all admired as fans long before they had become fellow professionals, Maiden actually turned up *en masse* to meet the Priest guys at a rehearsal that they were holding in Willesden a few days before the tour began, on 7 March. Laden with sacks of beers and brimming with pre-tour bonhomie, the Maiden boys were dismayed to find Priest guitarist KK Downing in taciturn mood. Upset by what he saw as Maiden's insulting attitude, they had been there less than five minutes before the plainly disgruntled guitarist had them all unceremoniously kicked out. "I just thought they were taking the piss," KK would confide to your author years later. "But they were just kids. They didn't know any better. And these days we're all great mates, you know?"

"In those days," says John Jackson, "you used to be able to break a band off another tour, especially if it was a rock band, because so much depends on how good they are live. And there had been some classic examples over the years – Lynyrd Skynyrd supporting Golden Earring to a half-filled Rainbow in 1974, then going back there and doing their own show a few months later and completely selling it out; or like when Little Feat supported The Doobie Brothers and completely stole the show. And the whole new wave of metal thing was really coming to the fore then, of which Maiden were rightly regarded as being at the forefront. All the older bands were starting to look over their shoulders and wonder what all the fuss was about. It was like the changing of the guard.

"But the fact is, I knew Maiden would go down brilliantly on that tour, and they really did. I mean, absolutely. Totally. And ever since then, Priest have had the hump with them." So much so, in fact, that Priest would later fire Jackson specifically because of his perceived allegiance to Rod and Iron Maiden. "But if anything they did me a big favour," John insists now, not unreasonably, "because it encouraged me to leave Cowbell and start my own agency, Fair Warning, in 1984. And of course my first big clients were

Iron Maiden." (It's worth noting that Fair Warning is now one of the biggest agencies in the world, representing more than 200 artists, including Maiden, Metallica, Black Sabbath, Guns N' Roses, Megadeth and Slayer, along with more household names such as Blur, Wet Wet Wet and Sheryl Crow, amongst many others.

Priest, for their part, were not happy with the situation, according to Steve Harris. "They made it difficult for us," he says. "Their sound man, Nigel, started mucking us around. It was bloody annoying, but if anything it just made us that more determined to deliver."

Rod Smallwood puts things into perspective. "We were delighted to get the Priest tour," he says. "I'd actually signed them to the MAM agency in 1972, although I left soon after and so did they. Maiden were big fans, so we were really looking forward to the tour. Unfortunately, Garry Bushell – then at *Sounds* – in his inimitable controversy-provoking style wound up Paul to make his fateful comment about blowing them away. We later found out that Priest were pissed off about this, and understandably so. I had called their manager, Jim Dawson, and asked if it was OK to take Maiden down to meet them, with a few beers, at their rehearsals. This was agreed, so we went down to Willesden, where they were in pre-production. Unfortunately, the management never told the band, so they mistook our visit as lack of courtesy and arrogance and we were promptly asked to leave.

"So you could say that we had a rocky start to the tour. This led to a few problems, but these just fired Maiden up even more. The result was poisoned relationships between the bands for many years, and we twice toured arenas in the US with them, in 1981 and 1982! It really is a shame that two great British bands who, despite the difference in ages, should have been friendly were at loggerheads due to a series of misunderstandings. In the long run, touring with Priest both here and in the States was immensely successful for us and made a big difference to Maiden's early development, and I thank them for that. And everything's OK between us now."

Maiden's last show with Priest had been at the Birmingham Odeon on 27 March. From 1-10 April, they completed seven final Metal For Muthas dates with Praying Mantis, Neal Kay and Tygers Of Pan Tang in tow. Then, on 11 April, the day after the final Metal For Muthas show at the Central Hall in Grimsby, EMI released the *Iron Maiden* album to the nation's record shops. A week later, it was in the charts – at Number Four!

"I was completely shocked when the album went into the charts," says Dennis Stratton. "We were in a pub and someone from EMI came 'round and said, 'You've gone straight in at Number Four,' and we all went out and started screaming! We got back to the record company and there were people shouting from the windows of EMI in Manchester Square, 'You've gone to Number Four!' It was real, but it wasn't real, if you know what I mean. It felt like you probably do if you win the National Lottery, only they don't give you a big cheque for it straight away. I mean, we had such a big live following that we'd been told the advance orders alone would probably put it straight into the chart, but we had no idea it would be so high. I don't think anybody did. Then, of course, when it went down the next week, we were all disappointed. It's funny how your expectations can change so much in just a few days. A week before, we'd have been thrilled if it had gone in as high as it then went down to, which was, like, Number 17 or something."

The album did fall back down the charts the following week, but it was another month before it disappeared from sight completely, by which time Iron Maiden had sold more than 60,000 copies, enough to earn the band their first silver disc. "We didn't expect it to go in that high," admits Steve. "We knew it was gonna go in the Top 30, possibly Top 20, you know, going by the pre-sales, as they call them, and all the other stuff they tell you. We'd done quite a bit of touring by then, and we'd really built up a real hardcore following. I mean, it wasn't massive then, it was still an underground type of thing, but because of that we were confident the album would do quite well. But to go in at Number Four! It was like, 'Bloody hell! You what?' At first, I thought someone had made a mistake. We thought maybe it was Number 40, or maybe Number 14 at best, you know? I made them go and check twice, and even then I still couldn't quite believe it."

Still fondly regarded by many first-generation Maiden fans as one of the finest albums the band would ever make, *Iron Maiden* comprised eight classic Maiden originals, five that Steve had written alone ('Prowler', 'Phantom Of The Opera', 'Transylvania', 'Strange World' and 'Iron Maiden'), two that he'd written with Paul ('Remember Tomorrow' and 'Running Free') and one that Davey had come up with, 'Charlotte The Harlot', which was "based on a true story". A more-or-less faithful representation of their early live set, all eight numbers had been brutally worked into shape by the endless parade of gigs that Maiden had performed over the previous twelve months, and it's a mark of just how immensely powerful and tempestuous those early shows were that, despite the brittle, rudderless production, *Iron Maiden* still jumps out of the speakers like a herd of angry elephants when you play it now, 20 years later.

"We'd been playing most of those songs for years, in one form or another, which was a blessing, because it meant we didn't have to mess around in the studio," says Steve. "We just tried to get our live sound down on tape. Because I think the production did really suffer, I don't think we really got it, actually. You listen to some of the live tapes from some of the gigs we did in them days and they blow the bollocks off the album. Don't get me wrong, I'm very, very proud of the first album. I think we recorded the songs the best we could, and at the end of the day that's how those songs will always be remembered by the fans, so I ain't knocking it. And I mean, it was our first, wasn't it? So of course it's special."

Questionable production values notwithstanding, the band play like angels with their wings on fire, transcending the limitations of their surroundings as they had learned to do in the countless pubs in which their music had grown to produce a work of rigorous, undeniable appeal. Paul Di'Anno's vocals are superb throughout, gritty but controlled, the aggression on up-front rockers like 'Prowler' or 'Running Free' teased out rather than shouted, the emotions expressed surprisingly tenderly on more reflective moments like 'Remember Tomorrow' or the charmingly effete break midway through the otherwise judderingly Zep-like 'Charlotte The Harlot'. Even when he hadn't actually written the words himself, you just knew that Paul meant every one of them.

"It was the best album I did with Maiden, without a doubt," the singer reflects today. "I didn't think the second album was a patch on it, personally. People go on about the production. I don't even notice it. All I hear is the band playing and me singing and how great the songs are."

Reviewing the album in *Sounds*, Geoff Barton wrote, "Heavy metal for the '80s, its blinding speed and rampant ferocity making most plastic heavy rock tracks from the '60s and '70s sound sloth-like and funeral-dirgey by comparison. A safety-pin/loon-pant hybrid? In many ways, yes!"

Malcolm Dome was even more lavish with his praise in his five-star review for *Record Mirror*. "It was everything that you hoped they would do," he says now. "For me, it marked the start of the '80s, in terms of where rock music was now going, and I still think it's one of the best things they've ever done. In fact, I'd say that and the album that followed, *Killers*, are still my two favourite Maiden albums of all time, and I've got them all."

And of course towering resplendent in full-frontal colour on the cover was the band's new-found friend, Eddie. Garry Bushell used to enjoy winding people up by telling them that the picture of Eddie on the cover of the first Iron Maiden album was actually inspired by a photograph of Neal Kay, and yet, hard though it is to believe, Eddie looked much, much worse than that. He looked like a corpse that had just been brought back to life by a huge surge of unholy lightning (the riff, possibly, to 'Phantom Of The Opera'?). Former *Metal Hammer* editor Jerry Ewing, now an author in his own right and in-house rock reviewer for *Vox* magazine, remembers "buying the album and sitting on the bus home just staring and staring at this picture of this...thing...on the cover. You obviously weren't meant to take it too seriously, and I liked that. So many rock bands up till then were very pompous about their album sleeves. It was all surreal images and heavy symbolism. Maiden wasn't like that. They had some big, heavy songs that were obviously supposed to be meaningful, but mainly they had this great spirit going for them, almost like a punk band. They just rode right over you and didn't give a fuck, and I thought that was great.

"I was still only a kid then, and I remember seeing bands like Judas Priest and Nazareth on *Top Of The Pops* and thinking, 'This is crap, just a bunch of boring old farts,' you know? But Maiden was new, was big, exciting, and they were the spearhead of a new movement, or so we kept being told. And you just had the feeling that they were going to be immense. People talk about the production or lack of production on the album, but as a kid buying his first Iron Maiden record I didn't pick up on any of that. I just played it and thought, 'Yeah! This fucking rocks!'"

8 Adrian

Iron Maiden's first major British headline tour was a massive 45-date jaunt with Praying Mantis and Neal Kay still in support which kicked off at the Drill Hall in Lincoln on 15 May and would culminate in the band's first appearance at the Reading Festival – then the biggest annual outdoor event in the British rock diary – on 23 August. Along the way, they would also headline their own show at London's Rainbow, another first, which EMI helped them celebrate by hosting an after-show party for the band and hundreds of guests at Madame Tussaud's Chamber of Horrors wax museum. EMI had also rush-released a new single on 16 May to coincide with the dates, the band wisely opting for a re-recording of 'Sanctuary', the Harris/Murray/Di'Anno track that they'd contributed to the ill-starred *Metal For Muthas* album, which was already a firm favourite with the Maiden fans who had seen them play it live.

Built around Dave Murray's police-siren riff and Paul Di'Anno's gruff, catch-me-if-you-can vocals, 'Sanctuary' is three minutes and 13 seconds of pure, unadulterated riffage, as catchy as a meat hook and sounding just as bloody. "It had turned into one of the songs that we played right near the end of the show," Dave Murray remembers, "and we still do, sometimes. I think the version we did for the single was ten times better than the original *Metal For Muthas* version, anyway." Certainly their growing legion of fans thought so, as enough of them dashed out to buy it during its first two weeks of release to send the single crashing into the UK charts at Number 33. And this time, unlike the album, a week later 'Sanctuary' had actually gone even higher, ticking like a bomb at the Number 29 spot in the nation's charts, once again without any radio support. (It would probably have gone even higher if they'd made a return appearance on *Top Of The Pops*, but strike action amongst the technical crew at the BBC had resulted in the show being off the air for several weeks that summer.)

And, of course, there was another special Eddie sleeve to go with the single. This time, however, Derek Riggs had managed to come up with an Eddie that not only captured the mood of the music it enfolded superbly but was also to cause no little controversy for the band. A knife-wielding Eddie is depicted crouching over the slain, mini-skirted figure of a woman that, on close inspection, appears to be Margaret Thatcher, the Conservative prime minister who had been swept into power in Britain at the 1979 general election. Judging by the scene, Eddie had apparently caught the malingering PM in the unforgivable act of tearing down an Iron Maiden poster from a street wall, a crime – in Eddie's mad, unblinking eyes – worthy of only one punishment. The blood is still dripping from his twelve-inch blade as we catch up with them. However, the single's release had coincided with a series of highly publicised real-life acts of violence perpetrated by the various disaffected members of the British public against several top-level Tory government officials. (Lord Home had reportedly been set upon by a gang of skinheads at Piccadilly Circus tube station and Lord Chalfont was given a black eye by another closely cropped youth while walking down the King's Road.)

"The artwork was very tongue in cheek, as usual," comments Rod. "At that time, Maggie had visited the old USSR and, following her tough stance with them, had been christened the Iron Maiden. Eddie took offence to this, and even more so when she started taking our posters down. It's still one of my favourite artworks. Just before it came out, I suggested to EMI that they black out her eyes, as this would give the tabloids an angle and draw attention to the single. It worked, and we got great coverage."

On 20 May, *The Daily Mirror* reproduced the uncensored version of the 'Sanctuary' sleeve under the banner headline "It's Murder! Maggie Gets Rock Mugging!" Soon questions were being asked in Parliament. "Premier Margaret Thatcher has been murdered – on a rock band's record sleeve," reported *The Mirror* in shocked tones. Hilariously, it quoted a ministerial spokesman as saying, "This is not the way we'd like her portrayed. I'm sure she would not like it." Carrying the same story in *The Mirror*'s Scottish sister paper, *The Daily Record*, the Scottish Young Tories were said to have found the sleeve to be "in very bad taste", accusing the band of cashing in on "a cheap gimmick". Paul Di'Anno would claim that the upset PM had gone as far as instructing her solicitor to send the band a letter expressing similar views, but as neither Steve nor Rod can remember ever receiving such a letter it's probably best to mark this one up as just another example of Paul's overactive imagination.

As their booking agent, John Jackson, has said, the Maiden tour that summer was a must-see for rock fans all over the country, and wherever Maiden turned up there were thousands of fans, old and new, waiting for them. The only immediate setback was the increasing tendency of Paul Di'Anno to lose his voice. The rigours of belting out the vocals in front of the loudest band in the land each night was partly to blame, of course. As Dave Murray says, "The way Paul sings, as well, it's full-throttle from start to finish, and it was, like, either he can do it or he can't. There was no in between with Paul." But what really loused up the singer's larynx were the long hours spent partying after the show each night. "I didn't know how to pace myself," he chuckles now.

"It got so bad that, at one point, it was like he was complaining about it every night," says Steve. "The trouble was that, with Paul, you never knew when he was putting it on. He'd started complaining that he was losing his voice on the Priest tour, but by the time we came to do our own tour he'd make such a big deal out of it, you'd really start to worry. Then, once he was onstage, he'd be totally fine. It was almost like an attention-grabbing thing. He wanted you to worry over him. I don't know if it was nerves, but some nights he'd literally be lying on the floor in the dressing room going, 'Oh, I'm not gonna make it. You'll have to go on without me!' But the last thing we want to do is go onstage without a singer, so then we'd spend ages fussing over him, trying to make him feel better."

But the boy cried wolf once too often when the tour reached the Central Hall in Grimsby. "Grimsby was the classic one," continues Steve. "I just called his bluff. We got to the soundcheck and Paul was already into one – 'I'm dying. I'm not gonna make it. We'll have to cancel the gig.' I went, 'Fuck that. We'll have to do it without him,' and we did go on without him. He was right choked about it, too. I remember him watching from the side of the stage, feeling sorry for himself 'cause not only was he not doing the gig but he'd made himself look a complete prat. I wasn't going to cancel a gig 'cause of his old bollocks. I think, at the end, he did come on and do a few numbers that night, but even then he was acting like he'd had to drag himself off his deathbed to be there. But we started going through different versions of this virtually every night in the end. Talk about a drama queen. He was starting to drive me barmy!"

"I was a kid, 22 years old, and here we were headlining our own big tour, and I didn't know how to handle it," Paul admits. "I didn't know nothing. I didn't want to know nothing! And of course I was doing a bit of speed and whatnot to keep me going, and I think that used to make it worse, actually, because you'd be awake for days but feeling really ill, and some nights I just didn't think I was gonna make it. My voice kept going, and that was nerves, too, but once I got onstage I was usually all right."

Back on the home front, headlining a sell-out tour and having a Top 30 single and Top Five album did not, as Maiden discovered, bring immediate financial rewards – the band was still taking home less than £60 a week each when 'Sanctuary' first became a hit.

Steve Harris: "Everybody knew that any money that was going to be coming in was gonna go straight back out again. We'd already talked about it with Rod and we'd agreed that he wouldn't take any of his commission from the management side and I wouldn't touch any of my royalties from the publishing side so we could use that money to help subsidise the band. I suppose it was a business risk, if you like, but you just knew you had to put it all back in, do all the tours and everything we needed to do and then hope for the best, basically. And it worked, you know? We couldn't have done any of the big tours we did that year if we hadn't, because we wouldn't have been able to afford it."

"To begin with, I didn't take my share of the commission at all," says Rod. "I just took what I needed for my running costs, which were very low, as I was always with the band anyway, and there were no office costs at the time, because Zomba owned a house next to their studios on Chaplin Road, Willesden, and they let me use it free. I had no secretary and did all the bookkeeping myself, so my overheads were hardly anything."

But while Rod and the rest of the band had learned to live reasonably well on their meagre "beer rations", as Paul fondly remembers them, Dennis Stratton wasn't so happy with his lot. Five years older than his new bandmates and with a wife and child to support as best he could, he claims now that he was actually worse off financially than he was before he joined the band. "Weirdly, the money I was getting was now less than before," he says, "because I had to give up doing session work and the odd-job manual work that had been keeping me going before I joined Maiden. I remember going to Rod's office with a phone bill and a shopping list, like a weekend's shopping for the family. My daughter, Carly, was two years old at the time and I simply just couldn't take care of her on the wages we were getting, so Rod coughed up a little more. It was more than anyone else was taking home at that time, but I had more responsibilities than the other lads. I had a kid to feed and look after."

Whatever money the band was making in 1980 was being channelled straight back into keeping them on the road. Like a shark, in order to stay alive, Maiden needed to keep moving. Having just spent the last twelve months touring Britain, the logical step was to try and get the band some extended live work in Europe, where *Iron Maiden* had now been released to a great critical fanfare that summer. From that perspective, winning the support slot on Kiss' European tour that year was not only a vitally important step for the band but also a considerable behind-the-scenes coup for both Rod (who persuaded EMI to foot the bill for the tour) and John Jackson (who somehow managed to persuade Kiss to let Maiden do it). Perhaps more famous for their lurid make-up and outlandish stage costumes than the brutally rhythmic music they make, Kiss were a legendary American heavy-metal band that had never toured extensively outside the US when they arrived for the first date of their European tour in Rome in August 1980. To join the band on tour as "special guests", as Maiden would that year, was a golden opportunity to shine before tens of thousands of people who had never seen or heard the band before. As John Jackson says, "No matter how much it cost 'em, it was one they simply could not afford to miss."

"We couldn't afford to do it on our own, because we'd spent all our up-front money on necessary equipment, clearing old band debts and keeping the band working up to that point," says Rod. "Now we needed them to help us, but it was a lot of money – around £30,000 – but it was going to be a long tour, and we'd play to over 250,000 people, so we had to do it. By now, Brian Shepherd had gone and the new A&R head, Terry Slater, just didn't understand or support Maiden, so politics had to be played. I just went around canvassing everybody I could, basically. There was a guy there called Charlie Webster, who was our product manager and who was right behind us; and Martin Haxby, of course, who'd been behind us from day one; and Richard Littleton, who by then was head of International; and I just went to them all and got them all so into it they managed to persuade each other to give us the money."

Before he began working in London, Richard Littleton had been managing director of EMI in Finland. He admits that he had never heard of either Iron Maiden or Rod Smallwood at that time. "It was the first day at my new job in London, and absolutely the first message on my desk waiting for me when I arrived was from a Mr Smallwood," he recalls. "Well, I didn't know a Mr Smallwood, but I called the number he had left and he told me he was the manager of this band that had just been signed to the label and that they were playing that night at the Marquee in London. He said they were the best band on the label and if I had any judgement at all I should make sure I see them. Well, you know, he was so pushy, but in a very charming way – he obviously really believed in his act – and so I thought I would go. And, well, coming straight from Finland, it was a bit of a culture shock, to tell you the truth. I went to the Marquee and I remember the place was packed with people and the floor was sticky from all the beer. It was an amazing atmosphere, and the band just tore the place apart. I remember a couple of kids at the very front fainted during the show and the rest of the crowd just passed their bodies back over their heads to where the security people could get to them. I had never seen anything like it before and found it quite incredible.

"The very next day, Rod came to see me and told me they'd been offered this Kiss tour in Europe and asked me if EMI was willing to help with the costs. I told him I would consider it and get back to him. Then I called Martin Haxby and asked for his advice. I was still relatively new to the touring side of the business – my background was mainly marketing – so I spoke to Martin and he said that, ultimately, it was my call, but that there wasn't much else going on at the label, certainly in terms of developing new artists, so maybe I should do it."

"For the Kiss tour, I think it was either 20 or 30 grand they needed," says Martin, "and Richard and I effectively championed this. We said, 'We've got to do it,' because it was clear this was a big chance for Maiden and I just felt Rod was worth it. This was as a relatively new guy, too, at that time, I should add. But the way I ran it was to try and be more artist-friendly, anyway. You fought like hell for your position and the company's position, but at the same time you were totally realistic. It was blindingly obvious to me the Kiss tour was a big, heaven-sent opportunity for Rod and the boys, and if it doesn't work... Well, people forget very quickly in this business, really."

"To keep us going, I'd work it all out in advance," says Rod, "how much we'd need and how much we had, in terms of pipeline royalties – money that hadn't been paid over to the band yet from overseas sales – and I'd go to Martin and Phil Roley and say, 'We've got a ten-grand pipeline in the black. Can I have some of it, please?' And we'd get five grand, and we'd run it like that. But because we were selling records from the off, there was always some pipeline. We could always get it. I was never worried. I never had any worries about Maiden at any stage, ever. It just seemed like this was it. I thought we were unstoppable."

The key, as Rod says, was "not to take the piss". Eschewing the common music-business practice of building extra costs into your tour budget so that, after you'd paid for everything, you ended up with some cash on top, Rod would routinely take every receipt into Martin Haxby's and Richard Littleton's offices, "just to show them where the money was going".

"Rod ran a tight ship," says Haxby. "We could see that straight away. He didn't let anybody spend anything, and he would bring in his bills and proof of purchases and say, 'Look, I don't want to bullshit you. You tell me, is this the right amount of money?' Then he would come in with the actual receipts and match them up to his budget and they would always match. In the end, we said, 'Look, it's OK. You don't have to keep doing that any more. We trust you.' And we did." Indeed, so tight were Rod's tour budgets that he had soon acquired the nickname Rod Smallwallet.

But the highlight of the year for Iron Maiden actually took place on the eve of the Kiss tour, when they made their first ever appearance on the bill at that year's Reading Festival. The largest, most prestigious outdoor event of the year in Britain, Maiden found themselves billed once more as "special guests", which in practical terms meant that they were second on the bill, following on from The Pat Travers Band and just before the Saturday-night headliners, UFO.

To build up their profile even further for the big occasion, the previous weekend Maiden had been the main feature of a TV documentary on the NWOBHM scene broadcast on *20th Century Box*, Danny Baker's weekend "yoof" show. Apart from an amusing appearance from Neal Kay ("I despise the term heavy metal," he told the cameras while sporting a T-shirt with the words "Heavy Metal Soundhouse" clearly emblazoned across its front), the programme focused on the three shows that Maiden had performed at the Marquee in the first week of July, yet again reinforcing the idea that, if any one band was going to emerge unscathed from being lumped in with so contrived a scene as the NWOBHM, it was going to be Maiden. Not that that stopped presenter Baker from taking the opportunity to ridicule easy targets like Rob Loonhouse and his cardboard-guitar-wielding chums. When *Melody Maker* also chose Maiden's debut Reading appearance to run their first feature on the NWOBHM, the band was again singled out as the Ones To Watch, except for one small niggling detail: the picture of them that the magazine ran was captioned "Saxon". The message was clear: the mainstream was still struggling to absorb the fact that, far from dead, British rock hadn't looked so alive for years.

The 1980 Reading Festival marked a turning point in the careers of several bands that day. It saw Slade's rebirth as a headlining live act in Britain; the beginning of the decline of UFO as a creative force to be reckoned with; and Iron Maiden's arrival onto the big stage. "Now let's see Iron Maiden follow that," Canadian singer Pat Travers had impetuously told the audience as he left the Reading stage that night. Big mistake. As Robin Smith's review in *Record Mirror* noted, "Iron Maiden proved to be the heroes of Saturday night. They even gave UFO a run for their money." Meanwhile, in *Sounds*, Geoff Barton called it "the performance of Maiden's lives". The ecstatic response that the band received the moment they walked out onto the stage confirmed it.

For Steve Harris, who had been a UFO fan since he was still at school, the chance to share the bill with his former boyhood heroes was all the proof he needed that, whichever way the media might want to read it, Maiden had now become the band he'd always wanted it to be. "Playing Reading Festival as special guests to UFO... I mean, that really was something I used to dream about," he says. "Then, to be doing it... I don't know. I was very, very nervous, I remember that. Not because UFO were there, but because we were. We were on a different stage – there were two stages, so that, as one band ended, the next started up on the other stage – and we went down really well. We didn't go down as well as UFO, you know, but it was still tremendous. We'd never played to so many people in Britain before, and at one point Dave Lights turned the spotlights on the audience and as far back as you could see there was people. Playing in pubs, you can see the whites of people's eyes, and that can be scary, if you're not used to it; but playing to 40,000 people, or whatever it was, when they turned the lights on and you could see them all, that really sent a shiver through me."

"After the first couple of songs, when Paul was tiring for a drink, I would walk up to the mic and start telling them what a great crowd they were," recalls Dennis Stratton. "But I remember, at Reading, I walked up to the mic and started saying to Dave Lights to turn on the floodlights, which we usually used at the end of show, during the audience-participation bit, but after three songs I walked to the mic and said, 'Light 'em up, Dave. Let's see what they look like!' And he lit up the whole of the crowd and it just blew my mind! I've still got a picture that [former *Sounds* photographer] Ross Halfin took from behind the drum riser just as I said it, and you get some idea of what it was like to stand there in front of all these people. It's my pride and joy, that picture."

Dave Murray: "I don't think I'd ever been so nervous before a show. I mean, we'd done a few big gigs by then – festivals in Europe and some TV stuff – but this was on our home turf, you know? And we didn't just want to do quite well; we wanted it to be brilliant, just the best that we could make it. And I remember the hours leading up to going onstage just seemed to crawl by for me. I think I had to down one or two shandies just to steady my nerves. Then, once we were onstage, it just whizzed by. It was like it was all over in a second. I remember the beginning, when we first went on, and I remember the end, and the only other thing I remember is when they turned the lights on the crowd and you could look out at them. It was like a sea of faces that just stretched into the horizon. And the noise! They were almost louder than us."

"We couldn't think what to do for special effects, so we had all these guys running around with Eddie masks on," says Dennis. "It was brilliantly unbelievable, but it worked. I've never seen anything like it in my life."

The day after the Reading Festival, still nursing their hangovers, the band jetted to Lisbon, Portugal, for their first show on the Kiss tour, another mammoth jaunt, and one which would find Maiden spending the next two months criss-crossing the Continent and playing nearly 30 shows in nine different countries along the way.

"We were lucky to get on the Kiss tour of Europe," says Steve. "Kiss were massive at that time, so we were going out to a big audience over there, 10,000 or 20,000 a night in most places. And the first album was doing well in Europe, too. We didn't expect it, but it was. It was strange – we seemed to be doing well everywhere. But EMI were a very good company and they pushed us in the right way, and also I think it's like the thing really spread from the UK. The prestige of doing so well in the UK had turned it into a word-of-mouth thing, and we'd turn up in places like Leiden, in Holland [where they opened for Kiss in the giant Groenoordhalle on 13 October], places we'd never even heard of, and they'd have these massive banners waiting for us with 'Iron Maiden Go Over The Top' written on them and all this. It was unreal."

Just like back home, however, the European Maiden fans seemed to be gripped by a strange hysteria. "We were playing these big stadiums in Italy and Maiden fans were fighting with Kiss fans," says Steve. "It was, like, 'What's going on? We weren't expecting any of this!' We didn't want any of the fighting, you know? But it was just really weird, and the reactions we were getting were incredible, totally beyond us. It was outrageous."

As usual, the hardships of touring had their funnier side. At the first show, in Rome, when the truck carrying the gear still hadn't arrived an hour before they were due to go onstage, Kiss kindly offered to lend Maiden some of their spare equipment. However, just as they were facing up to the prospect of knuckling down to doing their 45-minute set with unfamiliar gear, Vic Vella and the rest of the crew arrived to relieved sighs all round. The only problem was that, having received a panicky message when they arrived at the hotel to get their arses down to the gig pronto, Vic and the crew had assumed that there must be an emergency and had hurriedly taken a cab to get there, leaving all the band's gear still stuck back at the hotel. Only the helpful, last-minute intervention of someone from the Italian branch of EMI who had a very fast car and no regard whatsoever for the conventions of road safety rescued the situation, and the band finally took to the stage with their own instruments and amps to hand and barely a minute to spare.

Kiss proved themselves to be amicable touring partners, and the band were pleasantly surprised when Gene Simmons strolled into their dressing room during one of the earliest dates and began to tell them how much he liked their album. "I bet you ain't even heard it," Paul sneered sceptically. To prove him wrong, the burly bassist turned around and reeled off the title of every track and in the right running order. Later on in the tour, Simmons actually paid the band a much greater compliment after Paul once again challenged him on another visit to the Maiden dressing room, this time to ask if he could have an Iron Maiden T-shirt. Knowing the Kiss leader's reputation for making it a rule never to wear any other band's T-shirts but his own, Paul immediately jumped in with, "What d'you want it for? You'll never wear it!"

"True," Simmons demurred. "You don't often see me in anything other than a Kiss shirt. But if I had one with the name of a group that's going straight to the top, I wouldn't mind." And, as everybody knows, Gene Simmons' tongue is far too long to fit in his cheek, so he got his T-shirt.

When Kiss arrived for a week of dates in Britain at the start of September, Maiden – who no longer needed to support anyone in their own country – took the opportunity to have a short holiday and set up camp for the week in the Italian holiday resort of Lido de Jesolo. Situated on the sun-drenched Adriatic coast, the band looked forward to a welcome break, their first since Paul had joined the band two years earlier. What they didn't know, however, is that the Lido is actually known as a sort of Italian Bournemouth, a seaside home from home where elderly German retirees go to escape. "There wasn't much in the way of birds," Paul quaintly puts it, although there was a free-flowing bar situation, and on one particularly inebriated evening Davey and Rod got so smashed that they decided it would be a good idea to get thrown out of the hotel, which would mean that they'd get their deposit money back and be able to book into somewhere further down the coast that might be a little livelier. In order to achieve this, they decided to break into the hotel's bar after it was closed that night, using the aid of Paul's trusty flickknife. However, when the hotel security were woken from their slumbers by the alarm bells, Rod had to use all of his managerial charm to prevent the pissed-off security guard from calling in the local *polizia*, while Dave made sure that the switchblade was wiped free of fingerprints and hid it underneath a couch. Far from getting their money back, they awoke the next day to a bill for £300 in damages.

Joining back up with the Kiss tour in Germany on 11 September, the fun and games began to ring a little hollow as a new problem began to surface that was much more serious than any irate hotel security man and much closer to home. The problem was Dennis.

"There was a problem with Dennis, I think, right from the start, but it only really came to a head on that Kiss tour," says Steve. "It wasn't so much his playing; it was more his personality. To begin with, we got on really well, you know? He was another West Ham supporter, so that was all right, but to be honest Rod never really fancied him from the start. Rod saw straight away that he wasn't right for the band. He didn't say he didn't think he was right; he said he wasn't sure about him, that he wasn't convinced he was the right person for the band. I said, 'Well, you know, I think he is,' and that was it. The only thing I was starting to worry about was whether his heart was really, totally into what we were doing, but he said he was, and so you took his word for it.

"But later on, within a few months, I was beginning to think I'd made a mistake. I really think he was just into other things. I mean, he was into The Eagles and The Doobie Brothers and all this stuff. I mean, I quite liked some of that stuff, but it's not where my heart lies. I don't wanna play like that live, you know? But the sort of ideas Dennis was coming in with, or the sort of stuff he'd be messing around with at the soundcheck, it just made you notice the difference. Like, if I wanted to have a jam at a soundcheck, I'd be fucking playing Black Sabbath or Montrose or something like that, you know what I mean? Giving it loads! But he'd be there playing, like, 10cc and The Eagles and stuff like that."

The arguments began in earnest on the tour with Kiss, when, according to Dave Murray, "Dennis seemed to spend more time hanging out with the Kiss crew than us." Sometimes he even preferred travelling with the crew to sitting on the band bus, and the others took it as a slight – all of which, says Stratton, was nonsense, just another difference born of their age gap.

"I'm not saying he didn't like Maiden's music," says Steve. "I think he felt that it was good music, and he enjoyed playing it, but Dennis is the kind of bloke that will play any type of music and he'll enjoy playing it. But I didn't think his heart was 100 per cent into it, and it did start to cause problems. His general attitude started to get a bit weird. He just seemed to be negative about a lot of things. He liked a drink, which I had no problem with, because it didn't affect his playing, but he'd sometimes get a bit aggressive when he'd had a few beers. And some of the things he used to come out with, it made you think. Music-related things, just like the general direction we were going in. He questioned a lot of the fundamental things we were trying to do, and it became more and more obvious to everybody, not just me, that it was almost like he was trying to pull us somewhere else.

"It wasn't an age thing, either. One of the reasons I chose him in the first place was 'cause I thought, you know, 'He's experienced, he's a good player and we could do with a bit of that.' But it turned out he just wasn't Maiden. He just wasn't. His heart wasn't in it, I'm sure of it. He can say what he wants now, but that's what I thought at the time and, you know, I still think that."

Either way, the split, when it came, could hardly be described as amicable. "Because I'd been so used to working with major acts, like Quo, I knew what it was like to be on tour," says Dennis. "You can live in one another's pockets for so long you begin to get fed up with each other's company. The tour with Kiss itself was brilliant, because we were opening again and we had nothing to lose. But what happened was, we went into Europe and we were travelling a lot, sitting next to each other on the bus. And you know, it's like… You're tired, not getting to bed, travelling long miles, and it's easy to get irritable. That's when people cause arguments and fall out. Suddenly, little things count for a lot and tensions can build up.

"I listen to all kinds of music – The Eagles, Steely Dan, George Benson, as well as rock stuff like Van Halen, Journey, Toto. I'm a musician, and I just love to listen to the playing. And when I'm relaxing, I'm listening to all kinds of different stuff – you know, headset on at the back of the bus and just listen. [Former Deep Purple vocalist and Whitesnake frontman] David Coverdale is probably my favourite rock vocalist of all time, especially the more melodic, slower stuff, because with his voice he can really make those things sound spine-tingling. But travelling on the band bus, all you'd ever hear were these heavy-metal tapes and stuff. I mean, there was some great stuff there. Van Halen, Judas Priest, UFO – I can get off on all those bands, but not 24 hours a day, every day of the week, 52 weeks a year, do you know what I mean? So sometimes I liked to get off the tour bus and travel with the road crew instead. I just enjoyed spending time with the crew, anyway. They'd seen it all before, and I loved their company. They were so funny and so fair. I always lugged my own gear, anyway, and just loved helping out. I even drove the truck for a while, just to cut down on the boredom and to do something different. It can be pretty boring, travelling around on a bus every day, and I liked to pick things up if I could. I was always interested in how things worked, and the crew would show me."

All of this the rest of the band could understand, up to a point. However, when Dennis also began hitching rides whenever he could in the cars of any of the locally based EMI staff that would make periodic appearances throughout the tour, the others not unreasonably began to suspect that it was more than just the fact that Dennis liked hanging out with the crew; they thought that he just didn't like hanging out with them.

Stratton, however, strenuously denies this. "I just get on like a house on fire with people," he insists. "I'd hang out with Kiss, go out drinking and have a meal with the guys when they got their make-up off after the show. It was my birthday on tour, and the Kiss guys threw a party and gave me some great presents. I remember I got an American fireman's helmet from [Kiss guitarist] Paul Stanley. Like me, they were a bit older, and we just got on. And then it got to a point I used to enjoy travelling with them more than the band, which upset Rod, because he wanted all the band to be together all the time, like a gang. This is where the real problem started for me, because I couldn't stand that. I just can't do it."

Eventually, Rod took Dennis to one side and had a word. "I just asked him what the problem was and why he didn't travel with the rest of the band on the tour bus," he says. "I mean, he'd only just joined the band a few months before, and we're out on the biggest tour of our lives and he couldn't even be bothered to travel with the rest of the band. I just wanted to know what made him so special."

"I don't know if Rod thought I was trying to score points," says Stratton, "but I just get on with people. I'm interested in what goes on. Like, I'd spend hours just watching Kiss rehearse. They were still in their early make-up phase, and they had a great stage show, and I just wanted to see how they put it all together. Rod and Steve took it the wrong way. They thought I was trying to avoid them. But it wasn't true. Then Rod had words with me in the afternoon of one of the shows with Kiss. He made it quite clear he wasn't happy with me travelling with different people to the show or to the next town. He wasn't happy with the way I was acting. He thought I was avoiding the band. I tried to explain, but he wasn't happy. He said I was to travel with the band, and that was it. We had a bit of an argument. I mean, I just couldn't see it. My attitude was, 'As long as I'm there and I'm happy and I play, what's the problem?' But he didn't like the idea, so he said, 'You have to travel with the band.' It wasn't 'or else', but he made it quite clear that I was to do what I was told. He even started having a go at me about the music I was listening to. I said, 'I'm sorry, I can't help that!'"

So Dennis ignored Rod and continued to travel from gig to gig with whomever he pleased. It was to be the beginning of the end. Dennis Stratton's last show with the band was at the Drammenshallen Arena in Oslo on 13 October, the last night of the Kiss tour. He says now that, by then, the atmosphere in the dressing room had grown so bad that he secretly suspected that it might actually be his last gig with the band. "Even Davey Murray, the mildest-mannered, nicest bloke you could hope to meet, gave me a very cold reaction that night," he recalls. Nevertheless, the show went well, and afterwards, in his post-gig euphoria, Dennis began to tell himself that he was just being paranoid and that there would be even greater nights to come with the band.

"Because it was the last night of the tour, we all had a great laugh," he says. "Paul Stanley came on during one number and put a bucket over my head. Then I did the same to him later on, when Kiss was playing. I remember coming offstage and thinking that was great and just feeling generally happy about things. Then, as soon as I got back to the hotel, I remember being told by the crew that it looked like I was gonna get fired. It was then I realised I'd overstepped the mark."

His voice lowers to a hoarse whisper as he recounts those final scenes: "I went into my room, got my tape player, turned it to full volume and put *Soldier Of Fortune* on it by David Coverdale. Then I got in the bath fully clothed, me headset on, and turned the shower on and just sat in the shower and cried my eyes out. It was sad, because I had so much to give the band, but I was being held back. I could see the band getting bigger and bigger and I had so much to offer. Unfortunately, Steve and Rod saw it differently. I knew it was coming, but I refused to accept it, in my head. I thought, 'Wait till we get back to England and maybe we'll sit down and Rod will shout but give me a last chance.' But when I got back to London, Steve lived about five minutes away from me and I called him up and went over to see him. I said, 'Look, I hope you don't think I've got any problem with the band. It's just that I don't like living in people's pockets.' But he was very distant. Wouldn't discuss anything to do with me or him or the band."

Dennis' final engagement came a few days later at the video shoot for the band's next single, 'Women In Uniform'. "We all turned up and got ready," he says. "It was supposed to be like a live show. All the stage gear was set up and the lights. We did three or four run-throughs before I realised there wasn't a single camera on me. As we were playing, I kept looking, thinking, 'What's going on?' Then it came back to me suddenly and I knew. So, when we finished filming, we got changed, and I remember getting in the car and driving around the back to the stage door and the crew were there loading the gear – Pete, Loopy and Dave Lights – and they all came over and we shook hands and they must have known, but they said, 'Good luck. See you soon.' But at the back of my mind, I knew."

Dennis Stratton's dismissal from Iron Maiden was made official on 1 November 1980. "I got a call from Rod to come over to the office," he says. "I drove over there and, as I walked in, Steve was already there, sitting in a chair opposite. I shook hands, sat down and Rod said, 'I've got some points to make,' and he went through all the stuff again about how he wasn't keen on me not travelling with the band and not liking the music I was listening to. It was, like, 'I told you, you've got to be 100 per cent into this band or it won't work.' I said, 'I *am* into it. I'm 150 per cent into it!'" By then, though, Steve and Rod's minds were made up.

"I walked out of the office and went home and didn't really know what to do at first," Stratton says. "I knew they'd already contacted Adrian Smith, because I got a call that night from some friends I'd made at EMI in Germany and they told me. They also invited me out there for a few days just to cheer me up. So, the next day, I flew to Cologne, got picked up by the A&R guy and his girlfriend, went back to their place and had a big party. It was weird, but at least they saw what I was trying to say. But Maiden was still a very young band then, and maybe you have to experience these things yourself first before you see it from my point of view."

Maybe. Dennis would go on to form Lionheart, who would later land a long-term deal in America, and although he would continue his tirade in the press against Maiden in general and against Steve Harris in particular for many years to come (he cynically referred to Steve as "Sergeant-Major Harris"), he was, frankly, soon forgotten by the still-growing legion of Maiden fans who had barely had time to get used to him in the first place. His replacement saw to that. While Dennis had left to establish a presumably more mature musical relationship with his next band, Iron Maiden had finally made contact with a guitarist they could really relate to: Adrian Smith.

By the end of 1980, Urchin – the band that Adrian had formed with Dave Murray while they were both still at school and had subsequently steered to their own short-lived record deal with DJM – had finally fallen apart and Adrian was filling in time with a band of sub-glam East End reprobates called Broadway Brats while he decided what it was he really wanted to do. (In an interesting historical footnote, if Adrian had turned down their offer, the other guitarist that Maiden would have approached was Paul Di'Anno's old East End mate Phil Collen, who was then going nowhere fast with an even more glam-influenced London outfit called Girl. In the event, however, Adrian accepted Maiden's offer, leaving Collen free to take up the offer not long after to join those other leading lights of the NWOBHM, Def Leppard.)

"We were gonna give Adrian the job before Dennis joined," reminds

Steve Harris, "but Adrian was still very much entrenched with Urchin and they still had the deal and everything happening, so, you know, the timing wasn't right for him. At the time, he'd been with Urchin for five years or more, he'd formed the band, and I suppose it was a bit like me with Maiden – it was his band and he rightly wanted to stick with it and see if he could make it happen. And both bands came from the East End, and we'd done the same pubs and that. We'd been through a lot of the same bullshit, and I respected him, because we had overtaken them with the album deal and everything else, and so it would have been very easy for him, when we first asked him, to say, 'All right, I'm gonna join them and make some money.' But he didn't. He stayed with his thing and he tried to get things happening, and I thought, 'Fair enough. Good luck to you, mate.' Then, when we came back to him a year later, he was tempted, I think, 'cause he liked the band. He was a big mate of Davey's, and Urchin was over by then, anyway, so we all knew Adrian already, and when he finally made up his mind to go for it with Maiden, he slotted in really quick."

The hardest part for Adrian, as Steve suggests, was indeed simply making up his mind one way or the other, a task that he admits he's always had difficulty with, not just in relation to Maiden but also "with everything. Some days I can't even make up my mind whether to get out of bed," he adds with a small chuckle. He's joking, but only just. As Rod says, "Indecisiveness is Adrian's middle name. Even if you go out for a meal with Adrian, you'll be on the cheese and biscuits before he's even decided on his starter."

"Laid back" is how Adrian himself prefers to see it. "I never get too outwardly fired up. It's all going on inside, but I just don't always show it. I like to keep my cool, if I can." Suffice it to say that he's managed pretty well, so far.

Adrian Frederick Smith was born in Hackney Hospital on 27 February 1957. The son of a painter and decorator from Homerton, Adrian was the youngest child of three and has an older brother, Patrick, and a sister, Kathleen. As the baby of the family, he had what he describes as "a typically happy, pretty boring upbringing, I suppose. As a kid, I was into all the usual stuff, mainly football. I was a Manchester United fanatic when I was a kid, but when I got into music I stopped doing all that stuff and I didn't get back into football until I was in my mid 20s. But I'm not into teams as such now. It's all money now, football, isn't it? If anything, I'm more of a Fulham fan, because I used to live in a flat next door to the ground and I used to go and watch them play sometimes, so I always follow what they do now."

Adrian played for the school first team but, as he says, his interest in football "and everything else" dropped to below zero the moment he got into buying albums and learning the guitar. He was 15 when he bought his first album, Deep Purple's *Machine Head*.

"My sister used to go out with this guy and she used to borrow his records and leave them lying around the house," he says, "stuff like Purple, Free, Black Sabbath... Then she stopped going out with him, so I started buying the records myself. A lot of other kids I knew were into soul, which I quite liked, but it was party music. I liked the idea of an album you could sit down and listen to."

Adrian first met Dave Murray while browsing through the Rock section of his local record store. "Dave was the only other person I knew that was into the same sort of thing as me," he says. They would dress up in their finest rock-dude clothes and "hang out together, trying to be as different to everybody as we could. We were the blokes who always used to turn up at parties in their kaftans and beads and start rolling joints and putting Deep Purple's 'Highway Star' on the turntable repeatedly until it drove everybody else 'round the bend, at which point we'd usually get thrown out. 'Highway Star' was my anthem when I was a kid. My hair was long even in primary school, much longer than some of the girls'. I was always being told to get it cut and I never did. I don't think I had a proper haircut for years. First of all, I wanted to be a singer, mainly because I didn't have a guitar but I did have a microphone – my parents bought me a mic on my 14th birthday, for some reason – so it was me on the mic, Dave on guitar, and we used to do 'Silver Machine' by Hawkwind, because that was three chords and it was easy."

What finally gave Adrian the idea of learning the guitar himself was watching all the excitement it used to cause at school whenever Dave brought his electric guitar in. "He used to be surrounded by girls all day," Adrian recalls. "Having the guitar, even then I could see it gave you some sort of edge. Girls noticed you. So, I thought, 'Right. Well, I can do that.'" He began by picking up "this old Spanish guitar we had lying around the house, 'cause my brother had taken classical guitar lessons", but it was hardly the instrument on which to begin experimenting with 'Highway Star', "so I gave that a miss and borrowed Dave's spare guitar and began practising on that".

"It wasn't very good," Davey smiles. "It was this old solid-bodied Woolworth's job with an action about an inch off the fretboard, but I sold it to him for, like, a fiver and his dad fixed it up and he started to learn on that. I used to go 'round and play along with him, just to help him."

Soon the two were playing regularly together and had decided that they were going to leave school and form a band. "Once I'd learned a couple of barre chords, that was it, I was off!" says Adrian. "Of course, I was into Sabbath and Purple and bands like Santana, and I couldn't really play any of that to begin with, so I just concentrated on stuff like the Stones and Thin Lizzy, simple stuff that you could just sort of chug along to. I mean, you're not only learning your instrument; you're searching for some sort of identity, at that age. Whether it's musical or otherwise, it's at that time when you've got to make some sort of choice about your life, you're on the verge of leaving school and going into the real world, and so we used to talk about that sort of thing, me and Davey and all our mates, dreaming of what it would be like to make it in a band."

Such was his hurry to get his musical career started that Adrian left school at 16 without even staying long enough to sit the O-level exams for which he'd just spent the last five years studying. "I was off as quick as I could," he says. "I just thought, 'I don't need this. I'm going to be a rock star.' I don't think my parents knew where I was at. I mean, I've got kids of my own now, and I'd be horrified if one them said that to me one day!"

There followed a succession of awful jobs as the dreamy teenager filled in time waiting for his career to somehow miraculously take off by working, variously, as a trainee spot-welder, an apprentice cabinet maker and a milkman. (He used to take the milk float out with a Marshall amp strapped to the back, blasting out his favourite tapes at six o'clock in the morning.) "I had so many jobs because my attitude was always bad," he says. "They were very, very soul-destroying jobs, and I just couldn't get excited by doing them, so I used to just lark about, really, until they got rid of me or I'd had enough and left, which was usually when there was a gig coming up."

As soon as he left school, Adrian started his own band, which was originally called Evil Ways. Dave Murray was the guitarist, but, as Adrian says with a smile, "He tended to come and go." Adrian was always keen to have his own band and write his own songs and, although he would sometimes play for short periods in other bands, he always kept Urchin's loose line-up together.

"Davey was more into ringing up ads in the *Melody Maker* and going for auditions," Adrian points out. "I wasn't all that interested in joining a band, anyway. I just used to go to these auditions occasionally to test myself out, test my nerve to see if I could stand up there and play in front of a room of complete strangers. In fact, my first serious project was Iron Maiden. Before that, I was always in my own band."

He had abandoned the idea of becoming a full-time singer: "Once I picked up a guitar and started to play a little bit, that was it, really. I just feel more comfortable with a guitar than without one."

Of course, playing the guitar also meant that he could now write his own songs. "One of the first things I wrote was '22 Acacia Avenue', which of course ended up in a slightly different form on the *Number Of The Beast* album. I wrote that when I was 18, but I ended up working on it over a period of years with various different line-ups I had of the band. But it was weird how it came to end up as a Maiden song. Urchin did a gig in the local park and we played '22 Acacia Avenue', and it probably sounded completely different than the version we would later do in Maiden, but the weird thing was, Steve Harris was at the gig. I didn't even know him then, but he remembered it when I joined the band, years later. We were getting stuff ready for *Number Of The Beast*, and out of the blue Steve turned to me and said, 'What was that song you used to do in Urchin?' and he started humming it and it was '22...'. I mean, it had changed quite a bit since then, and we probably ended up changing it quite a bit again by the time we did it in Maiden, but it was weird how he'd remembered that one song all those years. It just shows you that nothing's ever wasted. We probably didn't even play well that day, and were probably really down afterwards, but because we had a go and did our best someone in the audience remembered. That's why it always pays off to do your best. Even if it seems like a dismal disaster at the time, you always come away with something from it."

Urchin actually got a record deal with DJM (former home to Elton John) and hired a manager long before Maiden had first set foot in EMI's Manchester Square offices. "It was the management that came up with the name Urchin," says Adrian. "They had this idea for an image for us. The thing was, we were all really young. I was only 19 when we got a deal." On signing with DJM, Adrian was given "one Hong Kong dollar, as they say". It was, he says, "a very dodgy deal. I mean, I knew absolutely nothing about the business side of things in those days, and I didn't want to know. All I cared was that one minute I was signing on and the next I had a record deal, you know what I mean? I thought it was that simple." The band were advanced £5,000, which they quickly used up with the purchase of a 1,500-watt PA "and a dirty great big coach for the band and the 'crew', which was basically a few dedicated mates". One member of the crew, however, was a welder, and he furnished the bus with customised bunk-beds and seats. "It was great, really comfortable, which you need, really, if you're going to be living in the thing for weeks on end." And Urchin did just that, playing, by Adrian's estimation, "over a hundred gigs that year".

The first Urchin single, a "motorbike epic" built around an old Deep Purple riff which they called 'Black Leather Fantasy', was released in 1978. "We didn't have a title for it, and I said 'Black Leather Fantasy' as a joke and it stuck. I remember the promo sleeve said something about the 'resurgence of heavy metal', but there was no one really doing it yet, at that time." The single "got a couple of good reviews in *Sounds* and *Melody Maker*, but didn't sell much. It's funny, 'cause Neal Kay at the Soundhouse used to play it, but by that time the record had been out two years."

Adrian says that he first became aware of Iron Maiden in about 1977. "I might have seen 'em before Davey joined," he says, "but it was when he joined them that I really began to notice them." But when Dave later rejoined Urchin after his bust-up with Dennis Wilcock, "I thought they'd really messed up, 'cause even I could see that Davey's style of playing really fitted in more with what Maiden were doing than what we were up to in Urchin, which was still hard rock but with more of a groove to it. We were into the more catchy sorts of rock songs." Dave would play on the next (and last) Urchin single, 'She's A Roller', eventually released early in 1980, but by then he had already left once more, to rejoin Maiden.

When Adrian got a phone call from Steve Harris soon after, asking him if he would also be interested in a job in Maiden, Adrian admits that he was sorely tempted. "I smoked my way through two packs of cigarettes thinking about that one," he says. "There were reviews of them in the music papers by now and quite a buzz building. I think they were on the verge of getting the deal with EMI, too, and it would have meant proper wages and all that, which I could have really done with. But I eventually turned the offer down. I had to, really. We had our tour bus and our deal and I thought about it for quite a few hours, but I phoned Steve back and said, 'Thanks for the offer, but I'm gonna stick with what I'm doing.'"

It was a decision that, he now admits, he would live to regret, as in the next year Urchin fell apart and Maiden's first single and album rocketed into the charts. "I remember bumping into Davey at some gig somewhere, and I remember thinking he looked really prosperous," says Adrian. "Not rich, but just…really together. He was wearing all these new leathers, and he just seemed really happy, like everything was going great for him. I wasn't seethingly jealous or anything, but I couldn't help feel a little bit envious. But I've known Dave all my life, and I was just really pleased for him. It's great when a mate does something. It makes you feel like there's a chance you could do something, too. So I thought it was great. I just wondered if it would ever happen for me."

Adrian drifted along. Without a regular band to play with, he couldn't rehearse, "so I just sat around writing songs and going to gigs, wondering what to do next". His publisher had suggested a collaboration with a professional songwriter "from up the West End", but Adrian abandoned it after just one meeting for the straw-clutching aberration it was: "I ended up sitting down with this bloke and trying to write with him, but it was really terrible, just not happening at all, and I came away feeling quite depressed. Then I remember walking home because I had no money for the bus and feeling really down about everything. I think it was probably raining, too – you know, the whole depressive cliché – and as I was walking along, looking at the ground, lost in my own thoughts, I literally bumped into Steve and Dave in the street. It was like fate! Practically the first thing Steve said was, 'What are you doing?' I said, 'Not much,' and he said, 'Listen, we're looking for a new second guitarist. Would you be interested?' I couldn't believe it. It was like something out of one of those really corny old films, like your fairy godmother suddenly appearing in the street. So I said, 'Yeah, that'd be great,' and they phoned me later and told me where to go for the audition. I must admit, I was surprised when they said they wanted me to do an audition. I thought, 'Well, Dave knows more about my playing than I do.' But I went along, 'cause I really wanted the gig and I thought, you know, 'Just 'cause Dave knows I can play doesn't mean the others will be ready to accept me, so maybe this is a good thing.'"

Indeed, the audition was a full-on affair, the first time Adrian had ever encountered that kind of atmosphere. What he couldn't know, however, is that, coming on the heels of the arch-individualist Dennis Stratton, both Steve and Rod were super-keen to make sure that whoever they got in this time was going to fit in perfectly with what they expected from a member of Iron Maiden.

"Rod was very suspicious," Adrian recalls, "because I'd turned them down the first time, I think. But I wasn't nervous or anything. Maiden were doing well for themselves – that was pretty obvious from the set-up – but they weren't stars to me; they were just another band from the East End that I'd grown up with."

"Adrian was into different kinds of music as well, but everybody's into different kinds of music," says Steve. "Dennis wasn't the only one. It's just that, live, you want to go out and beat the audience over the head, and that's where Dennis kind of fell off a bit. But Adrian, he was like us. He really loved UFO and stuff like that. You just know if someone's into it, and Adrian was. You could feel the difference straight away."

"I remember Rod interrogated me," says Adrian, "like, 'Can you play riffs? Do you play lead, too?' It was very intense. Steve was obviously very motivated, very serious about the whole thing. Dave and Paul seemed more easy-going about everything, but Rod was the most serious. Steve kept telling Rod off for interrogating me, which set the pattern for the next few years, really, Rod putting the pressure on and Steve deciding when enough was enough, sort of thing."

After the rehearsal was over, Adrian was asked to wait with the band's tour manager in the adjacent pub while the rest of the band talked it over with Rod before coming to a decision. "To be honest, I wasn't quite sure what a tour manager was," he admits, "but he took me to the pub and bought me a drink and I thought, 'Yeah, tour managers are OK.'

Then, 20 minutes later, they all came 'round and said, 'You're in.' It felt fantastic! Like being accepted into a family, almost. In fact, the main impression I got was that it *was* like a family they had together.

"They were obviously all really into it for the right reasons, and it was a buzz to become a part of that. Maiden really took care of their own, and once I was in they took care of everything. I really didn't have to think about anything except my playing the whole time I was in the band, which is a dream come true for a musician, really.

"It was the first time in my life that I actually got paid for playing, and I'd be lying if I didn't say the money was great. I'd never had any money before, so of course it was great. But it was also great to play with Dave again, and it was a real challenge, because Maiden was the first proper band I'd ever been in. You know, they had proper roadies and fantastic new gear. You really felt you had something to live up to. I mean, once the euphoria of being offered the gig wore off, and I started to think about what the job entailed, I admit I began to feel a bit intimidated, really. I'd always had control of every other group I'd been in – I'd always written a lot of the songs, playing with guys who really wanted to play with me – but when I first joined Maiden I was just the guitarist, and it was a lot different. I had to play things that I wouldn't normally play, because the kind of songs Steve writes tend to go off in all kinds of different directions, a lot of it quite complex with lots of time changes and different set parts that he wants you to play. It definitely made me a better guitar player. I was suddenly expected to be able to do stuff that was far more intricate than anything I'd been used to till then. I mean, anyone walking into Maiden would find it a big job, and I was only 23 then, which is probably a bit young to walk into something like that. But I always had a fair amount of confidence in myself, so I just gave it a crack, really."

The first thing Adrian actually did as a member of Iron Maiden was a TV show in Germany. "Never done TV before," he says, "but thankfully it was just one of those pre-recorded things where you zip in, do one number and zip out again, and I hardly had time to think about it." Back in England, the main task ahead was working on new material for the next Maiden album, which the band were hoping to begin recording in the New Year. "I think the first songs I actually worked on with them were 'Killers', which was the title track of the next album, and 'Purgatory', which later became one of the singles from it. I think it was reworked from an old song of theirs called 'Floating'."

Rehearsals were briefly broken off, however, in order for Maiden to finish the year as they had spent most of it: on the road. The idea was to get Adrian relaxed and give him time to gel with the band before going into the studio to start work on the next album. This final round of UK dates finished a twelve-month period in which, Dave Murray says, "we'd done more than we'd ever dreamed possible. Or certainly more than I ever dreamed possible, put it that way!"

"We broke off to do a tour, about a dozen gigs in December, which culminated at the Rainbow, which was an amazing experience, on a personal level," says Adrian. "I grew up going to gigs at the Rainbow. I saw The Who there, Rory Gallagher, Nazareth. Now, for me to actually be standing there, it almost didn't seem real, but the show that night was filmed, and when I watched it, sure enough, there I was. We rehearsed for the tour at what's now the Brixton Academy, a huge place down in south London, and I remember walking in and seeing this fucking great big lighting rig set up, and I thought, 'I can't fucking believe this! This is big time!'"

Adrian's first gig with Maiden was at Brunel University, in Uxbridge, on 21 November 1980. "Brunel holds about 2,000 people, something like that, and the place was jammed," he remembers. "I'd never played to that many people before. And their fans weren't like any I'd come across before. They were mad, some of them, mad and really into it. And if you were a fake, they'd suss you out in a second, you know? At that first gig, I remember I was pretty nervous just before we went on, so I thought I'd go outside and mingle with the crowd, say hello, sort of thing. Like, no big deal. And I remember one punter came up to me and said, 'Are you the new guitarist?' I said, 'Yeah.' He said, 'You better be good!' I thought, 'Fuck, what have I let myself in for?'"

He would soon find out.

9 Martin

Apart from the pre-Christmas flavour to the tour, the twelve-date trek that Maiden embarked on in November 1980 – their fourth British tour that year – was a useful way of easing Adrian's playing into the band's sound before work began in earnest on their next album. Emerging unscathed from his baptism of fire at that first gig in Uxbridge, Adrian had settled in remarkably quickly, a fact which surprised those onlookers who didn't know of the close personal ties that existed between the two guitarists, for while it would be hard to find two lead players whose styles were more unlike on the surface – Davey the king of improvisation, soloing off the top of his head all night with a mile-wide smile permanently creasing his face; Adrian the hunched figure with the haunted expression, his solos worked out well in advance – together these apparent opposites would clash in the most kaleidoscopic fashion, their styles complementing each other in a way that was, Davey says, "almost telepathic". With an empathy born of all the years they'd spent learning and playing the guitar together, in Iron Maiden they would find the most perfect vehicle for their expression that either of them would ever know. "I can't imagine ever having that two-way mental thing going like that with any other guitarist," says Adrian nearly a decade after he left the band that made him famous.

The final date of the tour had been a festive-flavoured performance at the Rainbow in London. The show was filmed that night and later released as a half-hour EMI video, directed by Dave Hillier, so for much of the show the band had to dodge their way around cameramen as they strode about the large stage. Not that the crowd minded. When one of the sound cables burned out before they were able to record such crucial numbers as

'Iron Maiden' and 'Phantom Of The Opera', Paul announced that, because of technical problems, the band would have to play those songs again after the show, and that if anyone wanted to stay behind they'd be very welcome. Not one fan left the building as the band powered through their unexpected encore.

As Dave says, "Once Adrian had joined and Clive came in, the band was really there, you know? Of course, with me and Adrian already being great mates, it made the whole thing ten times easier for me, personally. But I think musically we really started to take off from there. Playing live, he just fitted in straight away."

"It was such a great way to come into the band," agrees Adrian. "Everyone was very cool, very serious about the music but very easy-going about everything else. Being in Maiden was like being in a bubble – everything was just taken care of for you, so that all you had to worry about was making the show good. And it was all very matey, like one big family. I remember, before the tour, we all used to meet up for rehearsals at about eleven in the morning, have a few drinks – not enough to make you drunk, just enough to give you a bit of a buzz – then go in and start rehearsing. Then we'd all go out together afterwards, usually to places they knew, music pubs and gigs and that. Then, on tour, we were always going about together, going in the van to do interviews or whatever. We always did everything as a band. Clive was a good laugh. We used to go fishing together on our days off. Dave, too. Steve was often as not doing something – attending a mix or having a meeting with Rod, taking care of the business side while the rest of us just hung out together and played."

To promote the tour, EMI had agreed to release a new single. Unwilling to simply release another track from the *Iron Maiden* album, the band suggested that they record one of the new songs that they were planning on using on their second album, but they eventually dropped the idea when their publishing company, Zomba, urged them to consider another option: a cover version.

The track in question, 'Women In Uniform', had been a sizeable hit in Australia that year for an Aussie band unknown in the UK called Skyhooks. Zomba's logic appeared sound enough: this proven hit was unknown in the UK and might appeal to both the hardcore Maiden fans that they knew would buy anything the group put out and also to casual buyers who simply liked a good, catchy rock 'n' roll song. The hope was that the combination of the two would be enough to send the band spiralling into the Top Ten for the first time. The band's natural instinct was to reject the idea out of hand, but for the first (and, mercifully, last) time in their career Maiden refused to obey their instincts and, against all their better judgement, decided to give it a bash (although this probably had more to do with the fact that Steve didn't have a suitable new song ready than any desire to do a cover as an A-side).

Recorded in Zomba's own Battery Studios, in Willesden, while Dennis Stratton was still in the band and produced by Tony Platt (then known for his work with AC/DC), for the author and for many other Maiden fans from those days 'Women In Uniform' represented the first real low in the band's career, a worked-up-about-nothing rush through the most cliché-ridden bobbins this side of the last Spiñal Tap album.

"Zomba came and said, 'Do you fancy doing this song, "Women In Uniform"?'" says Steve. "When we first heard it, I thought, 'I don't know. It's not a bad song, but the original version, by Skyhooks, was very, very different,' so we said, 'Well, if you can easily sort it, then yeah, maybe we'll have a go at it,' and we did it, we rearranged it, and it was really pretty heavy, the way we did it. Tony Platt was the producer, who they'd got in to try him out with a view to maybe doing the second album. But the thing is, Zomba being Zomba, you know, they wanted to get a hit single, and instead of getting him to try and work with us they just told him to make it a hit. If I had known that, I wouldn't have fucking used him in the first place, but being as he worked with AC/DC and that, I thought, 'Oh, you know, fine. He's not gonna pull us in any commercial direction.' But they briefed him, supposedly, and said, 'Try and get a hit single.'

"So he was trying to pull us in a more commercial vein, and this whole fucking mix that they had – just from some overdubs Dennis and Clive had done when I wasn't around – had completely taken us away from what we'd done with the song in the first place. The original mixes were much heavier than that, and I just went fucking nuts! I had to walk out, I was that pissed off. I had to walk out, because I thought, 'I'm gonna deck him.' I said, 'You don't know nothing about this fucking band! You come in to do a fucking job. You've been told what to fucking do by the powers that be, or whatever. It's got nothing to do with this fucking band. You just know nothing about us, so you can fuck right off!'"

With Platt red-carded and Stratton one step closer to his own last call, Steve went back into the studio on his own and remixed the track. The truth is, though, the song stank and no amount of heaviness was going to disguise that. However, the band did make their first video, the infamous "as live" shoot onstage at the Rainbow, which would prove to be Dennis Stratton's swan song. (See if you can spot him in it.) It was extremely unusual at that time for any act to make a video – despite Queen's brilliant 'Bohemian Rhapsody', many years earlier – but Maiden always wanted to try out new ideas, and they managed to persuade EMI to pay for it. Despite the paucity of the material, the result is nevertheless a genuinely frolicsome representation of what the band were like in those young and nervy days. It's just sad and ironic that the only video from those times we're left to look at and ponder all these years later isn't something classic like 'Running Free' or 'Sanctuary' but this contrived second-rater. Unsurprisingly, it was not the big hit that Zomba had envisaged, scampering in at Number 35 and mercifully disappearing from sight a week later.

On the plus side, however, 'Women In Uniform' did contain the excellent Harris-penned 'Invasion' on the B-side and also came replete with another sleeve in the growing Eddie collection, this one depicting our skull-faced hero cavorting arm in arm with a nurse and a schoolgirl, while an armed and uniformed Maggie Thatcher – resurrected from her grisly end on the 'Sanctuary' sleeve – awaits in ambush around the next corner. The question was, could Maggie's motive be jealousy, rather than revenge? Unfortunately, not everybody got the joke, and Liverpool's *Daily Post* gleefully reported that a group of "screaming, chanting, banner-waving feminists" invaded the Student Union hall at Leeds University, where the band were playing on 22 November.

The single would also afford the band a return appearance on *Top Of The Pops*. Once again, the show's producers agreed to let the band play the song live but, almost as if their karma was already catching up with them, the performance was a disaster. Indeed, so disgusted were they by the experience that, despite more than 20 hit singles in the UK in the interim, it would be another 15 years before Maiden would ever be seen live on the show again.

"We did it live again and everything seemed fine," says Steve. "We rehearsed it in the afternoon and they let us play just how we would have done it, but when it came to go on and actually do the show they turned us right down, the bastards! Clive had to play so quiet he might as well have used brushes. It was a joke! It was an absolute disaster, and that's why we vowed not to go on there again."

As good as his word – although every video would continue to be a feature of the programme over the years – Steve Harris made sure that Maiden didn't appear on *Top Of The Pops* in the flesh again until their debut Blaze Bayley single, 'Man On The Edge', in 1995. "But by then," he points out, "it was a geezer called Rik Blaxill who was producing the show, and he was much friendlier towards rock bands in general. He just let us come on and do anything we wanted," he grins. "So we're all good mates again now."

Nevertheless, with the 20/20 vision that 18 years' distance allows, Steve admits that he regrets the decision to release 'Women In Uniform', although he suggests that, despite any minor damage it may have done to their reputation in the short term, in the long term they learned some important lessons, namely, "never, ever, *ever* to allow anyone outside to fuck around with our music again. Anything like that, I thought, 'I ain't fucking having it no more.' It's not like Zomba wanted to harm us; they just wanted a hit. That's their job, you know? And to be fair to Tony Platt, he's a nice enough bloke, really. He just completely missed the plot, as far as we were concerned."

Suitably chastened, the band now faced another difficult choice: who should they get to produce the new album? Clearly, neither Will Malone nor Tony Platt were going to be asked back for an encore. What they needed, as Steve says, "was someone who was genuinely into the band's music and who actually understood rock music and what Iron Maiden was supposed to be about, not someone just trying to make a quick killing." That someone was to be Martin Birch, a producer then in his mid 30s whose name could be found on many of the albums that Steve and the others cherished most, including some of the best by Fleetwood Mac, Wishbone Ash, Deep Purple, Black Sabbath, Whitesnake, Rainbow and Blue Oyster Cult. A producer who can also sing and play most instruments, Birch had started out in the mid '60s as a singer/guitarist in what he now describes as "a heavy blues sort of outfit" called Mother's Ruin. He first got an inkling of his true vocation when Mother's Ruin went into the studio for the first time to make a single.

"Don't forget, this was the '60s," he warns, "and in those days you went in the studio and played and sang, and when the voice on the other side of the glass said, 'That's good,' you'd stop. That was all the input the group got into the whole recording process. You just came in and played and they handed you your record at the end of it. And most bands were happy to accept that, in those days. They didn't know any different. But The Beatles had come and started to change all that, and I was always one of those guys who used to want to hear the tape back first. I'd always insist on going into the other room where the producer was sat at the recording console and listening to the playback with him, and if I didn't like it I'd say so. Of course, this didn't usually go down too well. In those days, the producer was totally in charge of a recording session and the band was just treated like the hired help. And frankly, some of them just didn't have a clue. They were these old record-company guys who'd probably been doing Engelbert Humperdinck the day before, you know? And I used to think, 'I'm sure I could do better than that.'"

When Mother's Ruin lived up to their name and began falling by the wayside, Birch landed himself a job as a "tape op" (recording engineer's assistant) at London's Delaney Studios, in Holborn. "I got to learn about engineering a record, and moving more into the production side just came naturally," he explains. "Because I was young, I understood where the younger bands were coming from, musically, and I was always introducing new sounds and effects. And just being able to talk to the bands on their own level, I knew what it was they were trying to achieve with their music, and after a time the bands started talking to me more than they would the producer."

The late '60s and early '70s was a golden age in British rock music, and Birch found himself working in the studio with some of the most successful rock artists of the day. One of the first bands he worked with as a producer was Fleetwood Mac. This was in 1969, during the final, turbulent days in the band of singer/guitarist Peter Green, the distressed boy genius who would become – along with Pink Floyd's Syd Barrett – the most public acid casualty of the '60s, drifting eventually into long-term mental illness and vagrancy. (These days, of course, the author is pleased to report that Green – although still very fragile – is again both playing and recording and apparently in decent health.) A time of great inner turmoil for the Mac, who feared for the sanity of their increasingly unpredictable leader, it was also astonishingly a period that found the band approaching its creative zenith, enjoying huge critical and commercial success with the singles 'Oh Well' and 'The Green Manalishi (With The Two-Prong Crown)' and the albums *Mr Wonderful* and *Then Play On*.

"The last thing I ever did in the studio with Fleetwood Mac was also the last thing Peter Green ever did with them," says Martin, "and that was 'The Green Manalishi'. By then, Peter wouldn't play with any of the other members of the band in the room. He'd become very paranoid and suspicious of everybody. But again – because I was young, I think – he didn't seem to mind me being around. So, when he did 'The Green Manalishi', that's how it was done, with just me and him in there recording his guitars and vocals and whatever else he wanted to do. Then the band came in later and added their bits. It was bizarre, but I didn't really think of it that way at the time. I just thought he was this great artist who had a certain way of working, if you know what I mean. I wasn't really aware of the drug side, at that time."

Before his name became forever entwined with Iron Maiden's, however, the band that most hard rock aficionados most closely associated with a Martin Birch production credit was Deep Purple, with whom he recorded a string of landmark albums in the '70s. It was, he says, "an extraordinary period in my life. We were all about the same sort of age and we just learned and grew together." Not surprisingly, after the eccentricities of Peter Green, dealing with Deep Purple's guitarist, Ritchie Blackmore, who was equally errant (although, it should be stressed, for entirely different reasons – Green had destroyed his ego, while Blackmore was still building his), was, says Birch, "really easy. Ritchie was great to work with, not awkward at all. Working one to one, the guy was a real pleasure. The whole point is the music. The kind of people I enjoyed working with may have been characters, but they all knew how to deliver the goods, and that's what it's all about, not what the rest of the world thinks or says about you." Working on such era-defining Purple albums as *Machine Head* and *Burn*, the producer recalls sitting around on his own after one session, playing the tape back and worrying. "I thought something must be wrong, because I kept thinking, 'Surely it can't be this good!' But it was."

By the time Iron Maiden caught up with him, in 1981, Purple had long since broken up and Birch had been busying himself producing groundbreaking albums in the careers of late-'70s survivors such as Ritchie Blackmore's Rainbow (*Rainbow Rising*), Black Sabbath (*Heaven And Hell*) and Blue Oyster Cult (*Cultosaurus Erectus*). The first time he ever heard of Iron Maiden, he says, "was the same as everyone else, through reading about them in *Sounds*. I didn't really know much about the so-called new wave of British heavy metal, but then, I didn't really know much about punk. I was so busy working in a studio that I don't remember where or when people started thinking of music in those terms. I just gradually became aware that there had been a moment when good music stopped being just good music and became heavy metal or punk or soul or whatever. It was all down to what they call niche marketing, and it became a very '80s thing. I just tried not to get involved. But I remember sitting in my kitchen at home in Denham, where I used to live then, and reading about this great new group called Iron Maiden that was going to blow all the old rock bands away, and I thought, 'Yeah, they sound good.'"

Birch was in Paris, finishing the *Heaven And Hell* album with Black Sabbath, when he read that Maiden was about to go into the studio to record their first album for EMI with Will Malone. "I thought, 'But I'd love to do that!' And I wondered why no one had been in touch. I thought, 'Well, maybe I should have called them.' And I kind of said to myself then, 'You know, maybe I'll call them next time.' Then, what really made my mind up was something that happened a few months later, when I was working on *Cultosaurus Erectus*. I was in New York and I went to visit Ritchie Blackmore, who lives out on Long Island, and I remember sitting with Ritchie and he said, 'Have you heard this new band?' and proceeded to play me the first *Iron Maiden* album. He just thought it was great, and so did I. About halfway through it, he just turned to me and said, 'Why don't you do them?' And I thought, 'He's right. I should be doing this band.' It was right up my street, exactly the sort of thing I enjoyed, and I could tell that the production didn't do enough for them on that first album. I definitely thought I could do better, put it that way. I just felt I understood what they were about, straight away."

When, by strange coincidence, he received a phone call soon after from Ralph Simon at Zomba, who managed Birch's affairs, asking him if he would you like to produce the second Maiden album, "It felt like, well, that's it, this is fate, you know?"

The first time Martin was introduced to the band was backstage at the Rainbow after their Christmas show there in December 1980. "I thought, 'I hope they're as good as the record,' but they were ten times better than that! I honestly thought they were the best new band I'd seen in a long time."

Later, over a drink, Steve confessed to Martin that he'd actually wanted him to produce the first album. "I said, 'Me too! Why didn't you ask me?' He said, 'We thought you were too big.' But we started talking about music and about some of our favourite albums and stuff, and it turned out we had a lot in common. I'd actually produced some of the albums that Steve thought of as his favourites, and we had the same sort of sense of humour, which is important, I think, if you're going to be working closely on something as personal as making music together. We'd always work very hard, but there'd always be room for a bit of pissing around. You've got to make it fun or it wears you out."

"We wanted Martin for the first album," confirms Steve. "We all talked about him, but we thought, like, 'We're not worthy.' That wasn't the phrase at the time, but we didn't think we were big enough, you know? We just thought, 'This is a top-notch producer who's produced most of our favourite bands – Purple, Whitesnake, Wishbone Ash and God knows who else,' so we just thought, 'Well, he's not gonna want to touch us.' Like, 'Who are these upstarts?' Then, later on, we found out that he had done lots of bands that weren't huge, stuff I had in my collection, like Stray. He didn't seem to care about the sales of the band or the status of the band, really; it was just whether he was into it or not. And apparently he'd been reading about us and he'd heard a couple of things and he liked what he heard. He said, 'You should have come to me before. I'd have loved to work on the first album.'"

Convinced that they'd at last got the right man for the job, Maiden went into the studios with Martin Birch for the first time in December 1981. The setting was Battery Studios, where they'd cut the last single, and the band already had the title and all of the tracks worked out well in advance. The album would be called *Killers*, and all Martin had to do was get it down right...

"In the early days, they were pretty raw," he says. "I thought the best way to handle them was to make them feel as comfortable as possible, so I set them up as a group in the middle of the studio and said, 'Look, just play the songs as you would live and we'll work from there.' Technically, we got around things the best we could and gradually made them aware that, if we did that for the time being, just recorded the whole band playing together, it would be a lot easier for them. I had always been interested in getting the natural sound a band produces themselves onstage, and with Maiden I tried to capture that as much as I could. And to begin with – especially on the *Killers* album – I would encourage them to take it step by step, rather than upset them by making them play one at a time and do endless overdubs. So, to begin with, we just concentrated on capturing their natural sound and put little overdubs on afterwards."

Before long, he was christened "the headmaster" for his strict studio discipline. "I'd never worked with a producer who was so totally involved in the whole process," recalls Adrian. "He was a good laugh, but when we were working, he cracked the whip. The band was tight, anyway, from playing on the road, but Martin came in and made it even tighter."

"It was pretty obvious from the off that Steve was in charge," says Martin, "but he gave people their heads and really let them go for it. Just, when it came to the final say, it was down to him. Which was good, from my point of view, because me and Steve would agree 99 per cent of the time. And because they'd worked most of these songs out on the road long ago, we were able to work quite quickly and it all came together really well. I always knew they'd be big, but I've got some very nice memories of that time, before it all really started happening for them. Considering what they later went on to achieve, it was a different world for them, back then. I remember on the *Killers* album they used to sit there saying to me, 'Oh, it must be great, going to America,' and, 'What's Ritchie Blackmore *really* like?' and they were just so young and good fun to be with, it made for a refreshing change from what I'd been used to up to then. I thought, 'I like this band. I hope we work together again.'"

As history now records, Martin needn't have worried. "I went from doing albums with bands like Whitesnake, Sabbath, Blue Oyster Cult...but within a few years, I was concentrating exclusively on Iron Maiden. In the end, it was just what I really wanted to do, and I was lucky enough to be in the position where I could make that decision."

Inevitably, Martin would be approached many times over the next ten years to produce "bands that just wanted to sound like Maiden", but being Martin he turned them all down. He even turned down Metallica. "They were another band that had been incredibly influenced by both Maiden and Purple, I think, and any other time I'd have probably been quite keen to do it," he says, "but I was putting so much energy into the Maiden albums, I thought, 'If I start trying to build up another band in the same way, I'll be completely knackered and I won't be able to give either of them 100 per cent,' so I said no."

Killers would contain ten tracks, nearly all of which had been written by Steve and had already become established crowd-pleasers in the band's live set. These comprised half a dozen full-on Maiden-style rockers – 'Wrathchild' (vastly improved from the original *Metal For Muthas* recording and earmarked as the next single), 'Another Life', 'Innocent Exile', 'Killers' (with new and improved post-tour lyrics, written by Paul), 'Purgatory' (destined to become the second single from the album) and the fiercely anthemic album-closer, 'Drifter' – plus two instrumentals: a one-minute-and-46-second-long intro piece called 'The Ides Of March' and, further in, the even more epic-sounding 'Ghengis Khan', a track which anticipated future full-blown Harris rock operatics (but this time with lyrics), such as 1984's 'Rime Of The Ancient Mariner' or, more recently, 'Sign Of The Cross'. The album also included two more last-minute numbers that Adrian Smith was now on hand to help them bash into shape: the first, a full-throttle piece of rock theatre in a similar style to the previous album's 'Phantom Of The Opera', called 'Murders In The Rue Morgue'; the second, the album's only reflective moment, the rambling, semi-acoustic 'Prodigal Son'.

Very much a companion piece to the first Maiden album, *Killers*, like its predecessor, was an album that essentially documented the band's earliest days. In many ways, the tracks on both records are all interchangeable, and while it may be fair to argue that *Iron Maiden* contained more of what are now regarded as the classic Maiden tracks from that era – 'Prowler', 'Running Free', 'Phantom Of The Opera', 'Charlotte The Harlot' and the grisly title track itself, 'Iron Maiden' – it was on *Killers* that the quintessential Maiden sound was first caught masterfully on vinyl. You don't have to be a recording engineer to hear the difference in sheer sound quality between the two albums, and in this respect, at least, *Killers* captures Iron Maiden at its Di'Anno-era zenith.

"Production-wise, it was chalk and cheese, compared with the first album," says Steve. "As for the quality of the songs, I think you could argue that the first album was the strongest, but I tend to disagree, really. The thing was, the first album was like a 'best of' from our live set, songs which went back years. It was difficult to choose which ones to do, and there were some really good ones that got left off. I mean, 'Wrathchild' had been in the set from the start, but that got left off, and that was an amazing song live. So, after we did the first album, we still had a lot of really good, strong songs, and we didn't want to lose them. I mean, what are we gonna do, put them on a B-side or whatever? You can't. They're not B-side songs. They were good enough to go on an album, so that's what we did. After that, though, that was it, there was no more, and we needed to write a whole load of new material for the next album."

And, of course, *Killers* boasts the most gruesome Eddie yet on the sleeve, depicted now as an axe-wielding maniac, his victim's hands still clutching at his shirt as its unseen body slips agonisingly to the ground, the blood still drooling from the blade, Eddie's sharklike mouth contorted into a hideous smile. "That was Dave Lights' idea, that one," Rod reveals. "Well, if you're going to call your album *Killers*, and Eddie's going to be anywhere on the cover, it's pretty certain something gruesome's going to be going on, isn't it?" he laughs. Cleverly, Derek Riggs had set this nightmarish scene in Manor Park, one of the tough East End neighbourhoods from the band's earliest days together, and if you look closely you can see, in the distance, both the Ruskin Arms, where Maiden used to play, and the Kinky Sex Shop next door, with Charlotte stripping off in the red-lit room above it. "Eddie was this fantasy figure, but the band always wanted something in there that was real, too, from their own lives," Riggs explains. "I've never been to these places, but they would tell me about them and I would just try to imagine them."

When *Killers* was released, on 9 February 1981, the critics did not look favourably on such subtleties, by and large, and for the first time Maiden found themselves viewed from the wrong end of the critical microscope. *Sounds*, of all people, gave it a devastatingly critical review, writer Robbi Millar slapping it with a one-star rating (the lowest possible) and characterising the album as "more of a failure than a triumph", with "far too few stormers to the inch", the only two worth the price of admission, in her opinion, being old stage favourites 'Wrathchild' and 'Drifter'. The rest of the album was, she reckoned, "well dodgy", consisting of little more than "tiddly-tiddly-tiddly guitar" and "slow-quick-slow" time changes. It was a savage attack that seemed laced with personal vitriol. Had the band done something to offend the young *Sounds* reviewer? Or was this merely the beginning of a critical backlash building against the band? As it turned out, it was both.

"Robbi Millar reviewed it in *Sounds*, and she didn't give it a very good review, but there was a story behind that, and I don't mind telling it," says Steve. "She was knocking Paul off at the time, and Paul gave her the elbow. We gave him a bollocking after that and said, 'You could have waited to dump her until after she did the review!' I mean, I would like to think it would have been the same review she wrote whatever happened, but I don't really believe that. It pissed me off at the time. I think it always pisses you off when you've just been in the studio working your bollocks off and come out with an album you believe in and someone knocks it. I mean, how long does it take to write an album review? And when someone writes it off just like that, yeah, it can be really annoying. But having said that, it didn't upset us that much, 'cause we believed in it and we thought, 'Bollocks to that,' you know, 'cause we obviously knew the other side of the story as well. So we couldn't really take much notice of it."

Paul Di'Anno: "I don't know if it had anything to do with me dumping Robbi or not, but I don't like *Killers* anyway. I thought it wasn't a patch on the first album. Don't ask me why. We all worked our bollocks off, but it just don't have the same magic for me as the first album. It just don't."

Certainly, whatever the relative merits of the new material, there were more than merely "musical" reasons behind the sudden shift in critical perspective of which Maiden now found themselves the victims. Malcolm Dome, who gave *Killers* the only positive review it would receive, in *Record Mirror*, certainly thought so. Pointing to both the relative disappointment of the 'Women In Uniform' single and the acrimonious departure of Dennis Stratton, Dome described what he calls now "the general feeling of the band having achieved too much too soon. There was a lot of jealousy surrounding them, too, at that point, I think. From the outside, it looked as if they'd had it pretty easy, just having hits straight out of the box, and I think there were more than a few people ready to believe Dennis Stratton and his Sergeant-Major Harris stories. And partly because of that, and partly because the whole NWOBHM thing was already becoming old by that point, it was almost inevitable that Maiden would start picking up bad reviews. It must have come as a bit of a shock, though, because up until then everyone had been saying how brilliant they were all the time. And it's a shame, because *Killers* was a great album."

When *Killers* debuted in the UK charts at Number Twelve, eight places lower than *Iron Maiden* had, it only added fuel to the critical fire lit under the band.

"I know some people looked at it like that," says Steve, "but I really don't think the reviews had any bearing on the fact that *Killers* didn't go in as high as the first album. It went in at Number Twelve, which was still great, and we actually sold more copies of it here in Britain, as well as many, many more abroad. But we didn't have a hit single before it this time, and maybe that had something to do with why it didn't go in quite so high as the first album. 'Twilight Zone' and 'Wrathchild' had been released after the album. And there were other factors, too, like the fact that a lot of other well-known bands were releasing albums at the same time... I mean, at the end of the day, the difference between four and twelve is actually very small, in terms of first-week sales. And like I say, we sold more copies of the second album overall, so it wasn't anything we were gonna get worked up about."

They might not have, but the critics were about to have a field day, knocking both Maiden and the whole NWOBHM culture from which they had apparently sprung down to size over the coming months – not entirely unjustifiably itself, either, in retrospect. Dante Bonutto is a former editor of both *Kerrang!* and its '90s' offshoot, *RAW*. These days, he is a highly regarded A&R man, responsible for bringing such cutting-edge rock artists as The Wildhearts and Entombed to the attention of the world. However, as Bonutto says, you didn't have to be a top record-company executive in 1981 to grasp that "the NWOBHM had already begun to burn itself out by the time Maiden released their second album, so anything they released at that point was bound to be viewed from that perspective". Rightly or wrongly, that *Killers* should appear to falter, however slightly, was seen merely as further proof that the edifice that NWOBHM had erected for itself in the media was about to come tumbling down.

"By 1981, a lot of the bands most closely associated with the NWOBHM scene had got major record deals and were all releasing their first albums," says Bonutto, "and once you had all those albums, it became a lot clearer who really had the goods and who didn't. Clearly, Maiden was still way ahead of the pack, with Def Leppard close behind them, but they were lucky to have experienced, professional management behind them, something most of their contemporaries clearly lacked. Angel Witch, for instance, was managed by guitarist Kevin Heybourne's dad, Ken, and Diamond Head was managed by [singer] Sean Harris' mum, Linda, and... Well, in retrospect, it's not difficult to see why those bands didn't get very far. You had to have talent but you also had to have some business savvy. Maiden had both, but a lot of the others didn't really have either. Or, like in the case of Diamond Head, they had all the talent in the world but no proper management whatsoever."

As an example of what Bonutto is talking about, it's worth relating the story of how Bud Prager, the American manager of Foreigner, had flown to London in 1981 to declare his interest in managing Diamond Head in the US only to be met with a blank "Never heard of you" from the singer's mum, who was then acting as the band's chief representative. Foreigner had enjoyed the biggest-selling album in America that year with their 4 album and attendant worldwide hit single, 'Waiting For A Girl Like You' (Top Five in the UK in 1981), and, as Bonutto says now, "It was the sort of gaffe that characterised the business dealings of most of the bands in the NWOBHM scene. If Bud Prager had taken Diamond Head on, with his contacts and experience, he might have been able to do what Rod Smallwood did for Iron Maiden and Diamond Head would still be around with Maiden and Def Leppard today. But unfortunately, those sorts of opportunities don't come along more than once every lifetime, usually, and it just became obvious, after a while, that most of these bands weren't really going anywhere."

"I suppose you could call it a bit of backlash," says Steve Harris. "But it didn't just seem to be us. It was Leppard, Saxon, Samson. We all got given some stick in the press that year. I remember we were away on the road for about six months, that year – out of the country, you know – and it wasn't until we got back and started getting all the papers again that I started to notice the change. We didn't care. We believed in what we were doing long before we got called new wave of metal, or whatever. It was a shame for some of the other bands, though. I was quite surprised how many didn't make it, actually, looking back. There were certain bands that we actually thought should have done more that didn't. Like Angel Witch, for one. They did an album later which I thought was really good, you know? But they disappeared after that. Or Wytchfynder, who I thought were quite good, too. And Diamond Head, who at one stage looked like they were going to be the next Led Zeppelin."

Even Neal Kay was feeling the critical backbite. As the man who liked to claim the credit for almost anything that moved under the NWOBHM media umbrella, his fate was to be that of a captain going down with his ship. By 1981, his profile boosted further by his touring with Maiden and his memorable (if nothing else) *Metal For Muthas* album, Kay had briefly become a hugely influential figure in the music business as more and more of the major labels in London began circling like sharks around the few still-unsigned bands linked with NWOBHM. When Kay complained publicly that he considered it a scandal that *Rock City*, the debut album by New York metallists Riot (and a much-favoured item at his Soundhouse gatherings) was only available in Britain as an expensive US import, the band's record company, Ariola, moved quickly and *Rock City* was promptly given a proper UK release.

But when the Bandwagon was taken over by new owners at the end of 1980 and Kay was unceremoniously ousted from his perch in the DJ's booth, not even *Sounds* would come to his rescue. When Maiden arrived back in Britain from the Kiss tour, in November, Steve immediately sent a letter of support to *Sounds*, which began, "On returning from a two-month European tour, we were very pissed to hear that Neal Kay has been kicked out of the Bandwagon by the management there," before going on to suggest, "all headbangers should write in protest to the Chief of Administration at Charrington Breweries to tell him what you think of his brewery and his manager." However, despite Maiden's open support and the brief appearance of picket lines outside the venue, the campaign – which *Sounds* pointedly refused to support – was unsuccessful and Kay was eventually forced to move his Heavy Metal Soundhouse to a new venue, in Harrow. The spell was now broken, however, and Kay's new home never really captured the imagination in the same way that his nights at the Bandwagon had. The final blow came when *Sounds* withdrew the Soundhouse chart from its pages and Kay's voice – once so persistent, so loud, so comically self-righteous – was permanently silenced.

"Because of the success, in particular, of Iron Maiden, Neal Kay had become quite influential," says Geoff Barton. "Let's face it, the major record companies didn't really have a clue about heavy metal, and to a large extent still don't, I suspect. And so for about five minutes they all decided Neal was the man who knew about this NWOBHM thing, and if they listened to him maybe he would guide them to the Next Big Thing. The trouble was, I think it all went a bit to his head, because he did lose the plot very quickly after that. I mean, that *Metal For Muthas* album was an embarrassment. But then you look at pictures of Neal Kay or myself at that age and you think, 'What were these guys on?' We were all very young, and the truth is Neal was very much in love with that form of music, and he was a great PR person for it, for a while. But he did lose the plot very quickly."

Indeed, Barton and Kay – once NWOBHM blood-brothers – had fallen out badly over the *Metal For Muthas* album. Kay was deeply affronted by the mauling Barton had understandably given it in his *Sounds* review, even going so far as to suggest that it was envy, more than critical judgement, that had poisoned Barton's formerly friendly pen. But then, as Malcolm Dome – who knew both men – says, "I don't think Neal could brook any sort of criticism at all. He took it all too personally. He'd discovered Iron Maiden and helped start the whole NWOBHM scene and he wasn't going to let anybody forget it. And that was the trouble with the whole scene by then, as always seems to happen: it stopped being just about music and became more about ego."

Meanwhile, back on the road, the release of *Killers* heralded the start of what would be Iron Maiden's first-ever co-ordinated world tour, a mammoth eight-month trek that would see them play a staggering 126 shows across Britain, Europe, Japan, Australia and North America, taking in 15 countries and headlining everywhere except America, where, like Japan and Australia, they were making their first-ever visit. The whole shebang kicked off at the Ipswich Gaumont Theatre on 17 February, with the British leg encompassing 24 shows, culminating with Maiden's first-ever headliner, at the Hammersmith Odeon, in London. The tour single was a double A-side, comprising a mid-paced chugalong that Steve and Davey had put together called 'Twilight Zone' and 'Wrathchild', from the new album. Originally intended as a B-side, the band liked the finished cut of 'Twilight Zone' so much that they decided to upgrade it to full single status. 'Wrathchild' was also made an A-side, but for a much more practical reason.

"The reason why we did it as a double A-side was because we had a live version of us doing 'Wrathchild' at the Rainbow, before Christmas, on video that we could use," reveals Steve. "We couldn't afford to pay for another video for 'Twilight Zone', so we did a double A-side, because we knew we were gonna be off touring a lot and, if by any chance they wanted us on *Top Of The Pops* again, at least we'd got a video for 'Wrathchild' we could give them. We thought, 'If we put a double A-side out, then at least we can cover our arses.' But the joke was, it didn't get shown on *Top Of The Pops*. So it wasn't a huge hit or anything, but we accepted that. We were concentrating on the touring so much that our minds weren't really on it, anyway."

Released in the first week of March 1981, as their UK tour neared its climax at the Hammersmith Odeon, 'Twilight Zone'/'Wrathchild' actually got to Number 31 in the UK charts, making it Maiden's second-highest chart single to date. *Top Of The Pops* almost certainly would have aired the 'Wrathchild' video, but the show was off the air again due to yet another strike by their technical crew.

Meanwhile, Rod and Derek Riggs had managed to stir up more media unrest over the latest ghastly Eddie image that they'd come up with for the sleeve. Angry accusations of gratuitous sexism began to fly their way again as several critics read all the wrong things into the image of young woman sitting before her bedroom mirror in her nightie while a ghostly Eddie hovers behind her frightened reflection. But if they'd looked a little closer, and listened to the lyrics, they would have noticed Eddie's picture framed on the girl's dresser, complete with the inscription "To Charlotte, love Eddie", and realised that Eddie is actually dead and trying to contact his girlfriend from the next world. That's why he's transparent. Geddit? True, he's contemplating bumping her off (spot Doctor Death making his first appearance here, too), so that she can join him in Hell, but this doesn't alter the basic fact that 'Twilight Zone' was Maiden's first (albeit somewhat disguised) love song.

The tour itself was an unequivocal success for the band. Playing their last show in Britain that year at the Hammersmith Odeon on 15 March, it was apparent that the band had shed much of the raw garage-band attack of their pub-filling days in favour of a far more professional two-hour show, but without forfeiting one iota of their energy. It was exactly the kind of show that you could see bringing down the house in arenas all over the world, as it had undoubtedly been built to. (Historical footnote: the support band that night was French avant-metallists Trust, then featuring one Nicko McBrain on drums. Watch this space!)

Six days later, Maiden had begun the European leg of the tour, in Lille, France. For the next seven weeks, they travelled all over Europe, sleeping on the tour bus and playing almost every night. The schedule was so punishing that they rapidly became confused about which country they were in and what language the natives were speaking. Adrian remembers Paul introducing the band to the audience in pidgin French at one show. "The only trouble was, we were in Italy at the time."

Their new tour manager, Tony Wiggins, who had only begun working for the band at the start of the tour, says that one of his earliest recollections of the band was when they stopped the bus for a toilet break at a garage in Germany and the garage owner took one look at the long-haired reprobates spilling onto his forecourt, panicked and put the "Closed" sign up on his door. Perturbed by this unwelcoming act, the band responded in kind by simply unzipping and urinating all over the forecourt in full view of the now-frantic manager's wife and daughter, at which point the owner became so irate that he ran from his office and threw a bucket of cold water over the lot of them. Bad move. Davey, already somewhat the worse for wear, hurled the bottle of brandy from which he'd been swigging through the garage's big office window and the owner went mad and called the police. Cue one mad rush for the bus. "We dived back on the bus and turned off the main road as soon as possible," Wiggins recalls. "We drove down these little roads for hours until we got back on the autobahn for Strasbourg." The tour manager, who had come straight to Maiden after working for cardiganed crooner Gilbert O'Sullivan, says that he was aghast. "I remember thinking, 'What the hell have I got myself into?'"

On a more serious note, the German leg of the tour, in May, was where Paul Di'Anno's "vocal problems" first became a euphemism for a much deeper and more worrying malaise. Back to his old tricks of staying up for days on end and then wondering why his tonsils wouldn't respond in the required manner, the band was actually forced to cancel five of the German dates while Paul rested his voice. Local promoters were not best pleased, and fans were mightily unimpressed, but the band just about got away with it by promising to return to play the cancelled shows later on in the tour (which they did, in October) and throwing in a few impromptu autograph-signing sessions at half a dozen different record stores, where the kids became so worked up that police had to be called in each time to quell what the hysterical German press later reported as "street riots".

Nevertheless, Steve, for one, considered this to be the last straw in his working relationship with Paul. Things couldn't continue this way, he decided. Something had to be done. Not now, mid tour – "We didn't want to have to cancel the whole tour; that would have been a disaster" – but soon. Very soon.

"Rod actually asked me, when he first got involved with the band, was there any potential problems that might crop up in the future he should know about?" recalls Steve. "And I said, 'Well, I've got to be totally honest, you know. There may be a problem with Paul, because sometimes his attitude is a bit weird.' Rod asked me what I meant and I said that it was weird little things, like sometimes Paul just hadn't shown the same commitment as the rest of us. He wouldn't have the money to come to rehearsals, sometimes, and things like that. Silly things that are trivial at the time but, when you're trying to pull your weight together, it means a lot. I had to get a loan out for him for this microphone he wanted, and he said he'd pay me back, but he never did. Stuff like that.

"But I always thought, like, 'As the band gets more successful, maybe he'll be more into it.' But if anything the bigger we got, the worse he got. I don't know. Paul seemed very nervous at times about how big the band was getting, and sometimes he'd be really negative about things. He was into it, but he seemed to be on this weird trip, like it all seemed to be happening too quick for him. It was like he was a bit threatened… He'd come offstage some nights and pretend to collapse unconscious. He was always fainting!

"I remember when we played the Nottingham Boat Club, right in the early days, it was the usual thing. Done the gig, crowd going berserk, absolutely mental reactions, you know? So we're gonna go back and do an encore…and Paul's fainted in the dressing room! I've never seen anyone faint so conveniently, either. He always managed to land on a chair or on a flightcase, never flat on his face. And this time, I went and slapped him. I was, like, 'Get up, you bastard!' And he just opened his eyes and went, 'You

The uncensored 'Sanctuary' sleeve

Maggie gets revenge? 'Women In Uniform'

Maggie finally asks to meet
Maiden. All is forgiven

A gift from the fans at
Leiden, Holland on the
Kiss tour, 5 October 1980

Eddie disagrees
with Ozzy biting
heads off bats

Pie-eyed on kids' television
programme *Tiswas*, 1981

The photo of Steve that *Sounds* used for their front cover, 1982

Maiden's last photo with singer Paul Di'Anno

The first official photo session with new frontman Bruce Dickinson

A note from Rod in the
official fan club
magazine, International
Edition 3, 1982

IRON MAIDEN

19th April 1982

Dear 'eadbangers,

What a start you've given us to 1982! We've just finished a sell-out
U.K. tour, and are halfway through the European stretch of "The
Beast on the Road" World Tour, which is also going great, and you
put the new album straight into the U.K. chart at No: 1 - where it
still is as I'm writing. Not many bands have got such great fans -
thanks. It's a bit too early to get chart positions from European
countries, but we'll let you know them next time.

As I said, the band are in Europe at the moment, just starting on
ten dates in Germany, finishing with a gig in Amsterdam on May 1st.
They have a short break then, before heading for the U.S. of A. on
May 10th. We'll be touring there with Rainbow and 38 Special first
off, but during the six months we'll be there, bands we'll be playing
with will change a lot. After that, it's off to Japan, and then back
home - hopefully for a rest.

Best wishes till then from us all,

Rod Smallwood.

P.S. Just heard the album is No: 54 with a bullet in the American
charts, after only 3 weeks!

West Ham fan Steve with his Leyton
Orient-supporting dad

Steve and Bruce in backstage high jinx,
Dortmund, 1983

Backstage during the
World Piece Tour,
1983, Nicko's first tour

Dave Murray at
Compass Point
studios, 1983

Nicko in the video for
'Flight Of Icarus',
Compass Point, 1983

Two sides of the story. Above: during writing
of *Piece Of Mind*, New Jersey, 1983.
Right: performing it on tour!

Dave, Steve and Adrian travelling light, 1983

Davey and long-time producer Martin Birch, Compass Point, 1983

First time at Madison Square Garden – SRO – 8 October, 1983

The Maiden squad that beat a Def Leppard XI 4-2 in Dortmund. L-r: (standing) Horace, Bruce, Dave, Loopy, Rod, Geoff, Steve, (kneeling) Dave Lights, Adrian, Roger, Mark and Titch

haven't got any sympathy for me, have you?' I was like, 'No, I fucking
haven't! Now get back on that stage!' And he just got up and sort of
staggered back onstage.

"I don't know whether he was seeking attention or what. I don't know
what the hell it was, but he wasn't really looking after himself, physically,
either. Someone who's singing has got to look after their voice, and you can't
be staying up all night smoking yourself stupid and taking speed and what
have you. You've got to look after yourself, and Paul wasn't, and so, at the
end of the day, we ended up cancelling gigs because of his problems, and that's
one thing, if you know me, I just can't tolerate. I'm not into drugs myself,
never have been, but I'm not against other people doing what they like, as
long as it doesn't fuck up their gig. Well, Paul was letting it fuck up his gig.

"Then, on our first European tour as headliners, we're in Milan, and it
was sold out, about 3,000 there and loads of punters locked out, and the
promoter suddenly tells us we'll have to do a matinee show as well or there
will be a riot. Basically, the guy had deliberately over-sold the gig to make
more money. But what he said was right – there were thousands of these
kids left outside, and if they didn't get in there was probably gonna be
trouble, so we didn't have no choice. But Paul was, like, 'I can't do the
matinee show! My voice won't hold up!' I said, 'Paul, just fucking take it
easy. Don't go overboard. Just take it easy in the afternoon gig and go for
it in the evening, or take it easy at both shows, if you like, but we've got a
situation here. We can't back out of it now.' So, anyway, he's done the
afternoon show, and it came to the evening gig, and he's done that. Then
it's time to do the encores and he's gone off and conveniently fainted on a
flightcase. I'm, like, 'Oh, fucking hell. Not now…'"

Enough was enough, they decided. "I think it occurred to us all at the
same time, about Paul," says Rod. "It was very sad – it was certainly not
what anybody wanted – but when we started losing gigs with Paul's voice,
something was obviously really wrong. I don't know if he had a death
wish, but he actually seemed to know that he was going to let the band
down, almost as if he was scared of success and the responsibility this
would inevitably bring and he couldn't live with that responsibility. In any
band, everyone should be responsible to each other. That's certainly the
Maiden way.

"But Paul had started to get a bit into the whole lifestyle aspect, shall we say, of being a rock star. We managed to keep most habits at bay for a long time, but then it's very hard to, in this business, particularly at that time. The first time I was aware that anyone was doing anything was when we were on the Kiss tour. Paul was getting up to stuff and I was, like, 'Well, you'd better control it. I'm going to be watching you.' I knew the only thing that could stop Maiden was themselves.

"Steve won't touch drugs. He never has, and the reason is that he's scared what they'll do in his mind. He's already got a very creative and open mind. He doesn't need any other stimulation in that department. Some of his songs, like 'Twilight Zone', are based on out-of-body experiences. 'Number Of The Beast' was a dream. If your head does this anyway, you don't need drugs. If anything, he likes something to cool him down, and a few beers will do that for him. But Paul was so over the top. He started having vocal problems, he smoked like a chimney, he drank brandy and, you know, now he's doing a bit of coke and speed, too, and he was missing gigs. And it's always been a Maiden thing that they've never wanted to let the fans down, and these things were starting to hurt us. We lost the whole German tour. I remember we sat up all night writing handwritten letters to all the main German magazines, because we didn't want anybody to think we were fuck-ups."

"It's no secret. I was pretty out to lunch on that tour, I suppose," Di'Anno admits. "It wasn't just that I was snorting a bit of coke, though; I was just going for it non-stop, 24 hours a day, every day. I thought that's what you were supposed to do when you were in a big, successful rock band. But Maiden had become so big by then that the band had commitments piling up that went on for months, years, and I just couldn't see my way to the end of it. I knew I'd never last the whole tour. It was too much. People ask me now, would I have done things different if I could go back and have my time over? Well, the honest answer to that is no. I was a kid. What did I know? You're not supposed to know anything. That's the beauty of it. The trouble was, Steve and Rod and the others didn't look at it like that, and I couldn't blame them. They had all these plans and, the way I was, I was starting to stick a spoke into them, I could see that. I just couldn't do anything about it. I didn't want to."

The band had learned to put a happy face on their difficulties and the tour continued, albeit with yet more cancellations at intervals along the way through Japan, Australia and on to their first-ever visit to America, a place that they'd all dreamed of playing since they'd first dreamed of playing. But even here, Paul managed to let himself and the band down.

"It was just a nightmare, really," says Steve, "but because the band was breaking big, we didn't want to lose him, you know? We wanted to carry on as we were. But we thought, 'The longer it goes on, the more we've got to risk.' And that's when it was decided we had to make the change. We didn't have any pressure from anybody; they just went with what we did. It was us and Rod and fuck everyone else, you know? So we all had a meeting – the band and Rod – and we said, 'Look, it's gonna have to change.'

"We carried on with Paul for a little while, still hoping that he was gonna do it, and we talked to him and said, 'Look, Paul, pull your fucking socks up, or else,' but it just wasn't happening and we had to knock it on the head with him. And do you know what? I think he was relieved. Who really knows what goes on in Paul's head? I'm not sure he does, half the time. But that's the feeling I got. He was a bit gutted, but he was also relieved that he didn't have to put up with all the hassle of being on the road and having all these things to do, these responsibilities to shoulder. Because it *is* a big job, being the frontman. But I still can't really understand it. It was almost like he had a death wish, when it came to success. And it's a shame, because I always thought of Paul as really talented, not just as a singer but with his songwriting as well. He didn't write tons of stuff, but 'Remember Tomorrow' and the lyrics to 'Running Free' and 'Killers', it was good stuff. He had it, but he just sort of threw it away."

"In the end, the split was totally amicable," says Rod. "Paul came 'round the office and the rest of the band were supposed to come 'round too, but no one else showed up. So I had to tell Paul, and he actually said to me, 'That's OK. I was gonna come in tomorrow and tell you that I wanted to resign, but I didn't know what to say.' And whether he said that to cover himself or it's true, I still don't know. He's a very complex character is Paul, very loveable, but sometimes he didn't seem to know reality."

"It's true, I was relieved," agrees Paul. "I was sad, too, but I'd had enough of it by then, I think. I'd had a bellyful. I didn't get into rock 'n' roll to keep to schedules and have meetings and make sure I get my eight hours' beauty sleep every night. Not that I'm knocking Maiden; it takes guts to do what they went on to do. But they had so many ambitions, I couldn't keep up, and I think, in the end, they made the right decision. When you look who they got in to replace me... I mean, that's the fella I'd have chosen, too. So then they were happy and I was happy, so it worked out all right in the end. People say, 'Don't you wish it had been you?' I say, 'It was me! I just didn't want it.'"

Losing their singer is a huge gamble for any rock band, let alone one battling for their credibility with an already hostile music press, but it was a risk that the band would have to take. As Steve says, "We knew there was no way we could carry on with Paul, but we honestly didn't know if we'd be able to carry on without him. We just had to wait and see."

They simply had to roll the dice and hope. Six...six...six...

10 Bruce

From the outside, sacking Paul Di'Anno when they did looked like a huge gamble for Iron Maiden. In fact, it turned out to be the best thing that could have happened to them. With the benefit of hindsight, it's not difficult to see that Maiden had gone as far as they could with the self-styled Cockney wide-boy leading the charge. They had successfully conquered Europe and Japan with Paul. Now, poised to take on the USA with their third album, it was imperative that they should have a frontman equal to the task. Clearly, Paul Di'Anno was not that man. Genuinely rattled by the ever-increasing demands placed upon his usually hungover shoulders, Paul had visibly shrunk from the task of helping lift Maiden to the next level.

On the other hand, Bruce Dickinson, the Samson singer that Maiden would eventually turn to, had no such hang-ups. Where Paul Di'Anno's dreams and ambitions ended, Bruce's were just getting warmed up. Like Steve Harris, he'd dreamed of nothing less than to be standing on the tallest stages in the world since he bought his first album, Deep Purple's *In Rock*, when he was 13. Known variously these days as author, pilot, video director, radio and MTV presenter, solo artist and father of three boisterous children by his second wife, Paddy, it's sometimes overlooked that Bruce Dickinson is also one of the greatest white rock singers to emerge on the international scene since the heyday of British blues rock vocal legends like Robert Plant, Paul Rodgers and his beloved Ian Gillan. Musically, you could say that he and Maiden simply belonged together. As Steve Harris says, "If I'm honest, I'd have to say it was probably more Bruce's style of singing that I really imagined singing my Maiden songs, right back in the early days. It's just that Paul came along first."

Paul Bruce Dickinson was born on 7 August 1958 in Worksop, a small mining town in Nottinghamshire. Although Paul was his proper first name, he always preferred to be known as Bruce, even as a child. His parents were still in their teens when they married, and baby Bruce's imminent arrival hurried the young couple into the kind of make-do-and-mend union common in pre-abortion '50s Britain. Barely out of school themselves and virtually penniless, the expectant young couple were initially forced to live with Bruce's grandparents, who would take on much of the responsibility for the child's earliest upbringing.

"I was a bit of an accident," Bruce admits. "My mum was 16 or 17 when she became pregnant and my dad was 17 or 18. They were subsequently married and I was born about four or five months later. My mum worked in a shoe shop, part time, and Dad was in the army. He was a motor mechanic, but he lost his driver's licence through being a general hooligan and so he just thought, 'Fuck it,' and he volunteered for the army. It paid more and he got his licence back straight away. My recollection is that I was pretty much raised by my grandparents, because my own parents were so young. My grandad was a coal-face worker at the local colliery and my grandma was a housewife who used to do a bit of hairdressing in the front room. My first school was Manton Primary, which was known as being a tough place in this fairly run-down area – all the kids from the local estate used to go there – but it never struck me as being tough. I had a great time, actually. I remember my childhood at that time as being extremely happy."

By the time he was ready to start school, however, Bruce's parents had moved out of Worksop and left him behind with his grandparents while they headed for Sheffield, the nearest city, where jobs were then plentiful.

"My parents had moved out, because the jobs were in 'the Smoke', as they called it, which was Sheffield," he says. "I didn't really feel like I had a mum and dad. My grandad was the closest thing I had to a dad. He was great. My grandad was probably in his mid 40s by then, which is a really good age, actually, to be a dad. I remember him teaching me boxing. He taught me how to fight before I went to school. He said, 'If anybody says anything at school, just whack 'em. Stick up for yourself and don't let anybody push you around.' And I got sent home from school a day later, 'cause I went 'round the school whacking everybody! And then he gave me a stern lecture on when to whack and when not to whack people. In many ways, I think, I was the son that he never had. But to my grandmother, I was always going to be the little bastard that had taken her daughter away from her. She said that when she looked at me she always saw my father, and I did look a bit like my dad, I guess, facially-wise."

A happy if solitary child who used to crawl behind the couch and refuse to budge whenever he was upset ("I didn't want anyone to see me"), Bruce's first experience of music was dancing in his grandparents' front room to 'The Twist' by Chubby Checker. "My grandparents used to put the record on and I used to do the twist for everybody, and of course at that age you think it's really cool." The first record he ever remembers actually owning, he says, was the single 'She Loves You' by The Beatles.

"We had a record player and a radio and I managed to persuade my grandad to buy me 'She Loves You', which was Number One for weeks and weeks and it was, like, one of those records everybody had to have, you know? And maybe because of that, I don't know, but I remember thinking I liked the B-side better than the A-side, and that's when I started listening to music and deciding what I liked and what I didn't like. I remember liking the harmonies on the B-side of a Gerry And The Pacemakers single, which was called 'I'll Never Get Over You'. Then there was a kid down the street who had an electric guitar and everyone used to talk about it in hushed tones. I must have been about five years old, and I remember seeing this kid with this electric guitar and it was, like, 'Blimey!' He was a teenager – he must have been all of 16 – and he just looked like a god to me. He had long hair – well, long for those days; it probably went down to his ears – and he had pointy shoes on and stuff. I mean, he looked like he'd just stepped off the telly."

Even though the amount of time he was actually allowed to watch it was rationed, as a child, "telly" would prove to be a crucial factor in the way Bruce's interest in pop music would develop. When he was growing up, his two favourite TV programmes were *Jukebox Jury* – the original pop TV quiz show, in which a panel of famous guests would be asked to review a smattering of the week's new record releases, voting them either a hit or a miss – and *Doctor Who*, the weekly saga of a time- and space-travelling "Doctor" and his long-running battles against such futuristic alien enemies as the Daleks and the Cybermen.

"I always watched *Jukebox Jury*, because it was on before *Doctor Who* on a Saturday night," he explains, "so *Jukebox Jury* and *Doctor Who* became inseparable in my mind. The excitement of seeing The Beatles or whoever on *Jukebox Jury* was kind of similar to the excitement I would get out of seeing the Cybermen on *Doctor Who*. They were both from a different world, to me.

"I wasn't particularly into science fiction. More science fact, really. I was incredibly obsessed with the moon and space, to the point where I remember getting huge sheets of wallpaper and drawing plans for my own spaceship, all the navigational equipment and everything. Really quite detailed plans, you know? The same thing with a submarine which I designed when I was about nine. It was going to be built out of dustbins welded together, about three feet long. I loved the idea of living under the water, like Captain Nemo, or floating out in space, or just about anywhere except for reality. I was really into the first landing on the moon, the first unmanned landing on the moon, in the very early '60s. I remember trying to tell my grandma how important it was, 'cause she was going to use the newspaper to light the fire with. I said, 'You can't throw this away!' I don't know what I expected her to do with it; I just felt it was too important to throw on the fire. But that was the '60s. Growing up at that time, I just felt that there was no limit to what you could do."

Except perhaps in Sheffield, where Bruce was eventually despatched when he was six years old, once his parents had set up house and found themselves regular work there.

"They never listened to music," he says. "My parents would be just totally focused on trying to make money. It was weird. They were quite strict. Then, later, I discovered they'd actually gone around the world or something. They worked as a duo in a performing-dog act with, like, poodles leaping through hoops. Mum used to do a lot of dancing, ballet dancing, and she looked great. She had a great figure and everything. She'd won a scholarship to the Royal College of Ballet and my grandmother wouldn't let her go, so then she got pregnant. That was like hell, and the dancing became her ticket out of there – out of Worksop, out of the shoe shop and everything. So there was this whole other life they'd had which I knew nothing about, as a kid."

The only clue was an old acoustic guitar that his father owned but didn't play any more. "It was a really, really crappy one, but I was fascinated with it. It was a dreadful, horrible old thing, completely unplayable. I don't think anybody could get anything out of it, so I used to grab hold of it and start bashing away, making this terrible noise and making my fingers blister."

When he'd first arrived in Sheffield, Bruce had been sent to a notoriously tough local primary school that made Manton look like something from the set of *Beverly Hills 90210*. "It was called Manor Top, and as far as I know it's still there," he says. "I don't know what it's like now, but when I went there it was like Colditz," he smiles darkly. As the new kid in class, he found himself beaten up and picked on so much that eventually his parents moved him out and sent him to a small, private, fee-paying school called Sharrow Vale Junior.

"I was at Manor Top for about six months, maybe," he says. "Then we moved. We were constantly moving house to make money. My parents would buy a house, do it up, sell it, then buy somewhere else and start again. For a lot of my life, I was living on a building site. But my parents had got to the stage where they were actually making some money. They had bought a boarding house, and then I think my dad bought a bankrupt garage and started running that, too. He was always selling second-hand cars off the forecourt of the hotel."

As a result of his parents' unceasing efforts to better themselves, as a teenager Bruce attended a "posh person's" private boarding school in Shropshire called Oundale. "I didn't mind going there," he says. "I didn't particularly enjoy being with my parents, so I saw it as an escape. They gave me the choice – like, 'Do you really want to do this?' I was about twelve, and I just went, 'Yeah.' I think it was because I hadn't built any real attachment to them when I was very, very young, and also the fact that they had real difficulty in relating in any sort of meaningful way to me as a person, as opposed to me as a child who it was their duty to look after and feed and clothe and shelter and educate, you know? The idea of picking me up and giving me a huge cuddle... I'm sure it happened, but I was never really conscious that it did, at the time.

"There were other times, though, when I was surprised how sort of understanding they were about things. I once nicked a small Dinky car toy out of some department store and got nabbed for it and got the full grilling from the police and everything. And obviously, you're eleven years old and they're trying to scare the crap out of you so you won't do it again. And it worked! They scared the crap out of me and I've never nicked anything since. But I remember my dad had to come down and fetch me and I was surprised that he didn't put me over his knee and give me a caning or something. On the other hand, he never talked about why I did it ever. Expressing your innermost feelings just wasn't on the agenda, in my family. My grandad – who was very ill – later swallowed a load of pills and tried to do himself in, but nobody ever talked about it afterwards, and he was living with us at the time. My grandparents had moved in with us at the hotel by then.

"But in some ways, I'm sort of quite grateful for the fact that I didn't have what you would think of as a conventionally sort of happy, uncomplicated childhood. It made me very self-reliant. I grew up in an environment where it struck me that the world was never gonna do you any favours, that if you stopped and let things just slosh you around that you'd end up being squashed. It was sort of drummed into me, because of the way my parents were. They were very self-reliant, hard-working people. They never stopped. And I had very few close friends, *very* few, because, you know, I never really met anybody for long. I was always moving. I don't think my dad had that many really close friends, either. The only one who had lots of friends was my sister, Helen, who was born not long after I first moved to Sheffield. She was the complete opposite to me, a complete social butterfly. She went riding and had hundreds of friends."

Bruce's private education was to come to an abrupt end, however, when he was expelled at the age of 17 for the somewhat surreal crime of urinating in his headmaster's dinner. "Basically, it goes back to this idea of me being a complete outsider, which I was becoming more and more aware of as I got into my teens," he explains. "I had no problem whatsoever with the idea of going off to boarding school, but the reality, when I got there… I mean, I hated it and wouldn't fit in at all. The way that everybody had a status, pre-ordained, when they went in there that you had to follow. I was just, like, 'But why? This is absolute crap.' So that didn't get me off on the right foot, because all these kids had been institutionalised for five years at other boarding schools before they got there, so this whole class system was already ingrained into them. You certainly didn't speak out against it, or you wouldn't be there."

As a result of his miscreant ways, Bruce was picked on and routinely bullied by the older boys. But these were not the simple fisticuffs that he'd encountered at state-run hellholes like Manor Top. "More like systematic torture," is how he describes it now. "You couldn't get away, that was the thing. At Manor Top, at least you got to go home at the end of the day." His chief tormentor was his dormitory captain, an 18-year-old, six-foot-tall member of the school rowing team "with the mental age of a twelve year old". Bruce tells how his dorm-leader's favourite trick was to "come in at about ten o'clock at night, grab a pillow, make it into a weapon, gather everybody around my bed and give me a lesson in self-defence by beating the shit out of me". It was a brutal regime that Bruce endured nightly throughout his entire first year.

"It was literally every night," he says, "and then you'd get in your bed some nights and it'd have six broken eggs in it and everything would be soaked, all the clothes would be soaked, everything ruined and impossible to sleep on... I knew I could have called my mum and dad, but that would have been bottling out, so I didn't do it. They found out after about a year and a half. In a funny sort of way, I thought that telling my parents and complaining to the teachers would be letting people win. I was just determined not to. You just don't let people get the better of you, that was my attitude. Even if you're lying there with all your guts kicked in, you can still go away saying, 'All right, you're bigger than me, you can beat the shit out of me if you want, but you're not superior. That's me, mate.' And that's what occurred to me. I used to cry my fucking eyes out in private, but never, ever, ever, *ever* show that sort of...of weakness in public, because then they really *have* won."

Bruce had grown up an only child, drifting between different homes, different schools, even different parents. He even felt distanced from his sister – as he confesses he still does to this day – because, as he puts it tellingly, "She was a planned child, you see? So I started to become aware that I was this outsider, and I just accepted it. But that's when I started deliberately doing, like, odd things. I remember they had this school army-cadet course that everybody hated, so I became in charge of it, and I could handle live ammunition and weapons and all these handguns and stuff. Me and this other kid – who was terminally uncool, too – decided that we would have our little revenge every Wednesday afternoon by blowing the fuck out of people. Oh God, we used to do stuff that was *so* dangerous! Setting little booby-traps for people. Not to hurt them, just to scare them.

"I was probably about 16 at this point, and we used to do this school exercise every year where all the schoolmasters and all the willing kids went out for an afternoon and played soldiers and then camped up for the night in some old milk sheds out in the countryside. We got permission to be 'the enemy', and it was just straight out of *The Dirty Dozen*. I remember, at four in the morning, me and this mate of mine went charging through this campsite, running all over the tents where the schoolmasters were sleeping, stomping all over them and letting off smoke bombs. It was our little moment of revenge."

The idea of becoming a singer was still some way off but one that he took his first tentative steps toward when he became involved in the school's amateur dramatics society at the age of 15. "The first time I stepped on a stage, I loved it," he says. "I felt really comfortable straight away, and so I started volunteering for every play going. I did two or three house plays, numerous school plays and sixth-form plays. I even ended up directing some, in fact. I loved it. It wasn't so much the dressing up; it was the language, and trying to get inside the head of what was going on, on the page. We'd do Shakespeare – the drama department was very ambitious, and I remember taking part in these quite elaborate productions of *Macbeth* and *Henry VI*. I used to really try and understand what was really being said on the page and give it something, you know?"

But music was never far behind acting in the adolescent Bruce's scheme of things, and he tells a familiar '60s tale of listening to tiny transistor radios under the bedclothes after lights out at night.

With visits to the record shop severely restricted, records became a common currency at school. "We were only allowed one hour of television a week, so really the only outside entertainment you'd have was music, and people were always swapping albums or selling them second hand," he recalls. "You'd go down the corridor and there'd be music coming out of every single study, and I heard this thing coming out of someone's room one day and I went in and said, 'Whoa! What's *that*?' And they just looked at me disdainfully and went, 'It's "Child In Time" by Deep Purple. Don't you know *anything*?' But I was too amazed to care. I was, like, 'Yeah, but where can I get hold of that?' The first album I ever bought was Deep

Purple's *In Rock*, all scratched to fuck but I thought it was great, and that's what started me off on buying albums and getting into rock music. That and the end-of-term concert. A band would come into school every term and play, and so three times a year you had a rock concert. The first gig I ever saw in my life was a band called Wild Turkey, and I remember there was an interview with them not long after in *Melody Maker* or something and they asked them how the tour had gone, and one of them said, 'Funnily enough, the best gig we had the whole tour was this boarding school.' I remember I went absolutely mad. My shirt came off!"

There were other pivotal moments as well, such as when Van Der Graaf Generator played there ("Peter Hammill, the singer, was an old boy at the school, and it was rumoured the headmaster used to keep a picture of him in his drawer, and if he saw the prospective parents had longish hair he used to whip it out and put it on the wall!") and Arthur Brown. "His album *Kingdom Come* had just come out and it was tremendous. The best singer I'd ever seen.

"It was always progressive, kind of album-orientated. That was my live-music input. But as far as albums go, I just snapped up the first Sabbath album, Deep Purple's *In Rock*, *Aqualung* by Jethro Tull, *Tarkus* by Emerson, Lake And Palmer – just whatever was around. I mean, I must have been a marketing man's dream, because every band I saw play live, I bought their album. Then I'd go back and listen to other bands that had supposedly influenced them, you know? But my favourite was definitely Deep Purple. I just thought *In Rock* was the greatest thing ever!"

But being a singer still hadn't crossed his mind. Instead, originally, Bruce fancied himself as a drummer. "Ian Paice of Deep Purple was my absolute hero," he says. "I just wanted to be Ian Paice. Specifically, I wanted to be Ian Paice's left foot. But I couldn't afford the kit. There was a couple of rich kids who used to have drum kits at school and used to have sort of a band, you know? I remember hanging out at the back, watching them rehearse and thinking, 'I'm sure I could do better than that.' And occasionally they'd let me have a fly around the drums, and I'd be useless, but I still knew I could do it better than they could. I could just hear it all in my head. I used to make myself a drum kit out of exercise books and things on my desk. I didn't have any sticks, so I used these two bits of square wood and bashed around on my bed at seven in the morning."

Eventually, he wheedled himself into the outer fringes of the group by "permanently borrowing" a pair of bongos from the school music room and "sort of sitting in the corner bashing along without asking. I'd made friends with the singer, who was this guy called Mike Jordan. We used to play war games together, but he won all these prizes for his bass singing – as in classical-type singing – so he was the singer in this group, and it was kind of painful. It wasn't very rock 'n' roll at all.

"I remember trying to learn 'Let It Be'. There was about two or three chords to it, so everybody was just about bashing through it. I was in the corner trying to sound like John Bonham on a pair of bongos, and it was diabolical. It sounded terrible! Red-raw hands, I had, bashing away, giving everybody a headache. It sounded like a shire-horse walking into a bunch of boxes, but poor old Mike couldn't hit the high notes at all, and I started trying to encourage him by singing along, only I could hit the high notes. I always sort of thought that I could probably sing. In fact, I knew I could sing, because somebody had heard me yelling away to 'Jerusalem' in the school choir and said, 'You've got a really good voice.' I sort of went, 'Bollocks!' you know? But it made me think.

"So I said, 'Let me have a go at singing and I'll shut up with the bongos and give you a hand with the top notes of 'Let It Be'. And so I did it and everybody went, 'Fucking hell! Where's this voice come from?' Unfortunately, the band split up about five minutes later. But there was this other kid, who was also terminally uncool, who was really into BB King and liked blues stuff. He was learning it all on acoustic guitar and I used to go in with him. Nick Bertram was his name, and he'd get his BB King songbook out and we used to wade our way through all these blues standards and things, him playing and me singing. And then I got myself thrown out of school for the famous pissing in the headmaster's dinner incident."

Ah yes, that. For the record then…

"The headmaster, the deputy headmaster, the housemaster and all the relevant school authority figures were having a dinner party to celebrate the opening of a new extension at the end of the house and the food was being cooked by the school prefects. They'd run out of cooking oil and they wanted to borrow the cooking oil in our study so we thought we'd, er, assist, me and this other kid. I think we'd had a couple nips of something alcoholic, and a tiny amount – like, less than half a teacup – actually went in. They had a sixth-form bar upstairs, so we went upstairs and had a couple of beers and started pissing ourselves laughing because we could see the silhouettes of everybody tucking in. Someone said, 'What are you two laughing about?' So we told him, and the next morning it was all over. The whole school knew. The worst thing about being expelled, though, was waiting for my father to come down and pick me up in the car. But my parents were silent on the subject, the same way they reacted when I nicked the Dinky toy out of the department store. They picked me up, didn't say anything about it, never mentioned it again. I did think, 'Bloody hell,' you know? 'Aren't they going to say anything?' But in actual fact, I went off and the next six months were really, really useful."

Returning home to Sheffield, he enrolled at a local comprehensive. "I loved it," he says. "It was brilliant. Everybody was, like, normal. There was no *Tom Brown's School Days*, and there were girls there, which freaked me out at first. Like, 'Fucking hell! I hope they talk to me!' Then, my first week or so, I remember these two kids at the back talking, going, 'What are we gonna do about the rehearsal tonight, then? The singer's quit. What are we gonna do?' I was, like, 'Christ! Shall I say I'm a singer?' because they'd only been hanging out in this guy's bedroom singing songs with an acoustic guitar. 'What should I do?' So I went up and said, 'I'll do the singing for you, if you like.' And they were, like, 'Oh, brilliant. Well, you're on, then.' So I went 'round, and it was actually a kid that I went to my old school with who was their drummer. It was in his dad's garage – drums, bass, two guitars. Very Wishbone Ash, because they'd learnt the whole of *Argus* note for note. So I started learning the songs, and they were, like, 'Fucking hell, you can really sing! Wow, we've got a singer!' So then I started thinking, 'I'll have to buy a microphone…'"

Bruce remembers buying his first microphone and "feeling like a dirty old man buying a porno magazine, because it was really strange. If anybody had asked me, 'Are you a singer, then?' I'd have gone, 'No, no, I'm not, no, no, definitely not!' and I'd have run out of the shop. I was so scared of looking foolish. I didn't want to do it unless I could nail every note like Ian Gillan. I didn't want to call myself a singer unless I could do that, and I didn't know if I could do that yet." He would soon find out.

"The first gig we ever did was at a place called the Broad Fall Tavern, in Sheffield, which still does gigs. They called themselves Paradox, and I said, 'That's a fucking crap name. Why don't you call yourself something big and mythical, like Styx.' And they went, 'That's a good name.' So we called ourselves Styx. We weren't aware that there was this big American band already called that. We were blissfully ignorant. But the band split up anyway, soon after, so that was that – except now I had a mic and an amp of my own. I thought, 'Well, I can always use them again somewhere else.'"

Leaving school at 18 with A-levels in English, History and Economics, at first he toyed with the idea of following his father into the army. He had already enlisted in the Territorial Army some months earlier, and his father in particular was very keen on the idea of his son having a proper career in the services.

"I didn't really know what I wanted to do," Bruce admits, "but I went home and I thought, 'Fuck it, I'll join the TA for six months.' I had a great time, but realised, in actual fact, that my fantasy that it was going to be like Rambo going *bang, bang, bang* was absolute crap, that there was just as many – if not, more – idiots in the army than anywhere else. Not necessarily the guys I was with, 'cause they were a great bunch of blokes. We'd go out into the woods and dig a bunch of holes, get fucking wet, get pissed on and then go back and get as drunk as skunks. I'd never seen men get that drunk and do such horrid things, and I'd certainly never seen so many loose women. I mean, I didn't do anything with them. I had no idea what to do! I remember this one woman trying to pull me and all I did all evening was play darts. I had no idea how to deal with it at all. But in the end I thought, 'This is really not a real career choice. This is like a bit of a fantasy, really.' It was a good way of escaping for a while, 'cause I didn't know what else I was gonna do. Like, 'I'm gonna be a rock 'n' roll singer? If that's not a fantasy, what is?'"

Instead, he applied for a place at university and found himself taking History at Queen Mary College in London's East End. "It was the first time I'd ever been down to London," he says. "My parents were, like, 'What are you gonna do when you get down there?' I'd told them that I was still gonna join the army, but that I wanted to get my degree first. That was what they wanted to hear, so that was my cover story. Then, when I got down there, I started immediately finding and playing in bands. I met this guy called Noddy White, who looked exactly like Noddy

Holder from Slade. He was from Southend, and he was a bit of a guitarist, bit of a bass player, bit of a keyboard player, bit of a songwriter, a bit of everything, you know? And he had loads of equipment – he had a PA, the lot. I was, like, 'Fuck me, man. Let's form a band!'"

The band was called Speed. "It had nothing to do with taking speed. We were a completely drug-free band. We just used to play everything ridiculously fast!" They would rehearse as often as Bruce could persuade Noddy to set up his gear.

"I got Noddy to give me a few guitar lessons and I just started writing stuff straight away," he says. "He showed me three chords and I'd write stuff just from those three chords. By now, punk was happening big time, and in the East End you were right in the middle of it. I got involved in the Entertainment Committee at college, and one day you'd be a roadie for The Jam and the next you'd be putting up the Stonehenge backdrop for Hawkwind, or whatever. I remember Ian Dury And The Blockheads played there and The Sex Pistols did some semi-secret shows there.

"Then we started playing a few gigs. We used to nick the college minibus, say we were borrowing it for a course outing and rip all the seats out, cram the gear in and go down to the Green Man pub in Plumstead. We got quite a nice little following going, in the end, and I got my first experience of what it was like to get up and sing in front of an audience. It was just one of those college things that don't last very long, but it was good for what it was."

But not quite good enough. Keen to expand his repertoire, when he spotted an ad in the *Melody Maker* – "Singer wanted to complete recording project" – Bruce, who had never been near a recording studio, replied immediately. Advised to send in a sample tape of his voice, he "wailed and wolfed and hollered and just made noises" onto a cassette and sent it in with a note that read, "By the way, if you think the singing's crap, there's some John Cleese stuff recorded on the other side you might find amusing."

"The tape came back and this guy said, 'We think you've got a really interesting voice. Come on into the studio.' So I went in and recorded this song called 'Dracula'. The track was for this obscure band called Shots, which was basically this bloke Phil Shots and his brother, Doug. God knows whatever became of it, but this guy, Doug, was freaking out, 'cause we multi-tracked the voices – doing, like, four-part harmonies – and he was, like, 'Are you sure you've never done this before in your life?' So we started talking and he asked me what music I liked, and of course I started saying, 'Ian Gillan, Ian Anderson, Arthur Brown,' and Doug goes, 'That's it! Fucking Arthur Brown, man! Sometimes your voice is a dead ringer for Arthur!' He said, 'We've got to form a band.' I was, like, 'Bloody hell,' you know? 'This guy's got a studio and he wants to form a band with me.' I was, like, 'Yes!'"

Bruce started gigging with Shots, "mainly pubs, but nobody was really interested", until one night, in a fit of pique, he semi-jokingly started lambasting the clientèle for not paying enough attention and got such a good response that he started doing it every night until it became a regular routine.

"We'd be playing in pubs to about five people and you'd be trying to do your stuff and no one was paying any attention," he says, "so I got into this thing where I used to stop the song halfway through and just start picking on these guys in the audience. I'd go, 'Oi, you! Yeah, you, you fat git! Everybody look at him. Is everybody looking at him? Fine. What's your name? Have you got a name?' Just taking the piss out of people. And suddenly everybody paid attention, 'cause they might be next! Then, before the guy had a chance to answer, we'd go right into the next song, only now everybody was listening. The first time I did it, afterwards the landlord of this pub was, like, 'Fucking great show, lads! See you next week!' So we started sort of building this bit into the show. And that was when I first started to get the hang of not just being a singer but being a frontman, too. I found out later that a lot of people can sing, but ask them to get up onstage and handle a crowd and they can't. They wouldn't know how. So this was important stuff I was starting to suss out about the job."

Bruce's first real break, however, came the night that the members of Samson paid an unexpected visit to a Shots gig, in Maidstone in 1978. Formed around the songs of Sidcup-born guitarist Paul Samson, the band had already released one album, *Survivors*, on the independent Lazer label and attracted a great deal of interest in the press, singled out with Iron Maiden, Saxon and Angel Witch as one of the leading lights of the then-burgeoning NWOBHM. Their chief claim to fame, however, was the fact that their drummer, Thunderstick (real name Barry Purkis, the same

Kiss worshipper from Maiden's earliest days), always wore a leather S&M mask onstage.

"They saw us at the gig and we had a chat afterwards and they said, 'What are you into?' I said, 'Well, I sort of really like Purple and Sabbath and Tull, but I really want to do things with a bit of a weird edge to it,' because by then Shots was becoming almost a heavy-metal comedy act. The show had completely taken over the music. But Thunderstick was really into The Heavy Metal Kidz, and he was going, 'It was just like seeing the young [Kidz singer] Gary Holton up there, just having a go at people and taking the piss. It was great!' I was, like, 'OK, I can do that, but I think there's a bit more to it than that.' But Paul Samson gave me his number and basically said, 'Listen, we've got an album out, we've got a record deal, but we need a new singer and we'd like you to be it.' I was about two weeks away from doing my History finals and I said, 'Yes, I would love to be in the band, but can you give us a couple of weeks? I've got some exams to do and then I'm yours.'"

Actually, getting his degree had never seemed important, until he realised that he might not even get the chance to take his final exams unless he put his extra-curricular activities to one side, at least for a short time.

"I dossed around at university for two years," admits Bruce, "done absolutely fuck all work, got pissed, got laid and just generally had a pretty good time. And then they tried to throw me out for non-payment of rent, because I spent all my college grant cheque on buying a PA for the band. I used to hide when the rent inspectors came round. Also, I'd failed all of my second-year exams, so they had a pretty good case, really. But I was Ents Officer for the Student Union, and in those days it carried a bit of weight, so they relented, and in the end I did six long essays in the space of two weeks that normally people took six months to do and got great marks in all of them, and they just let me stay in. And then, the last six months before my degree, I thought, 'Fuck it. I've got this far. It seems a shame not to actually go into the library and open a book and find out a bit about what history's all about.'"

Cramming like mad in the last few weeks leading up to his finals, Bruce managed to secure a 2:2, "which is what everybody else got, anyway". However, going straight from his final exam to his first Samson rehearsal proved to be a contrast too stark even for the indefatigable Bruce. "In fact, the first rehearsals I went down to with Samson pretty much set the scene for my entire time in the band." He was about to enter what he now jokingly refers to as "my let's-do-drugs days. I'd never really been into drugs – I just used to drink a lot in those days – but I went down there and the bass player was doing lines of sulphate behind the amps, Paul was smoking loads of dope and the drummer had done a load of Mandies [heavy-duty prescription tranquillisers popular with musicians in the late '70s]. And I'd been to the pub, of course, straight after finishing my exams, so you can imagine the racket at that first rehearsal. Thunderstick fell off his drum stool, 'cause he was so Mandied out of his head, but fortunately there was a wall behind him, so we propped him up against that and he managed to carry on playing. I didn't have a clue what was going on, really. I just went with it. Thunderstick was obviously really into Kiss – I could see where he came from – and Paul was into Leslie West and Mountain and ZZ Top and I was, like, mad into Deep Purple, so it was quite a combo."

Not entirely sure of his bearings, he decided that the best policy was to "just jump in and make the best of it. When in Rome, and all that. I left my girlfriend, who I'd been with for three years at university. I told her I was gonna turn into a complete arsehole. I thought it was what I was gonna have to do, frankly, so I could just communicate with the guys in the band, because it was not at all what I expected. In my naïvety, I thought people who were in rock 'n' roll bands were great artists, and it was a huge shock to the system to realise that they weren't, that they didn't even aspire to be, really. Some of them did, maybe, but some of them, like Samson, were very frightened of the idea. Some of them just wanted to have a good drink, a good shag and take some drugs, and I found that really, really difficult to relate to. I thought, 'I've got to find out if I'm gonna work with these guys and we're gonna make music.' And as soon as I sort of accepted that, I thought, 'Right, I'd better go down and find out what all this drug-taking and shagging's all about, then.'"

But Bruce was never into the hard stuff. When it came to illegal highs, marijuana was his biggest personal vice. "I did smoke a bit already," he admits. "Somebody turned me onto smoking a bit of dope at college, and I thought, 'Oh, that's quite strange.' I quite enjoyed it, you know? And then, in Samson, it was more of a habit. I mean, Paul used to light one up all day every day, and I discovered quickly that, if you were straight, you couldn't actually communicate with anybody. It was impossible. So I just thought, 'Oh, you'd better smoke a joint. Otherwise you won't be able to write anything.' And that's pretty much how it went. I more or less resigned myself to it. Like, I'm gonna turn into a person that I'm basically not for two or three years, you know? Because I really wanted to be a singer, and I thought it was just part of the price that had to be paid. To be honest, every single thing I ever did at that time I believed it was just another step towards my goal of just wanting to be a singer in a rock 'n' roll band. I think you have to have that level of belief. Or I do, anyway."

Bruce had to put up with a lot to get his shot at the big time. He even had to put up with a silly name, and he became known throughout his tenure in Samson as Bruce Bruce, a dreadful echo of an old Monty Python joke. "Their management were forever writing me dud cheques deliberately to take the piss," he explains wearily, "and one of their little jokes was making the cheque payable to Bruce Bruce, as in the Monty Python sketch. And it just stuck. I mean, I wasn't entirely happy with it, but it was, like, 'Oh well, OK. It's a sort of stage name, isn't it?'" Writing most of the songs with Paul, Bruce Bruce would make two albums with Samson: *Head On*, released in 1980 on the Gem label, and *Shock Tactics*, released on RCA after Gem went bust, in 1981. Neither album really showcases Bruce's vocal talent in the way subsequent Iron Maiden albums would, but by early-'80s standards they were both still good, solid rock albums. Neither were big chart hits, but then they weren't major-label releases, like Maiden's had been. Samson, it seemed, had the talent but not, perhaps, the luck.

"I think the *Head On* album could have been really good," says Bruce. "I just wish to God we'd had a decent producer, 'cause there were some great songs on there. And actually, funnily enough, speaking to Rod Smallwood about it later, Rod sort of admitted that the only band that he thought had any chance of doing anything to rival Maiden was Samson. He as good as admitted that he deliberately set out to make sure Maiden beat Samson to the punch. Not because of that, specifically, but because, before I joined the band, Samson had duffed over Maiden at some soundcheck or something and Rod had never forgiven them for it, which I can believe, because there were certainly a few egos flying around in those days."

Lumped in with the NWOBHM, it wasn't long before Bruce and Samson found themselves sharing the bill with fellow NWOBHM stars like Praying Mantis, Angel Witch and, inevitably, Iron Maiden.

"There was this thing called the Crusade For Heavy Metal, which Maiden was part of, and it was basically a travelling circus of bands which played the Music Machine, in Camden, every week," says Bruce. "Samson's management always claimed that the idea was theirs, so Samson were always there on the bill somewhere, and Saxon were on it and Angel Witch – all the bands that were part of that whole EMI *Metal For Muthas* compilation. So, you know, for better or for worse, it existed, and that was really my first experience of this idea that there was some sort of…er…movement. Up till then, I was unaware of it; but I first saw Maiden… I think it was at the Music Machine, in about 1980. We were actually headlining over them, but they showed up with all the tribe from the Ruskin Arms and the place was packed out and people were going mental for them. And I remember standing at the back, watching them, just taking in this whole vibe surrounding the gig, and I went, 'This is Purple!' That was the first thing that came into my head, that this was just pure Deep Purple. There was Davey Murray, obviously influenced by Ritchie Blackmore – he's got the Strat, the long, long hair – and the drummer sounds like Ian Paice. I mean, a dead ringer! I didn't notice the bass player that first time, but I looked at the singer, Paul, and I thought, 'Hmmm, I don't understand why he's there…'

"But I was watching, and they were good, really fucking good, and at that moment, I remember thinking, 'I wanna fucking sing for that band. In fact, I'm *going* to sing for that band! I *know* I'm going to sing for that band!' And it wasn't even a thing of trying to worm my way into it. I just thought it was inevitable. I just remember thinking what I could do with that band, 'cause I'd always been a huge fan of Purple and I just saw Maiden as another Deep Purple – not identical, musically, but maybe the same shiver up the spine. I just thought, 'This is really me. Not Samson.'

"Paul himself was kind of dismissive of them. I think a bit of it was sour grapes, a bit of it was genuine. He just didn't like it, couldn't relate to it at all. But I remember we had this kind of groupie we used to call Flannel Tits, and I think she was getting 'round the Maiden guys, too – she did a trick involving rubbing her tits on the end of your knob – and I remember she showed up once with a tape of a Maiden gig recorded straight off the mixing desk and she put it on and I went, 'Bloody hell, this is mad!' It made Samson sound like a joke by comparison. Our time-keeping was never great, but Maiden kept it really, really tight."

Generally, it was "the direction they were going for", more than a lot of the actual material itself, that Bruce says he found most exciting about Iron Maiden. He claims that he "didn't really listen to the albums a lot. It was just seeing and hearing them play live that did it for me. I mean, obviously I heard the albums, and some of it sounded cool, like 'Prodigal Son' and 'Remember Tomorrow'." As for his predecessor in the band, "Paul always sounded great on the record," says Bruce, "but when it came to the real thing, when the band were really slashing away onstage, he really had to get on top of it, dominate it, and I think that's when it didn't sort of happen."

His next run-in with the band that would one day make him famous was nearly a year later, when Samson were recording *Shock Tactics* in an adjacent studio to the one in which Maiden were then recording *Killers*. "There was a bar at Morgan Studios where we would all meet up," he says. "Martin Birch was doing their album and Martin was my hero. He'd done virtually all my favourite records, and just to lay eyes on him, it was, like, 'Oh my god!' And of course Clive Burr was there, too, who we knew 'cause he used to be in Samson before I joined, and Clive would pop 'round to our neck of the woods and we would go over and see him, too. So, anyway, I was in there one night, and they had just finished doing the mix, and Clive said, 'Come and have a listen,' and then he just turned the speakers up to as loud as they would possibly go and then just stood at the back of the room having a beer. I remember listening to this thing – I think it was 'Murders In The Rue Morgue' – and I went, 'Wow! It sounds amazing!' And it did. I'd heard the first Maiden album, and I thought it sounded like crap. And then, when I heard *Killers*, I was, like, 'This is more like it. This is really gonna do it for them.' And of course *Killers* was the one that the press was having a major grump about over here, but it was the one that everybody else in the world was, like, 'Hold on, this is the business!'"

Ironically, Samson had originally been booked to support Maiden on some of the dates on the European leg of their 1981 world tour that would precipitate the band's decision to fire Paul. "In the Killers tour programmes there was even an advert for *Shock Tactics* in the back," Bruce recalls, "but we pulled out at the last minute because the record company wouldn't pay the tour support, or whatever. I'm still not sure whether that was the reason, but whatever the reason was it was pulled at the last minute, and that was that. So Samson with me in it never actually played a gig outside the United Kingdom, ever."

It was the beginning of the end for Bruce Bruce and Samson. Gem, their record label, went out of business and *Shock Tactics* was turned over to RCA, "who did not give a shit about this unknown band from England. As far as they were concerned, it was, like, 'We'll just shove it out and who cares?'" Disillusioned with the way their seemingly inept management team had handled things, Samson fired them and suddenly found themselves in an even worse predicament. "We went about it the wrong way," explains Bruce, "probably because we were all completely stoned at the time." Slapped with an injunction which meant that gradually all of their equipment was reclaimed as they were actually touring, they couldn't even legally accept payment for their shows. "It was the end of the road, quite literally," says Bruce, "but we just refused to accept it."

Offered the chance to try and redeem their flagging public profile with a spot halfway up the bill of that year's Reading Festival, "we grabbed the chance with both hands and hoped for the best. It was the second time we'd done Reading and we went down really well. It got good reviews and everything. There's actually a live album [*Live At Reading, '81*] of that one gig, and we sound pretty good, actually. But by that point, the energy was very strange in the band. Paul was really wanting to go off and get more and more into his own thing, you know, the ZZ Top thing, which is what he did immediately after I left. He had a new manager by then, who was talking to A&M about getting a new deal for the band. We actually got as far as having publicity shots done up for A&M, but by then I'd already made my mind up that I was leaving."

What persuaded him was the presence at the Reading show of a certain large Yorkshireman. "Paul was still in the band, but I think everybody was aware that there was a problem," says Bruce, "and when I came offstage at Reading that day everybody knew that something was up. Funnily enough, there were these rumours that I was gonna join

Rainbow. I got this strange phone call once in the middle of the bloody night from Ritchie's roadie or somebody saying, 'Are you available?' I'm, like, 'Of course I'm available. Ritchie's my favourite fucking guitarist!' But I never heard any more about it. The first thing I heard about Maiden was that Rod and Steve were wandering around backstage at Reading. I found out they'd flown in especially from the south of France that day just to watch Samson. Of course, I didn't know what the background was, that Rod was still unsure. Apparently, Steve was, like, 'The guy's got a great voice,' or whatever, and Rod was, like, 'I don't care what kind of voice he's got. He's in Samson and they stitched us up.' But then Rod came and had a chat with me.

"Now, at Reading, there's this quadrangle of beer tents and stuff, you know, and right in the middle of it is a bloody great pole with arc lights and spotlights on it. We were the only two people in the whole place standing in the middle of the quadrangle, under the spotlights, with everybody at the Reading Festival staring at us, and I was looking at Rod, going, 'Do you really want to do this here?' But Rod was kind of oblivious, you know? It wasn't really much of a spiel. It wasn't like, 'We want you to do the job.' It was more like, 'We'd like to offer you the chance of an audition.' And I was, like, 'Oh, all right.' I remember being very self-confident at the time, though, and saying, 'But when I do it, I'll get the job, so let's talk about what's gonna happen when I get the job.' And Rod went, 'Oh. You'd better come back to the hotel with us.'"

"I'd never been much into Samson," says Steve Harris, "but I'd always thought their singer was good, and because we'd been having problems with Paul more or less from the start, I suppose I always had one eye open for singers. I just sort of had a sneaking feeling that Paul might let us down one day and we'd have to get someone else in. So I'd seen Bruce in Samson a couple of times and I thought, 'Yeah, the bloke's got a really good voice and he knows how to work a crowd.' I thought he sounded a bit like Ian Gillan, actually. Then, when the shit really hit the fan with Paul, he was one of the first people I thought of. Rod wasn't keen – he'd never forgiven Samson for stitching us up that time – but I didn't care. I just thought the geezer had a great voice. So I said, 'Stuff that. I want him!' And so we arranged to go to Reading to have a look and see if he was interested."

Bruce auditioned for the band at a rehearsal room in Hackney on the following day. "As soon as I walked in, I knew this was something entirely different from anything that I'd known up till then," he says. "They had proper, professional roadies; they had a proper monitor system; they had cars laid on. They had everything! I thought, 'Right, there'll be no smoking dope in the back of the tour bus any more, then.' As it happens, there was plenty of that, subsequently. But I mean, it was not the same sort of vibe at all as Samson or any other band I'd ever been in. I was, like, 'OK, well, this is now the big boys you're playing with, so you'll have to learn to play by big boys' rules,' and that was fine with me. I'd already bumped into Steve a couple of times. I'd had a few chats with him, but nothing that made any impact on me. I didn't think he was either the messiah that some people made him out to be or the ogre that other people said he was. I saw him as being a fairly personable sort of guy. He was very friendly, you know? But the whole thing that surrounded Maiden, that very intense, almost self-important vibe... I found it a bit stifling, I must admit. I thought, 'Is this really necessary?' But I guess it was, because you create that air around you, which is really important. It draws people like a magnet to you, fans and supporters in the biz. You get respect because you demand it. And that's what they had.

"So I started singing, and we did 'Prowler', 'Sanctuary', 'Running Free' and 'Remember Tomorrow'. Then we chucked in 'Murders In The Rue Morgue' and a few other things as well, but I think we just knew straight away. Everybody knew immediately, really. Then they wanted to put me in a studio as well, to see how I sounded in the studio, and Steve phoned up Rod and said, 'When do we have to go to Scandinavia? Can we get a studio this afternoon?' Then he turned to me and said, 'What do you feel about that?' I said, 'Fuck it. Let's go, mate. Whatever you want. Do it now, if you want.' So we got to the studio and I went in and sang on four tracks, and there was a bit of a confab, and I could see Rod in the corner going, 'Are you sure? Are you sure?' And everybody else was basically going, 'Oh, shut up,' you know? And that was it. We all went out and got roaring pissed and I was in Iron Maiden."

11 *Nicko*

News of Paul Di'Anno's "shock dismissal" from Iron Maiden when the band returned from the final leg of their first world tour, in October 1981, was broken in *Sounds*. A spokesperson from the EMI press office was quoted as saying that the decision had been made "on a totally amicable basis" and was due to "largely different attitudes towards the music and touring". Refusing to kick a man when he's down, the band chose not to make public the real reasons behind Paul's demise. "We always say something like 'musical differences' whenever anyone leaves," Steve Harris explains, "but it's more for their protection than ours. It's enough that they're not in the band any more. There's no need to rub it in, you know?" However, these admirable sentiments didn't deter *Sounds* from speculating that there were other, "more explicitly rock 'n' roll factors involved".

Wisely, Maiden didn't allow their fans time to dwell on this possible catastrophe. Determined to show that this was just a temporary setback, they hurriedly announced their first British performance with their new singer, Bruce Dickinson, who would make his UK debut with the band at the Rainbow, in London, on 15 November. In order to give Bruce a chance to acclimatise to the dizzy new heights that he was ascending, the band played five shows in Italy in the last week of October: Bologna, Rome, Florence, Udine and Milan. If the Italian fans had been perturbed by the loss of Paul, they didn't show it. Tickets for all five shows were sold out well in advance and audience reaction verged on the ecstatic each night.

For his part, Bruce says that he was surprised at how easily he seemed to fit in with his new bandmates. "I felt at home straight away," he recalls. "It just felt like one big family that I'd suddenly become a part of." The rest of the band were equally pleased with the choice that they'd made. Where Paul remained an unknown quantity, both onstage and off, Bruce could be relied on to give his best performance night after night. As Adrian Smith observed, "If he had nerves, he certainly didn't show it. He just came onstage and sang like he'd been in the band since day one."

The ultimate test, however, came with the band's appearance two weeks later at the Rainbow. Their first gig on home turf since Paul had been ousted from the band, even Bruce admits to feeling a tad nervous for that one. "I wasn't worried about doing the job," he says. "I felt I'd proved in Italy that I had that side of things already pretty much sorted. It was just more a question of whether their fans would actually accept me. It wasn't my fault that Paul wasn't in the band any more, but it was inevitable that any ill feeling in the crowd was almost certainly going to be directed at me."

He needn't have worried. Yes, there were some small sections of the otherwise wholly partisan crowd at the Rainbow that night who couldn't resist the temptation at the start to yell, "Bring back Paul!" but the catcalls gradually died as it became clear that Bruce was no mere Di'Anno substitute. He not only quite clearly had a better, stronger voice than his predecessor (no "you do the high notes and I'll do the low notes" to the audience with Bruce), but he commanded attention from his place on the stage in a way that Di'Anno's moody, aggro-merchant act never did.

The audience had been used to seeing Steve Harris whirl around the stage, carrying his bass like a machine-gun, strafing the audience with musical gunfire, his right foot up on the monitors, looking for all the world as though he were about to leap into the jungle of faces crowded around the front. Now, in Bruce, there was a competing athletic presence, as he literally galloped over every inch of the stage, climbing up the rigging one moment, racing to the lip of the stage the next. If there'd been a chandelier in evidence, you felt sure that Bruce would have been swinging from it. It was a radiantly charged, swashbuckling performance that banished any lingering doubts about the band's future. "He really knew how to work an audience," reflects Dave Murray, "and he gave it his all in a way Paul never did. Paul was great when he was actually singing, but he was a bit lost onstage, maybe, the rest of the time. Bruce just didn't stop moving around and giving it some, whether he was singing or not."

As a result, the Rainbow show was a triumph, the perfect rebuke to the critics who had gleefully jumped on the news of Di'Anno's departure as more proof that the band's days as a force to be reckoned with were numbered. As events would amply demonstrate, they couldn't have been more wrong, and the band ended the year in fine style by hosting a Christmas charity bash at the Ruskin Arms. Their first appearance for nearly two years in the tiny pub in which they had built the foundations of their current success, the gig was billed as an appearance by Ghengis Khan, which of course fooled no one, and the pub was spilling over with people hours before the band actually arrived. With all proceeds going to London's Barnardo's Children's Hospital, the Ruskin gig also served the purpose of allowing Davey to receive his first decent onstage pie-ing.

It's a tradition in the Maiden camp to deliver a good on-stage pie-ing to any member whose birthday happens to fall on the night of a gig, and Davey, being born on 23 December, had always managed to sneak out of it until then. Not any more, though. It was a deliciously low-key but heartfelt way to bid adieu to a year of some almighty ups and downs, twelve months in which they'd lost and gained both a singer and a guitarist; completed (just about) their first world tour, including their first trip to America; seen their second album demolished in the UK press yet go on to become a Top 20 hit in Britain, Canada, France, Germany, Japan, Sweden and Belgium; and in the process been awarded gold records for outstanding sales in Britain, Canada, Japan and France. The subtext was easy to read: now, with Bruce in the band, the future of Iron Maiden had never looked so assured.

Malcolm Dome: "Most people thought that Paul Di'Anno was a great frontman, and when he was fired it was assumed that Maiden was now in hiatus. Then Bruce came in and everything just immediately turned around. He was the perfect final piece of the jigsaw that would turn them into a huge international band. Had Paul stayed or Bruce not arrived, I think they would really have struggled to make it beyond the mid '80s. They needed something, and Bruce was that something. But you've got to give credit to Steve and Rod for even knowing that and making the right choice at that time. It would have been easy to fuck it up, like most of the NWOBHM bands eventually did, in one way or another, but Maiden didn't. They stuck at it until they got it right, and then there was no stopping them."

"I didn't have any plans about what I would do once I got onstage with them," Bruce admits. "I just let it all happen pretty spontaneously. The only thing I was sure of was that I wasn't going to try and be a Paul Di'Anno clone – not vocally, not visually, nor in any other way. The first time I spoke to Rod about the job, at Reading, I'd said, 'Look, I don't know what your views are on what I should do, but I have some pretty strong ideas on what I shouldn't do, and what I shouldn't do is what the guy before me was doing.' I said, 'If you want me to do that, then you should really get somebody else right now, because it's not even worth talking about it.' That Cockney-sparrow stuff Paul did, it just wasn't me. I didn't even think it was particularly interesting. Good when they played in Britain, perhaps, where they understood what he's on about, but a bit of a waste of time anywhere else in the world. I just thought the band was bigger than that."

"Bruce was one of the only guys who could have done it, really," asserts Adrian Smith. "He had the vocal range and he had the experience. As far as we were concerned, he was a proven talent who could definitely tackle the job. But we didn't really know for sure until we did those first shows with him in Italy and at the Rainbow, which were for us all to get comfortable with each other before we went into the studio. That was the final proof that we had done the right thing. Vocally, he fitted in perfectly, but personality-wise he was completely different to Paul. Not so Jack the lad and a bit more cosmopolitan, if you know what I mean. Like, whatever country we played in, Bruce would always try and talk to the audience in their own language, even just a little bit, just to let them know we were putting a bit of effort in, and the crowd loved it. It made a bit of a change to Paul's usual 'Awright! 'Ow are ya?' approach. After that, going in to make an album wasn't quite so worrying. In fact, it made us more desperate to get in there and show what we could do now."

But before they could begin recording the first Maiden album of the new Bruce Dickinson era, first they would need to write some new songs. Having used up the backlog of good material that they'd accumulated from their earliest days, for the first time Maiden started working on an album completely from scratch. In effect, they had three months to complete the task, working steadily on ideas together at the same rehearsal studios in Clapton in which Bruce had been auditioned, Hollywood Studios. It was an unusually lengthy period for the band to be off the road in those hectic, make-or-break days. But then, these were unusual circumstances.

"It was only by accident that we actually got so much time to write together," says Bruce, "because I was the new guy and everything was all thrown up in the air. But it was just as well, because the band didn't really

have any new songs ready yet. They'd used up all the good stuff they'd had
and they'd been on the road ever since. So it was quite good, in that way,
because I wasn't going to be asked to sing words that had already been
written by Paul or songs Steve had written with him in mind. It was all
fresh to that line-up, which is one of the reasons it's such a great album, I
think. We had time to think about the songs first."

They decided to call the album *Number Of The Beast*, after one of the
most completely realised Steve Harris compositions yet, the misleadingly
tongue-in-cheek 'Number Of The Beast', and for many long-time
observers this is where Maiden really began to come into their own as
recording artists. They had long been recognised as a live band of
startling power and yet, despite the plaudits that the first album had
received and the increased sales of the second, doubts persisted over
whether the band would have the creative ingenuity to spread their
appeal over more than a couple of albums.

Number Of The Beast scorched away those doubts like spittle off a
hot stove. Comprising eight mostly brilliant tracks, the obvious difference
is of course in the vocal department. Bruce's much greater vocal range
offered new options to both Steve as a songwriter and Martin Birch as a
producer, and he would become the conduit through which Maiden
would now be able to record some of its most ambitious and complex
material. Bruce's cod-operatic style – all manic vibrato topped off with
swooping, note-perfect flourishes – sounded as though it was practically
built in the laboratory for Steve's music. His great gift was to be able to
turn the most convoluted lyric into something sexy, something that you
could hum. (How would you approach the first line on the album,
"Longboats have been sighted, the evidence of war has begun/Many
Nordic fighting men, their swords and shields all gleam in the sun"?)

"Although he was excellent on the albums he did for them, and was
ideal for the time, I could always see Maiden going beyond what Paul was
capable of," says Birch. "From my point of view, I simply didn't think he
was capable of handling lead vocals on some of the quite complicated
directions I knew Steve wanted to explore. Bruce's was a voice that I could
work with much easier. He had a much bigger range, and he could carry
melodies, where Paul couldn't at all. So, when Bruce joined, it opened up
the possibilities for the new album tremendously. Paul just couldn't have

done it like Bruce, and for that reason *Number Of The Beast* was the turning point for Iron Maiden, as far as I was concerned. It was the album when I realised they would be what I hoped they would be. I remember saying to them, when it was finished, 'You know, this is going to be a big, big album. This is going to transform your career.' It just had all the magical ingredients: feel, ideas, energy, execution. And I think the response I got was, 'Oh, really?' I was, like, 'Yeah, really!' I mean, in their heart of hearts, I'm sure they were hoping, but I knew. As we were recording it, I could just feel it. I remember we spent ages getting the vocal intro to the title track right. We did it over and over and over till Bruce said, 'My head is splitting! Can't we move on and do something else and come back to this?' But I wouldn't let him do anything else until he'd got it perfect. He saw what I meant afterwards, but you could see he was struggling to begin with. But that's the thing about Bruce. He's a trier."

As for the material itself, if anything they had benefited from not having any left-overs from their past to fall back on. As a result, there is a new maturity to the songs, new rhythmic and melodic depths undetectable in earlier crowd-pleasin' fare like 'Charlotte The Harlot' or even 'Running Free'. With new Harris-penned mini epics like 'Hallowed Be Thy Name' (the dying note of a condemned man) and the track from which the album takes its title, 'Number Of The Beast' (inspired by the film *Omen II*), Maiden had entered new creative territory. They were starting to take risks, and it was starting to pay off.

Steve, who always preferred to write alone, came in with 'Run To The Hills', 'Invaders', 'Children Of The Damned', 'Number Of The Beast' and 'Hallowed Be Thy Name'. Bruce's recent addition to Maiden had also encouraged Adrian to become more involved in the songwriting process, and of the three remaining tracks, 'Gangland' was written by Adrian, with some help from Clive; 'The Prisoner' was by Steve and Adrian; and '22 Acacia Avenue', as we learned earlier, was an old take-no-prisoners belter from Adrian's Evil Ways days, resurrected here with help from Steve as the latest instalment in the chequered career of the band's beloved Charlotte. Bruce, who would contribute some of Maiden's most memorable material on subsequent albums, was denied an opportunity to write for the album, as he was still embroiled in the legal difficulties of which he had unwittingly become a part in the last, dying days of Samson.

"It wasn't until the next album that me and Bruce started gravitating towards each other as songwriters," explains Adrian. "Steve seemed to prefer writing on his own. He would come in with his songs already worked out right down to where each guitar break would be and even who would do the break. He knew how the vocals should go and had a real vision of exactly what he wanted the whole thing to sound like, whereas Bruce and I started hanging out and writing whatever took our fancy. Bruce has always had a lot of energy and enthusiasm for new ideas, you know, and so we teamed up. But it wasn't until after the *Number Of The Beast* rehearsals that we really hit it off."

For Adrian, "*Number Of The Beast* was definitely the best Maiden album, up to that point. The songs were all there and there was a much fatter sound." Steve Harris, however, isn't so sure: "I loved *Number Of The Beast*, but I didn't think it was our best album at the time, and I still don't. There's a couple of tracks on it which I think are not quite so good, and one of them is one of the ones I wrote!" The two tracks Steve is referring to are Adrian's Clive-assisted stomper, 'Gangland', and 'Invaders', which Steve wrote himself. "'Gangland' was, like, Clive's first attempt at songwriting," he explains, "and I should have just put my foot down and said, 'Look, this is a B-side,' because it should have been, really." Steve says that he would have preferred to see 'Gangland' replaced by a track that he and Davey had written (also with help from Clive) called 'Total Eclipse', which was used instead as the B-side of the first single from the album, 'Run To The Hills'.

"What happened was that we needed a single quickly, because we had a new singer and we had a British tour booked and ready to go, and it didn't look like the album was gonna be ready in time for it, so we badly needed a single out to try and cover all those bases," says Steve. "We just chose the wrong track as the B-side. I think if 'Total Eclipse' had been on the album instead of 'Gangland', it would have been far better. Also, I think 'Invaders' maybe could have been replaced with something a bit better, only we didn't have anything else to replace it with at the time. We had just enough time to do what we did, and that was it."

Unfortunately, as Bruce says, "What we gained on the swings we lost on the roundabouts, and when it actually came to the recording it was all done in one mad, unholy rush." In fact, because of the time it had taken to write all the new material, the album was recorded and mixed at Battery

Studios in just five weeks, including a break after the first week to record and mix 'Run To The Hills' and 'Total Eclipse', so that they could get a single out quickly, before returning to complete the rest of the recording as quickly as they could.

"We had to pick the single before we recorded anything, because of the schedule," he continues. "We were, like, 'Oh, fucking hell! We haven't recorded any of the songs yet. How do we know which one will be a good single?' I mean, they were all such killer songs on *Number Of The Beast*, we could easily have picked the wrong track completely. But the schedule said we had to pick a single, and so we asked Martin what he thought and he said 'Run To The Hills'. So, thanks to Martin's prize-winning ears, that's what we did, and it turned out to be exactly the right choice."

It did indeed. 'Run To The Hills' spiralled into the UK charts at Number Seven when it was released in February, Maiden's first Top Ten single in the UK. A new video was hurriedly pieced together by director David Mallet from live footage interspersed with comic extracts from old Buster Keaton movies (although Buster himself didn't appear, for copyright reasons), which *Top Of The Pops* showed in full, as did the newly emergent MTV, a bonus which would help attract new fans to the band all over America. And of course there was a tantalisingly tacky new Eddie sleeve to go with it, showing our abominable hero caught this time atop a hill (geddit?), locked in hand-to-hand combat with Beelzebub himself.

Back in the foothills of the studio, with the next British tour due to begin on 25 February, Martin Birch battled against the clock to complete the mix of the album in time for its release. "Rod would be outside the door of the studio with the sleeve and the label waiting to slap it on the plastic, virtually," Martin jokes now. However, in his rush to beat the clock, he nearly scuppered the whole album. "We rushed the album a little bit too much," he says. "I remember I was still in the cutting room when Rod booked a party for some of the EMI people to listen to it. I'd been up all night mixing, so it was hardly ideal, but I managed to do a pretty good mix for the track itself, 'Number Of The Beast', and 'Run To The Hills' we'd done already, but with the rest I simply had to rush and do the best I could. Then, at the party, when they played the album back, Steve came up to me afterwards and said he thought some of the mixes didn't really stand up to the mix on 'Number...' and asked me why that was. And I just told him,

'I'm sorry, but I just didn't have enough time.' So, of course, Steve was terribly unhappy about that and went off and had a big pow-wow with Rod. He just put his foot down, quite rightly, and insisted that I be given some more time to complete the mixes properly, which is what we did. We took the tapes back into the studio and mixed the rest of the album again. It was a complete last-minute thing, but if Steve hadn't stood up for it against the record company we wouldn't have even got that. We remixed, and this time I took my time. We used to ban Rod from the studio after that. 'Can I come in?' 'No!' We even put a sign on the door: 'No northern managers welcome.'"

As Martin suggests, amidst the tension and fury to get it right and finish it on time, the recording of *Number Of The Beast*, like any Maiden album, also had its lighter moments, none more memorable than the evening Rod sat down to phone actor Patrick McGoohan and ask for his permission to use a recording of his voice on the album. Taking its title from the name of the cult '60s TV series, the band had come up with the idea of prefacing 'The Prisoner' with McGoohan (who played the central character, known simply as Number Six) uttering his famous catchphrase from the show: "I am not a number, I am a free man!" DJ Tommy Vance had helped out by lending them an original recording of the quote from the show, but they still needed McGoohan's permission before they could go ahead.

Steve recalls how, for once, their unflappable manager looked almost star-struck as he nervously dialled the phone. "Oh, bloody 'ell," Rod moaned later. "It's all right dealing with these arsehole rock stars, but he's a real *bona fide* superstar actor. I was fucking terrified!" The rest of the band watched and laughed as Rod hesitantly began explaining the details to the actor, who was speaking from his home in Los Angeles. "What was the band's name again?" he asked. "Iron Maiden," Rod replied. "A rock band, you say," McGoohan mused. "Do it!" he snapped in the most imperious manner of his TV character and hung up the phone. So they did.

Number Of The Beast was eventually released in Britain on 22 March 1982, two days after their UK tour ended at the Hammersmith Odeon. But that small hiccup didn't prevent it from shooting straight into the album charts at Number One. The day that they received the news, the band were driving over the Swiss mountains on their way to Paris, but they didn't have time to celebrate when they heard the news, as the tour bus had broken down and all five of them were outside in the snow, pushing the bus. The tour manager, Tony Wiggins, looked on in astonishment: "Here we had five young guys whose album had just shot to the top of the charts in England pushing the coach to get it started, and no one thought twice about it. There were no moodies, no star trips. Then they got back on and we drove off as if nothing had happened."

To prove it was no fluke, their first-ever UK Number One stayed there for a second week as well. Even more impressively, the album was a Top Ten hit almost everywhere else in the world, selling well over a million copies worldwide in the first few months and going on to sell more than six million. In America, where the title of the album had caused a storm of protest from the emerging so-called "moral majority", a right-wing American political pressure group ludicrously accused Maiden of being Devil worshippers and of "trying to pervert our kids". As Steve says, "It was mad. They completely got the wrong end of the stick. They obviously hadn't read the lyrics. They just wanted to believe all that rubbish about us being Satanists." Nevertheless, the resulting publicity kept the band's name in the news in every town that they visited that year, as kids everywhere were desperate to check out for themselves this band that was putting the fear of God into their parents. Could they really be as good as all that?

They could. The next chapter provides a fuller picture of day-to-day life on the road with Maiden during this period, but suffice it to say that the Number Of The Beast world tour was Rod's and the band's most ambitious and successful yet, comprising 180 shows in 18 countries stretched over ten utterly action-packed months. This tour established a pattern that they would continue to follow and expand on throughout the rest of the decade as each album sold more and each world tour grew bigger, until Maiden were acknowledged as the biggest and most influential heavy-metal band in the world.

"1982 was definitely our year," remembers Bruce. "The band obviously built itself a huge base before I got there, but the *Number Of The Beast* album took it much further." Even the *NME* – the UK's self-styled weekly paragon of indie virtue and sworn enemy of anything with the word "metal" appended to it – put Maiden on their cover in 1982. More precisely, they put a snarling Eddie on the cover in April, when the magazine sent *überscribe* Paul Morley to interview them. Anticipating Morley's predictable cynicism, Rod had insisted that the band would only be interviewed if the magazine agreed to run it in strict question-and-answer format, thus avoiding the possibility of being quoted out of context or, as Rod put it, "getting stitched up". Reluctantly, the *NME* agreed, and the resulting piece was amusingly balanced between Morley's dour pronouncements on the band's "moral and intellectual complacency" and Bruce and Steve's responses, which were far more intelligent than he'd expected. "He was obviously really nervous," remembers Bruce, "because he got completely pissed and tried to steal a bottle of scotch."

With fame and critical favour came success on a scale previously unknown to the band. They headlined everywhere they went, except America, and even there they were now able to count on a fanbase nearing the million mark. *Number Of The Beast* had been the first Maiden album to go gold in the US (ie to register sales of at least 500,000), and for the first time in their lives the band were making money. Real money. Bruce Dickinson recalls how, when he joined the band at the end of 1981, "I was on about £100 a week, to begin with, which was just enough to get me out of this squat I was sleeping on the floor in and into a small flat with my girlfriend." But when they returned from the last leg of the Number Of The Beast world tour in Japan, just twelve months later, Bruce and the others would do so as extremely wealthy young men. "I remember we came home from that tour with a big bonus each," recalls Dave Murray. "It wasn't like we were millionaires, but we all had money, suddenly. Somewhere in the six-figure bracket, I suppose. More than we knew what to do with, really, put it that way."

"We'd been used to having nothing for so long, it didn't seem real at first," says Adrian Smith. "But we realised things were getting bigger in America when we were told we were selling more T-shirts than the bands we were supporting. People were getting into Eddie, and they were snapping up anything that had his mug on it, basically. It was great because, no matter who you are, whether you're The Rolling Stones or whoever, no one makes any money out of touring. You're lucky if you break even. Selling good quantities of merchandise, though, enabled the band to stay on the road and keep going for that bit longer than it would have been able to otherwise, because of the extra money."

This cash boost came when EMI agreed to renegotiate Maiden's deal with them. By then, Rod had been joined by his old Cambridge partner, Andy Taylor, and with the sizeable advance they would receive this time from EMI the two men set about putting the band's future on a secure, long-term footing. No more would they be reliant on dipping into their pipeline royalties for money to keep the band afloat. As Andy says, "From that point on, the band's never been in debt to anybody."

"Andy came in around the time of *Number Of The Beast*," says Rod, "because we were starting to do well but it was getting bigger very quickly and I needed someone like Andy to handle the business side more and more. In a rock band, your first problem is, how do we make some money? Then, when you've made it, your next problem is, what do we do with it, now that we've got it? Up until then, I did everything on my own. It was just me. Then Keith Wilfort came in to look after the fan club in about 1980, and Keith was always happy to answer the phones and help out as best he could. But after *Number Of The Beast*, it just wasn't enough any more, especially as I was always on the road with the band. I'd always planned to bring Andy in when it got to this stage, anyway, so that's what I did. Up until then, everything had to be ploughed back into the band. Now that changed."

"Maiden were never, to my knowledge, more than a £100,000 in the red to EMI at any time, until we renegotiated," says Andy, "when they went up to, you know, a very large figure, which cleared everything out and allowed them all to buy a house. Before that, I think they'd all been on about £100 a week. But now we had some money, the important thing was to look after it. We made a pledge to the band, where we guaranteed them that no one was ever gonna knock on their door again asking for a bill to be paid. We said, 'You'll never be on credit again. You'll never have a tax problem. Whatever you get, it will be yours to keep, and you'll never have a chance of losing it.' And that's how we've carried on. Nowadays, it's a much bigger situation again, and if Maiden was to end tomorrow, none of them would have to work again. But that's all because of all the careful planning Rod and I put into their money right from the word go. We like a laugh, but we don't fuck around."

For the first time in their lives, the five members of Iron Maiden – all from poor or deprived working-class families – enjoyed the kind of financial security that their parents couldn't have dreamed possible for them. As Andy says, each member of the band was encouraged to put their new-found wealth into property, which – with the exception of the notably indolent Adrian and Clive, who had very different reasons for wanting to hold onto their cash – they all did as soon as they returned from touring that year.

"I can't really remember what I did with the money we got after the Beast tour," says Adrian. "I was always accused of being tight, 'cause I never used to spend it. As long as I had enough money for a drink and some cigarettes, I just never bothered much. I did rent a nice flat in Fulham, which is one of the nicer parts of London, and I remember going out for a lot of nice meals, but I had no financial plan or anything. I didn't buy a car or a house. I just left it there. We were working away from home most of the time, anyway, so management just took care of everything."

One thing that their management could not control completely, however, was the personal lives of the band members, and once again the only thing that threatened the continued prosperity of Iron Maiden was the band themselves. Startlingly, Steve reveals that his main concern, as they set out on the groundbreaking Beast world tour, was whether Bruce was going to be all right.

"It was weird, and at first I thought I was imagining it, but there were nights onstage during the early part of that tour when Bruce used to, like, try and jostle me onstage. It was all done in fun, only you could tell it was a bit more than that, sometimes. It was, like, an ego thing, and it did make me wonder if he was right for the band. I don't know if he thought he had to sort of stamp out his territory, or whatever, but he didn't need to. If anything, we were pushing him to be more of a frontman than Paul had been, you know? We wanted him out there at the front. But whatever the reason, I don't think he really felt part of it for the first few months or so. I think things only really settled down after we did the next album and he started to write with us."

But if the band would have to endure a bedding-down period with their new singer, there was a much more serious problem looming. This time it was with Clive Burr.

"Clive was a great drummer," says Adrian, "an Ian Paice-type drummer, steady and solid and with a nice feel to everything. But Clive's drumming style wasn't the problem; it was keeping it together for the rest of us when he was having an off night, which he was having more and more as time went by, particularly on that last American tour together."

As Adrian says, touring America can be "too good to be true for some people". With its open-all-night clubs and its 24-hours-a-day, seven-days-a-week vibe – especially when compared to those pre-satellite days in Britain, when there were only three TV channels and Sunday closing – the allure of touring America was still bound up in their minds with one long party. As Steve points out, "America is not exactly the easiest place in the world to resist temptation, particularly if you're in a touring rock band and your album's anywhere in the charts."

In truth, as we will discover in the next chapter, nobody in Maiden – with the exception of Steve – was able to resist going for it on that American tour in 1982. The band were in the position where they were starting to attract all the attention but were still actually working as a support band. Obliged merely to turn in one tight, 45-minute-long set each night, they found themselves with plenty of time on their hands to kill and plenty of new American friends they never knew they had before who were willing to show them how to do it. Unfortunately, Clive – who was certainly not the worst offender – was the only one who allowed it to affect his gig and, as Paul Di'Anno had discovered to his cost, this was a cardinal sin that Steve, for one, could not forgive.

More than 15 years later, Steve still frowns and shakes his head as he recalls the night Clive "spent most of the gig throwing up into a bucket at the side of his kit. The main thing I was worried about at the time was getting through the tour. I thought, 'Well, if we're having problems with a 45-minute set, what are we gonna be like when we're doing our own thing and we've got to do a two-hour show?' That's what bothered me the most about Clive. It actually got to one point, in the States, where I went to Rod and said, 'Look, I just can't carry on like this,' and he had to really slap me about and persuade me to carry on. It's not like me to give in, but I just felt that it was wrong, going out and pulling the wool over people's eyes by not being as good as we could be. This might sound big-headed, but I think, with Maiden, even when we're not at our best, we're still good enough, in a lot of people's eyes. But to me, that wasn't good enough. It upsets me when we're not at our best, and on that tour we were really struggling, some nights, because Clive just couldn't hold it together. And it weren't just me Clive was pissing off; he was pissing everybody off."

"It got to everybody, in the end," agrees Adrian. "When you're in the driving seat in a band, like the drummer is, the pressure's really on you. It's key. And if you start fucking up, it fucks everybody else up, too. The bass playing, especially. So Steve was starting to get the needle a lot with him. Then Clive would be given a warning and he'd always be, like, you know, 'I'm sorry. I didn't realise it was getting so bad. I'll make sure it doesn't get that way again.' Then everything would be fine for a few shows, and then it would start again. Clive is a great drummer and a great guy as far as I'm concerned but, like Paul, after a while you could just see it coming."

Unfortunately, Clive Burr failed to respond to any of the numerous enquiries I made, via intermediaries, as to whether he would be interested in putting his side of the story to me for this book. He didn't refuse to speak, but neither did he agree. He simply didn't reply at all. In fairness, it would be wrong to try and read anything too deeply into this silence, but it's a pity, nevertheless, because Clive is still remembered very fondly by the members of the band who knew him in those days. "I still think he's the best drummer the band ever had," says Bruce. "That's not taking anything away from [present drummer] Nicko. Technically, Nicko's probably a far more competent drummer than Clive. It's just that Clive had incredible feel, and you can't learn that, and I regret that he wasn't given more time to try and sort himself out."

However, as usual, in the '80s time was the one thing that Maiden simply didn't have. Adrian, who was closer to Clive than anybody else in the band, probably best sums up the disappointment and tragedy of Clive's departure from the band: "Unfortunately, I didn't keep up that contact when he left the band, which is something I regret now. The truth is, we were away all the time, but there were still those other times when I might have picked up the phone, or whatever. But I don't think I knew what to say, really. The day we had to tell him, Dave and I had a couple of swift drinks before we went into this meeting, because it was terrible, it really was. It affected me more than I knew at the time, I think. I mean, me and Clive used to go out and get wrecked together on the road all the time, and there was a part of me that was thinking, 'How can the pot call the kettle black?' I thought it might be me next, you know? Which is probably another reason why I started to take things that little bit more seriously on the next tour. I still had a good time, but I started cutting down on the socialising on the days of gigs. Besides, I was tired of coming onstage with a headache."

Ironically, the drummer that Maiden would choose to replace Clive turned out to be one of the biggest-known party animals then in captivity, Nicko McBrain, or Mr Excess Everywhere, as he laughingly describes himself. An incongruous choice, surely, considering the nature of Clive's dismissal? On the surface, perhaps, but there was method in Maiden's madness yet.

"The thing with Nicko is that he's got this…I don't know what you call it, but this reserve bag of energy somewhere," says Steve. "He's just always had this thing that, no matter what he's been up to, it's never affected his gig. As I said, I don't give a shit what people do, and people sometimes get a bit intimidated by me because I've always been clean, I've never taken any drugs. But I really don't care. I'm completely non-judgemental about it – unless it fucks up their gig, whatever it is, whether they're in the band or working for it. And Nick has never let anything stop him giving 110 per cent onstage. And for me, as the bass player, that's really great. It means I never have a bad gig because the drummer let me down, which is what had been happening too much with Clive. So, even though Nick is Mr Party, it never bothered me, and it still doesn't. I know he'll be right on it the minute we step onstage, and that's priceless to me."

Most of the band had first met Nicko McBrain when he was drumming in Trust, who had supported Maiden on several shows in 1981. "They were all French, and Nicko's as English as baked beans," Davey recalls, "so he spent most of the time hanging around with us and we got to know him." But Steve always remembered Nicko best from a performance he'd witnessed the drummer give when he was still playing in a three-piece called McKitty, with whom Maiden had shared the bill at an open-air festival in Belgium in 1979. "In fact, it was our very first gig abroad, and we were still semi-pro at the time," he says. "The Gillan band were headlining, I think, and Nicko was playing with Donovan McKitty – who was a great Hendrix-style guitar player – and Charlie Tumahai – who used to be in Be-Bop Deluxe, who I loved – on bass. They'd done their set and there were all sorts of problems – Donovan McKitty's guitar got fucked up and Nick and Charlie did this bit of a jam thing together while he tried to fix it, and Nicko was just fucking amazing! Drum solos are usually pretty boring, but watching him go into this was better than watching the rest of the set.

"So I remembered him from that, and when Clive left he was one of the first people I thought of. I mean, he's always been a character, but I just knew he'd be the right man for the job. It was quite funny, because, years later, when [present vocalist] Blaze joined, Nick actually came to me and said, 'Look, I've heard this bloke is a bit of a party animal. Are you sure we're doing the right thing?' I said, 'Nick, hold on a minute. We hired you.' And he thought about it and he went, 'Yeah, that's true,' and we both started laughing, because he's earned his reputation for being Mr Excess, and quite rightly so, from the stories people have told me over the years! You never quite know which Nick you're going to get, 'cause he tends to change from show to show. One minute he's up and Mr Party and then the next day he might be Mr Depression, but that's just the way he is. But it never once affected his gig, and if it ever did then we'd give him a slapped wrist and he'd go off, sort of tail between the legs, and sort it out, you know? Nick's never been a problem like that."

Michael Henry McBrain was born in Hackney, east London, on 5 June 1952. It's hard to believe, when you look at him now and notice the battered, lived-in face and the fierce, arm-covering tattoos, but young Michael Henry was actually nicknamed Nicky as a child because, as he cheerfully confesses, "that was the name of my teddy bear, Nicholas The Bear. I was very attached to him, used to take him everywhere with me, and so my family just started calling me Nicky for fun. Unless I was in trouble. Then it was Michael."

He'd always wanted to be drummer. None of the family were particularly musical, but his father was a big trad-jazz fan, and young Nicky's big hero when he was growing up was Joe Morella, whom he discovered after watching the late, great jazz drummer play an extended break midway through a Dave Brubeck TV performance in the early '60s.

"When I was about ten, I used to get hold of all my mum's pots and pans and biscuit tins and anything else I could lay my hands on that made a good noise when you hit it, then get a pair of my mum's knitting needles and start bashing away," he says. "I used to pretend I was Joe Morella hitting the tubs. Or I'd go out into the kitchen and pick up a pair of knives and start hitting the gas cooker – this big, old, enamelled job – and of course all the paintwork started chipping off and my mum went apeshit."

Finally, in order to spare poor Mum's kitchenware, his dad relented and bought Nicky his first drum kit. "I must have been about eleven or twelve, and it was what used to be called a John Gray Broadway kit, which was basically one snare, one tom-tom, one cymbal, two drumsticks and a pair of brushes," he recalls. "I wasn't interested in no brushes – I just wanted to hit things – but my father made me learn how to play with the brushes as well as the sticks. He said, 'You'll have to know how to play everything if you want to be a proper drummer,' and of course he was dead right. So thanks, Dad, for that. But I just loved it. I was like a pig in shit!"

Inevitably, it wouldn't be long before young Nicky found his services much in demand. Drummers were hard to find, and when he joined his first school band he revelled in the new-found attention it brought him. "We used to play every Saturday morning," he recalls. "It was fucking magic! I can still remember it. All cover versions, you know. We weren't good enough to write anything yet. It was all early Stones songs and Beatles shit."

Musically, apart from his father's extensive jazz collection, Nicky began to dig the sounds of more contemporary '60s groups, such as The Animals, The Shadows and, of course, The Rolling Stones and The Beatles. Bizarrely, however, his earliest experiences as a stage performer of sorts also included a stint as a member of the Russell Vale School of Dancing, in Wood Green, where he used to go ballroom dancing every Saturday afternoon. "I was a dab hand at the old cha-cha-cha and samba," he chortles self-deprecatingly, but in truth he was a gifted dancer who went on to lead the school through several competitions. "That all went out the window, though, as I got more into being a full-time drummer."

By the time he was 14, he was regularly playing "pubs and weddings – semi-pro gear". As he got older and more accomplished as an all-round musician who could play not only pop but also the more complicated jazz styles, he began to pick up regular work as a session man, a species that was much in demand in those Tin Pan Alley, prefab-pop days of the '60s. He would load all of his gear into his father's tiny Morris Minor 1000 and trundle off into the night.

"I'm a right old slag, me," he confesses. "I'd do anything – pop albums, folk albums, religious albums or more rock-type stuff. I didn't mind. I could play anything, but I couldn't read music, so I tended to do more sort of pop stuff, and I used to do a lot of work for this label called Young Blood Records and sometimes with this bloke at EMI. There was me and this bass player called Brian Belshaw, and we were a bit of a team, like a portable rhythm section, and it was great experience. Most people in bands act very blasé about the session work they've done, like it's the most boring thing in the world, but actually I used to really enjoy it. Being a drummer, it's very hard to sit at home and just have a play on your own. It's not like being a guitarist. So I just used to like it 'cause it got me out and about playing with all sorts of different bands. And it stuck a bit of wonga in my pocket too, so that came in handy."

But while session work paid the rent, Nicky knew that it would never make him rich and famous and, as he says, "After a while, you want to do something that means something to you personally, and you can't do that at sessions. You need to be in your own band before you can start to get that out of your music, and so that's what I wanted to do." His first "proper" band was called The 18th Fairfield Walk, who became better known later on as Peyton Bond, a good, entertaining pub band that specialised in covers of Otis Redding, Beatles and Who material. "It was all right while it lasted," he says, "but it was never gonna go anywhere while it was doing just covers," so when he was offered the chance to join a more ambitious London outfit called The Wells Street Blues Band, "I jumped at it. It was still mainly covers, but it was a lot more interesting stuff, real hardcore, purist blues stuff." It was the late '60s, a time when a band's prowess could apparently be measured by how heavy they were, and it was only matter of time before The Wells Street Blues Band evolved into the much more progressive blues sound of The Axe, which they renamed themselves in 1969.

"The Axe was very sort of typical for that time. We were all influenced by John Mayall's Bluesbreakers and by what Eric Clapton, Jeff Beck, Jimmy Page and Peter Green had all done with that sound. We sort of saw ourselves in that mould, but it never really took off. We thought we'd made it when we won a local talent competition and the prize was a recording contract with Apple Records, which was The Beatles' label, or so they said! But nothing ever seemed to come of it. It was just a bunch of bullshit."

However, The Axe did finally start featuring some of their own material in their set. But then there was a big argument between the singer and the guitarist and that was that. "I liked it, but it was a bit over the top – three lead guitar players in one rehearsal room is a bit much for anyone to take, I think." Bowed but not broken, Nicky simply tried again, this time hooking up with a singer and keyboardist named Billy Day and his songwriting partner, guitarist Michael "Mickey" Lesley. "This was in about 1971, something like that, and I remember it well, because it was the first time I'd ever been put on wages. I got 50 quid a week, and I thought, 'Hey, this is great! I'm really starting to make it now!' But the wages also included driving the van, 'cause we didn't have no roadies and I was the only one with a driving licence – Billy lost his through being done for drunk driving – but it also meant that I got to take the van home at night, and of course I thought that was great. Here I am, got my first paid job in a proper band and I get a company vehicle, too!" he laughs.

It was also during his spell with Billy Day that Nicky suddenly became Nicko. "The boys had a publishing deal with April Music," he says, "which, through one thing and another, turned into a deal with CBS Records. So we were down at CBS Studios, in Whitfield Street, London, recording what was going to be our first album. Then, halfway through a session one day, the head of CBS decides to pay us an unexpected visit. Dick Asher was the head of CBS in those days, so we're all in there bashing away and Dick Asher comes in with Maurice Oberstein. It was just prior to Obie taking over CBS in England, and I think Dick was showing him around, or something.

"Anyway, Dick's come in. He's already met Billy, but he asks him to introduce him to the rest of us, and Billy was out of his brain as usual – he loved a drink, did Billy – and he decided it would be funny to introduce me for some reason as Neeko. He goes up to Dick and Obie and goes, 'I wanna introduce you to my Italian drummer. This is Neeko.' I thought, 'Fuck me, Billy, you are definitely over the top.' I tried to tell them different, but Obie then started calling me Neeko and it just went too far. So that was it. It stuck from there. I quite liked it, actually, only I changed it to Nicko so that it sounded more English."

Unfortunately, a new name was the most lasting gift that Nicko's association with Billy Day would produce. The band finally fell foul of the singer's inebriated working methods. As Nicko says, "The trouble with being a drummer is that you're left waiting on the sidelines quite often, waiting for the people in the band who are supposed to be coming up with the songs and the direction to get off their arses and get on with it. You start to sense very quickly when something's just not happening, and poor old Billy... He was a lovely guy and a great musician, and I learned an awful lot playing with him, but the band just weren't going nowhere. So, after a while, I thought, 'Right, that's it. I've had enough. I'm off.'"

There were one or two more short-lived attempts at getting a band of his own off the ground, but the first time the spotlight really hit the name Nicko McBrain was in 1975, when he joined Streetwalkers, the band formed by vocalist Roger Chapman and guitarist Charlie Whitney, who had both first found fame as being the leading lights of Family, much-respected authors of such landmark albums as *Music In A Doll's House* (1968) and *Bandstand* (1972).

"This is where it gets a bit complicated," says Nicko, "but basically I'd been in a band called The Blossom Toes, who looked like they were gonna land this big record deal, but then – surprise, surprise – it all got fucked up at the last minute. The guitarist in The Blossom Toes was a guy called Jim Cregan, and when things went pear-shaped he went off and joined Family. That was in about 1973. Then Family broke up in 1974 and Jim left to join Cockney Rebel. But before he did, he must have put the word in for me or something, but the next thing is, I get a call saying, would I be interested in auditioning for the gig in Roger and Charlie's new band? I'm, like, 'Yes!' I mean, I was a huge Family fan – I thought *Music In A Doll's House* was a fantastic album – so I was definitely up for it. They'd already done their first album, which was called *Streetwalkers*, but their drummer, Ian Wallace, had left and they had a tour coming up, and so that was that. I was in like Flynn!"

As chance would have it, one of Nicko's earliest tours with Streetwalkers involved a trip to New York, where the band were sequestered on the same bill as fellow Brit troupers Cockney Rebel, then managed by a callow ex-Cambridge graduate called Rod Smallwood.

"It was the first time I ever met Rod, and I'll never forget it," says Nicko. "We were playing at this club in New York called the Bottom Line, us and Cockney Rebel, and I just remember this big hunk of Huddersfield northerner walking 'round giving it the big 'un, as they say. Once you got talking to him, though, you discovered he was a lovely fella, loved a drink and a laugh. There was a big party after the gig, of course, and I remember everybody was screaming at each other and drunk. I don't think either of us had ever been to America before, and it was like British boys on holiday, a rock 'n' roll holiday. We actually met one another in a cupboard. It was one of those sorts of parties…"

"The first time I met Nick was in New York, and the first thing I thought was, 'Lovely guy, completely mad,'" recalls Rod. "And I don't think my opinion has changed of him since. Brilliant drummer, lovely guy, completely fucking mad. Even he'll tell you that."

By the time the two men met up again, in the early '80s, Streetwalkers – who had broken up soon after, when Roger Chapman went solo – was a distant memory and Nicko had been paying his way first as the drummer in The Pat Travers Band (that's Nicko adding the bones to Pat's guitar gravy on their *Making Magic* album) and then, latterly, in French socio-political rockers Trust. ("There was a lot of politics in their songs, but it was all in French, so don't ask me what any of it meant!")

Nicko says that he was well aware of the difficulties Maiden was experiencing with Clive Burr long before he was actually offered the gig. "I knew Clive, 'cause we'd all toured together when I was in Trust," he says, "and he actually rang me one night from America saying he'd heard they'd talked to me about replacing him and I was honest with him and told him straight, 'Look, Clive, they ain't gonna offer me the gig if you pull yourself together.' I remember I was still with my first wife at the time and she gave me a bollocking afterwards. She goes, 'What did you tell him that for? He'll pull himself together and keep the gig and you won't be left with anything.' But that's not how I saw it. I didn't want to steal another man's gig. He'd rung me to ask me for my opinion and I gave it to him as best I could. The rest was up to him."

Nevertheless, when it all proved too much for Clive and Maiden did end up offering the gig to Nicko, he admits, "I was well fucking pleased! I think it would be fair to say I had a small drinky-poo to celebrate that little bit of good news. I mean, I was out of work, so it was a life-saver. But better than that, I really liked the music. It was right up my strasse, as they say. I'd always been able to play powerfully, but Maiden was a real stepping stone in the progression of my style. It was a great experience, because of the pedigree of the players. You can't get better. At what they do, Maiden are the best there is, it's as simple as that. And when Steve writes a song, he always comes up with a beat I've completely overlooked, or he'll suggest something that I might not have thought of. And he's not even a drummer! But that's the beautiful thing about music – there's so many ways to represent it. But because he's the one that's written the songs, he knows better than anybody how they're supposed to go and what feel they're supposed to have, so I always listen and then try and give it something of my own that maybe he hasn't thought of yet. So it works really well."

"I know other drummers that have auditioned for Maiden that can't do it," says Adrian Smith. "You have to be a bit of an athlete, and Nicko is a fantastically athletic drummer. He always had the chops and the technique, but in Maiden he really exploded, to the point where a lot of stuff we did after he joined was then founded on his playing, all those busy patterns he does, displaying tremendous technique. It sounds daft now, but when he first joined I thought he might be a bit funky for us, because Nick can play anything. And he's tight. He's really at the front of everything, and Steve loves playing with him. Steve and Nicko used to work for hours, going over these bass and drum patterns. I mean, normal rules do not apply to either Nicko McBrain or Iron Maiden, which is why they've both always stood out."

The first thing Nicko actually did with the band was a TV show in Germany. News of Clive's departure had not yet been made public, and so Nicko did the show wearing an Eddie mask. Some might say that, metaphorically speaking, he has yet to take it off...

12 Uncle Sam

The next five years would be a time of unbridled success and prosperity for Iron Maiden. Having outlived the NWOBHM phenomenon, they now found themselves treated like rock royalty wherever they went. During this time, they released four studio albums – *Piece Of Mind* (1983), *Powerslave* (1984), *Somewhere In Time* (1986) and *Seventh Son Of A Seventh Son* (1988) – as well as their first live album, the double *Live After Death* set (1985). All five albums sold in their millions and all featured what is now nostalgically regarded by the critics as the classic Harris/Murray/Smith/ Dickinson/McBrain line-up. Martin Birch was also the producer on each occasion, and it's fair to say that, like all good captains, having painstakingly assembled his winning team, Steve Harris stuck to it until, by the end of the '80s, the Maiden trophy cabinet was stuffed with more than 100 gold and platinum albums from all over the world.

The band was now at its commercial zenith. By 1985, Iron Maiden was the biggest rock band in America, enormous stars able to fill 13,000-seater arenas like the Long Beach Arena, in Southern California, for four nights in a row, or 7,000-seater theatres like the sumptuous Radio City Hall, in New York, for five nights in a row, both of which they did that year. Meanwhile, at home in Britain, where their albums now routinely went into the Top Five, a dozen more hit singles had turned them into household names, replacing Purple and Sabbath as the familiar face of heavy metal to those who knew little about the music, and becoming the benchmark by which every subsequent metal-rock band would subsequently have to measure itself to those who knew anything.

"By that time, I'd moved on to edit *Kerrang!*, which had become a major magazine title in its own right," says Geoff Barton, "and as far as our readers were concerned at that time Maiden was just the biggest band in the world. I think they won just about every category of every annual Readers' Poll we ran from about 1983 to 1988. They were one of those bands that you simply couldn't put on the cover often enough. The more Iron Maiden we had in the mag, the more the readers liked it. For a long time, they simply couldn't put a foot wrong."

Creatively, the band was also at a peak, and some of their best-loved songs date back to this time: 'Run To The Hills', 'Number Of The Beast', 'Hallowed Be Thy Name', 'The Trooper', 'Revelations', 'Flight Of Icarus', 'Aces High', 'Two Minutes To Midnight', 'Rime Of The Ancient Mariner', 'Wasted Years', 'Stranger In A Strange Land', 'Heaven Can Wait', 'Can I Play With Madness', 'The Evil That Men Do'... The list is huge and impressive, with at least half a dozen of the titles on it still to be found in the Maiden live show today. That's not to suggest that absolutely everything that they recorded in those days was top-notch, of course. The sheer speed with which Maiden wrote and recorded most of those albums (in comparison, Def Leppard, the only other survivors from the now-barely-remembered NWOBHM days, produced just two albums during the same five-year period) meant that, inevitably, some tracks were better than others. (It's hard to imagine Maiden padding out an album now with a second-rate instrumental like the revealingly titled 'Losfer Words', as they did on *Powerslave*.) But the era was bookended by the release of two of the best albums that Maiden would ever make: *Piece Of Mind* and *Seventh Son Of A Seventh Son*.

The latter was the finest and most imaginative collection that this line-up of Maiden would produce, and is discussed in detail in the next chapter. However, it's the former work that most Maiden purists would probably cite as being the definitive recording of this unrepeatably prolific period. The first Maiden album to feature Nicko, *Piece Of Mind* actually begins with a big drum flourish, as if announcing the arrival of the Mad McBrain into their midst. Like Bruce with Paul, in terms of sheer technique, Nicko was a far superior performer to his predecessor, and his addition to their ranks allowed the band an even greater capacity to finesse what was now recognised as the quintessential Maiden sound: full-metal-jacket vocals, combat guitars, artillery-fire drums and the ever-present rhythmic pulse of Steve's manic bass, bulging like a vein in the foreground. The sheer strength of the material on *Piece Of Mind* reflected the fact that, in master technicians like Bruce, Adrian and Nicko, allied to the gutsy rock 'n' roll energy and emotion of Steve and Davey, Maiden now had all of the tools they needed to stretch out and begin to create their own first real masterpieces.

"For me, *Piece Of Mind* was the best album we'd done up to then, easily," says Steve, "and I carried on thinking that right up until the *Seventh Son...* album, which was five years later. I'm not saying the two albums we did in between – *Powerslave* and *Somewhere In Time* – weren't good, 'cause there's a lot of stuff on those albums I still think of as some of our best ever, but *Piece Of Mind* was just special. You can nearly always go back to an album and pick out things you might have done differently, or whatever, but I still think *Piece Of Mind* is good the way it is. It was Nicko's first album. We felt like we were on a high, and you can hear that mood on the album, I think. Most of all, though, it was just the songs. Between us, I thought we'd really come up with the goods this time."

They certainly had. As usual, a clutch of Harris-penned tracks provided the backbone of the album, including 'Where Eagles Dare', a sky-kissing paean to self-reliance and inner strength; 'The Trooper', a *Boy's Own* tale of wartime derring-do; 'Quest For Fire', inspired by the thought-provoking movie of the same name, released in 1982; and 'To Tame A Land', an epic album-closer with lyrics only comprehensible to readers of *Dune*, Frank Herbert's labyrinthine novel of space-age politics, love and war. In fact, the band had originally planned to call the track 'Dune', and had discussed using a spoken-word passage from the book as an intro, but then Herbert sent word via his agents that he was refusing them permission because, he said, "Frank Herbert doesn't like rock bands, particularly heavy rock bands, and especially bands like Iron Maiden." Ouch! "He just assumed that, because we were a rock band, we must be a load of morons," says Rod, nonplussed, "which, to say the least, is a pretty narrow-minded attitude."

Of the remaining five tracks, 'Flight Of Icarus' and 'Sun And Steel' were Bruce and Adrian numbers; 'Still Life' was a Steve and Davey tune; 'Die With Your Boots On' was a Bruce and Adrian idea onto which Steve grafted some ideas of his own; and 'Revelations' was a song that Bruce came up with on his own. All of them were superb, but two, 'Flight Of Icarus' and 'Revelations', deserve special mention. The former, a mid-paced growler that suddenly bursts into a multi-tracked vocal chorus straight out of the REO Speedwagon back catalogue, was the controversial first single from the album. An unbelievably cheesy piece or just unbelievably catchy, depending on your point of view, despite reaching Number Eleven in the UK in April 1983 and gaining the band their first single release in the US (where, unlike the UK, singles aren't released unless a record company is utterly convinced that they have a potential hit record on their hands), 'Flight Of Icarus' divided critical opinion, not least amongst the band themselves. "I don't think there's anything wrong with 'Flight Of Icarus' as a song," says Steve, "though I do wish we'd had more time to break it in live before we recorded it. It was a lot more powerful live, a lot faster and heavier." However, Bruce insists, "Steve never liked it. He thought it was too slow, but I wanted it to be that rocksteady sort of beat. I knew it would get onto American radio if we kept it that way, and I was right."

He was. 'Flight Of Icarus' remains the only Iron Maiden track ever to receive any real level of airplay in the USA, and climbed as high as Number Twelve in the Rock Radio charts in 1983. It was this radio success, plus the tour, which led to their first American platinum album. However, it was the storming follow-up single, 'The Trooper', which most Maiden fans from those days still recall first when you mention the *Piece Of Mind* album.

The only people who didn't like Bruce's 'Revelations', though, were the ones who weren't supposed to like it, the neo-fundamentalist religious groups in America who still accused Maiden of being Satanists. Ironically, what appeared to offend them most this time was the witty use on the sleeve of an actual quote from the Bible's Book of Revelations, chapter 14, verse one, which reads, "And God shall wipe away all the tears from their eyes; and there shall be no more Death. Neither sorrow, nor crying. Neither shall there be any more pain; for the former things are passed." However, where the scripture reads "pain", the band had inserted the word "brain" as a pun on the title of the album, itself a pun on the fact that a post-lobotomy Eddie is pictured on the sleeve of the album chained up in a padded cell, the top of his skull sawn off. It was a deliberate wind-up which worked only too well, and before long families all over the American South were again being urged to burn their teenage children's Iron Maiden records.

The band themselves found the whole situation so absurd that they couldn't resist really taking the piss, and at the last minute they inserted a few words played backwards between 'The Trooper' and 'Still Life' as a joke on anyone gullible enough to believe stories that accused bands like Maiden and Led Zeppelin of inserting evil messages on their albums that could only be revealed by playing the records backwards. Playing Maiden's little message on *Piece Of Mind* backwards would reveal a very different kind of devilment, one extremely drunken Nicko McBrain doing what he calls "my famous Idi Amin impression". He still laughs when he remembers the story.

"We were sick and tired of being labelled as Devil worshippers and all this bollocks by these fucking morons in the States," he says, "so we thought, 'Right, you want to take the piss? We'll show you how to take the bleeding piss, my son!' And one night the boys taped me in the middle of this Idi Amin routine I used to do when I'd had a few drinks. I remember it distinctly ended with the words, 'Don't meddle wid t'ings yo don't understand.' We thought, if people were going to be stupid about this sort of thing, we might as well give them something to be really stupid about, you know?"

The album was recorded at Compass Point Studios, on the beautiful Bahamian island of Nassau, in January 1983, and was their first recorded outside England. Apart from the relaxing atmosphere provided by the beachside studio, the main reason for this was financial. As Rod explains simply, "It was for tax reasons. We were still trying to save every penny. The problem with being a rock band is you're either earning a lot of money or you're earning nothing. And no matter how well you've been doing one year, you never know what's going to happen the next. It's not like a normal business, where you can fairly safely predict what the figures will be over the next two or three years; in the music business, you're only ever as good as your last record. Particularly in the early days, when you're still trying to build an artist's reputation, you can't just assume that everything you do is going to be as successful as the last thing you did."

Even so, Rod never personally doubted that Maiden would continue to enjoy ever greater success, as his ever-astute partner, Andy Taylor, now remembers: "You can't balance the books entirely on dreams, and we didn't want to end up with a big tax bill and no money to pay it. To save as much money as possible against that rainy day is the job of all responsible managers to consider, especially on those sunny days when no one else wants to think about it, so we recommended the band do the next album outside Britain."

"Rod said to me, 'We've got to record the album outside England. Where can we go?'" says Martin Birch. "The options were Air Studios, in Antigua, which later got blown down in a hurricane, or Compass Point, in Nassau. I went down and checked them both out and I liked Compass Point, so we went there. Personally, I would have preferred to go somewhere like the Record Plant, in New York, or somewhere in Los Angeles. It would have been easier and we might possibly have got better technical results. It was pretty bare bones down in the Bahamas, but it was sunny, we liked it and it was available, so we decided to do the recording there and then mix it later in New York."

Released in Britain on 16 May 1983, *Piece Of Mind* entered the UK charts at Number Three. Critical response in the UK had been lukewarm, compared with the fanfare that accompanied the release of *Number Of The Beast*, and although *Piece...* would outsell every previous Maiden album in the UK, it never quite reached Number One in the charts and remains strangely overlooked by the critics to this day. Only the readers of *Kerrang!* magazine seemed to get it, voting the album Number One Album Of All Time in their 1983 end-of-year polls, with *Number Of The Beast* just behind it at Number Two.

With no title track in evidence, for once, the title of the album was conceived around an idea that Rod and Steve came up with for the cover and which Derek Riggs had actually flown out to Nassau to paint for them while they were still recording, depicting a typically grotesque Eddie who has quite literally flipped his lid. "We decided to lobotomise him," Rod explains. "Originally, the working title was 'Food For Thought'. Then we were talking about it in this pub in Jersey, where they were writing before they went into the studio, and one of us – we can never remember who, because I think we were pissed at the time – said,

'Piece Of Mind,' and we both went, 'Yes! That's it! Quick, get Derek on the phone.'"

The world tour that followed in the album's wake took a similar path to the one established with the *Number Of The Beast* album, only this time it was even longer. When they began the tour, in Hull on 2 May, they were welcomed back onto the British stage as conquering heroes. Many of their fans were new and had barely heard of Paul Di'Anno, let alone Dennis Stratton, and Bruce lived up to his new nickname, "the air-raid siren", with all the added confidence that being a recognised and important member of "the family" now accorded him. But it was in America that the band really upped the ante. Against the advice of everybody (except Rod, who urged them to throw caution to the wind and "just bloody get out there and do it"), the band headlined their own US tour for the first time in 1983, a gamble that paid off handsomely as they watched, awestruck, as *Piece Of Mind* climbed into the US Top 20, their first album to do so, eventually settling at Number 14 and selling more than a million copies for the band, thereby earning them their first US platinum album.

With the band still regarded as new in America at that time, *Piece Of Mind* was perceived by the mainstream US media as almost an overnight success, but the seeds of Maiden's American breakthrough had been sown long before the band had even set foot in the country. Rupert Perry, who was then vice president of A&R at Capitol Records (EMI's American outlet) and who later became MD of EMI in Britain, recalls how "Rod did something very unusual early on which helped the band enormously in America, something which most managers wouldn't have thought of doing then. In those days, we had about twelve or 13 different sales districts in America, where we had sales teams and promotional people that looked after that specific geographic market in the US. It's such a huge country, America, with different time zones and different State laws. There's simply no other way you can run an operation of that size without breaking it down into manageable pieces. And what Rod did was, he actually went to America and went to every single one of those offices and introduced himself to anybody that would speak to him. And this was really early on, months ahead of their first tour there, and it was an amazingly astute thing to do, because these people didn't know Iron Maiden from Adam, and if you imagine you're the district sales manager in Detroit, you know, not too many managers are going to call you up and say, 'Hi, you don't know me but my band's on your label and I'm in Detroit and I want to come and talk to you about them.' But Rod went to every single one of these offices and sat with the relevant people – the district sales manager, the promotional people – and told them what it was all about, gave them all a T-shirt, then probably took them out and got them pissed... It was a great move, because right from the start he kind of had everybody in the company onside for Maiden, really wanting to help with the project. He created a relationship the band would never have had otherwise. I mean, how could you not fall in love with Rod Smallwood?"

The foundations firmly laid, Maiden were able to use the welcome mat laid out for them by Capitol to drive home their message in the best way they knew how: by relentless touring. Despite good support from the American end of the record company, it was, as ever, the live stage where the band really won friends. America had always loved British hard rock and heavy metal; Zeppelin, Sabbath, Purple, Priest and UFO had all known tremendous success in the US throughout the '70s, and Def Leppard would also enjoy enormous US success in the '80s. Given enough exposure, it seemed only a matter of time before Iron Maiden did the same. But that didn't mean it would easy. Breaking America remains the ultimate challenge for any rock band from England – just ask Oasis – and, as we shall see, success would come at a price. As Steve says, "Touring America is like doing a world tour within a world tour. Not only is it the biggest place in the world, it's also the weirdest."

The first time that Maiden toured America was in the summer of 1981, when they again opened for Judas Priest. Touring America for the first time was a dream come true for the five inexperienced band members, as they discovered what all English visitors to the US discover, that the reality surpasses even the wildest expectations.

"We'd actually arrived in Los Angeles, where we had a couple of days off before the tour started, and the first place we got taken to was the Rainbow, on Sunset Boulevard, this famous LA rock club that we'd all heard about," says Adrian. "We'd read that Led Zeppelin used to go there in the '70s, and it was pretty amazing, 'cause who's there when we get there? Jimmy Page! It was just full of other bands, famous bands, and lots of LA groupies. It was a bit mind-blowing, really, for a kid from the

East End. I remember, my first night there, I got introduced to Pat Travers and Pat Thrall, who were, like, two of my favourite American guitarists of all time. And I got introduced to Jimmy Page, which was really weird. He was talking to me as one bloke in a band to another, and I was standing there thinking about all those Led Zeppelin records I'd got at home. It was like we were on equal terms, which was a bit of a trip. Maiden were like 'the band from England' in the club that week and we were just surrounded by people. There were chicks all over us. I didn't even get time to finish me pizza!"

The band's first-ever American show had been in the fabulously incongruous setting of Aladdin's Hotel, in Las Vegas. "Now, that was unbelievable," says Adrian. "Talk about from the sublime to the ridiculous. As you arrived in the hotel lobby, there were slot machines everywhere, and you were just surrounded by all this glitz. I think Wayne Newton was playing there that night. Then you got up to your room and there's purple wallpaper and a gold bedspread. It was enough to give you a headache, honestly. But the show itself was a cracker. I couldn't believe how many kids were really into it and seemed to know the songs. I wasn't expecting that kind of reaction from the crowds on that tour. Afterwards, I remember this one kid coming up and going, 'You were really *baaad* tonight, man!' I'd never heard anybody say that in real life before. I thought, 'Blimey, they must really like us!'"

Finishing with two shows back in LA, at which they opened for UFO, Maiden's first US tour had lasted barely two months, but it was enough to see *Killers* reach Number 78 in the *Billboard* Hot 100 (the nationally recognised chart) and sell nearly 200,000 copies – not bad for a band making their first brief visit. By the time Maiden returned to America in 1982, however, *Number Of The Beast* had reached Number 33 and was fast on its way to going gold, and the band were starting to be treated like stars. Still touring as a support act, they spent six months swinging from one major tour to the next, opening for bands like Judas Priest (again), Rainbow, .38 Special and The Scorpions, plus two huge stadium shows with Loverboy and Foreigner, all the time introducing increasingly fanatical audiences to Eddie, now a twelve-foot-tall mobile monster.

Another monster that nobody could hope to tame on that tour, though, was the one that Bruce now refers wryly to as "Mr Party

Animal. We all turned into him at some point on that tour," he explains. "I was, like, ligger of the year. If there was a party, I was there in a corner doing something, you know? I did quite a bit of that early on in Iron Maiden, actually."

"Most of the time, if it was a really long journey to the next gig – and some of those journeys were, like, 16 hours long – we'd leave fairly soon after the show," says Dave Murray, "but nine times out of ten, we used to stay and watch the headline bands and just hang about, have a few beers and try to pull a few birds, that type of thing. It was good fun, and in a way it was nice, because we had no real responsibilities as the support band. You'd come offstage before nine, or something like that, and then you'd got all the night to do whatever you want. Everyone was doing their own thing on that tour, and it started getting a bit out of hand, actually. I mean, especially in the case of Clive, or whatever."

Their American fans were just as wild. Gangs of Maiden fans would travel in convoy from show to show, sometimes covering hundreds of miles for weeks at a time just to be with the band. One particularly notorious but fun-loving bunch christened themselves the Chicago Mutants.

"It was almost impossible to rest, because some of the fans were so ingenious," recalls Adrian, "they'd find out where you were staying and turn up at your door. The Chicago Mutants were best at that. They would always book rooms on your floor, and you'd get knocks on the door from them at one in the morning... I remember staying in this motel somewhere in the middle of nowhere, one time, and the room I was in was on the ground floor and it overlooked the parking lot, and I remember getting out of bed in the morning and opening the curtains and there was a car park full of kids out there. Hundreds of them! And there were cars with Eddie painted on them and kids with strange Maiden tattoos and a lot of weird stuff going on, and these kids were leaning through the window, going, 'Come on outside! Come and see my car,' just trying to get me to come outside and talk to them. It was mad."

As the Maiden machine became bigger and more successful, so the offstage craziness began to subside. The shows were now two hours long every night and they were no longer the new dicks on the block; they were headliners, and they had a responsibility to themselves and their new-found fans to put on the best show they could.

"The Piece Of Mind American tour was probably the start of the whole band becoming a little bit more sensible," says Adrian. "In the past, touring America had been be so easy. We'd do our spot early on and spend the rest of the night having a good time. Now we were headlining, and we couldn't really afford to piss around. People had been saying that we were wrong to go out as headliners in the States so soon. They said we weren't ready for it, and that we'd never be able to pull it off, so I think we wanted to show them, too, you know? We had something to prove. I think we all took it a little bit more seriously."

Nicko, however, who was then touring with Maiden for the first time, remembers things somewhat differently: "When I joined the band, everybody – with the exception of Steve and Bruce – was just fucking nuts! We were just going absolutely fucking crazy on everything we could possibly get our hands on. Nine times out of ten it was in the booze department but, you know, we'd have a bit of taboo and a bit of yahoo and a little bit of livening up here and there, a bit of the old disco dust, or whatever you want to call it, and we'd have these all-night benders. Not on the day of a gig, but you'd still find yourself in the dressing room thinking, 'Ah, fuck. I shouldn't have got so pissed last night.'

"It was weird, though, because we've had some of our best shows when we've been hungover. But I have to say, not at any time that I've known of in this band has anyone done drugs before a gig or got drunk before a gig. And that's not because there's a law in the band that says you cannot do that – you can do what the fuck you want, as long as you do the gig properly; it's just not something we get into before a show. There was only one occasion on the Piece Of Mind tour that we did all have a few drinks before we went on, and that was a bit of a celebration, 'cause it was the last night of the American tour. It was after that, on the Powerslave tour, that things got a lot more serious."

Whenever it was, exactly, that Iron Maiden stopped being young tearaways and metamorphosed into seasoned pros, there's no doubt that their fifth album, the all-too-aptly titled *Powerslave*, was a watershed in the band's career, the moment when, ready or not, the boys in the band were forced to become men. Recorded once again at Compass Point Studios and released in September 1984, *Powerslave* was to become Maiden's second million-selling album in the US, where it reached

Number Twelve. (In the UK, it was only kept from Number One by a compilation album, which would today not be eligible for the chart.) It also heralded the start of the biggest, most successful tour that they would ever undertake. Dubbed the World Slavery tour, Maiden would be on the road for 13 consecutive months, performing over 300 shows in no fewer than 28 different countries. It was a memorable journey, and one that would take in such highlights as their first tour behind what was then still known as the Iron Curtain and an appearance on the same bill as Queen, before 250,000 people, at the first-ever Rock In Rio Festival in Brazil. However, it was also a punishing schedule, and one that would leave them all in a state of physical and nervous exhaustion by its conclusion. "It was the best tour we ever did and it was the worst," says Bruce now. "It nearly finished us off for good."

The *Powerslave* album itself was a gloriously packaged yet ultimately somewhat patchy collection of material. Of the eight featured tracks, only three tracks – 'Aces High', 'Rime Of The Ancient Mariner' and 'Two Minutes To Midnight' – really ranked alongside their previous best efforts. The latter was the best example yet of the growing songwriting partnership between Bruce and Adrian and a far more groove-laden affair than anything Maiden had released since 'Sanctuary'. It was also the first single from the album, smashing into the UK charts at Number Twelve in August and winning the band yet more new fans. "I could knock out stuff like that all day," Adrian says now, "but it didn't always fit into the kind of fantasy-horror thing that Maiden had going for them. In the early days, I needed Bruce to help me make things more how Maiden would want them. 'Two Minutes To Midnight' is a perfect example of that. I had the right riff and Bruce had the right words."

The other two stand-out tracks were both top-drawer Steve Harris compositions. The first, 'Aces High', was a soulful call to arms in the tradition of 'Where Eagles Dare', only punchier, angrier, the *rat-a-tat-tat* of the guitars and Bruce's swooping vocals uncannily like that of a mid-air dogfight, while the second, 'Rime Of The Ancient Mariner', remains, for the author and many other Maiden fans, the most fully realised of all of Steve's self-consciously epic songs. There have been others since that have come close ('Seventh Son Of A Seventh Son', 'Sign Of The Cross'), just as there had been others before ('Phantom Of The Opera', 'To Tame A

Land'), but none of them captured so eerily or so accurately the strange, other-worldly place summoned up for us by Steve in 'Rime Of The Ancient Mariner'. Inspired by the famous 18th-century poem of the same name by Samuel Taylor Coleridge, and nearly 14 minutes in length, it's a masterful evocation of a complicated mood piece that would become the dramatic cornerstone of the Maiden show for many years to come.

Of the five remaining tracks, only Bruce's scathingly autobiographical 'Powerslave' and Steve's suitably swashbuckling 'The Duellists' really cut the mustard, such was the standard that the band had now set themselves. Bruce's 'Flash Of The Blade' just about qualifies, too, but surely one song about sword-fighting is enough per album? And no Maiden fan's life would be any the poorer, surely, for having skipped Bruce and Adrian's blusteringly histrionic 'Back In The Village' or Steve's lamentably vacuous instrumental 'Losfer Words (Big 'Orra)', neither of which could claim to be anything but sub-standard album fillers.

"I still think it's a really, really strong album," insists Steve. "I think there are four stand-out tracks on there, all of which we did live, and that's 'Rime Of The Ancient Mariner, 'Two Minutes To Midnight, 'Powerslave' itself and 'Aces High'. Of the other tracks on there…there are some good ones. There's the 'The Duellists', which I still think is good, you know? It's musically interesting. But if you put the 'The Duellists' against 'Rime Of The Ancient Mariner and 'Two Minutes to Midnight'… I mean, it's just, no way. But they weren't filler songs or anything like that. I just think those four particular songs were really strong."

Equally impressive was the Ancient Egyptian motif around which the album sleeve and stage show was based. Bruce's title song of power-lust amongst the pyramids had inspired Derek Riggs to create his most sophisticated artwork yet, with Eddie's ghastly immortal visage replacing that of the ancient pharaohs as he sits Sphinx-like on his enormous sand throne, a monument to megalomania, as self-absorbed as the sun. Onstage, it was simply a question of bringing the album sleeve into three-dimensional life, topped off with a 30-foot mummified Eddie, eyes shooting fire, to close the show with. As Steve says, "It could have been totally cheesy, because you think of Egypt and the pyramids and really, how do you portray that without looking like Hawkwind? But the set was really good. It looked fantastic, and it was probably the best stage show we ever did."

"I still think that was the best show that Maiden ever put on," agrees Bruce. "It was just the right combination of epic stuff, but it wasn't too overblown and it wasn't so hidebound by the sort of technology and loads of hydraulics and inflatable things that occurred later, all of which had the possibility for Spiñal Tap-type fuck-ups on a regular basis. Virtually everything on the World Slavery tour – the whole set, apart from the lights – was done musical-hall style. It was all boxes and ropes and two blokes pulling levers. It was so simple, it was like pantomime. You could set it up in small theatres or big arenas and it would always look fantastic. "

One viewing of *Live After Death*, the classic video directed by Jim Yukich which captures the band onstage in America in 1985, will confirm that view. There would be bigger, more elaborate Eddie-ised stage sets as the years swept by, but never again would there be one quite so eye catching or quite so right for the moment. As Bruce says, "The song 'Powerslave' is more than just about the ancient Egyptians; it was also about us, the band, and what was happening to us. We were slaves to the power, whether, you know, musically, or in terms of just chasing success. We were both. Especially, as it turned out, on that tour. I never thought it was going to end."

Having broken into the Top 20 for the first time with *Piece Of Mind*, *Powerslave* was the album in America that, as Bruce says, "you just had to have, even if you never bought another Iron Maiden record again." Maiden were the happening new band of the moment, and the American leg of the World Slavery tour became the must-see rock event of the summer. Consequently, dates were continually being added to their itinerary, until the band – led by Bruce – quite literally told Rod that he would have to call a halt to proceedings, "or I was gonna jack it in. I guess it was the first time I really thought about leaving. I don't just mean Iron Maiden, I mean quitting music altogether. I really felt like I was pretty much basket-case material by the end of that tour, and I did *not* want to feel that way. I just thought, 'Nothing is worth feeling like this for.' I began to feel like I was a piece of machinery, like I was part of the lighting rig."

"I'm really surprised we got through that tour," says Nicko, "because that was the heaviest-scheduled tour I think we ever did, even today. It was, like, go, go, go, go, go, go, 'cause we were at the height of our success, especially in America, and we were doing four shows on the trot, then one day off, four shows on the trot, one day off... I think there were a couple of times we did five shows running on that tour. It was insane! I remember, about three quarters of the way through, we just went onto remote control, we were just in this no-man's land, and by the end we were all completely burned out. Bruce was especially done in, I think. He was almost ready to give up playing and go home. When you get to that stage, it's just not fun any more; it's becoming too tedious or too difficult, emotionally... I mean, it nearly destroyed the band."

"At the time, it just seemed endless," says Adrian. "Six months? Fine. Nine months? Fine... Then it got extended, and then extended again, and we were getting burnt out. These days, when bands take on 14-month world tours, they build in gaps for recuperation, but there were no breaks on that tour, no real gaps, just a day off here and there. We were all a bit jacked off with it at the end of it, to be honest. You're gone for a year and your whole life goes out the window, basically. As for keeping long-term relationships going – whether it's with friends or lovers or whoever – I mean, forget it. I know it goes with the territory, but it was tough. By the end, you don't know how to act properly any more. You don't know who you are or what you're supposed to be doing. I remember I went to see my parents when I got home and I knocked on the wrong door. Honestly!"

"The thing you've got to remember is that Rod is an ex-agent, and I don't mean a secret agent," says Steve. "You know, he doesn't like to see an empty diary. But that tour was a bit like getting your darts out and throwing them at the board and that's it, that's where you're going next, sort of thing. As a manager, he wanted to keep things really boiling, but we just we told him in the end, 'Look, we can't carry on like this. We're gonna be all right till the end of the tour, but if we carry on another, say, three or four months, then who knows what's gonna happen?' I thought it would be the last straw, basically, because Bruce was really in a bad way by then. He sort of turned into a hermit after it was over."

Recorded over two nights out of the four they actually headlined on that tour, at the Long Beach Arena in California, in March 1985, *Live After Death* was that rare and exotic thing: a truly indispensable live album. There had been occasional live recordings included as the B-sides of singles, and there was the ramshackle live four-track EP 'Maiden Japan' with Paul Di'Anno in 1980 (originally a Japanese-only release which was later made available in the UK), but never had there been such a lavish live Maiden collection as this. The album comprises twelve tracks that not only faithfully reproduced the frenzy and excitement of the band's most recent American tour but which all uniformly outstrip their recorded templates by some considerable distance. Released in November 1985, replete with the flame-licked corpse of a defiant Eddie rising from the grave on the sleeve, *Live After Death* went straight to Number Four in the UK and became the band's third straight million-seller in the States.

"We wanted to do a proper live album, 'cause that's what we've always been about, playing live," says Steve. "I think we've always had the problem in the studio – still do, to a certain extent, I suppose – of trying to recreate what we do live. When you listen to a live version of one of our songs, nine times out of ten it's much better than the original recorded version. It's very difficult to create the same atmosphere when you go into the studio. We used to joke that we should get a load of cardboard cut-outs of a crowd and put them in there to make us think we're doing a gig, just to get us in the right vibe."

They certainly found the right vibe on *Live After Death*. Playing to 52,000 people over four nights at Long Beach Arena, somehow they managed the marvellous trick of, as Steve says, "turning it into like a massive club gig. We only taped two nights of the four. We thought that, if we buggered it up anywhere, we could use stuff from both nights, but I think we actually ended up using all the stuff from the one night. We still recorded two nights for the video, just to get as many extra shots as possible to cut in later, just so you got a real idea of what was going on. But basically the album is just us going for it on one particular night. No overdubs or nothing. We were still actually touring when Martin went in to mix the tapes. He'd send them to us, like, two tracks at a time, and then he'd wait for us to say yes or no, so there was no chance of adding anything anyway, even if we'd wanted to. We were really anti all that, anyway. We were very much, like, 'This has got to be totally live,' you know?"

The success of both the *Live After Death* album and video had the knock-on effect of buying the band a little much-needed time to recuperate before beginning the arduous task of coming up with a credible follow-up to their most successful quartet of albums yet. It was their first real break of any length since they'd signed to EMI five years earlier.

"We were supposed to have six months off, which quickly became four months," says Bruce. "I was just sitting around and I gradually started to come back to some sort of sense that, well, OK, as long as we're not doing any more of these crazy tours, you know, let's see how we go. Because to me the touring thing just wasn't enough. Going out and playing in front of 10,000 people – OK, great, but that's not what I got into music for, exclusively. I got into music because I wanted to tell stories and I wanted to explore the inside of my head and communicate it to people, and I thought, 'Well, what would really give me a buzz to go off and do another twelve-month tour would be if we had another fucking record that I really felt was ground-breaking,' you know? Like, 'Where's our "Kashmir"? Where's our "Stairway To Heaven"?' So I went off into acoustic world and I wanted to do almost like an unplugged record for the next Iron Maiden album, except this was years before MTV started doing it."

Somewhere In Time, their sixth studio album, may not be the best Iron Maiden album ever, but it was certainly the most expensive. "We went a bit crazy," Steve shakes his head. "We recorded the bass and drums down in Nassau, at Compass Point, then went to Holland – to Wisseloord Studios, in Hilversum – to do the guitars and vocals, and then Martin took it back to New York to mix it at Electric Lady Studios. It was crazy, but we were just desperately trying to get it right without hurrying it for a change and, well, you learn from your mistakes, I suppose," he smiles.

Technically, it was certainly their most ambitious recording yet, with Steve, Adrian and Davey all experimenting for the first time with the latest generation of guitar synthesisers that had then just come on the market. It lent sweeping, new textures to the Maiden sound, somewhere between the warm layers a keyboardist might bring and the cruel edge only a technologically enhanced guitar drone can give you, allowing the band's already epic sound an even greater panoramic quality.

But if it was their most expensive album, *Somewhere In Time* was also their most successful, reaching Number Three in Britain when it was released in October 1986 and becoming the first Maiden album to sell more than two million copies in America. It also had one of their best-ever album covers, with Eddie in his now-infamous guise as the mutant offspring of Arnie in *The Terminator* and one of Doctor Who's Cybermen, a rogue time cop, half alien and half human, armed to his pointy teeth with futuristic weaponry. The scene is some far-flung half world where the Ruskin Arms meets the control deck of the *USS Enterprise* (and, if you look closely, where West Ham appear to be beating Arsenal seven-three, a sure sign that this is not Earth as we know it!).

The theme, in case you hadn't noticed, is one of space and time, with several of the tracks – 'Wasted Years', 'Heaven Can Wait', 'Deja-Vu', 'The Loneliness Of The Long Distance Runner' and the rampant demi-title track itself, 'Caught Somewhere In Time' – all reflecting earnestly from different vantage points on the brutal march of time and how it makes victims of us all. In this respect, *Somewhere In Time* could be described as Maiden's first dedicatedly conceptual album – except, of course, it wasn't meant to be anything of the sort. As Steve cheerfully now admits, "It was just a way of reading the songs after they were already done. We certainly never went in there and said, 'Right, let's write a load of songs on the subject of time.'" However, Adrian points out that, "If you think about what we'd just done and where we'd just been, maybe it wasn't so strange that most of the songs we seemed to come up with had something to do with time, either time wasted or time spent learning something that cost you a lot. It's all there, if you read between the lines."

Steve weighs in with his usual quota of heavyweight material: 'Caught Somewhere In Time', the lengthy, fuse-burning opening track; 'Heaven Can Wait', another seven-minute opus destined to become a stage favourite, with its football-terrace chanting and live-for-today message; 'The Loneliness Of The Long Distance Runner', which, for the author, is one of the weaker moments on the album, being over-wrought and over-long and nowhere near as good as any of the other three tracks Steve contributes to the album, the last of which, 'Alexander The Great (356-323 BC)', also closes the album. Not quite in the same league as 'Rime Of The Ancient Mariner', but trying very hard to be, it's a fittingly ambivalent conclusion to an album that is so nearly very, very good.

Of the remaining four tracks, 'Deja-Vu', with its soaring chorus and double-take lyrics, was an otherwise fairly standard rocker written by Steve and Davey, although it was the final three tracks that really caught the connoisseurs' attention: 'Wasted Years', the first gloriously upbeat (read "catchy") single; 'Sea Of Madness', an angular blood-and-guts rocker full of crooked lightning; and 'Stranger In A Strange Land', the wonderfully paranoiac, mid-paced second single from the album, its title and story lifted wholesale from Robert A Heinlein's classic novel of the same name. They were all great tracks, and they had all been written by Adrian alone. Indeed, perhaps the most glaring feature (or should that be omission?) of the *Somewhere In Time* album is the absence of a single Bruce Dickinson writing credit on any of its eight tracks.

This came as something of a surprise to the author when the album was released, having spent an evening with Bruce a few weeks before recording was due to begin, when he gave me "a sneak preview" of at least three songs he had recently written, he told me, specifically for the album. He sang them for me while playing an acoustic guitar, and I recalled being surprised at how folksy they were, more like something from Led Zeppelin's semi-acoustic third album than anything by mid-'80s-period Iron Maiden. But then, as Bruce says now, "If I'd had my way, the album would have sounded very different. *Powerslave*, for me, felt like the sort of natural rounding off of *Piece Of Mind* and *Number Of The Beast*, that whole sort of era. I remember listening back to it and I thought, 'Ummm, this is great, but I don't know how much more we can do of records that sound in this kind of vein.' I felt we had to come up with our *Physical Graffiti* or our *Led Zeppelin IV*, or whatever, that we had to get it onto another level or we'd stagnate and just drift away. It wasn't so much that it had to be acoustic; I just felt that we should be leading and not following. I felt that we were right there, at that point, that we had the whole world literally at our feet, waiting for what we were gonna come up with next, and I felt that, if we came up with the same old thing, people would accept it and people would buy it; but I felt, if it was me, I'd be… There'd be a tiny bit of disappointment there, too, you know? I just thought the time was right for us to do something audacious, something vast and daring, and I didn't feel that we did that with *Somewhere In Time*. We just made another Iron Maiden album."

Based on the simple, folksy material that he had been working on at home, Bruce had suggested that Maiden should make a more acoustic-based album, but the proposal – along with his acoustic guitar and his songs – were rejected out of hand by the others, particularly Steve, who says, "I just thought he'd lost the plot completely. Bruce just wasn't himself at the time. We didn't realise it at first, but he was probably more burnt out than anyone at the end of that last tour. Then, when we came back to do the next album, he just couldn't seem to get himself together with any of the writing or anything. He came in with a few ideas which didn't really suit. It wasn't 'cause it was acoustic, necessarily, or even that it was very different sort of stuff; it was just that we didn't think it was good enough, really. And I could see he would feel bad that his songs were rejected, but he seemed to accept it quite readily at the time, 'cause he realised that he was…not on a different planet, but he was sort of edging that way. He knew he was feeling a bit strange, so he just sort of let us get on with it, and luckily enough Adrian came up with some strong stuff on his own, and that was that."

Adrian says that it was just a sad coincidence that he happened to begin writing fully formed songs again, with lyrics of his own, just as Bruce's own songs seemed to be biting the dust with the rest of the band. "We'd had a little lay-off and Bruce just wasn't around for a while," he says, "and I think he had pretty definite ideas about what he wanted to write next, anyway. So I was just sort of left to my own devices and the songs just came with the words already there. It didn't mean me and Bruce wouldn't write again. I mean, he came in with some songs of his own, and it could have been those that were picked and then I wouldn't have had anything on there, so I don't think he can really complain about that. But the manner in which he found out… I regret that. No one really said anything to him directly, I don't think."

Nobody, that is, except Martin, who actually broke the news to Bruce one afternoon at Compass Point. "I always sensed a slight danger of too much input from Bruce and Adrian," he says, "because they were always in danger of kind of taking it away from what Maiden really was. Some of their songs just weren't suitable – like a Bryan Adams-type thing that Adrian came up with called 'Reach Out', this sort of US stadium rock which just wasn't what Maiden were all about. They eventually used that one as a B-side, but to have let the band put something like that on the album would have taken away from the whole point of Iron Maiden. Neither Steve nor I ever envisaged the band as anything other than what they were. The other songs Adrian wrote for that album, like 'Wasted Years', they were great, but even they walked the line a little bit, I felt. As for Bruce's songs, they were all acoustic and they just didn't fit. They had to go. Not because they were acoustic, but because they just weren't right. But we didn't make a big deal about it. Bruce has written some great songs for Maiden and we knew he'd write more. These ones just weren't right."

But despite the reassurances of the producer, Bruce took the news badly. As was his habit since a child, he did his best to hide his hurt and knuckled down to work on the songs the band did want him to sing. But the feeling of rejection, he says, "left me squashed inside for a long time. I felt very much like a fly being swatted. This was in the Bahamas, when we were recording the album, and Martin told me that the others didn't like my songs. So I went away and thought, 'Well, what shall I do here? Shall I throw a wobbler and pack up my toys and go home?' But I'd gotten far enough away from the state of mind I was at, at the end of the Powerslave tour, to go, 'Well, who knows? They could be right. Maybe I am a basket case.' And so I convinced myself that I should just go with it. And the more I convinced myself I should go with it, in a way I felt like I was just unburdening myself of responsibility."

But the seed of discontent had been sown, and although the 1986-87 world tour was one of Maiden's most successful and stress-free affairs, it was also during that time that some observers (the author included) first noticed that Bruce either seemed to be slowing down some nights onstage or just didn't seem to be...well...trying as hard any more. Not every night, just certain nights. I think, at the time, that most of us who made that observation probably thought that we were imagining it, that our expectations had perhaps been unfairly raised by the lightning-fast edits of the *Live After Death* video that were still fresh in our minds. But as it turned out, we weren't imagining anything. The band may not have changed radically since the last time we'd seen them on the Powerslave tour, but Bruce most certainly had.

13 Janick

Musically, *Seventh Son Of A Seventh Son*, the seventh Iron Maiden album, far exceeded even the band's expectations, and for a great many fans it was, and remains, quite simply the best album they would ever release. Certainly, it was the best that this particular line-up of Maiden would release. Nobody could have guessed, however, that it would also be their last.

Recorded at Musiclands Studios, in Munich, during February and March 1988 and released in May, *Seventh Son...* became Maiden's second Number One album in the UK, the first time they'd hit the top of the charts since *Number Of The Beast* five years and as many albums earlier, spawning no fewer than four Top Ten singles along the way. Indeed, it was their biggest-selling album everywhere in the world except America, where sales unexpectedly dipped slightly from the two million plateau of *Somewhere In Time* to a still highly respectable 1.2 million, thus winning the band their sixth platinum album in a row, with *Number Of The Beast* having also well exceeded the million mark. Steve Harris admits that he was disappointed: "Not so much by the sales – you can't argue when they give you a platinum record. It was more that they just didn't seem to get it."

America didn't take readily to the far more finessed sound that Maiden presented to the world on *Seventh Son...* The country was then in the thrall of a new wave of ultra-heavy street-metal bands, groups like Metallica, Megadeth, Slayer and Anthrax, all of whom had been inspired by early Maiden but were all now attempting to do what apprentices must and outmanoeuvre their masters. As Steve says, thrash metal, as this new US metal was dubbed by the press, "made what we did sound almost commercial". Maiden was even criticised in some sections of the US rock press for their increased use of synthesisers on the new album. The implication was that they'd gone soft.

"I thought it was the best album we did since *Piece Of Mind*," says Steve. "I loved it because it was more progressive – I thought the keyboards really fitted in brilliantly – 'cause that's the influences I grew up with, and I was so pissed off with the Americans, because they didn't really seem to accept it. *Somewhere In Time* had done far better. But you can't just go by album sales – they might buy the album and not like it, and maybe some of the American fans that bought *Somewhere In Time* didn't like it and so didn't buy the next album. I don't know. Who knows what the real reason was? But it didn't do as well in America, and I just couldn't understand it, because I really thought it was our best album, at that point. Everyone said afterwards it was a very European-sounding album. I'm not so sure about that. What's a European-sounding album? To me, it's just a Maiden-sounding album. It is whatever it is. And I thought, 'Well, if you don't like it, bollocks. I don't care!' There is no other way of looking at it, really. I remember thinking, 'Fucking Americans. They just don't fucking understand us.'"

But the very qualities that may have confused some American fans delighted the rest of us. This was still very much the quintessential fire-and-brimstone Maiden sound but here done up in all the colours of the technological rainbow, and it was a beautiful thing to behold. The cover artwork also reflected the band's more rounded approach, with Derek Riggs' splendid new ice-age Eddie seen only from the torso up, his lower regions dissolving into brittle ice bones, fingers of flame reaching from his exposed brain to the pale and distant sun. It was an eerily ethereal image a million head-miles away from the grisly, leather-jacketed fiend of earlier releases.

Once again, there was also a loosely conceptual feel about the album, although Steve is honest enough to admit that, again, this was more by accident than design: "It was our seventh studio album and I didn't have a title for it or any ideas at all. Then I read the story of the seventh son of the seventh son, this mythical figure that was supposed to have all these paranormal gifts, like second sight and what have you, and it was more, at first, that it was just a good title for the seventh album, you know? But then I rang Bruce and started talking about it and the idea just grew."

"I remember Steve rang me to tell me about this idea he'd had for the next album," confirms Bruce, "all about this seventh son of a seventh son stuff, and I thought, 'What a great idea! Brilliant!' And of course I was really chuffed, too, because he'd actually rung me to talk about it and ask me if I had any songs that might fit that sort of theme. I was, like, 'Well, no, but give me a minute and I'll see what I can do.'"

Unlike *Somewhere In Time*, on which the songs had been fairly evenly split between Steve's and Adrian's, on *Seventh Son...* the band had never appeared more integrated as songwriters. Of the eight tracks on the album, only three are written solely by Steve, and they are all top-drawer tracks: 'Infinite Dreams', with its spacey Hendrix-ish guitar and sudden vaulting gallop into full-on headbanging metal dementia; the title track, at almost ten minutes long the most epic interlude on a superbly over-the-top collection, an unexpectedly worthy successor to 'Rime Of The Ancient Mariner', Steve's previous most affecting opus; and 'The Clairvoyant', an irreverent romp through the spirit world, destined to become the third Top Ten single from the album.

Of the remaining five tracks, two were actually credited to Bruce, Adrian and Steve, both of which – the appropriately eccentric 'Can I Play With Madness' and the poundingly compulsive 'The Evil That Men Do' – were not only possibly the two best tracks on the album but also the two biggest hit singles Maiden had ever had up to that point. The final three tracks were evenly split between one number penned by Bruce and Adrian, the soaring, anthemic 'Moonchild'; one song by Steve and Davey, 'The Prophecy', which was easily the guitarist's finest contribution since 'Charlotte The Harlot'; and one final number by Steve and Bruce, 'Only The Good Die Young', which again is one of the most finely wrought chunks of blood and sweat that the two would ever create together and a fittingly salutary ending not just to the album but also to the do-or-die decade from which both it and its creators sprang.

With its swooping, harmonic vocals and irredeemably catchy hook line, 'Can I Play With Madness' was released as the first single in April and stunned everybody by leaping straight into the UK charts at Number Three, where it stayed, even more astonishingly, for another three weeks.

As Adrian says, "It was, like, our first proper hit single. 'Can I Play With Madness' actually started life as a ballad I had been working on called 'On The Wings Of Eagles'. Then Bruce had a verse for it but wanted to change the title to 'Can I Play With Madness'. I must admit, it did sound better that way. So we took that one in and Steve liked it, too. It was Steve who came up with the time change in the middle and the instrumental passage, which again gave it that lift it needed. I was surprised when it was such a big hit, though. We'd had singles go into the charts before, but they flashed in and straight out again, usually. But this hung around there for ages, and they actually played it on the chart run-down on Radio 1 on a Sunday afternoon, which is something they'd never, ever done before. And it used to go down really well onstage. I think people were amazed when they saw us sing the opening part. We weren't exactly known for our harmonies. If I'd suggested harmonies when I first joined the band, I would have got beaten to a pulp, but me, Bruce and Steve would sing the harmonies live. It was quite simple, really, but very effective, and the audience loved it – they'd jump up and down from start to finish. Despite the title and whatever Bruce meant in the lyrics, it became a feelgood kind of song for the band and a real highlight of the show on that tour."

The Seventh Tour Of A Seventh Tour, as it was inevitably dubbed, also broke with tradition in interesting ways. For the first time, there would be a live keyboardist playing with them on certain numbers. Nicknamed the Count because of the ludicrous dark cape he donned for these occasions, he was in fact an American musician named Michael Kenney, who had been employed as Steve's bass technician since 1979. However, news of his inclusion in their ranks – even for just a handful of the newest numbers – caused enough of a stir to encourage the band to even have their picture taken with their newly christened sideman.

Also for the first time, there was no humanoid Eddie to run amok onstage at the end of each gig. He was instead represented in even more gigantic form, rising from the rear of the Arctic-themed stage, an ice giant, his eyes weeping fire, his crooked jester's mouth gaping. It was a more stately form of menace than a mere stagger around the stage biffing people, although perhaps not quite as much fun.

The band's offstage entertainment had also grown more stately, more mature, and although the Seventh Tour Of A Seventh Tour was still one of the biggest they would undertake – 25 countries in seven months – they had learned from their mistakes, and from now on all of their tours would be paced a lot more sensibly.

Steve, who had married his girlfriend, Lorraine, in 1983 and was now the proud father of two infant daughters, had taken to bringing his young family out on the road with him, travelling across America in their own tour bus while the rest of the band either flew or took a separate bus. "I thought, 'I can't take my kids on the road and have screaming babies in the middle of the night,'" he says. "It would be very selfish of me to say, 'Look, lads, can I bring the family?' So that was the start of me getting me own bus, which was bloody expensive, but I thought, 'Well, at the end of the day, it's either that or not seeing my family and seeing my kids grow up,' especially when we were in the States, 'cause I don't really like flying, anyway. And we got to do a lot of different stuff you just don't do when you're in a band normally. Like, if we were in Texas, rather than being stuck in the centre of town in a high-rise hotel, we'd sometimes go and stay on a ranch just outside town or somewhere where there was something happening for the kids. And, because of that, I actually got to see more than just the bloody hotel and the gig."

As a result, as Steve says, "the tongues started wagging", suggesting that there was a growing rift between the captain and his troops. But that, he insists, "was all bollocks. Everybody started getting into their own things, just to stay sane." Bruce took to entering fencing competitions dotted around the tour schedule; Nicko learned to be a pilot, flying his own twin-engine Cessna jet; and golf began to overtake booze and birds as the activity of choice on the band's days off, of which there were now many more. The years of six gigs a week were now far behind them.

"I was always into flying aeroplanes," says Nicko. "That was my extravagance. That and golf. I'd never been into either of them before. But then, I'd never been able to afford to buy golf clubs and go out and pay for flying lessons before. It was great, because that was the financial state of stability that we had achieved in the band by then. We were on our fourth big tour of America and, even though it was as big as

Somewhere In Time, Seventh Son... was, like, our biggest album everywhere else in the world. And we'd learnt from the Powerslave experience, and from all the previous tours, that we had to build in some space for ourselves where we could just get away from it all for a day or two and do something completely different. Steve had his soccer and Adrian liked to go fishing... There was a lot of escapism on that tour."

Maiden also surprised their fans by announcing a world tour that, for once, would begin in America first and would then wind its way around the rest of the world back to Britain, rather than the other way around, which is how they had always previously done it. But there was method in their madness. The band had something special planned for the UK: their first headline appearance at Castle Donington.

On paper, it was a dream gig. In 1988, Maiden and Donington seemed made for each other. The latter had overtaken Reading as the largest, most prestigious outdoor rock festival in Britain, an annual showcase for the world's biggest heavy-metal bands, then in its eighth year, which regularly attracted crowds of over 50,000 and had subsequently been imitated all over the world. (By 1988, more than a dozen countries, including America, were holding copycat festivals under the same Monsters Of Rock motif.) And of course the former were by now the biggest British heavy-metal band in the world and had also by now inspired their share of imitators. Only AC/DC had ever headlined Donington before without having played there lower down on the bill at some point first. "Maiden had been offered Donington many times before," remembers agent John Jackson, "and Rod was always keen for them to do it, but we had always turned it down, because we wanted them to wait until they could headline it. We wanted the first time they ever did it to be right at the top so that it was really special, and we wanted to make sure we put the best bill ever together for them, too, which we managed to do, I think. We wanted it to be the biggest ever, and it was!"

It certainly was, and is still regarded as the finest bill ever to grace the stage at Donington. Supporting Maiden that day were some of the biggest names in '80s rock – from the top: Kiss, David Lee Roth, Megadeth, Guns N' Roses and Helloween

"Maurice Jones, the promoter, had been on at us for years to do it, but it's like John says, we knew we'd do it one year; it was just a question of trying to pick the right year," says Rod. "Like everything with Maiden, we wanted to wait until the time was absolutely right, and 1988 was it, absolutely, without a doubt. Great bill, great crowd... It should have been their crowning glory."

And so it was, in many ways. With 'The Evil That Men Do' released as a single in time for the show and their second from the album to go Top Five, over 100,000 people came to Donington that day, the biggest attendance ever recorded for the event, before or since. Maiden played a blistering, nearly two-hour-long set, climaxing with a massive fireworks display that held the spellbound, chanting crowd enthralled for a good half hour after the band finally left the stage. As Rod says, it should have been their proudest moment. Instead, as they filed back into the dressing room, they discovered that the biggest day of their lives had also been the worst.

It was Rod who broke the news. Earlier that afternoon, two young fans had been crushed to death in the crowd at the front of the stage. It had been raining on and off all day, and the front area of the sloping field where the Donington stage was set up had become a mudbath. During the excitement and frantic jostling for position that ensued as Guns N' Roses took to the stage at 2pm, two young lads – 18-year-old Alan Dick, from Rhu in Dumbartonshire, and 20-year-old Landon Siggers – lost their footing and fell into the mud, where they were unwittingly trampled underfoot. Security crews realised that something was wrong within minutes and managed to get a signal to Guns N' Roses to stop their set while they worked at retrieving the bodies from the mud. Both lads were immediately whisked to the emergency medical room beneath the stage, but it was too late. It was a ghastly accident for which no one was really to blame, but that didn't stop everybody looking for scapegoats. In a letter to *Kerrang!*, Maurice Jones, head of the festival's promoters, MCP, insisted that the size of the crowd that day had nothing to do with it, pointing out that the site was less than half full when the dreadful incident occurred. "This incident could have happened with a crowd of 5,000-10,000," he wrote, "and may happen again unless people respect fellow human beings." Jones reckoned that, out of the total crowd, "maybe 40 or 50 people created a problem. Were they the same people who smashed up the toilets and destroyed

100 metres of campsite fence and chopped down trees after we had spent £5,000 on firewood?" he added accusingly.

The truth is that nobody knows. None of the bands were informed of the tragedy until after Maiden had finally clambered offstage more than eight hours later, and in retrospect a more pertinent question might be, should the festival have been allowed to continue once the deaths had been made known to the organisers?

"When we did Donington that year, it felt like the cap on all our achievements," says Adrian. "But my main memories now are pretty tragic, because the deaths of those two kids just overshadowed everything. It's got to. But we weren't told until right afterwards, so my main memories of the show itself is of it being such a big gig. The pressure built up to an almost intolerable level in the days leading up to it. We were in England and all we heard for days was, 'What do you think of Donington?' It was what I imagine it must be like playing in the cup final, maybe. I remember it started to rain again just before we went on and the stage was really slippy, and it was nearly the full Spiñal Tap – I thought I was gonna come on for the biggest gig of my life sliding across the stage on my arse. But I managed to keep my balance, somehow. Then, for the first 20 minutes or so, it was so nerve-wracking I don't really remember anything except fear. Then we settled down and the songs started coming together and we really started to play, and by the end we were all really enjoying ourselves, really going for it. The crowd were incredible. We turned the lights on at one point and as far as you could look out you could see people. All Maiden fans. It was an unbelievable thing to stand there and see. Afterwards, they just gave us a chance to catch our breaths and then someone came in and broke the news."

"The crazy thing was, earlier on in the day I was on the side of the stage watching David Lee Roth and I remember the security trying to get his attention, because there was people obviously in serious trouble down the front," says Steve. "Some security guy actually climbed on the stage to get Roth's attention and he went fucking mad, like, 'Get the fuck off my stage!' He obviously wasn't paying attention to what was going on. So I thought, 'Fuck this. Someone's gonna get seriously hurt here,' so I rushed off to get Stuart, who was the promoter's assistant, and I said to him, 'Look, you've got to get Roth to make an announcement or do something, because someone's gonna get seriously hurt.' And so, when we were told after the show that two people had died, I thought it was during Roth's set. It wasn't – it was earlier in the day, during the Guns N' Roses set – but who knows? If I hadn't gone and said something at the time, it might have even been worse. I don't know."

John Jackson had been standing at the side of the stage during the Guns N' Roses set when the accident happened. "You could tell fairly quickly that there was a major problem," he says. "When a band's onstage, there's always a lot of swirling around, and because it was so muddy the kids just lost their footing and went down. It's impossible, looking down from stage, to see if people are actually on the floor, but I knew something was going on. The security guys had spotted something, and they immediately relayed that there was a problem to the crew on the stage, who quickly got a message to the GN'R guys, who were fantastic. They were 15 minutes into a storming set, second band on, and suddenly they were told to stop, which they did. They couldn't have had any idea what was going on, but they cooled the set down completely. They stopped and did some slow, rambling, ad lib bluesy thing to calm the audience down and, in effect, ruined their own set. But thank God they did.

"The kids were taken into the St John's Ambulance unit, but my head told me they were dead straight away. I can't remember exactly when it was confirmed to me that deaths had occurred, but it wasn't long after. Very, very few people realised the extent of the tragedy until later, so it wasn't necessarily discussed that the show should be called off, one of the reasons being that the crowd had settled and we didn't want to start more trouble. I've got an aerial photo of the audience actually taken around the time of the tragedy, and there was loads and loads of room on the site still, plus you could see people still coming up the roads and through the turnstiles. It wasn't a question of a crush; it was a question of people losing their footing because of the mud."

Had either he or Maurice Jones actually considered cancelling the rest of the show, though? "I don't think so," he says. "It would have been very difficult to tell that many people that the show was cancelled. It could have caused an even greater crowd problem. Over 100,000 people turned up that day, and nearly half of them were still on their way at the time of the tragedy. The previous record attendance had been 66,500, for AC/DC in 1984, so it was a huge crowd. More than 35,000 people just turned up on the day expecting to buy tickets. Rod knew, but we decided Maiden mustn't know. I don't believe that any of the other bands knew until afterwards, either. When we told the Maiden boys afterwards, I could see in their eyes that this was going to crucify them. The atmosphere after the show was horrible, really rotten. There was no after-show party or anything like that. We couldn't. Most of us just sort of hung about for a while and then just drifted off separately. After what happened to those poor kids, or what the families must have been feeling, there's not really a lot you can say in situations like that, is there?"

The tabloid press, of course, had a field day in the immediate aftermath of the tragedy, calling for not just Donington but all large outdoor music festivals to be banned, a ludicrous notion, but tellingly it was the last time you would ever be able to just turn up on the day and buy a ticket for Donington. From then on, the audience limit was capped by court order to 72,500. As John says, "If any good could possibly come out of those kids dying, in the future the organisation was always much more closely looked at. People will always go to festivals. They can be great days out for everybody. You look at how many there are every year in Britain and how many people go, and there's very little trouble. You can say it's only music, but it's important to people; it has a special place in their lives. Driving on the motorway is dangerous, but you've still got to get where you're going. Another kid, who had been pulled from the mud and was in a coma for a while, still came down to the next gig. He was one of the lucky ones, I suppose. But we brought him backstage at the Sheffield City Hall on the proper tour we did that winter and made a fuss of him. Thank God he, at least, made it."

Maiden headlined the Monsters Of Rock bill all over Europe throughout August and September. Then, after a brief break in October, the band set out on a brief thank-you tour of Britain at the end of November, ten dates that would see them undertake their first headline appearances at much larger British arenas, like the Birmingham NEC, where they played for two nights, and Wembley Arena, where again they played for two nights. The NEC shows were filmed for a new live video, which would be co-directed and edited by Steve, and the tour finally came to an end on 12 December, back at their beloved Hammersmith Odeon, scene throughout the '80s of so many Maiden triumphs. Now suddenly it was goodbye to all that. Although no one could have known it then, it would also be Adrian's last-ever gig as a member of the band, and another major turning point in their career was about to be reached.

Although Rod and the band had decided to make 1989 an official year off from any Maiden-related activities, events were about to take on their own momentum. With Steve locked away in an editing suite for the first six months of the year, splicing together the live footage that would eventually comprise the *Maiden England* video, and with Davey busy setting up a new home in Hawaii for himself and his American-born wife, Tamar, the rest of the band didn't remain idle for long.

Adrian was the first to break rank with the announcement that he was to release his first solo album, the short-lived *ASAP* (short for *Adrian Smith Album Project*). According to him, "The idea for it all began about two years before, when we had a bit of time off before starting the *Somewhere In Time* album. It all began when Nicko got bored and decided to rent a little rehearsal room just so he had somewhere to go and bash the drums. It's not the sort of thing you can really do on your own, so he rang me up out of the blue and asked me if I wanted to go down and just have a jam with him, just to stay in practice sort of thing. So I said, 'Yeah. What about if I bring a couple of mates down with me?' But give a bunch of musicians a rehearsal room for ten minutes and before you know it they'll turn it into a gig, and that's sort of what happened."

The result was a one-off bit of nonsense that Adrian and Nicko dubbed The Entire Population Of Hackney. "It was me and Nicko, Andy Barnett – who's the guitarist in FM now – and another guitarist mate called Dave Caldwell, who plays in Bad Company now," says Adrian. "Then we had another mate of theirs called Richard Young on keyboards, and basically we just did a couple of gigs for a laugh – a pub in Gravesend called the Red Lion and the Marquee, where loads of the Maiden mob turned up, too. We'd written a few songs together, and I was doing most of the singing, and it was good laugh. But that's all it was, at first."

Ironically, he says that the first time he felt encouraged to take the idea somewhat further was when Maiden picked up on two of the songs that Adrian had first previewed with The Entire Population Of Hackney – 'Juanita' and 'Reach Out' – and used them as B-sides to the singles from *Somewhere In Time*. "That was when I started making demos of songs that Maiden wouldn't have been interested in," Adrian explains. "Up till then, I would tend to discard ideas unless they were obviously gonna work for Maiden." Two years later, Adrian's stockpile of "stuff Maiden wouldn't be interested in" had grown into a vast catalogue of half-finished songs and different ideas. And so they might have stayed, if – further irony of ironies – Rod hadn't expressed so much enthusiasm for the demos when he heard them.

"I thought they sounded a bit like Bruce Springsteen or Bryan Adams," Rod explains now. "I didn't see it as a challenge to Maiden at all, because it was so different from what Maiden would do. It would also allow Adrian to get some of his more commercial leanings off his chest." Indeed, Adrian now says that Rod thought that the possibility of the guitarist actually having an American hit single would reflect well on Maiden's own status. "He said it would be great if we had a hit there, because it would help throw the spotlight in America back on Maiden," Adrian says.

However, despite being "given a shitload of money by EMI", the *ASAP* album failed dismally to make an impact on either side of the Atlantic. Recorded in London with Queen and David Bowie producer Steven Stewart Short and released in September 1989, it was a lacklustre affair with none of the material reaching anywhere near the heights of Adrian's more disciplined writing for Maiden. There had been a short ASAP club tour in the UK, with Zak Starkey (Ringo's son) replacing Nicko on the drums, and Adrian spent two weeks promoting the album with interviews in America, but all to no avail. He blames the album's lack of success now on the fact that "it wasn't metal enough for metal fans, and the fact I was in Maiden didn't cut any ice with the potential new market. I mean, basically it was a non-starter, commercially. Completely out there on its own."

The band had reconvened for a brief get-together in November 1989 for the release of the *Maiden England* video, a far more faithful reconstruction of the live Maiden experience, perhaps, than *Live After*

Death from four years earlier. Out went the lightning-fast cuts and zippy editing and in came the more steady eye of the true connoisseur – in this case, Steve himself, who had both directed and edited the final cut. EMI and Sanctuary threw a lavish launch party with a strong British theme – the hall was decked out with Union Jacks and the assembled media guests tucked into traditional English grub: fish and chips and warm, dark bitter. The launch had been a great success, and *Maiden England* became one of the biggest-selling video collections of the year in Britain.

After having spent the last six months working, Steve was intent on enjoying some downtime himself and repaired to the villa in Portugal he had "treated myself to when we first made a bit of dough". Bruce, meanwhile, was about to become very busy indeed. Like Adrian, he says now that he'd never seriously considered the idea of making a solo album until an uncontrived set of circumstances prevailed upon him to take what was, in retrospect, an almost inevitable step for the ambitious singer. Unlike Adrian's low-profile sortie, however, the repercussions of Bruce's headlong plunge into a solo project would effectively change the face of Maiden forever.

Rod had called him and said that Zomba were looking for somebody to do a track for the movie *A Nightmare On Elm Street, Part Five*. There was a budget, a studio and a producer, which was Chris Tzangarides, and when Rod asked if Bruce had "anything kicking about, I was, like, 'Yeah, definitely!' You know, lying." But he phoned up his mate Janick Gers, a former guitarist in Deep Purple singer Ian Gillan's solo band, Gillan, who had returned to college to do a degree when the band broke up, in 1983.

"Jan was an old mate who hadn't really done anything for a while, and he was getting so depressed he told me he was gonna sell all his gear," says Bruce, "and it made me really cross, 'cause he's a great player, Jan. He just wasn't having any luck at the time. So, when Rod told me this, I went, 'Me and Jan will do it.' So I phoned him up and said, 'You can't sell your fucking gear now. I've got something for you to do.'"

Janick Robert Gers was born in Hartlepool on 27 January 1957, the eldest of three children (he has a younger brother and sister). "My father had been in the Polish Navy, which is how he came to England, where he met my mother," says Janick. "Then he went into the British Royal

Navy after they were married, and then he went into the Merchant Navy after that. When I was born, he was still at sea for the first year, and then he had to stop and come back. There was a lot of Polish people living in that area, because there were big docks in Hartlepool, so he met my mum and they got married and Bob's your uncle."

As a child, little Jan's favourite activities were "swimming, football and music, in that order. I've always loved the footie, and still do, but swimming was the big thing when I was a little kid. I used to go training every day. Then that all just suddenly stopped when I got into music. I couldn't play, but I loved posing in front of the bedroom mirror with this plastic Beatles guitar my mum and dad had got me. In primary school, when we did the school play, me and my mates were always the band. We used to make cardboard guitars and colour them in, and we all dressed up and pretended to do *Top Of The Pops*, just miming to the records. We must have been about nine, and we kept, like, this little imaginary band going for years. I was the guitar player always. I wanted to be John Lennon. Then the first proper guitar I got was when I was about eleven, a little old acoustic. Terrible action! It was so hard to play."

He first got his hands on an electric guitar, what he calls "a little Woolworth's jobby", when he was 13 and immediately discarded the acoustic, but it wasn't until he was 18 that "I got my hands on the real deal", a white Gibson Fender Stratocaster. "That was my first proper electric guitar, and it's the one I'm still using now," he says. "I got it second hand from a guy in Darlington for 200 quid. I saved most of it up from a paper round. Then, 'cause it was coming up to my 18th birthday, my mum gave me some money towards it as well. It felt brilliant the moment I strapped it on. I remember thinking, 'Wow, this is fucking *it!*' Of course, once I had the Strat, I could join a real band. We did covers, and at our first gig at the school there was a big fight before we went on because we had to wear school uniform and we said we wouldn't, but the teachers wouldn't let us on in our stage clothes, so we all put our school ties on and went on like that as a sort of compromise."

After The Beatles, Janick got heavily into rock. It was 1970 and he loved "the wild guitar playing and the long-haired look" and began collecting albums and reading the music papers. "I really liked Deep Purple, Rory Gallagher, T Rex," he says. "Folky stuff, too, like Lindisfarne. Later on, I got more into Led Zeppelin. At first, I couldn't get into Robert Plant's voice – it was a bit high, to me; I thought he sounded like a girlie – but I really loved Ian Gillan, because he had this scream, and it was like everything I felt, the aggression that came out, and I identified with that. And because of that, I got off on Ritchie Blackmore's playing as well, and that really started me off. I was always doing solos, because I could never play chords, that was the thing. I'm not one of those that thinks about what they do before they do it. Certainly not playing live. My timing isn't particularly brilliant, but to me music's not mathematical; it's to do with your heart and how you're feeling. And if you play solos, you can go, like, 'Fuck the timing,' and just express yourself. Sometimes the mistakes are better than what you would have tried to think up, anyway."

He used to "just sit and play all the time, really" with his electric guitar and amplifier permanently set up in his bedroom. "I must have driven everybody mad. The only other thing I did was play football, and I was never a very good footballer."

Then he answered an advert in *The Hartlepool Mail*. "It was just 'Guitarist Wanted'," he recalls, "but I went along, and I think we played 'Strange Kind Of Woman' or something by Purple. I remember we were in a church hall, it was a Saturday afternoon, and this woman with her curlers in burst in and went, 'Will you shut that racket up?' I felt like saying, 'Excuse me, this is no racket. This is our music.'"

The band was White Spirit, a five-piece who first came together in the summer of 1975, just as Janick was studying for his A-levels. Featuring two guitars, keyboards and harmony backing vocals, their roots lay deep in the Deep Purple/Uriah Heep/Rush axis, a splendid mix of hard rock and synthesised prog that would eventually win them a deal with the independent label Neat Records, who issued their debut single, 'Back To The Grind', in 1978.

"It was quite a big deal in the Northeast, but I was just going to enjoy it while it lasted," he says. "We went out and toured and earned enough money just to keep going. We were all still on the dole. Then, later, after we did the album, the dole office got on to us and were, like, 'Come on, you must have been earning a fortune,' but we weren't. It's amazing how little you can survive on when you're young and just desperate to keep playing."

Picked up for a major deal by MCA, their debut album, *White Spirit*, was produced by Gillan bassist John McCoy and released (although to much less commotion) in the same year that Maiden released their debut album, 1980. "That whole NWOBHM thing just passed us by, really," he says. (Historical footnote: 'Midnight Chaser', the first single from *White Spirit*, bears a striking similarity to 'Two Minutes To Midnight'. "When I played it to Steve, he couldn't believe it," Janick grins, "but it was Number One in Neal Kay's Bandwagon chart for a long time. And I'm not saying Adrian heard it or ripped it off, just maybe it was buried in his subconscious somewhere.")

"I remember there were three pages in *Sounds* about the Bandwagon: Samson, Iron Maiden and somebody else, making it seem like there was a real scene going on," he recalls, "but it really wasn't as big as what everybody imagined. We were part of it, I suppose, but it was never written. It was only when people looked back that we got lumped in with the rest. We were just doing what we'd been doing for the last five years, and I'm sure Maiden were doing the same thing."

The band were offered the chance to support Gillan on their 46-date British tour that year, when for the first time Janick met Ian Gillan, his hero, at the opening show in Derby. "It was like getting to meet Father Christmas when you're a kid," he laughingly recalls. But Santa had more in his sack than just good wishes, and when Janick got a call from the Gillan camp some months later asking him if he'd mind actually joining Gillan's band, "I thought it was someone winding me up. I thought, 'Ian Gillan wants me to be his new guitarist? Fuck off!'"

However, it was true. Gillan's own guitarist, Bernie Tormé, had packed his bags after a row and left the band stranded in the middle of a German tour and, as Gillan himself later explained, "Janick was the first bloke we thought of. We'd all really admired his playing in White Spirit when they toured with us, and it was fairly obvious from talking to him that he was into my music, and so we thought, 'Well, let's give him a call and see if he's doing anything.'" With White Spirit's career flagging in the shadow of more-talked-about new British rock bands like Maiden, Saxon and Def Leppard, Janick grabbed his chance with both hands.

"I've been fairly lucky in my career," he admits. "I never intended to join Gillan or Iron Maiden. I can swear that point blank. It crossed my mind to play with Bruce, but it never crossed my mind in the slightest to join Iron Maiden. They'd got Adrian and Dave. What would they want three guitarists for? That was my attitude, until they told me different."

Janick would record two albums with Gillan: the live *Double Trouble* album, a Top Ten hit in the UK in 1981; and *Magic*, another Top Ten entry, in 1982. The band broke up not long after, however, when the singer's interest waned enough for him to accept an invitation to join Black Sabbath, who were then still a major band in America, where Gillan hadn't known success since he had left Deep Purple ten years earlier. By then, however, the young guitarist he left behind admits now that "I probably would have left the band myself sooner or later, anyway". Janick was the young rocker who wanted to lay down the law with his riffs; Gillan was the veteran frontman who, as he says, "had been there, done all that and bought the T-shirt" and was now more interested in recording covers of unlikely material like Stevie Wonder's 'Living For The City' and 'Cathy's Clown' by The Everly Brothers.

"I remember the first time *Number Of The Beast* was on the telly and I dragged Ian to watch it," Janick remembers. "I said, 'That's what we wanna do. That's where I'm at. That's rock 'n' roll!' And Ian said, 'Yeah, I know, but I've done that.' And he had a point. He *had* done it. But I was saying, 'I want them lights! I want that dry ice!'"

When the end came, Janick found himself unemployed, although considerably richer for the experience. Unsure what to do next, though, and with the phone ominously silent, he decided to go back to college and take a degree in Humanities. "I never gave up playing," he says. "I still kept all my gear, but it was a long while before I really got going again."

There had been several stop-and-start attempts at getting back into a full-time situation. In 1986, former Twisted Sister singer Dee Snider approached him about joining his solo band, which also contained one Clive Burr on drums. "He rang me up and we talked, but I remember saying, 'There is no way in this world that I am wearing make-up or anything like that. I'm just not into that shit.' But we had a chat, and he seemed a nice enough guy, but I never heard back from him."

Then there was the time he joined forces, briefly, with Paul Di'Anno in the ludicrously named Gog Magog. "Out of the blue I got a call from Jonathan King, who gives me this spiel about this sort of concept which he was trying to sell to America for a lot of money, this heavy-metal band called Gog Magog," he says. "It's out of the Bible, apparently. Gog and Magog were the two beasts that stand at the gates of hell. And basically he wanted to put a band together of people who had been in major bands. He says, 'I've got Clive Burr and Paul Di'Anno from Iron Maiden, I've got Pete Willis from Def Leppard and Neil Murray from Whitesnake, and we want to complement it with you.' So I said, 'Yeah, fine. I'll do that.' So he arranged some rehearsals and some recording time and we all got together and had a really good laugh. Pete Willis was a lovely little lad, Neil I've known from before, Clive I'd already met, and Paul, who's a lovely fella. Got a self-destruct button which he likes to push a bit too often, but a really lovely lad."

In the end, however, the deal crumbled with King's failure to land the sizeable deal he was after to launch the band. The original Gog Magog demo tapes later surfaced as a twelve-inch, four-track EP on the independent Food For Thought label but, as Janick says, "There was no money in it."

In 1987, however, Janick accepted an invitation that would change his outlook dramatically when what began as a guest appearance onstage with Marillion at Wembley Arena for the Prince's Trust concert in 1988 turned into an invitation to help Bruce Dickinson record his first solo album.

"I'd known Bruce since Samson days, and we'd always been really pally," he says. "We lived 'round the corner from each other in Chiswick, and we'd go to gigs together sometimes or parties, and we'd both got to know Fish and the Marillion boys. I always thought Marillion were a brilliant band. Like me and Bruce, Fish was an old Deep Purple/Ian Gillan fan, too, so we all had things in common. Then, when we got invited up to play with them at this Prince's Trust gig, Bruce was all for it, but I wasn't so sure. It had been a long time since I'd played live. Not since Gillan, in fact. But we did it, and it was tremendous. We did three songs, all covers: 'All The Young Dudes', by Mott The Hoople; 'The Boys Are Back In Town', by Thin Lizzy; and the Joe Cocker version of '(I Get By) With A Little Help (From My Friends)'."

When Fish left Marillion not long afterwards, he invited Janick up to his farm in Edinburgh to see if they could write together, and although it wasn't destined to be a long-lived a partnership, Janick co-wrote and played guitar on 'View From A Hill', possible the best track on the first Fish solo album, *Vigil In The Wilderness Of Mirrors*, released in 1989. "The first time I heard it," says Bruce, "it just knocked me out. I thought, 'Fish is mad to lose this guy. He can really write as well as play.'"

"Bruce called me and I went 'round to see him and he brought out this song that sounded AC/DC-ish," says Janick, "and I said, 'Nah, it wants to be more like...' So I put the chords in and then we re-did the chorus. He was trying to get away from the Maiden sound, so he was very open to ideas. And we went in, we recorded it in a day, two days, whatever, and it was great. I really liked it, you know? And that was 'Bring Your Daughter To The Slaughter'."

"I wrote it in about three minutes," says Bruce. "I don't know where the title 'Bring Your Daughter To The Slaughter' came from, but it just popped into my head. I thought, 'Bloody hell, straight out of AC/DC!' And I thought, '*Nightmare On Elm Street*. Yeah, that'll do.' Zomba went absolutely mad. They were, like, 'This is fucking great!' The guy called up the office and says, 'I can't believe this. Have you got any more stuff like this?' And I went, 'Well, yeah. There's a few things kicking about.' Lying through my teeth again. I said, 'Look, how about if we do an album?' He said, 'Fuck it. Yeah, all right.' So I called up Jan and said, 'You definitely can't sell your gear now, you bastard. We're making an album!'"

The intention, says Bruce, was not so different from Adrian's, "To do something you wouldn't in Maiden. Otherwise, what's the point in doing it?" Only this was to be a spontaneous combustion of songs, not something that they'd worked on meticulously, as Adrian had for months. The whole album was written and recorded in two weeks. "The quickest two weeks of my life," laughs Janick. A mixture of Bruce and Janick originals spiced with covers, *Tattooed Millionaire* is certainly a far more entertaining album than the earnest-sounding *ASAP*. From the bluesy Bad Company style of 'Son Of A Gun' to the quiveringly powerful version of 'All The Young Dudes' (a more potent re-enactment of the Prince's Trust performance, which also provided Bruce with his first solo hit single in the summer of 1990) to the upbeat Stonesy swagger of the title track (itself another Top 20 hit in the UK), Bruce had proved – to himself, at least – that he could live without Maiden. He even managed to squeeze a four-week tour of America out of it with his own band, comprising Janick on guitar, Andy Carr on bass and Fabio del Rio on drums. "We didn't do any Maiden songs, either," recalls Bruce. They encored each night with Purple's 'Black Knight' and AC/DC's 'Sin City'.

Ironically, the one Bruce and Janick song that didn't end up on *Tattooed Millionaire* was the one that had caused all of this commotion in the first place. Steve had intercepted it. "There was no way I could do it," he says, "'cause I was busy trying to finish the *Maiden England* video, so Rod asked Bruce if he wanted to do this film soundtrack and the next thing he comes up with 'Bring Your Daughter...' I said, 'Fucking hell! That's a great song! That would be great for Maiden. Don't do it on your solo album. We can do it for Maiden.' And he was happy that I said that, I think, 'cause he was quite pleased that he'd written a song that we wanted to do for the band."

"Steve heard the track before I'd even thought of putting it on the album, and he was, like, 'I want that song,'" says Bruce. 'So I was, like, 'All right, great.' My version – which only came out on the American version of the soundtrack album – is quite substantially different to the Iron Maiden version. The arrangement is identical, but mine's kind of...slinky. Maiden's just really goes for it. But I was happy that Steve liked something that much. In actual fact, I wandered back into Maiden to start the new album a very happy-go-lucky little leprechaun, so there was no intention whatsoever of leaving at that stage. If anything, the joy of doing my own album had made me sure I was happy where I was."

The first Iron Maiden album of the '90s, and the first to be produced on home soil since *Number Of The Beast*, seven years earlier, *No Prayer For The Dying* was recorded with The Rolling Stones' mobile studio in a converted barn on the side of the grounds of Steve's mansion in Essex in early in 1990. Before the first note could played, however, it became apparent that not everything in the garden was rosy. The thorn in the band's side this time was Adrian, who it quickly became obvious was not happy. Writing for the album had, as ever, proceeded swiftly. Steve, the only prolific songwriter in the band not to make a solo album in the intervening years between *Seventh Son...* and *No Prayer...*, had a hatful of new numbers that he wanted the band to work on, and by the time he was ready to call in The Rolling Stones' mobile Adrian realised that he himself had so far only contributed to one track, something that he and Bruce had been working on called 'Hooks In You', which did actually end up on the album but with Janick now playing Adrian's parts.

"The plan was to spend three months writing together at Steve's, taking our time and getting a vibe going," says Adrian. "Then, after what seemed like just a couple of weeks, it was suddenly decided to get the Stones' mobile in and start recording, and I was completely thrown by the idea. I wanted more time to finish writing the songs. I'd had the time off with *ASAP*, and maybe I'd used up some of my creative energy on that, but I think maybe *ASAP* had shocked a lot of people, too. It perhaps sent the wrong signals to the band in some way, like they were worried that I wasn't into doing metal any more."

He was also reluctant to go down the stripped-down, more "street-level" road that Steve was planning to take for the next album: "The vibe was, 'Let's go back and make a really raw-sounding album like *Killers*,' and I didn't want to do that. I thought we were heading in the right direction with the last two albums. I thought it was a step backwards to strip it all down again. I thought we needed to keep going forward, and it just didn't feel like that to me. But my attitude wasn't, 'Right, I'm leaving!' I just wasn't 100 per cent about things. And that was it. Once I'd expressed some doubt, Steve said, 'You don't really seem like you want to be in the band. If you're into it 110 per cent, that's fine, we can continue. But don't forget, you've got to hack another year on the road. Are you sure you want to do that?' And the more I thought about it, the more I thought maybe he was right. You can't go through all that if you're not 100 per cent happy. It would be a disaster and not very fair to anybody."

Steve, however, thinks that Adrian had been unhappy for a long time: "There was always something wrong. Sometimes he'd have his head down and we'd pull faces at him – you know, trying to cheer him up – but he wasn't having none of it. Then, before going in and doing *Seventh Son...*, I said to him, 'Look, do you want to be on this next album?' and he was, like, 'Yeah, yeah. Course I do.' I said, 'I just wanted to hear you say it, that's all.' But we did the *Seventh Son...* album, did the tour, and he seemed a little bit more up. But towards the end of it again, and going into the next album, Adrian seemed really negative about a lot of things. He just didn't seem to have the passion any more, and so it came out again, the six-million-dollar question, 'Do you or don't you want to be in the band?' And he was, like, 'Well, I don't know. I haven't had time to think about it.' And I thought, 'Well, hold on a minute,' you know? 'All I want to hear is, "Of course I bloody do. Don't be stupid."' That's the sort of answer we wanted. I know he's quite indecisive, to say the least – his nickname on the tour was Willy Orwonthe – but this was serious."

"It was decided to have a band meeting," says Adrian. "It was mainly Steve that did the talking. He said, 'You don't seem happy or into it any more,' and I said, 'Well...' and took a deep breath and went on for about an hour, talking about how I felt. I'd just done an album really expressing myself, really happy singing and playing. I knew Maiden was its own thing, and I was still happy to contribute to that, but it didn't look like I was going to get much of a chance to do that on the next album. I felt we needed more time to work on new songs, but the mobile had arrived and I hadn't written any songs and I was just very unhappy."

"So we sort of said, 'OK, you know, perhaps we'd better make the decision for you, then,'" says Steve, "and we said, 'If you're not 100 per cent, then you can't do it.' And he sort of shrugged his shoulders and said, 'I was hoping it was going to go the other way.' He was hoping that we still wanted him. But he had to want to be there first. It was awful for me, 'cause I really like Adrian. Personally, I was probably closer to him than anyone, and it gutted me. It gutted me that he didn't want to be there any more, but I thought, 'We've got to be strong about this. We can't keep someone there just hanging,' you know?"

"I wish I could have just gone in and said, 'Yeah, great, whatever,' you know?" says Adrian. "But life is not black and white. There's always doubts, especially as you get older, and it all happened over a couple of agonising days. There were lots of long phone calls. It was all very emotional. Maiden had been my life for ten years. It had become like a family to me. It felt strange at first, I admit – I didn't have that day-to-day involvement any more that I'd lived on for so long – but at the same time it felt like it was a weight off my shoulders. The truth is, I was unhappy. I felt stifled, after doing my own album, and coming back and not having any new ideas... It just got to me in the end."

A replacement would have to be found, and fast. "Bruce would never mention what was going on," says Janick, "but I knew Davey and I knew Adrian and I really liked them both, so I knew everybody in the band, but I didn't know what was about to happen. Then I got a phone call one afternoon from Bruce. He said, 'Would you learn some Maiden numbers?' The first thing I said was, 'No,' because we'd agreed we weren't gonna do any Maiden songs when we toured. So I said, 'Why do you want to do Maiden numbers?' He said, 'Well, somebody's leaving and we'd like you to come and rehearse with the band.' I said, 'Well, who's gone?' He said, 'Adrian.' I was, like, 'What? Say that again?' I mean, I was really shocked. My girlfriend said I was as white as a sheet when I got off the phone. She thought someone had died or something."

Janick auditioned for the band at Steve's barn three days later. "They said, 'What do you want to do first?'" Janick remembers. "I said, '"The Trooper".' I thought, 'We'll do that one. It's fast and furious. I'll be all right. Then me and Davey sort of charged into the first notes of 'The Trooper' and it just worked! It was just like *that*. The whole thing just took off. When we finished, I was shaking with the adrenaline, and I remember Bruce saying, 'Shit! That sounded incredible!' So we did another one – it might have been 'Iron Maiden' – and then 'The Prisoner' and maybe one other, I can't remember. Then they just huddled up in the corner and had a talk. Then Steve came over and said, 'You're in. And we start recording tomorrow.' I was, like, '*What?*'"

Sure enough, they began work the very next day, rehearsing the material with their new guitarist in the morning and recording in the afternoon. Martin Birch was again producing and the whole thing was done and dusted in under three weeks. Musically, the results were, it's fair to say now, mixed. As advertised, the sound is distinctly low key, compared to the kitchen-sink ambience of their two previous albums. Gone are the synthesisers and concepts, replaced by the warm hiss of room-temperature guitars cranking themselves up into a fever.

However, if the production is restrained, the playing is anything but. The band never sounded so "live" in the studio before. In places, the album sounds almost like a well-heeled demo. There are ten tracks in all, including just three songs solely by Steve this time: the melancholic title track, a far more mature and reflective piece than anything he had done before; 'The Assassin', which again is much more inward looking and mature than perhaps its shock-horror title suggests; and 'Mother Russia', in truth not one of Steve's more compelling epics, which closes the album on a disappointingly bleak note. Interestingly, some of the strongest material was written by Steve in conjunction with Bruce: the rip-roaring 'Tailgunner', which opens the album in fine, fire-spitting style; 'Holy Smoke', the *bravura* first single from the album, which crashed into the UK Top Ten in September 1990; and 'Run Silent, Run Deep', a melodramatic bit of pomp that steals attractively from Zeppelin's 'Kashmir'. The remaining four tracks comprised Bruce and Adrian's 'Hooks In You', which, compared to earlier Smith/Dickinson classics like 'Two Minutes To Midnight', is strictly second-rate fare; Bruce and Davey's 'Public Enema Number One', which, despite its truly dreadful title, is actually a neat piece of social commentary; Steve and Davey's 'Fates Warning', another moody, affecting piece featuring some of Steve's most thought-provoking lyrics ever; and finally, of course, the wonderful burlesque of Bruce and Janick's 'Bring Your Daughter To The Slaughter', perhaps the greatest track that Alice Cooper never recorded.

Released on 1 October 1990, *No Prayer For The Dying* crashed straight in at Number Two in the UK and went on to repeat its success everywhere else in the world, with the exception of America, where – although it went gold – its 500,000 sales was a drop from the five previous platinum albums. As we shall discover, the tide of popular opinion was turning not just against Iron Maiden but also the whole '80s heavy-metal ethos as a whole, to be replaced – at least temporarily – by a new, more self-conscious strain of heavy rock: grunge. But America – just like Heaven – could wait.

Released as the second single from the album, in January 1991, 'Bring Your Daughter...' also became Maiden's first-ever UK Number One single, where it stayed for three wonderfully *Top-Of-The-Pops*-perverting weeks, an astonishing feat made even more commendable by the BBC's churlish attitude to the record, refusing to playlist it on Radio 1 and showing barely 90 seconds of the live video clip on the aforementioned programme.

"I've never really been into singles," says Steve, "but seeing 'Bring Your Daughter...' go to Number One, I've got to admit, did make me feel proud. Even after all this time, it just made me feel excited again, like it really was all worthwhile, like a vindication that we must be doing something right. Musically, we'd got a little...not overproduced, but we just tried to get the album to sound as live as possible, 'cause we liked the sound in the barn, here, the actual room itself, and we thought, 'Well, we can't really get more live than this. We'll get a mobile studio in and just keep it as raw as possible.' For me, it didn't quite come off. I think if we'd had audience noise it would have made a hell of a difference. That's what we should have done. But again, it depends who you're talking to. Some people think it's our best album and some people think it's our worst album. Me, I don't think it's our best, but it's certainly not our worst. There's some bloody good songs on there. You could tell by how the audience reacted when we played stuff like 'Holy Smoke' and 'Tailgunner' live."

After not treading the boards for almost two years, the No Prayer On The Road tour got under way with a "secret" gig in Milton Keynes on 19 September 1990. After the mammoth production of the previous tour, like the new album it was a back-to-basics approach this time around, with a minimum of stage set and lighting. However, with Janick – the original whirling dervish of the stage – they didn't need any props. His high-maintenance nightly performances rubbed off on everyone, especially Davey, who himself suddenly began to spin into areas of the stage he'd forgotten about.

"We thought the Seventh Son... stage show just got a bit out of hand," reflects Steve. "I mean, the actual Eddie and the backdrops I thought looked amazing, but the giant icebergs and stuff were a bit naff, I think, and we just wanted to get away from all that and turn everything into like a massive club gig again, which we really managed to do. And having Janick in the band gave everybody a much-needed kick up the arse, too, because, being new, he was so enthusiastic about everything. I think it made us all open our eyes a bit and look at things in a new way."

This was just as well, for the '90s had only just begun, a new decade which didn't belong to them but to those who would come after them, and Maiden would soon have to face their toughest challenge yet.

14 Blaze

Only America had failed to fully embrace the new stripped-down Iron Maiden that had coincided with the arrival of Janick Gers. Although it went gold, *No Prayer...* was their least successful album in America since *Number Of The Beast* had first propelled them into the Top 40 there, seven years earlier. It was a period of great upheaval in American rock music, the very culture that supported it changing almost beyond recognition as both the music and the fans mutated into ever more specialised niches. Maiden found their appeal threatened on the one hand by the competing success of self-styled thrash-metal icons like Metallica, Megadeth (who both enjoyed their first Number One albums in America in the early '90s) and Slayer and on the other by an entirely unforeseen enemy: the '90s itself. Out went the big shows and long hair of the '80s; in came moody, minimalist stage sets, thrift-store clothes and despair-ridden Generation X anthems as newly emerging stars like Nirvana, Pearl Jam and Soundgarden began to redefine the way in which hard rock and heavy metal were both perceived and presented. The critics, as ever, had a name for it, grunge, and although Maiden themselves had returned to more down-to-earth production values, they were one of many '80s rock giants to be felled commercially in the US by the new rock reality.

However, everywhere else in the world – especially back home in Britain, where grunge was also the new ruling passion – Maiden's star continued its ascent apparently unabated, and their next album, their ninth, *Fear Of The Dark*, would become one of their best sellers. Preceded by the excellent Number Two single and manic, chest-beating opener, 'Be Quick Or Be Dead', *Fear Of The Dark* became Maiden's

Bruce Dickinson
flanked by
Sanctuary founders
Rod Smallwood
and Andy Taylor

The World Slavery Tour, 1984

Backstage in
Poland, 1984

A mummified Eddie
backs Steve Harris on
the World Slavery Tour,
1984

Maiden with comedy metal band Bad
News, Jimmy Page and Brian May
following their charity gig at the
Hammersmith Odeon, October 1984

The World Slavery Tour began in
Poland on 9 August, 1984 and
finished 190 dates later in
California on 5 July, 1985

Mummy Eddie on the World Slavery Tour, 1984/85

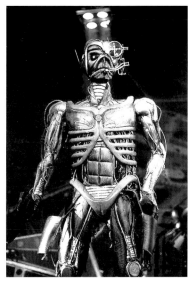

Tokyo, 1987, Somewhere On Tour

No Prayer On The Road, 1990

X Factour, 1995-6

A promotional shot of Steve, 1987

Rod shows his affection for production manager, Dickie Bell, Japan, 1987

Somewhere On Tour, 1986-7

Lars Ulrich helps out Nicko at New Jersey's Meadowlands Arena, 8 July 1988

Right: Bruce is desperate to get to the 1988 Monsters Of Rock festival where Maiden are headlining

Below: So are a record 107,000 fans

Janick Gers replaces Adrian Smith in January 1990. L-r: Janick, Dave, Bruce, Steve and Nicko

Janick in action

Dave at Donington, 1992

Steve wants more! Donington 1992

Mr Excess At All Times

Factor X: former Wolfsbane frontman Blaze Bayley replaced Bruce in 1993

Blaze-era Maiden with the star of stage, screen and now computer video game.
Ed Hunter, 1998

Back together: the first studio shot of the reformed line-up featuring Adrian and
Bruce, 2000. L-r: Dave, Nicko, Bruce, Steve, Janick and Adrian

Headlining at Rock In Rio III, 19 January 2001

The Metal 2000 Tour hits Europe. L-r: Nicko, Dave, Steve, Bruce, Adrian and Janick

third album to go to Number One in the UK, when it was released in May 1992.

Despite the turbulence that lay beneath the surface, the musical emphasis of the album was firmly on the positive, and to underline their commitment to the new decade Maiden took the unprecedented step of inviting other artists, as well as Derek Riggs, to contribute ideas for the new *Fear Of The Dark* album sleeve. "We wanted to upgrade Eddie a bit for the '90s," explains Rod. "We wanted to take him from this sort of comic-book horror creature and turn him into something a bit more straightforward so that he became even more threatening." The new Eddie was eventually selected from a design submitted by the previously unknown Melvyn Grant, who submitted an image of Eddie as some sort of Nosferatu tree figure leering at the moon. In truth, it was hard to see any real difference in style or even content from any of the earlier Eddie designs, except that this one lacked the same familial touches (no secret messages to Charlotte embedded in the picture) and displayed little of the same warped Riggs humour. "It was just our attempt to do something new," Steve shrugs.

Thankfully, the content did contain all the expected colour and detail: twelve tracks recorded in Steve's newly installed home studio in Essex. Despite the usual quota of gloomy epics you'd expect to find, *Fear Of The Dark* was easily the most entertaining Maiden album since their first, twelve years before. For a start, there were 50 per cent more tracks than there were on any previous Maiden album, the band responding to the demands of the new CD age by cranking out a more diverse range of styles than at any time before, from the bluesy, singalong boogie of Steve's 'From Here To Eternity' or Bruce's and Davey's 'Chains Of Misery' to the Zeppelin-esque grandeur of Bruce's and Janick's 'Fear Is The Key' or their razor-tongued 'Be Quick Or Be Dead', by way of the bleak, other-worldly Gulf War poem that is Steve's 'Afraid To Shoot Strangers' and his vivid, galloping, confessional title track itself. There really is something here for every Maiden fan of every era.

Of the remaining half-dozen tracks, 'Childhood's End' and 'The Fugitive' were both better-than-average songs from Steve, while 'The Apparition' and 'Weekend Warrior' were Steve and Janick efforts more worthy than memorable. 'Judas Be My Guide' was a woefully titled piece of self-absorption concocted by Bruce and Davey, while 'Wasting Love' – a ditty by Bruce and Janick dating back to his solo album – was an appealing piece of whimsy that contained the revealingly autobiographical line, "Maybe one day I'll be an honest man/Up till now I'm doing the best I can." Bruce, it seems, was finally starting to lay his cards on the table, for if, on the surface, *Fear Of The Dark* was a return to form of sorts for the band, it would also prove to be another – in retrospect, not unexpected – watershed in the band's career: the last album that Maiden would ever make with Bruce.

"When Bruce came back from his solo tour, in 1990, I realised then that he didn't have the same fire onstage with Maiden as he did with his own band," says Steve. "It seemed like he was going through the motions a bit. So I asked him then, you know, 'Are you still happy?' And he assured us that he was totally 100 per cent still there, which I think he was on the *Fear Of The Dark* album. Ironically, by then, I actually felt he was a lot more into it again, and on the first part of the tour that year his performances were better than ever. He just seemed more back into the vibe, you know, with the writing and stuff as well. I must admit, I'd been worried when he first did his solo thing. I thought he might leave then, but he didn't, so now I really thought he was back into the fold."

The Fear Of The Dark Tour opened in Scandinavia in May and wound its way around the rest of the continent throughout the summer. Several of the shows were also taped, for the band planned to release a live album mid tour. The highlight of that summer tour was the band's second headline appearance at Castle Donington in August. If the bill this time around lacked the high-profile allure of its predecessor four years earlier – replacing legends like Kiss, David Lee Roth and Guns N' Roses with less illustrious though no less worthy new faces like Skid Row, Sepultura and Thunder – Maiden surprised everybody, themselves included, by putting on an even stronger, more explosive performance than their 1988 appearance. They knew what to expect this time around and were far less affected by nerves. The entire show was filmed for yet another live album and video, both released in the following year.

The crowd was smaller than the one in 1988 due to the new restrictions imposed by local government authorities on promoters MCP after the tragic events four years earlier, but proportionately Maiden's second headline appearance there in 1992 was, and still remains, the second-best-attended Donington festival ever.

"After what had happened in 1988, they'd slapped a 72,500 crowd limit on it and they stopped the walk-up on the day," says Steve, "and I think we did something like 68,500 in advance. We were about 4,000 off a complete sell out. Since that second Donington, no fucker has done that amount either. No one. And musically, it was a lot better than the first Donington, I thought. The reaction and everything was better. We didn't expect that, to be honest, because we thought, 'It's not gonna be as good as the first one.' But maybe because we were more relaxed, I don't know, it was just better. It was still a good, strong bill, but it wasn't as strong, because we wanted to get Van Halen but they said they couldn't do it, 'cause they were gonna do their own UK tour pretty soon afterwards."

There was one person in the crowd that day who had decidedly mixed feelings about Maiden's performance: Adrian Smith, who joined the band onstage for the encores. "The first time I saw the band play after I left was at Donington, in 1992, and they were so good it felt bad, it really did," he admits. "Mind you, I'd probably picked the wrong gig to go and see. To see the songs I used to play, that I had written, being played and I wasn't there with them onstage… I felt torn in two. Part of me will always be in the band, as long as they're playing my songs. But Steve said, 'Come down and have a jam and play "Running Free" with us on the encore,' and so I did that, and it was great. It kind of rounded things off nicely and showed there were no bad feelings between me and the band, and it gave me a chance to say goodbye to the fans, which I hadn't had, because of the way things turned out."

The first leg of the tour ended on 4 November in Japan. The plan was to take a two-month break, during which Steve would oversee the mixing of the live album and prepare it for release in time for the second part of the tour, which was due to begin in the New Year.

"The Fear Of The Dark tour was always going to be in two parts, because we wanted to approach a live album in a different way," says Steve. "We wanted to do lots of different shows and pick the best songs from them and just, like, have a load of different audiences on there. The only thing I didn't really like about *Live After Death* was that the audience weren't loud enough – I mean, when you think of the amount of people that were there. And they were bloody loud at Long Beach, but they just weren't mixed loud enough. And I wanted loads and loads of audience. I thought, 'If we go to all different places, it means that a lot of the fans will say, "Whoah, that was the gig I was at!"' That was the idea of it, anyway."

But while Steve was busy mixing the album, Bruce was busy laying his own plans. "I always thought of myself as more than just the singer in Iron Maiden," he says, and by the start of the '90s it was a claim he could back up by pointing to the two novels (the Tom Sharpe-influenced tales of a preposterous character called Lord Iffy Boatrace) he had written and the various TV and radio work he had done, from being guest presenter on MTV to ringmastering serious BBC documentaries. In his spare time, he not only continued to enter and even win numerous fencing competitions around the world but also, like Nicko, qualified as a pilot. Now, with the success of his first solo album behind him, he began to think of himself even more as master of his own destiny and slowly began to resent having to "pen myself in, trying to conform to the established Maiden routine".

Despite the success of *Fear Of The Dark* and the triumph of that second Donington, Bruce was, in short, "bored and desperately looking for other things to do". Faced with the prospect of an enforced lay-off while Steve finished mixing the live tapes, when Sony enquired whether Bruce was interested in making a follow-up to *Tattooed Millionaire* they didn't need to ask twice.

"Sony, my label in the USA, were making noises, saying they wanted another one," he says, "and there was going to be this big gap in the middle of the tour while the live album was being mixed. I was writing a load of stuff and I borrowed Skin to be sort of the backing band. We got as far as doing all the backing tracks and then Rod pulled me to one side and said, 'Look, if you're going to do a solo record, don't just glibly do a solo record. Do a really fucking good one.' And that's when I realised I was just going along with the flow, making my solo album in the same way we were motoring on with Maiden. So I went, 'Right, full stop,' and pulled the whole thing."

Bruce still wanted to make a solo album, but "I wanted to do something quite unusual and quite mad". He flew to LA, where he began working with American producer Keith Olsen, who was then much sought after in the wake of the staggering ten-million-plus success of the Olsen-produced *Whitesnake 1987* album.

"One of my favourite albums was Peter Gabriel's third album, tracks like 'Intruder' and 'Self Control'," says Bruce. "In a funny kind of way, I found that to be a very heavy album, very intense, and I wanted to make that kind of thing, a very dark and intense album. I don't think Keith was really the right guy for it, because I don't think he really understood what was going on, but nevertheless off we went and we came up with a lot of very different stuff together. We came up with a couple of tunes that I would never play to anybody, but we also came up with some stuff that was really very interesting. It sounded almost like Bowie."

One track in particular, called 'Original Sin', which was about Bruce's relationship with his father, "became a turning point for me as an artist. I suddenly thought, 'Well, that's probably the most honest I've ever been on a record,' and at that point I think I realised that I had reached a creative fork in the road, you know? I thought, 'If you want to, you can stay with Maiden, but things are sure not gonna change.' Or I could take a chance and go somewhere else. Potentially, I knew I could be facing the prospect of commercial oblivion, which didn't scare me at all, because, for one, I've had a great living and career out of Maiden, which is more than anybody could possibly ask, and also I just thought, 'If that's as far as I'm supposed to go in this lifetime, if that's all I'm destined to do, then that's fine with me.' But I wanted to find out. I realised there's so many other things I could be getting on with in my life. And that was when I decided, 'I have to leave now. I have to tell people now and then I'll try and decide what on Earth I want to do later on, if anybody understands.'"

After much soul searching, Bruce broke the news to Rod while his manager was visiting him in the studio in LA. "I wore a groove in the kitchen floor," he admits, "spending hours thinking it through and stuff. And however I tried to play devil's advocate with myself, I just came back to the thing of, 'What do you *really* want to do?' It had to stop for me, because it was getting false. It wasn't a shared dream any more. So Rod had flown out to LA and I played him some of the stuff and I could see the look on his face, so I sat him down and went, 'As you can hear, it's quite different. That's the good news. The bad news is that I'm gonna leave the band.' He was, like, 'I suppose you've thought about it?' And I said, 'Yeah, I thought about it, and I want to leave the band.' Rod didn't really say anything. I said, 'I might end up doing OK or I might end up fucking up – that's my problem. But I'm doing this 'cause I can't continue. It's just a feeling I have. I've got to do something different.'"

Bruce's mind was made up. In the short term, however, this bombshell left both him and the rest of the band with another difficult decision to make. Should they finish the tour or call the whole thing off? "I gave them the option," he says. "My very words were, 'I understand that this puts everybody in kind of an embarrassing situation, but I'm gonna be completely honest about it, so if you like I'll call Steve.' And Rod said, 'No, no, no. Whatever you do, don't call Steve. I'll tell him.' I said, 'Well, do you want me to call Janick?' He was, like, 'No, no, no. Don't call anybody.' So Rod told everybody. But I then said I would do the tour, basically, 'cause I didn't hold any kind of grudges or malice, so I would do exactly what they wanted. If they wanted to do the tour, I'd do the tour. If they wanted to record one last studio album, I'd do that. And if they wanted to call it all a day, I'd do that, too. Whatever they wanted to do I'd go along with in good faith as well, absolutely. That's what I said."

"We had this break, and in the break Bruce has gone off to LA to do this solo album," recalls Steve. "Anyway, about two or three weeks before the second part of what was the Fear Of The Dark tour, I'd finished mixing the live album and I'd gone down to Portugal for a week to have a rest before rehearsals, and suddenly Rod says he's coming down there, too. I thought, 'That's a bit odd, Rod coming down to see me here.' I knew something was up. And that was when he told me that Bruce wanted to leave. Apparently, to be fair to Bruce, Rod told him not to call me. I don't know why, 'cause I would have rather heard it from him, to be honest, but Rod had told him not to. Rod wanted to tell us himself. And I mean, that didn't bother me, really. I wasn't totally surprised that he was going, to be honest with you. We all knew the reasons. It was obviously the solo albums, and he's into just about everything else you can think of – I mean his books and his TV stuff and everything else – and we knew that, well, something had to give sooner or later."

What really rankled, though, was the timing – mid tour; dates sold out weeks in advance; a live album about to be released. For Steve, this was totally against the grain, a fatal compromise to the integrity of the group. "I thought, 'Oh, shit. What are we gonna do about the tour?' Most of the gigs were sold out. And Rod said, 'Well, he's agreed to do the tour, and he says he's gonna go out with a bang,' and all that sort of thing. But first of all, I said, 'How can we go out and tour and look people in the eye and know there's someone up there that doesn't want to be there?' But Rod said, 'He says he's up for doing it and he's just gonna leave at the end, and it'll be like a nice sort of finale,' and all that. And I said, 'OK. If it's taken in that light, then that's OK.' Of course, I totally regret it now."

It was a very bad time for Steve personally, anyway. "I was still going through the divorce thing, and so I was down anyway, mentally," he says. "I was down and I thought, 'Fuck. The others are gonna look to me for the strength to carry on and I just ain't got it at the moment.' So I was feeling a bit sorry for myself, if you like. I spoke to Davey on the phone and I suppose, at that point, I did have a doubt as to whether to carry on or not. It was because I was so down. Normally, I'd have been, like, 'Bollocks to him! Let's just get someone else,' but at that particular time I was so down anyway. I thought, 'I just don't have the strength at the moment.'"

The turning point was after a few beers at a Bruce-less rehearsal one day, with more drinking being done than actual rehearsing, when Davey, of all people – the one who had always kept his head down – finally suddenly said what needed to be said. "We were all really down, Steve especially, and we were even talking about packing it in," says the guitarist. "But after a few beers, you know what it's like, the old bravado comes back. And we were all sitting around talking. It was probably the first real long, serious talk the four of us had had together in ages, and I can't remember what was being said, but I suddenly just got fed up talking about it and went, 'Look, why the fuck should we give up just 'cause he is? Bollocks to him. Why should he stop us playing?' I hadn't really thought about it. It just came out. But everybody just sort of went, 'Yeah, fuck that! We don't have to stop. Why should we?' And the whole mood changed and we had a few more drinks and started having a good old laugh again."

"Davey sort of gave me the strength to believe we shouldn't give up," says Steve. "I thought, 'Yeah. You know, I was stupid to even think it.' I hadn't decided that I was gonna give up, but I thought I just didn't have the strength, at that particular time. But in the end, the strength came from Davey. Once he spoke up, it was, like, 'Yeah, he's going. So what? Let's get on with it.' And from then on in, it was all right."

But their good mood wouldn't survive for long, once Bruce actually rejoined them on tour, in the spring of 1993. "It was OK to start with," begins Steve. "We did the press conferences and it was all right. We got on OK and stuff. But then, when we got out on the tour... I mean, I never ever expected him to go out there with any real passion, as such, because he's going, right? So I didn't expect that. I didn't expect him to go out there and look at the crowd in the eye and whatever, you know? I expected him to just go out there and be professional and sing. And I've got to be honest with you, we all thought he was really out of order and that he wasn't performing. And the worst thing was, if he'd been fucking crap over the whole tour, you can sort of understand it, to a certain degree, but this was specific times. It was so calculated, you know? I really wanted to kill him. I mean, we had a meeting and said, 'We don't want any of this bullshit or fighting or anything to go off, 'cause if it does then the tour is just gonna be over, and we've got to try and think of the fans. We've got to go out there and finish this tour off, and we've got to be strong about it.' But we played in Paris, for example, where there's loads of press. It's a big-profile gig. Then he'd perform, you know, pretty well. But if he played somewhere like Nice or Montpelier or somewhere like that, where it doesn't really matter, he was terrible. Fucking terrible. He was mumbling, hardly singing at all. One night, I went up to the monitor man and said, 'What the fuck's going on? I can't hear him!' And he pushed the fader up to full and said, 'Look, there's nothing there. He's just mumbling into the mic.' It's no word of a lie. You ask any of the rest of the guys about it."

"I know the sea of wisdom from Steve was that I didn't give a fuck," says Bruce. "I think my position in the whole thing was that I thought it wouldn't be a problem to go out and do the shows at all. It could be great, be a good vibe and everything else, but it wasn't a good vibe at all. And this is not necessarily from the band; this was when we walked onstage and it was like a morgue. The Maiden fans knew I'd quit, they knew these were the last gigs, and I suddenly realised that, as the frontman, you're in an almost impossible situation. If you're, like, 'Wow, this is really fucking cool tonight, man,' they're all gonna sit there going, 'What a wanker. He's leaving. How can it be cool?' Or do you go on and say, 'Look, I'm really sorry I'm leaving – not to put a damper on the evening, but I am quitting'? I mean, what do you do? And I suddenly realised that I didn't have a clue exactly how to play it, because every single person in that audience must have felt pretty ambivalent about the whole situation, as I did and as the band did. I think for them to assume that you can just turn on a performance like a tap is... In a sense, it's kind of symptomatic of the whole thing, you know?"

"Bruce says he couldn't face it, but he never seemed to have a problem when we were playing the big shows in London or Paris or wherever," insists Steve. "When all the press were there, it was a different story. He had no problem turning on a performance then. I mean, none of us expected Bruce to be 100 per cent – he couldn't be, or he wouldn't be leaving, would he? – but I swear, some nights all he did was mumble through the songs. You couldn't hear him at all. He may as well have not turned up at all, some nights. And that's when we all really began to feel bitterly towards him. Not because he was leaving, but because he really fucked that last tour up for us by not giving it everything he could have, which he promised us he would."

Bruce sees it differently: "That's crap. That's absolute crap. The singing was always really, really good. What I did do at shows was decide that I was not going to make like Mr Happy Face if the vibe wasn't right. What was the point in me wandering around trying to make myself indispensable when I wasn't going to be there in six months' time? I realised that, as we started doing the tour, I suddenly realised what I'd let myself in for. I was probably naïve to put myself in that situation in the first place, but that's my reply to it: yes, I was trying, actually. I was trying as hard as I could, every single night, but as hard as I could some nights it was impossible. A rock concert is supposed to be a celebration. It's not supposed to be a wake."

For the record, with the exception of Janick, who still maintains a good personal relationship with the singer, every other member of

Maiden insists to this day that Bruce was a shambles on that last, ill-starred tour in 1993, pulling himself together onstage only at the most prestigious, profile-raising dates and lapsing into incoherent, half-hearted performances for the rest of the time, charges that Bruce steadfastly refutes and will no doubt continue to do so until his dying day.

For a more impartial eye-witness account of what really happened on those last dates, I turned to tour manager and long-time Maiden associate Dickie Bell for his recollections. "When he was good, he was very, very good, but when he was bad, he was fucking awful," is his version. "He didn't even bother with the singing part some nights, as far as I could see. But I tried to stay out of it. It was obvious to everybody that they weren't getting on. Bruce was always the last to arrive for the show and always the last to leave the dressing room to go onstage each night, which in my experience with bands is nearly always a bad sign. But Bruce does play mind games – he acts like he doesn't really know what's going on around him half the time, but he never misses a trick. I think basically, though, the time had simply come for him to leave. Hanging around was doing neither side any good."

Bruce Dickinson's last public performance with Iron Maiden was the televised *Raising Hell* show, filmed at Elstree Studios in August 1993, a pay-per-view "music and magic show", the band's last show with Bruce bookended by the conjuring antics of well-known TV magician Simon Drake, which was televised live on MTV throughout the world.

"I actually really enjoyed that show but, do you know, I don't recall saying goodbye," says Bruce. "It was a very strange way of parting. After the show, I had a couple of beers and went home to bed. Because it was at Pinewood Studios, you got that feeling where you're on the back lot of a movie set sort of thing, and you move around at three in the morning after the party and it's dark and kind of lonely and stuff, and it was… Yeah, it was sort of melancholy."

Steve's own feelings, once the show was finally over, were inevitably soured by recent events, and his memories now are tinged with bitterness, feelings that both Nicko and Davey share. "Everybody was saying how sad it was, but by then we couldn't wait to get rid of the guy, to be brutally honest with you," the drummer admits. "We just wanted to get it over with. I mean, it was a great show, and Bruce was on top of the game, completely. Of course he was. The cameras were on him! Afterwards, I think we just got pissed. I can't even remember. It wasn't exactly the happiest last night of a tour we've had."

A press conference had been called at the start of the second leg of the tour, in March, when the old "musical differences" line was adhered to. Now, in the immediate aftermath of the split, there was some bad blood spilled in the media, particularly by Bruce, who seemed determined to completely distance himself from the band.

"OK, I know what it's like to do interviews and get misquoted," says Steve. "I understand all that. But it was just happening everywhere. We just had the attitude that we were not gonna rise to the bait and we weren't gonna start getting into a slanging match. The only reason we'll talk about it now is because it's for the book and it's important to set the record straight. At the end of the day, though, we thought he was fucking himself up, because basically it's the Maiden fans he's insulting, too, if he's having a go at Maiden. He was trying to belittle his past."

"There was a little bit of that from both sides, yeah," says Bruce matter of factly, "but that's probably par for the course, really. But whatever my feelings about Steve, he is what he is – he's a very talented guy and he's very honest. That's one thing I can say about him. I don't think there's a crooked bone in his body. And all of them... I mean, none of us are perfect, thank God. I've got my faults and my lunacies and my going off on tangents and all the rest of it that people accuse me of doing. Everybody has their own little skeletons. But everybody in Iron Maiden are, basically, really decent human beings. I think things just do get worn out after a while, especially in something like a band. I mean, twelve years, we were together, and I sometimes think that perhaps I should have left in 1986, before *Somewhere In Time*, you know? But that's just history now."

In the middle of all this, the good news for the fans was that Maiden managed to release two excellent live albums, *A Real Live One*, issued on 22 March 1993, and its companion in hell, *A Real Dead One*, which followed on 18 October. Both went to the Top Ten in the UK and both were, as advertised, vastly improved aural snapshots of the band in action onstage than their predecessor eight years earlier. All of the crowd warmth and sultry room ambience that got squeezed out of *Live After Death* in favour of sheer power and velocity was expertly captured and installed on

Maiden's latest live offerings, and while *A Real Live One* featured eleven of the most crowd-pleasing moments from the band's post-1985 period, *A Real Dead One* dug deep into the vaults for twelve tracks which dated back to their earliest days. Recorded during the first half of the Fear Of The Dark world tour in the summer of 1992, Bruce sounds magnificently cogent, and the band have never sounded so thumpingly good. You would never guess that it was all about to blow up in their faces.

One other change that Maiden's brace of live albums marked was the departure of producer Martin Birch, who had decided to retire altogether. "I'd already made my decision by the time Bruce announced he was leaving, so it had nothing to do with that," he says. "In fact, with *Fear Of The Dark*, I thought the band were really back on track. But even then, at the beginning, I was thinking maybe it was time for a change of producer for them. But once we got working, I was totally immersed. I loved every minute, and I thought it turned out a terrific album. But after that I spoke to Steve about it again. We'd been together a long time, and I just asked him, you know, 'Is it time for you to change the producer?' He looked at me, a little bit taken aback about it, I think, but that's how I felt. It was more down to me than the band. By that point, I'd had enough of making records, and shortly after that I stopped working altogether. I felt that, if I didn't really want to go in the studio, then it wasn't fair to them to do so. I wouldn't want to be anything less than 100 per cent for Steve and Maiden. We'd been making records for years together, but there comes a time when you just need to move on." From that point on, Steve, who had always worked so closely in the studio with Martin, would oversee production of all of Maiden's recordings, with the help of Nigel Green, a long-standing engineer and now a producer in his own right.

"Martin decided to retire," confirms Steve. "He'd had, like, 25 years of just album upon album, you know? He'd go straight from doing us into doing a Whitesnake album, or whatever. The list of the people he's worked with is as long as your arm, and I think he just got to a point where he wanted to do his own thing and play golf. So that's when I mixed the live stuff, the two single live albums, and since then I've been producing all our stuff with Nigel Green. I mean, basically, to tell the truth, I co-produced the last couple of albums with Martin anyway, so I knew what I was getting into. It was like a natural progression, really."

The most pressing business at hand, of course, was finding a new singer. They'd advertised for a replacement for Bruce as far back as March, when they first announced that he would be leaving, and they had subsequently been flooded with literally thousands of tapes, CDs and videos from hopeful Maiden wannabes from all over the world. With the tour now finished, it was time to actually sit down and sift through the mountain of recordings that had piled up. It was a mammoth task that would take them over four months to complete. "We listened to every single tape we got," says Steve, puffing out his cheeks and blowing. "I think it was one of the hardest jobs we've ever had to do. There were some excellent people but no one that was 100 per cent right for Maiden. There was one bloke who sounded just like Geoff Tate from Queensrÿche, who's got a great voice, but we didn't want a soundalike. Then there was another guy who sounded like [former Rainbow and Black Sabbath singer] Ronnie James Dio on one side of his tape and [former Deep Purple and Black Sabbath singer] Glenn Hughes on the other, and they're both fantastic singers, obviously, but I said to him, 'I don't wanna hear Ronnie James Dio or Glenn Hughes. I wanna hear you.'"

And yet, when it was finally announced in January 1994 that Bruce Dickinson's successor in Maiden was to be one Blaze Bayley, who until then had been a singer in a Birmingham-based band of punk-metal reprobates called Wolfsbane, very few Maiden insiders were surprised. As *Metal Hammer* writer and renowned Maiden archivist Dave Ling says, "It didn't take Nostradamus to predict Bruce's eventual departure. Nor was it any great shock when Blaze replaced him, as Steve had made no secret of his admiration for Bayley." The band had first come across their future singer when Wolfsbane supported Maiden on their 1990 British tour and Blaze – who even bore a strong physical resemblance to Bruce, back in the days when Bruce still allowed his hair to grow long – had made an instant impression on both Steve and Nicko, albeit for different reasons.

"I used to hear him practising, warming up his voice before a show, and you could tell that, as a singer, he was capable of doing much more than he was doing in Wolfsbane," says Steve.

"I just thought he was a total party animal," says Nicko.

In fact, he was both of these and a whole lot more besides, and as such was always the favourite to get the job. Indeed, Blaze had been one of the first potential candidates that Steve had contacted personally in the weeks that followed Bruce's shock announcement, but with Wolfsbane then just about to release a live album and embark on their own UK tour Blaze had reluctantly declined. He was flattered, he said, but the timing was simply not good. Steve understood perfectly, band loyalty being a quality he always held in high esteem.

What he didn't know until much later, however, was that Blaze changed his mind "almost as soon as I'd put down the phone, I think". Loyalty was one thing; outstaying your welcome was another. Blaze already knew in his heart of hearts that "Wolfsbane could never make it". After three studio albums, one live album, a mini album and a handful of half-remembered but always well-reviewed singles, Wolfsbane had, he says, "used up all its bullets". Nevertheless, he clung on right through one last tour, and it was only when the band began to sit down and discuss material for their next studio album that Blaze realised that, in their search for fresh ideas, the band were now veering so far away from "real pounding heavy metal" that what they did "just didn't fit my voice any more". He reached for the phone.

"It was a few months later. We'd done the tour and were supposed to be going in to do another proper album, and I just knew I didn't want to do it," says Blaze, "so I phoned up Steve and said, 'Look, have you found anybody yet? Because I really want to come and audition for the band. I really want to do it.'"

"Blaze is the one I had in mind to definitely try out," says Steve, "but obviously he was still in Wolfsbane and we had time on our hands and we weren't planning to do another album just yet, so we thought we'd just take our time and make sure we got it right. But I always felt that Blaze could be the one. To be honest, a couple of others in the band weren't so sure. They knew he was good onstage, and they accepted all of that, but they weren't sure about whether his voice would suit Maiden. But there's a quality in his voice I'd noticed, a richness, which sometimes got a bit lost with Wolfsbane. Don't get me wrong, I thought Wolfsbane were really good, but it was just a different way of singing, and I thought he could be really good for Maiden. And I knew he was a nice bloke and everything, 'cause I sort of hung about with him on the tour a bit."

By the time that Blaze called back, only one other serious candidate had emerged to challenge him, a young Brit singer with "a superb set of pipes", as Steve recalls. The young hopeful's name was Dougie White. "We did recordings of them both singing to a couple of Maiden tracks with Bruce's vocals wiped off. Then I played both the recordings back to the rest of the lads and Nicko hit the nail on the head straight away. We'd heard the first tape and we all agreed Dougie had a great voice, but we weren't quite sure if it sounded quite right for us. Then we played Blaze's tape and Nicko just went, 'Now, that's Iron Maiden, ain't it?' And I just said, 'Yeah, it just feels right. It fits. It feels really right.'" Maiden knew that they had their man. Meanwhile, Dougie would later join Rainbow.

"Blaze may be not as technically good as Dougie, but I think his sort of area is somewhere in between, say, Paul and Bruce, and that's why maybe it suited so well," explains Steve. "The only worry, I think, was that Blaze had never done a really long set or tour. I think the longest set he'd ever done was about an hour. I didn't know what a two-hour set every night for a year would do to him. He was worried about it, too. But all you can do is go out and go for it and see what happens. And as luck would have it, it worked great. He's great to have in the band, 'cause his enthusiasm is just unbelievable. I mean, with Janick there as well, and Nicko's a nutter anyway... I mean, it's a good job me and Davey are quiet, you know what I mean?"

Roughly the same height and stocky build as his predecessor, and exuding much of the same wide-eyed, manic intensity, the obvious similarities between the two belied the great gift that Blaze would bring to Maiden: the fact that he was so different from Bruce. The latter may have had more vocal panache, but it was the voice of the former that contained all the passion. And where Bruce always appeared to be looking beyond Maiden, unwilling to be pinned down, Blaze displayed all the confidence and grandeur of a king who has waited long to sit upon his throne.

Blaze Bayley (real name Bayley Cook) was born in Birmingham on 19 May 1963. "I usually lie about my age," he smiles. "You'll only know the truth if you read this book! Blaze was my nickname at school, and so I used that when we first started off. It was all glam-metal bands, like Mötley Crüe, and we were all wrapped up in that whole kind of scene, just trying to be outrageous, and we'd invent stupid names for each other, and they just stuck. I don't really know really why they called me Blaze. We called the bass player Slut Wrecker, which didn't take much working out. People always thought my first name was my last, anyway, so I just thought I'd keep it, and I started to be known as Blaze from then on, really. I even call myself Blaze now."

In Blaze's own words, the Cook family "was a bit of mess, really. I didn't have any brothers and sisters till I was eleven, so on my dad's side I've got one younger brother and on my mother's side I've got another younger half brother and sister. I lived with my mother when I was growing up. Both my mother – who's passed away now – and my father were married to separate people and…I think that's part of making my character the way it is. I think a lot of people from… I don't like using the term 'broken homes', but a lot of people from families that aren't complete or normal – whatever normal is – a lot of them seem to end up doing creative things. It puts, like, a different slant on them, you know what I mean?" One has only to consider the troubled early family lives of both Bruce Dickinson and Paul Di'Anno to see his point.

Like both of his predecessors in Maiden, Blaze grew up feeling like an outsider. "It definitely made me an outsider, and I think it's been part of my ambition, and it's also been a source of some of my demons as well, you know, having to deal with that."

At the time that he was born, both of his parents were barely into their 20s, and they found the unexpected arrival of a baby almost impossible to deal with. "My father was a drama student at the time, and they were very, very young," he explains. "My mum was probably about 20 when she had me. I mean, I'm much older than both of them were when they got married, and with the relationships I've been through and things that have happened to me, I think, 'God,' you know? 'What must their situation have been like?' Two kids still themselves, a baby, trying to get a life together… I just can't imagine how hard that must have been."

As a result, his parents' marriage didn't last long and, although he kept in touch with his father, Blaze lived alone with his mother until he was eleven, when she remarried. "Before my mum married again, my grandfather had a piece of land which he kept with some ducks and geese on it, and my mother had rented a caravan, so we just lived there," he says. "We were quite poor. We didn't have a television until I was about nine. We used to just listen to the radio. It was just me and my mother, and it was all right, I think. You don't realise, when you're a kid, that you're poor. It's only now, when I look back, I see that we were absolutely broke."

What saved the day was a sudden, overwhelming passion for music, specifically punk rock, which overwhelmed the British music scene when Blaze was 14. "Suddenly there was Blondie, The Sex Pistols and The Damned and The Jam," he says. "It all just melted into one with being an adolescent for me. Everything was raw. Everything was alive. Everything meant something. It just got into your brain. I wasn't allowed to use the record player in our house, because of the person my mother was married to, so I used to have to go 'round my friends' houses, and it was through doing that that I discovered all this other music. I used to rifle through their record collections and we'd listen to the first Black Sabbath album or *Led Zep IV*, and I couldn't believe it. I thought it was just incredible! Like, how can something sound like that? And all that got mashed up with really liking the energy and attitude of punk. It was all the same to me. I didn't feel you had to choose. We just listened to everything that was around, really, everything that was loud."

A natural playground show-off, it wasn't long before the teenage Blaze began to fancy himself as a singer. "I always talked about being in a band, just the same as everybody at school," he reveals. "Then, when I was 16, I thought I'd go and live with my father, because the situation with my step father was getting quite nasty at times, but I didn't really get on with my real dad very well, either. He wasn't somebody that was good at conversation or interested in music. He was very dark, very short tempered, a person who, I think, was very frustrated inside himself. So the situation was very... It kind of made me think in different ways."

He left school in 1980 with an O-level in Art (for ceramics and pottery) and "a fairly bad attitude, I suppose". Uninterested in anything outside becoming a full-time rock singer, he had begun his working life by drawing the dole. Enrolled soon after on a compulsory YTS (Youth Training Scheme), he found himself "working for pennies" as a warehouseman in a furniture factory. "It was just awful. It was absolute darkness and pain, just humping three-piece suites into the backs of trucks, sending them off, then waiting for the next truck to put more three-piece suites into and being abused by the foreman. It was horrible."

He landed on his feet, though, when he found himself working as a night porter at a hotel in Tamworth. It was "the perfect job for someone who didn't really want one. After about two in the morning and before about five, there was this magic time – things are quiet, you're quiet in yourself, there is absolutely nothing you can be doing – and it was during one of these moments when I just thought, 'My life is fucking going nowhere at all, absolutely nowhere.' And because you'd have the place to yourself all night, I'd just be listening to tapes of music. I just borrowed tapes and listened to absolutely everything that was going. Anything and everything that was rock, I listened to. I'd get a move on with the hoovering, then get the tapes out and start singing along."

His favourite singer was former Rainbow and Black Sabbath vocalist and subsequent solo star Ronnie James Dio. "The greatest voice in rock, without question," he claims. "I've got everything that he's ever recorded, right from his first band, Elf. I got to meet him once, but it took me, like, an hour before I could speak to him. But it was great, singing along to one of his albums during the middle of the night at the hotel, 'cause you could really belt it out. No one was around. I've always loved singing – it's such a natural, beautiful thing – and I started to write loads of poems then, too. I just spent hours really listening to music, writing words and stuff and really singing. Not just to records, but just by myself as well, just hearing the sound of your voice in a big room, singing."

But a singer needs a band, and in that department Blaze had so far been spectacularly unsuccessful. "I'd auditioned for a few bands, but I think I was just too over the top, too full on, and it overwhelmed them a bit," he admits. "But I was just being what you think a rock star is when you're that age. I mean, I'm not a quiet person anyway. I have my quiet moments, but I'm a nutcase most times. So I got a gig in a band called Child's Play and they said, 'We'll give you a month and see how it works out.' They played a kind of Thin Lizzy style of music. But we did a few rehearsals and after a month they said, 'Sorry, it's not what we're looking for. We want a different kind of voice.'"

His first real break came via the small-ads section of the local paper,

The Tamworth Herald. "It was the name I noticed, Wolfsbane," he remembers. "What it is, I later found out, is a purple-flowered plant that only comes into full bloom in the moonlight, and it's a highly poisonous plant, but it's got some medical properties as well. Of course, I didn't know that when I went to audition for them. I just thought it was a cool name."

A four-piece that first came to the attention of the music press in the mid '80s, Wolfsbane was a Van Halen-style, high-energy rock band that thrived on punishing tour schedules and full-tilt, audience-inciting performances. The creative core of the band was bassist Jeff Hately and guitarist Jason Edwards, with Blaze supplying most of the words. The drummer in the band was originally Blaze's girlfriend, but within a year she had opted out, to be replaced by the more appropriately monikered Steve Danger.

"The thing was, they couldn't get another singer and I couldn't get another band, so we were just thrown together," smiles Blaze. "None of us were good enough to get into anybody else's band, and I think really that's what kept us together and what made us progress so quickly. We were a total outrage band, a total shock band, abusing the audience and everything. We were never processed or manufactured or pre-digested. We were forged from battling through live gigs, when all you've got is what you stand up in. But because of that, we had a certain amount of people that would come to see us or buy our records on a regular basis."

In a chequered recording career, Wolfsbane were never short of support from the music press, and by the time Rick Rubin's then newly established Def American label signed them in 1988 Wolfsbane had already graced the covers of both *Kerrang!* and *Sounds* magazines. Their first somewhat patchy album for Def American, *Live Fast, Die Fast*, was recorded in Los Angeles, at Rubin's insistence, and released to loud media trumpeting in the summer of 1989. However, despite the critical hoopla, it was pointedly not a major chart hit. "The album didn't do that well, in terms of sales," says Blaze. "I think it might have sold about 25,000 copies or something like that, not too bad, and we had more press than you could shake a stick at, but it was more the whole thing, the fact that we were this vicious, outrageous band and we were with Rubin, who's perceived as the guru of what is cool. We were on his label, so we must be cool."

In 1990, the band released the six-track mini album *All Hell's Breaking Loose At Little Kathy Wilson's Place*. Again, despite glowing reviews, it failed to set the UK charts alight, although the band did enjoy one piece of good fortune, landing the support spot on the UK leg of Iron Maiden's No Prayer For The Dying tour.

"It was a dream come true for us," says Blaze. "And I liked Maiden. I had a few of their records, and I'd seen them on tour two or three times before. I thought they were a great band. On the old night shift at the hotel, I always played *Number Of The Beast* and *Piece Of Mind*. I had them on the same C-90 and used to play them back to back all the time. But that tour was the first time I met Steve. The first thing he said was, 'It's good to have a young band who might shake us up a bit,' which I didn't expect at all. It was refreshing. And he still says that now, whenever we get a new young band opening for us. He's, like, 'Great. You went down really well tonight. We've got something to do now.'"

As things turned out, the tour was a tremendous success for both bands. "We had encores nearly every night, and it was just the most brilliant time in my life up to that point," says the singer. "When it came to the Hammersmith Odeon, the last day of the tour, and having to go home afterwards, it was just horrible. I didn't want to go home at all. I wanted to carry on opening up for Iron Maiden everywhere."

However, that didn't prevent Blaze from trying to best his successor at the mic stand each night. "On that tour, my mission in life was to absolutely destroy Bruce every night," he says, "so I would carefully watch his performance, listen to what he said, look at the way he did things, and the next night in my performance I would try and totally outdo him. Bruce is one of the greatest frontmen of all time, so let's preface this by saying that. He's been all over the world, he's played some of the biggest shows in rock, he's fronted one of the best bands and he's recorded some of the classic album tracks of all time. He's a great frontman. But we were just totally arrogant. We knew no fear. We worked to blow anybody away. So I just said, 'Well, if he climbs on the side of the speakers then I will try and get on top of the speakers. If he puts his foot on the monitor, I will try and get down in the crowd. If he moves about the stage, I'll run about the stage.' I was just immersed in this whole thing of trying to outdo Bruce, which is weird, when you consider what came later."

A second, full-length Wolfsbane album, *Downfall Of The Good Guys*, was released in 1992, but by then even the critics were starting to grow impatient with the band's consistent lack of chart success, and when it too failed to improve on the situation Blaze says that he knew "the writing was on the wall". There would be only one more Wolfsbane album, the live *Massive Noise Injection*, released in 1993. "It was us at the Marquee, and it's a live album in the greatest tradition of live albums," Blaze says. "Complete chaos!" Before work could begin in earnest on what would have been their next studio album, however, Blaze was offered the gig with Maiden and immediately announced his departure from the band. In effect emphasising the frailty of the situation that Blaze left behind, Wolfsbane effectively disintegrated on the spot.

"It was hell," he says now. "Everybody but me thought I was the obvious person to take over from Bruce in Iron Maiden, but my loyalty to Wolfsbane was so much that I couldn't even think about that. Wolfsbane were stuck together, just glued together by all the tough times that we'd fought our way out of together, but by the end of that last tour we did I just knew Wolfsbane could never make it. The stuff that Jeff and Jase were thinking of doing was more like a punky Manic Street Preachers type of thing than real pounding heavy metal, and it just didn't fit my voice. That was when I phoned up Steve."

Blaze is not shy to admit that joining Iron Maiden "totally changed my life. They let me know a couple of days before Christmas 1993. Steve phoned me at home and said, 'Come down and have a meeting with me and Rod.' He didn't say, 'We want you in the band.' It was something like, 'Well, you're in if you want it.' Something like that. Just typical Steve – you know what he's like. And I felt stunned, really. Just stunned. I was really happy that I got the gig but just stunned because suddenly I was faced with a totally different life. I've hardly got any other life outside music and being in a band, and up to that point I was Blaze Bayley of Wolfsbane. Now it would be Blaze Bayley of Iron Maiden! So it was a weird experience. It took me a long time to come to terms with everything. I suppose I was euphoric. I remember there was a bottle of champagne that I'd kept under the sink for quite a while and I cracked it that night and got bladdered on my own, got bladdered and started looking in *AutoMart* to see how much Jaguars cost."

In January 1994, work began on writing the first album with Blaze as singer. Recorded at Steve's own ever-improving home studios (now christened Barnyard), the new album would take over a year to complete.

"We didn't want to write anything until we'd got the new singer in," explains Steve. "We knew it was going to be important, whoever it was, that they feel part of the writing process. Blaze actually said to us, 'What direction do you wanna go in?' We just laughed. We explained that we don't go for a direction; we just write the best songs we can. There is no direction. Whatever comes out comes out, and if it's good, it's used. And if it's not good, it's used as a B-side or kicked out. He couldn't fucking believe it – like, 'Fucking hell. This is amazing. Just to be in a band and do exactly what you want.' I said, 'It's not because we're in a situation where we can afford to say that. We've just always done that. We've never taken any notice of any bastard.'"

That was just as well, because when *The X Factor* was released in October 1995 it was greeted by some of the most scathing reviews that the band had ever received. Not since *Killers* had they been under such heavy critical fire, with the critics taking exception to everything, from the new singer to what they perceived (not altogether inaccurately) to be the "dark tone" of the material.

Even long-standing Maiden supporters like Dave Ling were left baffled by the unforeseen direction in which the new album had apparently taken the band. "Personally, I thought it was a big mistake, and still do," he says. "Despite the fact that I was one of Wolfsbane's sternest critics, I was kindly asked to write the record-company biography for *The X Factor* and was played three presumably carefully selected tracks in the Sanctuary boardroom, which caused me to eat my words. I went away raving. I even congratulated Blaze on his performance at the album's launch party. However, upon hearing the whole album, the immensity of their folly was apparent."

After spending a year working hard on what Steve Harris still now regards as "one of the three best albums we've ever made, the other two being *Piece Of Mind* and *Seventh Son Of A Seventh Son*", the band was confused and hurt by the depth of the criticism that *The X Factor* received. What made it even harder for them to understand was the fact that, despite the terrible reviews in Britain, *The X Factor* won Album Of The Year awards in both France and Germany and revitalised the band's career in America.

"I thought it was a special album," insists Steve. "Like it or not, we had this extra pressure to succeed, 'cause we'd got this new singer, and so we really went out of our way to try and make it as strong as possible. We actually ended up doing 14 songs and we used eleven, which is very unusual for us. Usually we used everything we recorded, you know? But we did a double album's worth of material, really, which is why it took so long, and to me it's like an extension of *Seventh Son...*, in the sense of the progressive element to it. I suppose it *is* quite a dark album, partly 'cause I was going through so much personal shit myself at the time, so some of that has come out lyrically, no doubt about it. But it's not just me. I mean, Blaze has got a very dark side to him, also. He can be Mr Party, but he's also got that Mr Dark Man side to him as well."

There's no question that *The X Factor* was the darkest, most adult-orientated album that Iron Maiden had ever produced. It was hardly surprising, then, that so many of their (much younger) critics in Britain would have a hard time coming to terms with it. Out were the comic-book horror stories and the drive-in-movie sci-fi of Bruce-era Maiden and in came the true-life reflections of people now in their mid 30s with something more to say about life than the vicissitudes of time travel or the wonder of the pyramids.

Steve, for one, had been going through a painful divorce, his marriage to his childhood sweetheart, Lorraine, having ended after 16 years together. With four growing children to look after – Lauren, then just ten; Kerry, eight; Faye, six; and George, four – he admits now that "it was probably the toughest time I've ever faced in my life", and Bruce's untimely departure merely exacerbated the situation. "I found it very hard to cope with everything. Like I say, if it hadn't been for Davey and the others being so strong, I don't know if I'd have made it through."

As a result, of the eleven tracks on *The X Factor*, at least ten of them can be read as desperate diary entries from Steve's own personal hell. Of the four tracks that he wrote alone, three of them – 'Sign Of The Cross', the eleven-minute-plus gloomy opus which opens the album; 'Fortunes Of War'; and 'Judgement Of Heaven' – are all specifically about not just the break-up of his marriage, nor even the break-up with Bruce, but about the even more painful and confusing break-up that was occurring within himself. Doubts surround him like a cloud of flies in lines like, "I've felt like suicide a dozen times or more/But that's the easy way, the selfish way/The hardest part is to get on with your life," from 'Judgement Of Heaven', or, "Why then is God still protecting me/Even when I don't deserve it?" from 'Sign Of The Cross'. More poignantly, his fourth solo contribution, 'Blood On The World's Hands' addresses his fears for the future of his own children, both metaphorical and actual: "Somewhere there's someone starving/Another savage raping/Meanwhile there's someone laughing/At us..."

It's ironic that, just as Bruce Dickinson left the band because he felt that they would never break out of the comic-book-metal niche that they'd so successfully occupied for years, Steve would reach a point in his own life where he, too, would need to discharge some of the emotions and feelings of his own drastically altered circumstances into the music that he was creating with his new singer. Even the tracks in which Steve is only a co-conspirator – 'Look For The Truth', 'The Aftermath', 'The Edge Of Darkness' and '2am', which he wrote with Blaze and Janick, and 'Lord Of The Flies' and 'The Unbeliever', which he wrote with Janick – seem, on closer inspection, to be about the same thing. Musically, too, the band had never sounded so ominously calm and studied, unleashing the full force of their power in bleak gales that erupt only occasionally, the perfect seismic counterpoint to the loneliness and desperation of the lyrics.

It was perhaps no coincidence that the track chosen as the first single from the album, Blaze and Janick's comparatively upbeat 'Man On The Edge', was the only track that Steve didn't have a hand in writing. Crashing straight into the UK charts at Number Ten, it also prompted the band's first in-the-flesh *Top Of The Pops* appearance for 15 years. "The show had really changed by then and the new producers really encouraged us to go for it," Steve says. The band wouldn't play live, though, having long ago accepted that the BBC engineers simply couldn't do their voluminous sound justice, although Blaze did sing the song live, because there's not too much you can do to upset a vocal performance.

Despite this success, however, the album itself only reached Number Eight in the UK charts, their first studio album not to make the Top Five since *Killers* 14 years earlier, a fact which still rankles with the group. As Steve says, "The album came out the same week as Prince, Madonna and a few other mega-sellers we just couldn't hope to compete with." But as Blaze points out, "I think some of the boys were a bit disappointed the album only got to Number Eight, but I was, like, 'Number Eight! We're Number Eight! That's fucking fantastic!' I'd never had a Top Ten record before, so I thought it was great."

Rod, however, wasn't the only voice close to the group who said that he thought the album "too dark" for mainstream appeal. But that was no longer an item on either Steve's or Maiden's agenda. "I think those strong situations where you really have to push yourself, where you really don't know if you're going to make it out to the other side, are good," says Steve. "They bring certain emotions out of you. I remember years ago someone reviewed a Todd Rundgren album, *Hermit Of Mink Hollow*, and they said that you feel all this emotion coming out of him because he'd split up with his wife just before he recorded it, and the reviewer said maybe he should split up with people more often, because it was a wonderful album. And it was that kind of thing, I think, for me with *The X Factor* – it came out of a lot of personal pain. I think 'Man On The Edge' is the only one you can really sing along to, but I love it that it takes you a bit longer to get into it. The best albums are all usually like that."

The first show in Britain by the new Harris/Murray/McBrain/Gers/Bayley line-up took place in the packed surroundings of London's Brixton Academy in November 1995. Described by Steve now as "hand on heart one of the best shows this band has ever done", the Brixton show proved two things: that Maiden had made the right choice with Blaze and that they were now a better band than they had been prior to his arrival. With Bruce and Adrian – the arch-deviants, always looking to pull the band down more commercial roads – now replaced by Blaze and Janick, who were both almost monk-like in their devotion to the cause of both Maiden and heavy metal, love it or hate it, the band had never looked or sounded more completely as one.

"We tailored the live set to what Blaze was capable of doing," says

Steve. "There were a couple of songs that we did actually keep away from, like 'Bring Your Daughter...', for example, which was more associated with Bruce, and 'Run To The Hills', also because it was Bruce's first big single with us, so we kind of side-stepped that one. But now that Blaze has been in the band for some time, we've done an album and a world tour with him and people I think have accepted him a bit more. Now I think we can do anything we want. Rod actually thought we shouldn't be doing 'Two Minutes To Midnight'. He thought that was more associated with Bruce than 'Bring Your Daughter...', but I disagree with that. I think we can do anything we like now. I mean, Blaze wants us to do 'Phantom Of The Opera'. He loves that, and we may well do that on the next tour."

As long as any other world tour they'd done in the past, but this time far more diverse in its scope, the X Factour saw Maiden playing a number of new territories. "We've always enjoyed visiting new places," explains Rod. "In 1984 we took a full production into Poland, when it was still Eastern Bloc. We always ask JJ [John Jackson] to find new places for us to go, and this time we had good reason. The brief to JJ was, 'We need to do ten or twelve shows away from the prying eyes of the press.' We wanted Blaze to have a fair shot. This was 1995. Metal was on the floor, and you could hear the media sharpening their knives. We just wanted a few gigs for the band to fully gel and for Blaze to find his feet, and JJ delivered big time."

"Keeping the band away from the usual areas was quite a challenge," admits John Jackson, "but in the end we started with three shows in Israel, then three in South Africa, then into eastern Europe, playing Bulgaria, Slovenia, Romania and Czechoslovakia. In each case it was the first time Maiden had played that country."

"Talk about baptism by fire," recalls Blaze. "The first time I went onstage with Maiden was on *Top Of The Pops* and the second was the opening gig of the X Factour – in Jerusalem, of all places. The opening of 'Number Of The Beast' really sent shivers down my spine!"

Maiden had even planned to do some shows in Beirut, but the Lebanese government withdrew their visas at the eleventh hour and, despite intervention through diplomatic channels, failed to change its mind.

As Blaze says, the tour started in Jerusalem on 28 September 1995 and finished almost a year later, on 7 September 1996, in Mexico, also taking in Chile (for the first time), Argentina, Brazil, all of western Europe, most of eastern Europe, Japan, Canada and a lengthy tour of the US, comprising 139 shows in all.

"My experience of touring was three weeks 'round the UK," admits Blaze. "Wolfsbane never toured outside of Britain, so this was something else. Sometimes I didn't think I'd survive. Other times I wanted it to go on forever. It was an unforgettable experience.

"Everywhere we went, the fans were really kind and generous to me. They knew Bruce had upped and left, but they also knew I'd give it my very best shot. I was so grateful for the support they gave me. Without that, I'd never have made it."

"It was tough for Blaze," confirms Steve. "It was a new experience, but the fans really took to him. He's very honest and loves the music, and this communicates to the fans, who love him for it.

"And we were careful on the tour. Depending on the territory, we kept the size of the halls to between 2,500 and 9,000, except for South America and the USA and some European festivals that we headlined in the summer of 1996. This meant we pretty well played to a sold-out crowd every night, so the atmosphere generated by the fans helped everyone. The caution really paid off. In the States, we played about 35 shows, but we were even more cautious, due to the state of the market, so we kept to small theatres and large clubs of around 1,500 to 2,000 and did something like 95 per cent sell out over the tour. Not bad, really, considering everything. But in South America, as usual, we let rip, playing anything from 15,000 to 55,000 people.

"For one of the last shows, we headlined Monsters Of Rock in São Paulo in a massive 55,000-seater soccer stadium – the Pacaembu Stadium, I think. Packed to the top, it was. Incredible. And the reaction we got was just amazing, absolutely spine chilling. I just looked back on the difficulties of the last few years – Bruce leaving, personal stuff, finding the new singer, spending a year producing the new album – and, I tell you, it's gigs like that that make it all worthwhile. We'd got our new band, everything was working, it was all systems go and I thought, 'Blimey! It ain't over yet, you know.'"

15 *Virtual Reality*

If *The X Factor* had divided critical opinion, it became more apparent – certainly musically – where the new Blaze-era Iron Maiden fitted in with the release of the exemplary 27-track, double-CD compilation *Best Of The Beast* in November 1996. The first major Maiden compilation ever commissioned, the journey from Paul Di'Anno's wonderfully original out-of-tune Spaceward demo version of 'Strange World' to Blaze at his most volcanic on 'Sign Of The Cross', via Bruce-era juggernauts like 'Number Of The Beast', made sudden and startling sense.

Tellingly, however, the most controversial track on *Best Of The Beast* was the newest, 'Virus', a nasty six-minute piece of vitriol that Steve, Blaze, Davey and Janick had cooked up together back at Barnyard in September 1996. Recorded after returning from nearly a year on the road, the energy and fire palpably crackle as the band hurtle through the song, hitting back at the critics who had tried to write them off, Blaze spitting out the words like rotten pieces of meat: "They want to sink the ship and leave/The way they laugh at you and me/You know it happens all the time..."

"We're all there to be shot down, but some of the reviews we've had over the years have been malicious," says Steve. "You can tell they've made their minds up about us before they've even listened to the records. We always say, 'Oh, we don't care,' but it's not always true. If you've just spent a long time making an album, trying hard to do your best, and someone just completely writes it off, it can be soul destroying. 'Virus' is kind of our go back at the people who have enjoyed putting us down over the years. Like, 'You've had your say, right. Now we'll have ours.'"

With *Best Of The Beast* having laid waste to the world's charts right through the Christmas period, the first few months of 1997 were a quiet time for the band. It wasn't until late summer that they finally reconvened at Steve's Essex studio to begin working on a new album. Seven months later, the enigmatically titled *Virtual XI* was released. On the surface a much more accessible collection than its daunting predecessor, both lyrically and musically, the material thankfully still retained the more adult, X-rated perspective that the Blaze-era line-up had ushered in. Now, however, the darkness was leavened with a fine, contrasting light, reflecting a new sense of optimism. And while tracks like the biting 'The Educated Fool' spoke of a knowingness bordering on the deeply cynical, others, like the upbeat first single, 'Angel And The Gambler', were full of fun and mischief, pointing the finger but laughing where previously they had scowled.

"Everyone said how much brighter it sounded than *The X Factor*," says Steve, "but it wasn't deliberate. Like everything we've ever done, it just sort of reflects where we were right then. With *The X Factor*, there was so much shit going down in my personal life, and what with Bruce leaving and Blaze coming in, I think we really felt the pressure was on to try and prove ourselves again. So there was a lot of that sort of...anger, I suppose, and fear in what came out. This time, we were all a lot happier with what we were doing, less worried, and just sort of going with the flow. I was certainly a lot happier, and so some of my songs are far less personal. Though not all of them."

Taking it track by track, then, 'Futureal', says Steve, "is something I wrote and that Blaze came up with the words for. Basically, he's talking about being locked up in virtual reality – whether that means on a computer game or in real life, you don't know. There is more than one meaning to the phrase 'virtual reality', if you know what I mean. Musically, I suppose it's a quite straightforward rocker but done Maiden style."

In retrospect an obvious choice of single, Steve bafflingly vetoed its release, making the extravagantly lengthy 'Angel And The Gambler' the single everywhere except in America. "I had a bit of a battle with Steve over 'Futureal'," admits Rod. "I thought it would have been a much better single than 'Angel...', but Steve put his foot down."

Written by Steve, 'Angel And The Gambler', he says, "is the story of these two characters, one guy who's been a bit of a rogue, a fly by night, and an angel who gets sent down to try and put him right – except he isn't having it. Afterwards, someone told me 'the angel' is supposedly the term for someone who backs a gambler, who stakes them the money they need to gamble with. So that was weird. Musically, though, the album version is over ten minutes long, and so we've had to try and cut it down a bit on the single. But it's still about six minutes long. It's kind of like The Who and 'Won't Get Fooled Again', that epic sort of single."

The next track, 'Lightning Strikes Twice', was written by Steve with Davey. "It's a never say never-type song," explains Steve. "Davey had the slow intro and I wrote the chorus and the words. Dave really liked the title, so we kept it. It's a very positive, hopeful song which you can read in lots of different ways."

'The Clansman' follows. At over nine minutes long, it's another patented Harris classic. "I wanted to imagine you're in the Scottish highlands – the loneliness, the mood – and then tried to create an anger and aggression in the rest of the song. It's about what it's like to belong to a community that you try and build up and then that you have to fight to stop having taken away from you. Musically, it's all about light and shade."

'When Two Worlds Collide', an upbeat singalong that Steve said he could "see going down well live", was written by Davey, who came up with the intro; Blaze, who penned the words; and Steve, who wrote the instrumental sections and the chorus melody. "Lyrically, I think Blaze was trying to write about the different sort of worlds he's lived in," muses Steve, "and maybe about how his world has had to change and adapt to the world of being Iron Maiden's singer but at the same time trying to keep his feet on the ground and still be who he really is. He's a very deep, dark person at times, Blaze. He can be an out-there, nutty sort of bloke one minute and very serious the next. And when he's had a drink, he turns into Ghengis Khan!" he laughs.

Perhaps the most telling track on the album, though, was 'The Educated Fool', another of Steve's solo efforts, this one about "getting older, realising there's other things going on." He stares off into space. "There's a reference to my father in there as well – 'I want to meet my father beyond...' It's about growing older and everyone expecting you to be wiser but how somehow the older you get and the more you know, the less you have the answers for any of it.

"It's like I've always been the one that took the band by the reins and pushed it in the direction I thought it should be going. I took the responsibility for that, and after a while the band just got used to me dealing with everything and expected me to do it. And I ain't complaining – I want to have that responsibility – but that doesn't mean it's always easy or that I think I'm always right. And, like, I've got three younger sisters and they all tend to look up to me more and more, especially since my dad died. And, of course, now I've got four kids of my own, too, so, though you shouldn't look at it like that, sometimes it *is* a pressure, because deep inside you know that you're only guessing half the time."

'Don't Look To The Eyes Of A Stranger', which follows, is cut from a similar dark cloth. "That's about my kids and my fears for the sort of world we're bringing them into, where every stranger is a possible threat," says Steve, "and how you have to teach them not to trust people, which is sad, you know? Really, really sad. I know that, when I was a kid, I was always told, 'Don't talk to strangers,' but I wasn't afraid to get on the bus and go and see West Ham on my own when I was nine or ten, you know? The world was safer then."

The last track, 'Como Estais Amigos', was an idea from Blaze which loosely translated means 'How Are You, Friends?'. "Blaze wrote the lyrics and Janick wrote the tune," says Steve. "It's basically about the Falklands War. Kind of a lament. Not just for the British soldiers that died, but for the Argentinean ones, too. It all goes back to when we toured Argentina with Blaze for the first time and Blaze was just blown away by how beautiful the people were and how amazing the whole place is, so friendly and that. And it's about just how everyday people get caught up in these things and they don't want to be.

"At the end of the day, though, it doesn't really matter what we wrote the songs about. I hope the music and the playing's good enough for people to read their own things into them. I think it's great when people come up with their own meanings to our songs. I've had letters from fans telling the things they've got out of some of our stuff and it's stuff that's never even occurred to me, sometimes. But when they explain it, I can see exactly what they mean, and then I start to think of the song in a new way, too. That's the amazing thing about music, it's like reading a good book – your imagination can run riot and you sort of fill in all the blanks yourself. That's why, when you go and see the film of the book, it's never as good the book. That's because it's never going to be as good as what you came up with in your own mind."

Released in May 1998, the title of the new album, *Virtual XI*, was inspired by two things: the parallel release of a Maiden computer game, *Ed Hunter – The Game*, and the fact that in June that year the England national football team would be competing in the World Cup finals in France. As Steve says, "We figure our fans are pretty much the same as we are, with pretty much the same interests, so we thought, 'It's World Cup year in '98. Let's get the football involved in the new album.' And we were already working on a computer game at that time, so we thought, 'Well, let's bring that element into things, too.'"

To help launch the record, they undertook a string of promotional football matches against all-star pro-celeb teams. "It was crazy," Blaze recalls, wide eyed. "Five thousand kids turned up in Spain just to watch the band play football. We had to have a police escort just to get into the ground!"

"Travelling 'round the world, seeing fans wearing West Ham scarves at our gigs in places like France or Germany, it gives you goosebumps," says Steve. "Football's such a common language now wherever you go. When we were in South America on the last tour, we were given all these different club shirts by the fans, and it felt like such an honour. I remember I wore an Argentina shirt onstage in Buenos Aires and the crowd went mad! And it gave me the idea then, really. So many fans relate to football, and everybody knows we're into it, 'cause we've always put 'Up The Hammers' on our album sleeves. And this being, like, our eleventh album, and there being eleven players in a football team... Well, it was perfect for combining two of my biggest loves together."

As part of the game, the band also amassed their own computer-enhanced virtual XI, a virtual footie team decked out in specially designed Maiden strips and comprising some of the most famous faces in football, including Paul Gascoigne, Ian Wright, Patrick Vieira and Marc Overmars – and, of course, several players from 'Arry's beloved West Ham. "A few of the lads came 'round to the house after the shoot and we had a drink and got a bit out of it," Steve chuckles. "[West Ham captain] Steve Lomas ended up singing along to a Kenny Rogers song on the karaoke machine. It was hilarious!

"As for the game itself, it's the most amazing thing I've ever seen. I don't get shocked very often, but *Ed Hunter* was so good. It's like walking into a 3D version of the *Somewhere In Time* album cover, like going into the bar at the Ruskin Arms, only full of aliens and stuff. You go in and we'll be, like, holograms playing in the corner, or sitting at a table gambling. And then you've actually got the game itself, which is, like, this big shoot-'em-up chase through space and time to catch Eddie. It's brilliant."

Bits of the game featured in the video for 'Angel And The Gambler'. "It's supposed to be, like, the biggest gig in the universe, and we're on this asteroid playing," Steve grins. "Eddie's like this Clint Eastwood figure standing in this *Star Wars*-type bar – it's along those lines. And for pyro, we blow up a planet!" With the band's own official fan club website (http//www.ironmaiden.co.uk) already one of the most popular official band sites on the net, *Virtual XI* also marked Maiden's emergence as one of the first fully computer-literate metal bands.

Suitably prepared, they thought, for whatever the future might bring, the Virtual XI world tour kicked off in Lille, France, at the end of April 1998 and continued right through to the following Christmas. Europe, Central America, North America, Europe (Part Two), Japan, Australia South America again... It was a Maiden trek in the old-fashioned sense: vast, sprawling, adrenaline driven.

"After two years off the road, it was, like, 'Get me on the tour bus!'" says Steve. "I love it. We all do. It's the most alive you ever feel in a band, playing every night to your fans." On tour, new songs like 'The Educated Fool' and 'The Clansman' quickly established themselves as show-stoppers in the new set. "The tour started great in Europe," says Blaze. "We got some amazing reactions from the crowds, some of it totally unexpected. We were just starting to see the end of grunge. When *The X Factor* came out, they were saying grunge had taken over and killed bands like Maiden. Now, three years later, it was like things were really looking up. I remember we sold out this huge ice-rink in Stockholm and the promoter told us we'd sold more for our concert than when Prince had played the last time. It felt like things were really going in a positive direction."

When the tour began in America later that summer, however, dark clouds suddenly began to loom on the horizon. "I had vocal problems," admits Blaze. "I got ill and we had to blow out a few dates, which is never good. I hate cancelling shows." A recurrence of the same problem he'd experienced on Maiden's previous US tour, it seemed like Blaze's voice was simply not up to the rigours of a full-on Maiden tour. As Steve says, "Being the singer for Maiden is very tough, when it comes to the gigs. You're talking about two hours, five nights a week, for months on end. And singing the stuff we do – that's very, very tough, and Blaze *did* find it tough. Some nights, he was great, and other nights, he...wasn't so great."

"It's a tough set for anybody," Blaze shrugs. "I mean, it was tough, but I was ill. And if you're going to have proper vocals and put your heart and soul into it every night, you're always in danger of doing your voice in. It's just rest – that's all you need. Maiden always did have a tough schedule. It's always been one of things the fans love about them, that they tour so hard. But when you do that, you run risks, especially the singer – I can't unstrap my voice and put it back in a box at the end of the night."

It wasn't just his intermittent problems in handling the vocals, though, that privately concerned the rest of the band. Accepted in Europe – particularly in France and Germany, where *The X Factor* was a major hit – and adored in South America, where the band had rarely been in their previous incarnation with Bruce, Blaze's reception in both Britain and America had always been mixed, to say the least. It wasn't just the rigours of touring that damaged his vocals, either; it was the strain of delivering songs originally written for Bruce. Both physically and metaphorically, Maiden's voice was slowly growing weaker.

By the final three dates of the tour, in South America at the end of 1998, Blaze says that he began to notice "an atmosphere kind of developing. There were some funny vibes at the end of the tour. When we got to Brazil, we did what I thought was a great show in Rio, but for some reason we didn't do an encore. I was standing by the side of the stage while the rest of lads went to the dressing room. It all felt a bit...contentious. It didn't feel right."

At the next show, in São Paulo, the local promoter had neglected to erect a safety barrier, and so the show had to be cancelled. "It was in really bad weather, too," remembers Blaze. "It was an accident waiting to happen. Somebody could have been killed, so it simply couldn't go on. But I remember the fans were very upset, so that didn't feel good, either. Then the last show was in Argentina, and... I don't know, it was heavily raining again. Anyway, I thought we did really well, but afterwards I had a sense there was some kind of funny vibe. At the time, I put it down to an end-of-tour kind of vibe."

At what point, then, did the band decide that it simply wasn't working and that a change would have to come? So far, Steve has been reluctant to discuss the matter in any depth in the various press interviews that the band has given since Blaze's departure. However, as he told me in an interview for *Classic Rock* magazine in April 1999, "It's kind of a delicate situation, really, because I've got a lot of respect for Blaze. I really like the guy, we all do, and it's just one of those situations where we don't really want to start saying the whys and wherefores until Blaze has had a chance to say something himself."

Two years later, and with the original honesty-at-all-costs intention of this book in mind, Steve says this: "Letting Blaze go was one of the hardest things I've had to do since I started this band." Would they have definitely replaced Blaze, though, even if Bruce hadn't come back? "Difficult question," sighs Steve. "In my mind, I'd like to say no, but there was talk and worry about Blaze because of the inconsistencies onstage, and it was getting to the point where something had to be done. But I actually enjoy working with the guy, and I don't make albums to try and be Number One; I just try and make the best albums I can. Maybe things had not been going as well as they were in the '80s, but metal was down, anyway, during the period Blaze was in the band.

"The fact is, I still stand by the albums we made together, particularly *The X Factor*, which is still one of my favourite Maiden albums. It's just a pity it didn't work out better on the road." Bruce coming back, Steve insists, was "completely unplanned for. I thought we'd get a completely new singer, if anything."

Once the decision had actually been made, how did Blaze take the news? "He took it very well, really," Steve says. "We'd had some discussions here and there already, so I don't think it was like it was totally out of the blue. But it was a very tough thing to do."

Blaze kept an understandably low profile for many months after. "I didn't want to say anything unless I had something positive to say," he says now. "If all I'd got to say was, 'I'm not in Maiden any more,' it's a purely negative thing. But if I can say, 'I've got my own band and album,' that's something to talk about."

He also admits now that his dismissal from the band came as more of a shock to him than Steve may have realised. Returning home at the end of the Virtual XI tour in time for Christmas 1998, Blaze insists that he was "quite positive, thinking about the next album. I'd written 'When Two Worlds Collide' with Davey and I was thinking we should try doing some more stuff together. Then we got through Christmas and I thought maybe, with it being the New Year, maybe everybody would get back into it again. Then, in January, I got called into the office for a meeting. I thought it was for a regular band meeting, but when I arrived everybody was already there. There was a bit of a weird vibe straight away. Then, as soon as I sat down, they told me."

How did he feel? "Oh, I was gutted to begin with, really upset, like anybody would feel when you're leaving something you've been a part of for a long time. Five years, two albums, and I'd always given 100 per cent in everything I did with them, from the writing to playing live, and I really enjoyed it. So no, it didn't feel good. But Rod said, 'The band wanna do something else, go in a different direction, carry on without you.' I asked if that meant Bruce was coming back, but they said nothing had been sorted out yet. I found out a week later. But it was better than hearing they were getting another unknown in. I felt like, 'OK, it's like a line-up thing, the classic line-up.' I mean, I still care about the band and, upset as I was, I thought, 'At least I know the band will carry on OK.' And I thought it was a really good move to have Adrian back as well."

He says it took "a couple of months to get over it. Everybody said it was nothing personal – they did it for the good of the whole band. What got me off my arse in the end was going through my notepad of lyrics and my Dictaphone tapes, where I keep all my little ideas for songs. I also got a lot of letters from fans saying they were gonna support me, which was an amazing boost. I started to flesh out ideas, and that's when I started seeing all the positive things I had taken out of Maiden. I'd seen what it takes to really make a band as successful as that. I'd learned from them how to stay focused. Before, I wasn't able to translate my ideas into the finished song, where with Steve that's something he's really good at, and I learned that from him. I learned a lot of things – how to be a better singer, a better writer, how to show leadership…"

More at peace with himself now that he has his own band, a solo career which has so far seen the release of one critically acclaimed album, *Silicon Messiah*, and ironically a growing reputation as a weighty live performer, in 2001 Blaze is philosophical on the subject of Iron Maiden: "I don't know if there's anything I would have done different, but I certainly learned enough to know the things I would never do again. Like when Bruce left Maiden, he kept a high profile, he was all over the place, while I hardly bothered at all. One thing I would have done is maybe made a bit more of the fact that I was now the singer of Iron Maiden, got my own name about a bit more. But I just didn't think like that then. I was just happy to be in the band.

"I know people will never stop talking to me about Iron Maiden. There's people who still ask them where Dennis Stratton is. It's like being in Kiss or something. The fans are so into the band they'll always want to know, and I'm really proud of that. We made two Top-Ten albums and had a Top-Ten single together, and I'd never done that before, so I'm very proud."

"The thing about Blaze," says Rod, "is he's fiercely proud of what he achieved with Maiden, and rightly so. It was no mean feat, stepping into Bruce's shoes – not just in the studio, where he did great, but also onstage, where he did start to struggle a bit sometimes on a long tour. With Steve, although he takes everything about the band incredibly personally – everybody knows Steve's put his blood and guts into this band – he's not so blinkered he can't see the big picture. One thing we've always shared is the ability to make decisions which are for the good of Iron Maiden, not any one individual. Over the years, it's what's made them tick – avoiding egos, putting the band first. That takes some doing over 22 years! To keep a fairly stable line-up through all that, not just the band but the crew behind them, the oldest of whom have been with the band since the very start – that's the key to it all. Even the ones we call 'the kids' have been with us for over ten years now.

"So when I asked Steve to consider the possibility of Bruce coming back, I knew what I was asking. It was never going to be something Steve would decide on the spot. There was a lot to take into consideration, and even then he wouldn't commit to anything either way until he'd actually sat down and talked to Bruce again. Once he got past that – I think he was really taken aback by how up for it Bruce was – Steve was able to see clearer how it might benefit the band."

Meanwhile, having emphatically set out to distance himself from heavy metal in general and Iron Maiden in particular, Bruce had thrown in the towel after both of his immediate post-Maiden albums – *Balls To Picasso* and *Skunkworks* – failed to excite either new or old audiences and did a complete musical about-face for his 1997 solo album, *Accident Of Birth*, teaming up again with Adrian Smith to record his most stridently metal material since his Maiden heyday.

"I'd always talked about doing an album with Bruce," says Adrian. "Then he rang me and started telling me about the stuff he'd been doing with Roy Z, enthusing about getting back to metal. I said, 'Come around,' and he brought some demos with him. I really liked the heavy, guitar-oriented songs, but I also had a couple of ideas, like the riff to 'Into The Pit', which was exactly what he was doing. And that's when we wrote 'Road To Hell', and from there everything started to snowball."

Adrian admits that he was "glad of the excuse to get off my arse and do something. I don't think I did anything at all for about the first two years after I left the band." Financially, he was set for life after seven years' virtual non-stop touring and recording. "I think I just needed a complete change of scene." And so, instead, he retired to the English countryside with his beautiful Canadian wife, Natalie, and started a family. "I don't think I even looked at a guitar for a while," he confesses.

It was only after getting up on stage with Maiden at the second Castle Donington show, in 1992, that Adrian began to think seriously about playing again, and within 18 months he had formed his own band, the somewhat esoterically monikered Psycho Motel, and begun recording their eponymous debut album, eventually released early in 1996 under a new deal that Rod had negotiated for him with Castle Communications, the independent London label that also signed Bruce in the post-Maiden era (now owned by Rod's Sanctuary Group). But Psycho Motel never really caught on, despite supporting Maiden on the British leg of the X Factour, and Adrian had, he admitted, temporarily shelved the project while he and Bruce worked together on the *Accident Of Birth* album and subsequent tour.

Bruce even had Derek Riggs design a special Eddie parody sleeve, which the shameless vocalist sarcastically dubbed "Edison". "I did it deliberately, of course," he told me with a dark chuckle. "I wanted to out-Maiden

Maiden." Steve's reaction was typically stoic: "Bruce would make a country and western album if he thought it would sell."

Adrian had always remained on friendly terms with Steve and the rest of the band. "I've kept up with everything they've done since I left," he said, "partly through curiosity and partly through some sort of weird devotion. I still like to know what's going on. I still care, in some weird way. I suppose I always will. You can't escape it." He says that he was "pleasantly surprised" at how well the band made the transition after Bruce: "I thought *The X Factor* was quite good, actually, the sort of thing Maiden's built on, really."

Exactly the sort of thing, in fact, that the critics were now saying about his own work with Bruce. But, as Adrian points out, "It couldn't help but have that sound. Of course it was gonna sound like Maiden. Roy [Z] was the real link between Bruce and myself and what was happening at street level. Roy knew a lot of real Maiden fans. He was more in touch with that side of it, and he said, 'Metal fans in LA want you and Bruce to make a metal album.' So we thought, 'For the fans out there, let's give them what they want but do a really good record.'"

When they also began to feature a selection of Maiden songs in their live set, it didn't take a rocket scientist to predict the reaction: wouldn't it be great if they got back with Maiden?

Adrian: "When we were putting the set together, we only had ten songs, only seven of which could be done live, so the logical thing was to include Maiden songs, stuff we actually wrote, like 'Two Minutes To Midnight', 'Flight Of Icarus', 'Be Quick Or Be Dead'... It was great to play them. Seeing the audiences' reaction every night was really gratifying." After that there was another Psycho Motel album and an even more scintillating follow-up with Bruce, *Chemical Wedding*, in 1997.

Adrian: "It was only after we'd been on tour with the second album, where we talked to a lot of people and they all kept saying the same thing: 'Why don't you get back together?' It made you think. At the same time, I used to get annoyed, 'cause it was an insult to Maiden and Blaze, the fact that people thought we could just go back into the band. So, although a lot of people said they'd like to see it, never in a million years did I think it would actually happen."

Little did Adrian know that Rod had secretly been trying to talk

Steve into considering the possibility of taking Bruce back into the band, or the repercussions that this would have on his own career.

"That's how it was for some time," says Steve. "Rod was being his bombastic, bullying best, 'cause he knew I wasn't into it at all. Whatever was happening with Blaze, I thought he was really good. Live, there was inconsistencies, which I really would like to have tried to sort out, but if it wasn't possible then you have to think again. But all the while Rod was going on about Bruce, I just wasn't into it. I didn't think it would work, and I didn't think Bruce would be up for it, either. At the same time, though, there were so many rumours flying around that Bruce wanted to come back. It was like it just kept coming up. Because he was doing metal albums again, I suppose."

For Bruce, it was a question he'd been dodging for years. "Well, it's come up in interviews every year since I left," he says. "I'm not completely in the loop over what happened with Blaze, but clearly there was something that happened on the last tour that fuelled further things like that. So the rumour mill started going and people started asking questions. But I have to say that, at that time, I tried to keep a discreet distance from it, particularly with the band. I was still bumping into Janick and going down the pub, and we'd talk about everything else except an Iron Maiden reunion, because we didn't think it was appropriate."

At what point, then, did Bruce returning become a serious idea? "When Rod first mentioned it, I wasn't really into it," says Steve. "I thought, 'Well, why would he wanna come back? Plus, I've always had the view that you don't look back. You look forward. But then I thought, 'Well, if the change happens, who would we get?' The thing is, we know Bruce and we know what he's capable of, and you think, 'Well, better the devil you know.' I mean, we got on well professionally for, like, eleven years, and so...after I thought about it, I didn't really have a problem with it."

Unbeknownst to both sides, Rod had privately pursued a similar line of inquest with Bruce. "It was Rod who took me aside and said, 'How do you feel about putting it back together?'" Bruce recalls. "I said, 'Well, you know, there's a couple of things that concern me, but 90 per cent of things that I think are massive opportunities.'" What concerned Bruce specifically, he says, "was whether we would in fact be making a real state-of-the-art record and not just a comeback album. In other words, if we were back together, then potentially Iron Maiden is looking at being nothing less than the best heavy metal band in the world again, and I really wasn't prepared to compromise on that idea."

Once Steve had at least agreed to discuss the idea with Bruce, a secret rendezvous was arranged in January 1999. "They all came down to my house in Brighton," Rod revealed. "We had to do it a bit off the beaten path, because we didn't want anyone to know. It was important they both be comfortable and not feel they had everybody's eyes on them, so we did it in the lounge at my house."

It was the first time they'd spoken to each other seriously since 1993, and initially, says Bruce, "It was strange. I think we were both a bit nervous. But as soon as we walked in the room, we gave each other a big hug and it evaporated. Literally, like, *boof!* Gone. And we both just chatted away."

"Obviously, the first question to Bruce was, 'Why do you wanna come back?'" says Steve, "and the second question was, 'How long are you gonna stay for?', 'cause it's no good if he's going to bugger off again after 18 months. I wanted to make sure he was gonna be with us for the long haul."

Steve admits now that he was sceptical right up until the moment he walked in the room. "I hadn't spoken to Bruce for five years or more. I thought we'd have the meeting and that it wouldn't work. I thought we'd all be grown up about it, but that would be it. Then we actually had the meeting and it really changed everything. His enthusiasm was 100 per cent, so I thought, 'Well, maybe it *is* the right thing to do. Maybe I need to take a back seat on my own personal worries and make the right decision for the band as a whole.'"

"He was, you know, a bit like, 'I'm still not sure exactly why you left,' sort of thing," remembers Bruce. "He said it a couple of times, and then he said, 'but that doesn't matter now'. And I went, 'Oh, but it *does* matter!' And so I told him, like, 'This is why I left.' I can't remember exactly what I said, but at the end I said, 'Does that make sense?' And he went, 'Well, yeah.' I thought, 'OK, well that's all right, then.' I mentioned that I didn't plan to make a country and western album," he adds, tongue in cheek, referring to Steve's earlier comment. "We all had a good giggle about that. It's just one of those things, like having a bit of a family set-to over the dinner table. And then, of course, we all ended up going down the pub. One thing led to another and we all woke up with thick heads the next day."

There will still be more solo albums, he maintains. "This doesn't mean an end to making records with Roy Z or with Adrian. What it may mean is that I don't have to go out and do club tours to promote them. I can't say I would mind giving that up." One of those performers whose personality and charisma – combined with remarkable athleticism – only truly fulfils its promise on the very biggest stages, Bruce describes the clubs and theatres he had grown used to performing in as a solo artist as "like performing in a jam jar. You feel like an angry wasp." He freely admits that the chance to step out onto the largest stadia in the world was also a big part of his motivation for returning to Maiden. "Well, it certainly wasn't anything to do with money," he says. "If money was the only motivation, we'd probably all have retired years ago. It's not about money for Maiden, at this point; it's about living the dream again." If they were to get back together, Bruce said, he would want them all to see it as "a huge opportunity for Maiden to kind of take the high ground again – not necessarily to do a commercial album or something dreadful like that, but actually to do a real heavy metal record and blow everybody's balls off, live. As long as that was the aim, and we all agreed on it, I was really into it. What I didn't want was for us to end up gradually, like, lolling back into complacency." That, after all, had been what had forced him out in the first place. "Well, precisely. But, thankfully, when we talked about it, it was like everybody sort of had the same idea. Steve was really into it, too. He doesn't want to see this as some sort of comeback. To him, this is, like, just the next step in Iron Maiden, and that's exactly how it should be. How it is."

"Bruce came down and explained why he'd left in the first place," remembers Rod. "Then Steve said his piece, which was basically, 'Why do you wanna come back now?' Bruce said, 'Because I'm sick of doing clubs. I want to do big things again. I want to finish off playing to 20,000 people, not 2,000.' Bruce said he'd always loved the band and wanted to make another killer Maiden album. And then we went down the pub," he beams.

"It was great," remembers Steve. "Adrian was the only one who wasn't there, but I rang him on my mobile to tell him. I remember standing in the pub car park on the phone. I laid it all on the line. I said, 'I want you back, 'cause it takes Maiden somewhere else, musically.' Then, the next day, Rod called him to confirm."

"They did their first photo session together two days later," Rod beams. As simple as that? "Yes and no, really," he says. "Nothing is ever that simple. The fact is, Bruce and Steve are never going to be the types that go out for a drink together. They have different interests – Bruce has no interest in football, Steve none in aeroplanes – but it's that difference that makes them tick as performers. It's the differences between them that make the creative sparks fly sometimes, that gives it that edge."

Having made their decision, the band were not slow to start making plans. Big plans. By the time the news was officially announced, in March 1999, rumours of some sort of reunion had grown so vociferous that it only confirmed what many fans were already hoping to hear, that Bruce was back with Maiden. What hadn't been anticipated was the dual announcement that Adrian was also returning to the fold. Yet there it was, in cold black and white on the official press release, which read simply, 'Bruce Dickinson and Adrian Smith are back in Iron Maiden,' followed by a few brief bullet points – that this would be the first time Maiden had had a three-guitar line-up; that they would be touring America and Europe from July to September 2000; and that there would be a new studio album in early 2000, followed by a full-on world tour. There was even an updated version of *Ed Hunter* on the way.

"When Rod first spoke about the Bruce thing, I said, 'Well, if Bruce is gonna come back, why don't we get Adrian back, too?'" recalls Steve. "He said, 'That doesn't mean you want Janick to go, does it?' I said, 'No, I don't want Janick to go. I think Janick's great. But why don't we have a three-guitar thing?', because, years ago, when Davey first joined, we were a three-guitar band. Then the other two left and we ended up bringing in other people to partner Dave, who could do the work of two guitar players. And I've always valued Adrian's writing. I think maybe Maiden lost something when Adrian left. 'Two Minutes To Midnight' is a superb song. 'Stranger In A Strange Land' was different again, as well. He adds a different dimension to the band."

Steve was also persuaded, he says, by the memory of Adrian's guest appearance with the band at Donington in 1992. "We did 'Running Free' and it just felt great. So I think it's quite exciting, not just having him back but the three-guitar thing, too. It just opens the thing up.

There's certainly enough guitar parts on the songs for three guitar players. And it's not like Adrian doesn't know them, is it?"

How had Dave and Janick taken it, though? "Dave was great about it," says Steve. "No problem whatsoever. Him and Adrian have been mates since they were kids. I think Janick was a little nervous to begin with, though – not once the decision was made but while it was being made – but I said, 'Look, this is not an audition, absolutely no way.' I told Janick he was a really important part of Maiden now and, if it means it's not working, that he was the one who stays. By the time we actually got on a stage together, though, we'd written some songs, done interviews, and it just felt totally natural."

Nevertheless, when the call actually came, Adrian confesses that he suffered "a violent mixture of emotions. I thought, 'But if I come back, who leaves?' Or would it be like I play half a set and Janick plays half a set? Whatever, I wouldn't have been happy if Janick wasn't into it." When the message came back, via Rod, that it was to be a three-guitar combo, Adrian was even less assured. "I thought, 'Three guitars? That's never gonna work!' Then I thought about it some more and decided, 'Why not?' Steve, being unorthodox in his thinking – which has always been Maiden's greatest strength – had suggested it, so I thought, 'Well, at least you should give it a go.'"

The first time they all actually got together again professionally was for the first photo session, arranged just days after Steve and Bruce had met at Rod's house. "We were all making jokes about what we were wearing," says Adrian. "It was exactly the same as I'd left it, really – Nicko was telling Jimmy Jones jokes, Steve was a bit quiet, Davey the same. Janick I'd known for some time anyway – he's always been a mate of Bruce's, and we used to play five-a-side football together. In fact," he adds, "having Janick there has given the band another ingredient. If I had gone back and it had been the same five guys, there would have been a lot of baggage, but having Janick there seems to make it all fresh again. It's not the old band; it's a whole new thing, which makes it great."

It was also an opportunity to repair some memories, Adrian says. "You always say, 'If I'd known then what I know now...' Well, this was a chance to go back and do things properly this time. We're not hung up on certain things like we were in the past. Now we just appreciate it all for what it is."

In April 1999, the band went to Portugal, ostensibly to write but really just to spend time together again. "I got there, set up and started to write immediately," says Adrian. "The first thing I put down was the music to 'The Wicker Man'. Everything just seemed to fall into place." There was a palpable air of expectancy surrounding the early sessions. "We all just threw ourselves into it," says Bruce. "That was when stuff like 'Fallen Angel' and 'Ghost Of The Navigator' came up."

Setting up in an old disused aircraft hangar, they listened to each other's ideas for new songs. "I stuck my tape in and I was really nervous," Adrian recalls, "but it was the riff to 'The Wicker Man', and ten minutes later we really tore into it live. Steve suggested some arrangement things, but that was it. And that's when we started working together again properly as a band. By the end of the day, we had a rough version of our first new song together."

It was a psychological victory, says Bruce, an important hurdle overcome. "We had this honeymoon period where everybody was leaping around with the big hoopla about us getting back together. And though we were all feeling pretty good about what we were doing, I think we all also realised deep down inside that the real proof of the pudding would only come when we actually got together on a stage again and tried doing it.

"I don't think we ever doubted our own abilities for a second, but it wasn't until we did actually get up and have a play together in Portugal that it really hit home to us how right this was. It was so good to be all together again. It just felt right, and that's when we knew for sure we'd done the right thing."

The brief two-month tour of the US and Europe which would follow in July was planned to be, according to Bruce, "basically like a greatest hits set, which actually takes a fair bit of pressure off us, because we can just get together and go out and do the most amazing live show and people, I hope, will come away from that going, 'Fucking hell!' And that's gonna put us in a great vibe and a great frame of mind for going in and just transferring that in the studio when we come to actually do the album. The important thing is that, when we had our initial get-together – myself, Steve and the band – my concern was, how did I know we were gonna make this great record? And Steve immediately said, 'Well, I think we need a producer, and I don't think we can do it in the same studio. We've got to do it in a state-of-the-art studio, the best studio we can possibly get.' By which point you could have picked me up off the floor! I was like, 'Well, that's bloody great!', because that was the single biggest worry of mine, that we would do all this and put all this effort in and that we wouldn't make the album that we were capable of making. But I really feel confident now that we're well on the way. We've got the right attitude. We still have to decide on a producer, but there's plenty of time. We're not recording the album until the end of this year."

It would have been tempting to invite Martin Birch back to produce it, which would have been the icing on the cake for long-standing fans, but according to Rod it was never an option. "Martin's retired now and has been for a few years," he said. "After spending most of his life buried away in the studio, he's enjoying the golf course now. So it was never going to happen, really. Plus, the band definitely see this as a chance for something fresh. They'd agreed they needed an outside producer this time, someone really strong who understood what they were trying to do, but someone new, too, who could bring something fresh to it."

Besides, it wasn't like they were short of takers for the gig. "Several producers have already come up," Bruce told me in Portugal, "from the most cutting edge and modern to classic producers and people like that. But all of this is speculative. We're still listening to tapes and talking with people. There's no hurry on this and we're not going to make a rushed decision, because it's important."

That was something else new. In the old days, recording a Maiden album was done very quickly. "We're determined that this is not going to be like that," said Bruce. "We want to work hard and we will be working hard this year. We've got a very, very big schedule for the whole of this year and indeed for the whole of next year. Next year is going to get quite silly, in terms of concerts and globe-trotting, and that's nothing that I mind, but the thing you don't want is to be rushing and tripping over your own feet when you're making the album.

"We're not gonna make the kind of album that's gonna be flavour of the month and sell 15 million copies. If we sold two or three million albums and we made a fucking brilliant Iron Maiden album, that's the album to make!"

Bruce was also keen to try and distance his and Adrian's return to Maiden from the many other comebacks that had littered the rock scene in the past few years (not least those of Black Sabbath and Kiss, to name just two). "I don't want to be in a classic rock band," he said. "I want to be the leader of the pack. There's a whole generation of rock fans that have never seen this line-up. As a result, they'll really wanna come and see what all the fuss is all about. Plus, hopefully there will also be older fans who will be interested again, too. We're gonna pull from every section of the rock audience, especially live. Maiden's live performances are legendary."

The show would be "bigger than it's been for some time," Bruce insisted. The 2000 tour would be "bigger even than that, the biggest Maiden show there has ever been. This is not about nostalgia at all. It's like they say in *The Dead Poets Society*, you know? 'Seize the day.' Well, we've grabbed everybody's imaginations now, and I think people are going to really pay attention to what we do next, and that's a very nice feeling. It really gives you a spur to...well, seize the day!"

Although quietly optimistic, Steve wasn't counting his chickens, as befits his role as team leader. He knew that there was still a lot of work to be done before this line-up of Maiden would be ready to stand up against the best of them. "There's always two sides to the coin," he said in Portugal. "Of course there's people out there that are happy Bruce has rejoined, but we've also had letters from people asking why Blaze has gone. I think you've just got to do what feels right, and at the end of the day it just seemed the right thing to do. It just feels right, at this point. Whether or not it still feels that way in two years' time, who's to say? But we've got to go with what feels right now. And it's not just Bruce coming back but the three-guitar thing, which gives it a different sort of angle altogether and takes it maybe into a different area. That's what I'm excited about – taking it somewhere else and trying different things."

They would still be performing some of the songs from the Blaze-era albums, Steve explained, just as they had continued playing Di'Anno-era material when Bruce first joined. "We don't know yet which songs from those albums are gonna suit Bruce's voice, but yeah, I'm pretty sure we'll do stuff like 'The Clansman' and maybe 'Man On The Edge', stuff like that. I mean, it's not like it's a reunion, where we've split up and reformed again; we've been an ongoing concern. It's not like the Black

Sabbath situation, as such. With us, it's more picking up where we left off, if you like. We just thought we'd give it a go and see what happens."

There would always be cynics who decried the whole thing. "There always has been, right from the start," said Steve. But since when had Maiden ever cared about the cynics? "It's been suggested it's been done for money," says Steve, "but it's not that. I think you know us all well enough to know it's not that. I mean, if there's some bonus coming in, you're gonna take it. Of course you are. But, at the end of the day, we're in a situation where, if we retired now, we'd still be OK, you know? So it's not like we have to go out and do it for that.

"At the end of the day, it really is just about one thing: the music. The band. That's always come top of the agenda, which is why we've never sold out, never compromised. As far as Bruce goes, we get on a lot better now than we ever have... We always got on professionally, but we actually get on now a lot better personally, too. I think we've grown up, on both sides of the fence. He's always been professional, but now he's got the hunger back for it he's incredible again, which is why I'm excited about the album we're gonna make together. If the combination works right and naturally feels right, which I think it will do, the spark will be there. I just think it will be. When you look who's in the band now, I don't think you can question it. It will be strong stuff. You just need to put these people in the same room together and see what happens."

16 Brave New World

The Ed Hunter tour kicked off in Canada on 13 July 1999. The first ports of call were Montreal's Molson Center Amphitheater and the L'Agora in Quebec the following night, and then the new-look Maiden descended on New York's Hammerstein Ballroom for what would inevitably be two highly scrutinised shows. Fans and media had jetted in from all over the globe to witness a landmark gig in Maiden's long history.

"In New York, I was absolutely shitting myself," revealed Bruce Dickinson a few days later, "and in Montreal, on the first night back, it was the same thing. Musically, though, it was as good as everybody had hoped. It was pretty funny, because we got offstage and it had been as good or better than everybody had expected. In fact, the only things we whinged about were the usual things like follow-spot cues, mistakes by lighting engineers or how much the sound had changed from the soundcheck. The audience loved it – they were freaking out. But by New York, things were really happening."

I caught the band in Milwaukee nine dates into the tour, and by then they had really hit their stride. The evening's show at the Pine Knob Music Theater in Detroit was little short of revelatory. Some months earlier, the fans had selected the tour's set-list over the Internet, and the results had paid dividends. But besides the impressive way in which Dave, Adrian and Janick had gelled onstage and the choice of material on display, what really struck home was the sense of camaraderie within the band. For these North American dates, Bruce revelled in his role of piloting Steve Harris, Nicko McBrain, Rod Smallwood and the tour manager from city to city in a twin-propped light aircraft while the three guitarists chose to travel either by domestic flights or by tour bus. Steve would sit contentedly in the plane's rear, reading and joking, while Nicko – himself an experienced pilot, of course – would either join Bruce in the cockpit or blend in with the rest of the passengers.

On the afternoon that I travelled with the band *en route* to Detroit, it was the little things that registered most, like Bruce's offer to buy a pilot teddy-bear for Nicko and Steve's unexpected warmth towards his returning vocalist. The flight from Milwaukee to Detroit was a short one, but black clouds were closing in and all on board were mightily relieved when Dickinson brought the craft down safely onto the tarmac before the thunderstorm broke. Following the full red-carpet treatment, we transferred into a minibus as the first drops of rain began to fall. As Steve remarked, reclining comfortably in his seat, it was "the only way to travel."

The Pine Knob show provided everything that the fans had hoped for and more. Although Maiden had already written some new material, it was quite rightly felt that going out with all guns blazing was the best way of blowing away the cobwebs. 'Aces High' (complete with recalled Winston Churchill intro tape) and 'Wrathchild' opened proceedings magnificently, after which 'The Trooper' and 'Two Minutes To Midnight' burst forth. The triple-guitar onslaught worked surprisingly well, with Adrian's return providing an extra lean, melodic edge to songs like 'Two Minutes To Midnight', 'The Evil That Men Do' and 'Wasted Years'. Meanwhile, Bruce interpreted Blaze-era songs such as 'Futureal', 'Man On The Edge' and particularly 'The Clansman' with the charisma that the critics had suggested lacking in his predecessor.

The set was rounded out with vintage songs such as 'Killers' and the epic 'Powerslave' before delving way, way back to 'Phantom Of The Opera' from the first album, winding up with 'Fear Of The Dark' and perennial set-closer 'Iron Maiden'. The crowd then wouldn't let the group depart without a three-song encore – 'Number Of The Beast', 'Hallowed Be Thy Name' and 'Run To The Hills'. And even before the house lights returned, the sweaty, smiling musos were back on the minibus and heading back for the airport.

At the Milwaukee hotel after the return flight, Steve Harris remained tight-lipped over the reasons for Blaze's departure. And because most of what the bassist had to say at the time was affected by this most fundamental of issues, it often made straight talking very difficult. Harris duly acknowledged that an understanding of the current Maiden situation depended on the way the previous line-up had dissolved, but still he kept his silence. "If Blaze hasn't spoken about it yet, then neither will I," he insisted to anyone who asked. "That's what we agreed."

Although the bassist was clearly relishing proceedings, to his credit he continued to remain loyal to Bayley. "I don't see much difference between this American tour and the last one with Blaze," he insisted. "There's been a few gigs with a few more people, but as far as reactions go there's not much in it. Last summer we played this venue to eight and a half thousand people. Tonight we had over ten thousand. It's a difference, but not a huge one."

At this early stage in the tour, Harris still seemed to share the shock of the fans that Maiden were back together with Bruce and Adrian again. "I think that Bruce is a changed man," he said. "A lot of that's to do with him sorting out his personal life and being back in the band. We've been pretty much on the same wavelength since the start. His attitude has been exactly where I wanted it to be. My only worry has been that he was acting that way because he knew that's what we wanted to hear. But with all this enthusiastic stuff he's been saying onstage each night, he'd look pretty silly if he just baled out at the end of all this."

Although Rod Smallwood has been credited as being the driving force behind the return of Bruce and Adrian, it seems that certain members of the band had also reached the same conclusion. In Detroit, Nicko offered his own perspective, which was that, if Dickinson hadn't returned, maybe the band would have called it a day at the end of the *Virtual XI* campaign. "If we hadn't got Bruce back, there was a possibility we'd have 'ung it up, and I didn't want that," he said. "We knew Bruce needed us and we needed him, so I finally brought the subject up with 'Arry. He took a bit of persuading, but even he knew it, underneath. First time around, it had become a bit like a marriage that was going down the tubes – if you stop communicating, things go wrong – but now both Bruce and Adrian are back and we're able to sit down and talk about things if there's a crisis."

Harris bridled at the drummer's comments. "Did Nick really say that?" he frowned. "Naaah, even if Blaze had stayed in the band, we'd still have been touring this summer and making the next record abroad, even looking for a producer, because Nigel Green's not available to do it."

Eventually, Steve summed up the early part of the tour as he saw it. "I'm not the type of bloke who goes shouting about things from the rooftops," he mused. "I prefer to take my time and see how things go. We've not done enough gigs or an album yet, but this line-up has the potential to be Maiden's best ever."

Dickinson agreed. When I told him that I was genuinely surprised to see the current line-up playing together after all the negative talk of the previous few years, he chuckled knowingly. "That's great, I suppose, because it adds drama. But I'll tell you what, it's all very grown up and we're working together more closely now than at any other point in the band's history, maybe with the exception of the *Number Of The Beast* album. We're actually talking to each other now. It's not like, 'Oh, hi. Did you get drunk last night?' We're really having real conversations about things that matter. It's really exciting."

Bruce also shed some light on how the band were going about writing for the next album. "We've been setting the gear up in a circle and everyone's been making suggestions and modifying what comes up," he revealed. "Sure, it can get a bit lively at times, but constructive argument is good, because it shows that people care. The vibe is really happening. You could touch it."

When asked whether there had been a lot of issues to resolve in order to get to that stage, he shrugged: "No. Honestly, no."

And were there any things still left unsaid?

"Again, no. All these things have resolved themselves. It's all just little details, and those things are relatively easily ironed out. Lots of things have changed. We can have a laugh, for a start. Wherever we've been playing, I've been telling the crowd, 'Scream for me, Long Beach!' [the line first coined on the live double *Live After Death*], and people love all that, because it was part of their growing up."

However, Dickinson became animated at the mere mention of the word *nostalgia*. "That's fucking horrible," he almost hissed. "It makes me quite angry when people keep on talking about the past. That's not what I rejoined this band for. I just wanted to make a great record. What this tour is all about is kicking everyone in the fucking bollocks. It's not about making Limp Bizkit and all these other bands have respect for what Iron Maiden once were but about what we are and what we're going to be."

The tour rolled on through North America until it reached the Bronco Bowl in Dallas on 8 August. Then, after a month of recuperation, it picked up at the Omnisport de Bercy in Paris before heading through Holland, Germany, Finland, Sweden, Italy, Spain and Greece, concluding at the Peristeri football ground in Athens on 1 October 1999. British fans were understandably less than chuffed at being omitted from the group's itinerary, although they were offered a ray of hope that Maiden would revive the Castle Donington festival in the following year. The much-missed bash had last taken place in 1996, headlined by Kiss, but if anybody could have revived the beast then Maiden would have been the band to do it. "I'd love to do Donington again, because it's a tradition that shouldn't have died out," Steve told me, "but it's something we'll have to talk about."

"For every person that would want to see the Iron Maiden reunion, there's an armchair critic," pointed out Dickinson. "The UK's a very unfriendly place for metal, and in that respect it's far behind the rest of the world. But who knows? By next summer we may have organised something for the British fans. And it won't be a gig at Reading!"

The Paris gig on 9 September was among the most easily accessible for Brit-based Maiden supporters, and bus after bus descended upon the French capital for the Omnisport de Bercy show, where the headliners were backed by Megadeth. The 17,000-capacity venue had sold out in six weeks.

When Maiden took to the stage that night, the reaction was so loud that it sounded as though a bomb had gone off. As the six-piece blitzed triumphantly through their 17-song set, which adhered to the one they'd played at Pine Knob, even long-time observers like myself had to admit that the band were performing as well as ever before and perhaps even better. At the gig's conclusion, hundreds of inebriated, ecstatic Brits trudged up and down the Champs Elysees waving Union Jacks and chanting, "Maiden! Maiden! Maiden!" What the locals made of the scene one can only wonder.

Following those triumphant images, it was fitting that the new album would be recorded in the same city. In November, the six-piece decamped to Guillaume Tell Studios with no firm idea of how long it would take them to create the anxiously awaited CD. They kept the producer's identity secret for several months, but word began to spread that it would be Kevin Shirley, nicknamed "Caveman". This was an inspired choice, as Shirley's previous work with The Black Crowes, Aerosmith, Dream Theater and Silverchair, among others, had established him as the hottest new name on the scene.

By all accounts, the sessions for what became *Brave New World* were extremely pleasurable. Shirley was firm but fair and more than willing to listen to everybody's suggestions, and relaxing evenings were spent quaffing inordinate quantities of French beer.

One of the album's main strengths was the diversity of its material. Although Steve was responsible for co-penning at least two of its finest songs – 'Dream Of Mirrors' and 'The Nomad', with Janick and Dave respectively – and writing 'Blood Brothers' on his own, the credits reflected significant input from Bruce (who was involved with four songs), Janick (also four tracks), Dave (three tracks) and Adrian (two). "Everybody was pretty cool and laid back about getting their songs onto the album or not getting them on," Dickinson stated later. "Everybody was aware that there had to be a bit of give and take. We had pretty much planned out the year so we would peak – a bit like the way athletes do – as we went into the studio. And, of course, when we did the songs in the studio, we pretty much did the entire album live."

Although it wasn't directly inspired, the opening track, 'The Wicker Man', took its name from the film of the same name and was built around a prime-cut Maiden riff. 'Ghost Of The Navigator' was the first of the album's songs to display the group's increasingly progressive feel and 'Brave New World' itself opened deceptively quietly before elevating into a thoroughly stadium-stomping chorus.

There are tenuous parallels between the next track, 'Blood Brothers', and the previous album's 'The Clansman', inasmuch as both boast strong Highland influences. The former's gently picked guitar motif proved that Maiden still knew the merits of light and shade, and the seven-minute epic gave away Steve and Bruce's long-avowed admiration for Jethro Tull. Half jokingly, Bruce revealed that he had sung the lyric on one leg in reverence to Tull's Ian Anderson.

A full three minutes more concise than the previous song, 'The Mercenary' relates the tale of those who kill for money and was later described by Bruce as "a fairly conventional, tuneful rocker, comparable to 'Die With Your Boots On'."

Nine minutes and 21 seconds long, 'Dream Of Mirrors' is without doubt the disc's most ambitious piece. Ebbing and flowing like the sea, it takes the listener through a variety of emotions as it chronicles the feelings of a man too terrified to sleep. Harris' chorus of "I only dream in black and white/I only dream 'cause I'm alive/I only dream in black and white/To save me from myself" prompted Bruce to chuckle, "Oh man, he's a tortured motherfucker!"

Adrian wrote the music and Steve supplied the lyrics and melody line to the tasteful if somewhat dark little rocker 'The Fallen Angel', which is overlaid with an enormous riff and some intricate lead breaks. Maiden then really pushed the boat out with 'Nomad', an Eastern-flavoured paean to the Bedouin, the warrior tribes of the desert. Another nine-minute song, 'Nomad' allowed the three guitarists to stretch out and show how versatile they could be.

"A bunch of aliens have destroyed their own planet and now they're coming to ours to destroy us" – that was the concept that Bruce revealed as being the inspiration behind 'Out Of The Silent Planet', a fine mid-tempo rocker that once again focused on the ability of the guitarists to texture and prioritise their rhythmic slabs and razor-sharp solos, while the album closed with 'Thin Line Between Love & Hate', a rhythmic and slightly soul-searching anthem that brought to mind Steve's old heroes Phil Mogg and UFO. Both song and album conclude with some beautiful interplay between Dickinson's soaring voice and an ethereal guitar line before dropping back into what sounds like an off-the-cuff jam session.

The reviews were ecstatic right across the board. Plainly, the new Iron Maiden line-up had lived up to both their own lofty expectations and those of their audience.

Live, the band were determined to live up to all the hype by returning with their most action-packed show yet. No Donington yet, though. Instead, the band announced that the British leg of the tour – dubbed Metal 2000 – would begin on 16 June in suitably gargantuan style at London's cavernous Earls Court arena, the scene of past triumphs for Led Zeppelin, Pink Floyd and Genesis. All 20,000 tickets had been sold out within three days, before Maiden had even announced opening acts Slayer and Entombed.

"There was an offer for us to do Donington. The date was the Saturday [the next day] after we did Earl's Court, and it was the day England played Germany in Euro 2000," revealed Bruce. "That was what clinched it for us. It would have been mad to play Donington – at which nothing less than a complete and utter sell-out looks good – on a day like that."

The Metal 2000 show was generally regarded as one of Maiden's very finest since they made their line-up changes. Now able to draw on a brand-new studio album, many of the older songs were given a rest, and all but three tracks – 'Nomad', 'Out Of The Silent Planet' and 'Thin Line Between Love & Hate' – from *Brave New World* were eased into the set. To make things even more interesting, 'The Sign Of The Cross' was added, a Blaze-sung track from *The X Factor*, and a grinning Bruce delivered the tune as he descended from the ceiling sporting a set of angel's wings. The show's production was large, and at its conclusion Bruce cajoled the crowd into burning a set of virgins in a cage.

Of the new songs, 'Dream Of Mirrors', 'Ghost Of The Navigator' and 'Blood Brothers' were especially inspiring, and although some griped at the lack of oldies such as 'Run To The Hills', 'Aces High' and even 'Running Free', the band were defiant in the face of such criticism. "As far as I'm concerned, if people want to hear 'Run To The Hills', there are plenty of Iron Maiden tribute bands," reasoned Bruce. "Too much nostalgia would overshadow what we're doing now."

After the Earl's Court gig, Maiden turned their attention back to North America again. Newly signed to Sony Records for *Brave New World*, they were overjoyed to learn that all 14,000 tickets for the tour's showcase event – a date at New York's fabled Madison Square Garden – had sold out in just two hours, even before the support acts of Queensrÿche and Rob Halford were announced.

"When Rod called and asked us how many tickets we'd sold in the first hour, we reckoned maybe 4,000," Nicko told me proudly on the day of the show. "We couldn't believe it when he said [erupting into harsh Yorkshire accent], 'No-o-o-o-o-o. Six and a half bloody thousand!' So we opened a book to see how many we'd sell within the first day, but he called back and said the bet was off; it was a sell-out within two hours. We thought he was having us on."

The vibe around the group was now completely different to that of their last Big Apple show with Blaze Bayley, which had seen Maiden headline the Roseland Ballroom. "Without a doubt," agreed Nicko. "We had two great tours with Blaze, but the last one was a struggle all 'round. But we still went out and performed as Maiden always do. We've done some great tours in the past, but this one tops them all. The whole vibe's so positive and everyone's getting on so well after all that stuff that happened six or seven years ago. People grow up. They change. Sure, we were a little worried about Bruce's reasons for coming back on board, but he's so into being in this band again. It was something he had to do."

So determined were the band to decry the nostalgia tag that they bravely retained the set they'd played in the UK. "I'm all for keeping these new songs in the set," stressed Steve afterwards. "Bruce and Adrian have been off doing their own solo albums and things for years, but it's refreshing for the rest of us to play something new, not to keep living in the past."

"It's important for us not to become a parody of ourselves," adds Janick. "I've seen it happen to so many other bands. I love playing the old stuff, but if you stick to the old stuff then old is all you'll become. We don't want to become a fucking cabaret band."

After the spectacle of Madison Square Garden, Steve was more upbeat about Maiden's continued longevity. "I'm as pleased as I can possibly be at this point in time," he stated. "If I've appeared to have my doubts, that was partly because we were still playing the bloody 'best of' [ie the Ed Hunter] set, which felt a little bit cabaret. I'll be honest, I found that difficult. But, as it stands at the moment, everyone's enjoying it and we all seem to be getting on well. So hopefully, yeah, it'll last."

Bruce, on the other hand, is quick to defend the Ed Hunter dates. "I really, really enjoyed those shows, because they were the best of all possible worlds," he explains. "We were playing a no-brainer of a set, a real killer, and it was in front of an enormous audience that you were giving exactly what they wanted. There wasn't a huge amount of stress, because we'd played them hundreds of times before. There were no arguments and no grief within the band, because there were no decisions to make. More than anything, that laid the trust and the foundations for the album."

In November, aware that not many had been able to get along to Earl's Court or even to Europe for the Ed Hunter performances, the band returned to the UK for three more dates in Glasgow, Manchester and Birmingham. Again, Rob Halford opened the show.

For Janick Gers, these were among the most enjoyable concerts of the Brave New World tour. "The ones like Madison Square Garden tend to be pressure gigs," he says, "but I'm from the north of England and I still remember the times when the big foreign bands would come to the UK and you'd get one show in London. If you were lucky you might get a show at Newcastle City Hall, but you'd go along and get the feeling they really weren't turning it on for you. I'm very aware of that, and I take it with me wherever I go. Wherever you are, you always try to make it a bit special for people who've paid their money. Every gig is as important as Earl's Court. In fact, maybe gigs like Earl's Court are slightly less important to me than the rest of the band."

In November, after months of conjecture, Maiden were finally confirmed to headline the Rock In Rio III Festival on 19 January. This was the opportunity of a lifetime, with a stellar international cast that included Britney Spears and the returning Guns N' Roses and an expected audience of one and a half million over the event's week-long duration, plus world satellite viewing figures that were likely to exceed a billion.

Before heading off to South America in early January 2001, Maiden took the chance of playing two relatively small warm-up dates at west London's Shepherd's Bush Empire. "To play in a smaller venue like this, where the crowd are right in your face, is going to get us all fired up before we head out to South America and Rock In Rio," Bruce explained. "A few of us saw The Who perform at the Empire earlier this year, and we just thought the atmosphere was fantastic."

Over the Christmas 2000 period, with a final batch of gigs in sight and the prospect of a lengthy rest throughout most of the following year, it was a logical time for everybody to sit back and take stock. "We haven't really stopped working since I came back to the band, and it's now almost two and a half years," pondered Adrian Smith. "It's been back-to-back tours and an album in between. But, although it's been a lot of fun, I think everybody's ready for a bit of a break now. We're planning on going back into the studio to start work on a new album at the end of 2001 or the start of 2002. I don't have any definite plans for my year off, but I'm sure I'll get up to something or other.

"Having had a break from it for a while, it's still a huge thrill to walk out onstage in front of 10,000 to 20,000 people each night," continues Adrian. "But the guys had done lots of touring directly before Bruce and I came back, so I understand why they want to take a break."

For Janick, who had played more of a front-seat role in the *Brave New World* album and tour, it had been a particularly enjoyable experience. "I was happy to contribute so much this time, and the album was a real band effort," he said. "Having a new producer come in was a real breath of fresh air. But to me, it's more about the overall chemistry of the unit. When I first heard that Adrian was going to come back with Bruce, the only thing that worried me – and I'm sure Adrian felt the same about me – was how it was going to work out with three guitarists and six people in the band. But it couldn't have been any better. We travel together and hang out, and the styles of the three guitar players have meshed together in the same way as our personalities."

According to Janick, no particular pecking order has materialised. One player is no more likely to demand a more melodic solo, and nor would another soloist claim to be more adept at heavier-sounding ones. It's all down to whatever feels right. "A lot of nodding goes on, signalling for somebody else to take over," he laughs. "Adrian's very rhythmical, Dave's probably more bluesy and smooth and I suppose I'm a bit off the wall, but we can all play the different types of solos if we have to. There are no set rules with Maiden. It's like every band I've ever been with – I never know what I'm gonna do until I do it!" As Rod adds, "The reason why three guitarists works so well for us – along with all three being great players – is that their combined ego is zero. We call them the Tres Amigos – they travel together, drink together and just get on great."

Speaking of which, Gers insists that, despite all of the line-up fluctuations, he never felt that he was in danger of losing his job: "I just don't think of things that way. I never asked to join Iron Maiden; they asked me to join them. So, if they'd asked me to leave, I would quite happily have gone along with what they wanted. I love playing with the band, because they're lovely guys, but when you start worrying about where your place is in the scheme of things, that's dangerous. I've never seen music that way. While the band want me, I'm more than happy to be there."

However, Janick admits that personalities within the band have changed. "We've all mellowed a lot," he says. "Maybe it's an age thing. I'm not as edgy as I used to be, and Steve's definitely more easy-going than he was. There are six very strong personalities within the band, but all have mellowed towards each other. Possibly, in the past, Bruce has tended to see things his own way, but after he came back that's also changed."

It's a subject on which Adrian agrees. When asked if the success of the revamped Maiden has allowed him to mentally dismiss the reasons why he left during the '80s, the guitarist shrugs. "I've not completely forgotten, but you've got to look forward," he says. "None of us want to look back and dig up the little things that might have got under our skins in the past. Everybody's a lot more mature now, and we all get to express ourselves. Obviously, a lot of it's still Steve's vision, and I understand that a bit more now than I did, but it's been interesting, observing the band from the outside. I've come back with a different perspective. I still think it was right for both me and the band to have parted company when I did. This probably wouldn't have been happening now had I not done so."

He admits that there were a few teething troubles at the beginning. "There were some disagreements," he reveals, "but it turned out to be a positive thing. Opinions differed on the tempos of certain songs, but, whereas before we might have brushed them under the carpet, this time we faced up to them and resolved them. Everyone was happy and nobody was left brooding in the corner."

Bruce says that it was important for him personally to have settled his differences with those bandmates with whom he fell out upon leaving the band. "It would have been silly to have continued with any bad feelings," he states. "The two people who were the most upset with me were Nicko and Steve. And I suppose I've discovered Steve's sense of humour for the first time, really. In some ways, Steve and I are more similar than either of us would probably care to admit. The differences between us are what sometimes make things spark, but we've also got to the point where we both realise that we're not trying to do other people down by having the opinions we have. I'm trying to do things that I think will advance the cause of the band. Now, if we disagree, we at least agree that we have the same aim in mind, which is just fine.

"I've chilled out a lot as well," he adds. "Having a solo career and developing it piece by piece has really helped me to mature. There's a flexibility now that's ongoing, and it has come about through trust. There might always be a bit of Steve that needs to feel a bit of paranoia, but that's part of the package. I'm not sure you can say Steve's completely happy unless he's kicking a ball around. That's just the way he is."

Confident that he has laid all doubts concerning his future involvement with Iron Maiden to rest, Dickinson goes on to stress his contentment with Maiden's current state of play: "If you were to wind the clock back to the Fear Of The Dark tour, and perhaps even beyond that, the band is playing wonderfully, better even than it was back in the *Live After Death* period. It's awesome."

Bruce also admits that he's more than happy with sales of more than a million and a half copies of *Brave New World* worldwide. "A certain amount of cynicism exists about Maiden. Some people just don't get it at all," he rationalises. "Because of that, they refuse to believe that there are people out there who do like us. Consequently, they hear we've sold a million and a half copies and they automatically assume it must be lies. It's amazing how many people in the record industry don't even know how many records Maiden sell. They can believe what they want. We've got the figures to prove it.

"Whilst it's true that there are a lot of nu-metal bands out there that are being very successful, Maiden is still holding up extremely well. When you consider that at our peak, back in the '80s, we were selling two to three million in a market that was completely crammed with metal of this style, one and a half million is absolutely fucking amazing. And the best part is that a lot of our audience is largely comprised of younger fans, especially in Europe and South America."

While we're talking statistics, some 250,000 fans were drawn to the Rock In Rio Festival, at which the band filmed and recorded a DVD for release later in 2001. "Rio was an absolutely incredible experience," Bruce says, "way better than the first time we did it [in 1985, in front of 200,000 people]. That one was full of angst and insanity, but this time we played a blinding gig. There was so much going on, it would have been easy to drop the ball just a little bit, but the band played one of the best gigs of our lives. And, of course, that was the time do it, as we were recording. The DVD will be the Rio show in its entirety, and Kevin Shirley, who's mixing it, tells me it sounds amazing. We were there for three days and the place was besieged with fans and press, but although we did some photos in locations, I pretty much locked myself in my hotel room or spent most of the time at the gym. For the 24 to 48 hours before the show, I was mostly lying down on my back, thinking about it."

In January 2001, Maiden were shocked and ever so slightly amused when 'The Wicker Man' was nominated for a Grammy for the year's Best Metal Performance. It was the second time they'd been honoured in such a way, after the live version of 'Fear Of The Dark' from *A Real Live One* had been chosen in the same category back in 1994. This time, 'The Wicker Man' was up against The Deftones' 'Elite', Marilyn Manson's 'Astonishing Panorama Of The Endtymes', Pantera's 'Revolution Is My Name' and 'Wait And Bleed' by masked metal marauders Slipknot. Although Adrian and Dave attended the televised 43rd annual ceremony at the Staples Center in LA, The Deftones walked away with the prize.

"It's jolly nice to be nominated for something like a Grammy, but I felt the timing was extremely odd," Bruce chortles. "Some of these categories – Best Heavy Metal Band On A Tuesday Morning – are hilarious. I couldn't fathom how we were in such eclectic company, so it was either put together by someone who had diverse tastes or by someone who had no idea what they were talking about. The words 'Jethro' and 'Tull' sprang to mind after Metallica were beaten to their award by Ian Anderson."

What meant far more to Maiden was the winning of the International Achievement award at the Ivor Novello award ceremony in June. The Ivors, as they are known, are given in recognition of outstanding songwriting and are voted on by fellow songwriters. Maiden's award commemorated album sales of an incredible 50 million copies worldwide. Bruce, Adrian and Janick attended the ceremony at London's super-plush Grosvenor Hotel, where tennis legend and long-time friend and fan Pat Cash presented the award. Cash told the throng – who included such luminaries as Pete Townshend from The Who,

Stevie Wonder, members of The Clash and composer John Barry – how, during his playing days, he would rush from the world's largest tournaments just to get to a Maiden gig on time.

Accepting the award, Bruce told the crowd, "Without the fans, none of this would be possible. We never get played on the radio and we are a traditional band in the sense that we play the shows, people hear the music and, if they like it, they buy it. This is indeed a great honour, and we owe it to them."

The Ivor award and the Rock In Rio concert set the seal on a triumphant three-year period for Iron Maiden. Not only had they taken their career to a newly credible high but they had played an integral part in restoring heavy metal to the mainstream. "It's great that Maiden have put metal back in the public eye," says Bruce proudly. "Having a band like Maiden doing what we do has given an awful lot of encouragement to a lot of other bands. Now some bands are more inclined to stick to what they would really like to do, as opposed to whatever the media feels is appropriate. Having a band like Iron Maiden around, who are pretty clear-cut in what they do, is a very good thing, because it gives like-minded people a little focal point. Even if they don't sound like Maiden, at least they can look at our attitude and realise that they don't have to compromise."

So the country and western album's still on hold, then?

"As we speak, yes, it's well and truly on hold for the time being," he laughs, "but I'm keeping that pedal-steel guitar in the closet."

Although they will spend most of 2001 recharging their batteries, Maiden won't exactly be fading from the limelight. "Steve's made it very clear that he wants a complete twelve-month break," reveals Bruce, "so you can take it that, once he's finished his involvement with the *Rock In Rio* double live album and DVD, there will be a year of inactivity. But there will be things going on throughout that period – there will be a new box set, and back catalogue is going to be reissued for the band's 25th anniversary, so we're not exactly going to be rolling over and lying down. We'll start writing and recording a new studio album, and I guess we're looking at 2003 for the next tour. To me, that's about right, because I'll be doing my own solo album in September, and if I get to tour it then it should lead right back into Maiden again."

When asked for his observations about the most recent stage of Iron Maiden's career and to speculate on the group's long-term future, Bruce already knows where his own sights are set. "As a band, Iron Maiden have played some incredible, fabulous concerts and made an album that the band are very proud of," he states. "We've seldom sounded better than we do right now, but there's still so much more music within us. To be honest, I don't think people have any idea what this band is truly capable of, and even some people within the band don't understand what we can achieve. So much of it, unfortunately, is down to chance. If we're in the right phase of the moon and all the planets are aligned, God knows what could happen. The band will always do really well, but we can still explode to unimagined heights in the future, and there's no way you can manufacture these things."

Dancing with Death in 2003: L–r Adrian, Janick, Steve, Bruce, Nicko and Dave

Bruce never looked better! The reissued (live version) of 'Run To The Hills' is unleashed in support of the Clive Burr fund

Inside the Ed: The delicious packaging for the collector's box reveals three double-disc CDs, an Eddie-approved shot glass and an exclusive parchment 'family tree'

Edward The Great makes an appearance as Janick and Steve prepare to do battle

Backstage at the Brixton Academy in March 2002 with Clive Burr

The Maiden battle bus! Journalists were treated to an exclusive preview of *Dance Of Death* as the Maiden machine rolled across Europe during the summer of 2003

Beastial visions: Eddie pulls out the stops for the finale of Download 2003

'Scream for me, Download!' 40,000 starved Maiden punters let rip

'Rainmaker' video shoot, the Roundhouse, London, September 2003

The Triple-Axe Attack: The three amigos – Janick, Dave and Adrian – take a bow

17 Rock In Rio

When Maiden headlined the enormous Rock In Rio festival on 19 January 2001 the band played in front of over 250,000 fans, the largest single crowd that they had ever performed for. The Rock In Rio festival holds such a place in the Brazilian nation's heart that it is beamed live on national television and syndicated to every South American country. With the additional Asian TV rights it has been estimated by the event organisers that nearly one billion people will have seen at least one evening's performance from the six separate shows that made up the third Rock In Rio festival. That's a lot of people!

Maiden headlined the fourth night of the festival which, unlike the previous week-long events, was this time held over two separate weekends. Playing under Maiden that day were Judas Priest singer and heavy-metal legend Rob Halford, local heroes Sepultura and eclectic rockers Queens Of The Stone Age. Previous performances at the festival had included boy band NSync, an all too rare live appearance by a rejuvenated Guns N' Roses, Papa Roach, pop queen Britney Spears, Sting and Britrock oiks Oasis. The night after Maiden, the Dave Matthews Band and Neil Young performed and the festival was closed on Sunday evening by the Red Hot Chili Peppers, supported by Silverchair and Deftones.

If Maiden were looking for a grand statement to finish off what had been the band's most successful world tour in years then Rock In Rio would provide the perfect backdrop. Unlike other festivals Rock In Rio is not an annual or even biennial event – you're lucky if you get to see one even once a decade! The last Rock In Rio festival – only the second ever – had taken place ten years before in 1991 at the Maracana stadium and been headlined by the original Guns N' Roses. Having played the opening day of the first ever Rock In Rio festival in 1985 as part of their World Slavery tour (as special guests to Queen during the blazing heat of the day), Maiden knew just what to expect from the intensely passionate Latin crowd.

Needless to say, offers of headline slots at Rock In Rio festivals are a rare event and as soon as Maiden's performance had been confirmed, in the previous autumn, plans were set in motion to record a live album and Iron Maiden's very first home concert DVD to commemorate the event. If anyone was looking for an appropriately giant-sized exclamation to underscore Iron Maiden's worldwide legacy then nothing was likely to top a show of this size!

"For me Rock In Rio was a chance to show how good this band can be," says Bruce, rolling his eyes at the very thought of Maiden's headline show. "We desperately wanted to do it but the stress level was exponential. It was genuinely one of the most intense gigs of my life for a whole variety of reasons," he gasps. "The whole day before the show I locked myself in a room and just didn't come out. I went down to the gym. I didn't party and I didn't sunbathe. I shut the curtains and lived in a cave and thought about the gig, just like a championship boxer before a title fight – because that's what it takes to play a gig that size. When I went out and finally did the show, it was like all hell breaking loose!

"I remember that I was so jazzed up when I ran up onto my little catwalk, and the first thing that I saw was all these damn cameras stuck to my ladder that I'd usually climb and I took an instant dislike to them. I thought, 'Fuck this!' and I ripped them off in a fit and threw them all off the back of the stage. The camera guys went nuts! But that was my little temperamental moment, and you have to have one every now and then otherwise it's just not real enough," says Bruce, flashing a mischievous grin.

"The energy that we expended that night was just incredible. I've never been so exhausted in my whole life, not just physically – I was tired but that was easy. It was an emotional and mental tiredness to the extent that I felt like someone had sucked all the marrow out of my bones 'cause I had never felt like that before. I remember sitting there at four in the morning after the show in a daze. The whole band was like that.

Normally after a show we all go have a few beers and say, 'Yeah, what a great gig', but after that one we all sat there dumbfounded, which is very rare for us and I've never seen everybody that way before or since," laughs Bruce. "But what a fantastic way to end the tour!"

Steve also has vivid memories of the pressure the band faced going into a show that would provide Maiden with their very first DVD and a third double live album.

"We all thought we'd played well. But we had to – the pressure was huge: live on telly to millions and filming a DVD too, but we tend to do well under pressure," he says confidently. "We usually like to get right in people's faces but we just couldn't that night. I remember running out to the edge of the stage to get the crowd going but the PA on the side wasn't working, so I couldn't hear a bloody thing out front and that meant I had to stay firmly within my area for the whole night," remembers Steve, with just a hint of frustration. The sheer size of the crowd demanded respect from the members of Iron Maiden but, reckons Steve, having played the event once before in broad daylight the number didn't affect everyone in the same way.

"They'd made a big deal about the size of the crowd and we'd flown in over them in the helicopters so we'd seen just how big a quarter of a million people looked like, but – and I know this is gonna sound odd – you just can't really differentiate between 100,000 people and 250,000 people – it's just a bloody lot of people! And at night with the spotlights on them you can't really illuminate the entire crowd anyway so you just get on with it. That said, the crowd that night were amazing and they made all the difference."

Though Janick had been to Rio before with Iron Maiden it was the first time the guitarist had played the Rock In Rio festival. Unlike Steve, Janick was more than aware of the butterflies in his stomach.

"I remember going up and seeing Jimmy Page stood on side stage and thinking, 'Of all the places he had to be he decides to stand next to me tonight!'" he laughs with a mock groan. "I think everybody gets a bit nervous doing shows that are important, it's quite a daunting task. There were all those thousands of people there at such a weird time of the night – because of all the delays with the various camera crews for our DVD, the TV broadcast and our recordings for the live album I think we ended going onstage at two in the morning or something daft like that. Everybody gets a bit nervy when you are plonked in front of all that gear knowing full well that every mistake will be seen and heard by millions of people! But the fans that night were incredible. There are so many different kinds of music there anyhow that everyone is prepared to listen to you and that gives you the ability to play. They are great fans."

"Flying in over a crowd that size made a huge difference to me," admits Nicko. "When I sat backstage I truly appreciated the enormity of the humanity there for us. Once we kicked into the motions I got on with it and held back the nerves, but at the back of my mind I just kept thinking, 'God there's quarter of a million people out there – don't screw up!'"

Tempting as it might be to see the band's headline show at Rock In Rio as a perfect end celebration to Bruce's return to the fold, Nicko is adamant that such a view doesn't capture how close the band had really become by that point.

"It might be tempting to frame the event as a perfect ending to Bruce being back, but for me that moment happened two years earlier when we all came together to do the promo shoot to announce it and start planning for the Ed Hunter tour. *BNW* [*Brave New World*] was a new chapter for Maiden as a whole and we all felt that way, including Bruce. I do remember Adrian turning round at one point in Rio and saying to me that it just felt like he'd been away on holiday and that made me feel good to hear him say it, because then it was like a journey that we'd all been on had finally been completed."

Having seen almost as many gigs as the band have played, even Maiden's tough-as-boots manager Rod Smallwood was moved by the momentous event in Rio. "The great gigs are when the band feel inspired by the occasion and the hearts of the crowd, the love of the audience. That feeling of identity and loyalty with the band is quite inspiring. And I think when you have a lot of people and everything is running smoothly, it tends to lift into something that you are never going to achieve in an arena. Donington in '88 was 107,000 people, Rock Am Ring in 2003 was about 75,000 but Rio was 250,000 people! It is strange when an audience that size becomes one whole animal, when hands all the way to the back are all raised, all being involved. It's an almost religious feeling."

18 Rock In Rio: The Album And DVD

When the resulting *Rock In Rio* DVD and double live album finally emerged over 12 months later in February 2002, it easily matched the band's previous live records in terms of performance. However, with the aid of state of the art 5.1 digital technology it knocked spots off any of the band's previous live video or audio releases, both sonically and visually.

Both the album and DVD featured 19 tracks representing all eras of Maiden's history, with no less than six numbers from the current *Brave New World* album. It also features early classics 'Sanctuary' and 'Wrathchild', the crowd pleasers 'Two Minutes To Midnight', 'The Trooper' and 'The Evil That Men Do' and includes Blaze Bayley-era favourites 'Sign Of The Cross' and 'The Clansman'. According to Bruce, the *Rock In Rio* collection's value to the Maiden canon is made all the more remarkable when you consider the intense pressures involved with getting anywhere near perfection in just one take.

"If you take the gig in its entirety, to know that you have only one shot at doing a DVD and that it's going to be in Rio and you know that everything else about it is going to be bloody amazing such as the crowd and the scenery and everything is set up and all you need to do is play a blinding gig, which you will only get one shot at doing, well, yes, then I am bloody amazed we did it, what else can I say?" he says with exasperation.

However good the band's performance on the night was, all their hard work might have come to naught due to some unfortunate "styling decisions" made by the editing company hired to produce the DVD. Originally booked for a 12-camera shoot, footage from two cameras mysteriously failed to turn up at the New York editing suite where the clips were due to be run together. Sadly for Dave Murray it was mostly footage of him that had been lost, even though the live TV broadcasts had clearly shown the guitarist ripping his way through many a flamboyant solo on the night, a situation repeated to a lesser extent on Adrian who also lost many of his filmed solos too. To compound frustrations, when Steve Harris arrived in New York to meet producer Kevin Shirley – to finish off what the pair believed would be final mixes for the DVD's soundtrack – to their horror they discovered that none of the so-called "final edits" were in the least bit satisfactory. Deciding there and then that if the project wasn't up to scratch then it would have to be delayed Steve took it upon himself to personally take over the editing of the DVD. Steve takes up the tale:

"It nearly killed me! I was pretty burnt out and ready for time off but it just didn't look right. The first three songs we were given were awful; the final mixes just horrified us. Some of the shots they were using were just bizarre too, like deliberately out of focus shots of the lighting rig! The thing was that the live TV broadcast had used 12 cameras on national TV so if the production crew had just started there and edited in their extra bits they would've done really well. I really don't know where their heads were at," he sighs.

Steve's sacrifice in the name of Iron Maiden's long-preserved quality control wasn't lost on the others, as Bruce remembers: "I'm not so nearly as picky about things as Steve is, but if he wants to be picky then that is OK by me, 'cause that's his time and so be it. As long as I can look at something and think it has a good vibe then we can go with it. But the soundtrack to the DVD was devastating. There was an edit being done and it was just awful, and even when Steve took it over then there was this whole technical cock-up in the transferring of the tapes, and that took even more time to sort out. So although Steve spent a lot of time editing it, he also spent a fair amount of time dealing with equipment crashes and bullshit, too. In the process he taught himself incredibly complex digital editing systems. He taught himself software that people take year-long courses to learn and I give him total respect for that."

Unsurprisingly, Steve still visibly shudders at the thought of the time spent locked away piecing together Maiden's moment of South

American triumph. "I really could have done without that DVD at the point it landed on me because it came at the end of what was a three-year cycle," he sighs. "The reason I didn't offer to do it in the first place was because I specifically didn't want to. Having already edited the *Maiden England* video and the *Donington 92* live footage I wanted a fresh pair of eyes on Maiden. I was after someone else's input and direction over my style," he says. "I told Rod that it was gonna take six or seven months to edit a two-and-a-half hour show plus documentaries. When you think about it, it's more than a movie – we certainly had more cuts and edits than your average movie anyway."

Steve ordered all the necessary editing equipment and had it installed into the former Maiden studio in his barn at home. Essentially the bass man taught himself how to use up-to-the-minute digital editing programs and graphics packages that professional video editors use.

"If you actually look at it as a piece of editing, and there are over 8,000 separate edits on there, then it's a master work," booms a proud as punch Rod. "Everything is to the beat as Steve wanted it and every shot is spectacular. It's a complete dedication to the cause. I mean, would you want to spend six months sat in a small room with equipment all by yourself? Incredible!" But once the finished article was in his hand Steve could look upon the package and know that he had helped create something of a landmark in Maiden's 25-year history.

"I really do think *Rock In Rio* is way better than *Live After Death*," states Steve. "I would say that I know, but if you'd reversed the two records in time then I think people would still celebrate the historical one because it's had time to bed in. It's just my personal opinion that *Rock In Rio* is better because we show the development in our songwriting and the progressive side of Iron Maiden is definitely there."

19 *Clive Burr*

In February 2002 a unique event in Maiden's history took place when the band announced a series of shows at London's Brixton Academy in aid of former drummer Clive Burr. Clive had come to recent public attention via a documentary DVD that traced the history and impact of the *Number Of The Beast* album (part of the acclaimed *Stories Behind The Album* series). Though Clive did not feature in the TV broadcast of the programme, he was included on the expanded home DVD version. Knowing this, Clive had contacted the programme's producers and had asked that the viewers be made aware that he was suffering from Multiple Sclerosis, which might explain some of the physical hesitations to his responses. The producers in turn informed Sanctuary management. The news sent shock waves around Maiden's inner circle, as the band members themselves were totally unaware of Clive's condition. Manager Rod Smallwood takes up the story:

"We had sort've of kept in contact, or at least you mean to, but the band were always busy and I've got four kids of my own now which keep me occupied, so inevitably things fade a little bit. The day after I was told of Clive's condition I mentioned it to Steve because I knew that he would have had no idea. Obviously we were concerned for Clive because he is family, a long-lost member may be, but still part of the Maiden family. So both Steve and I were in agreement that we should do something to help him."

Caught up in the middle of a year off, and scattered around various points of the globe, it wasn't simply a case of ringing the six members of Iron Maiden and asking them to turn up for a show a few weeks away. In addition to the band there were valued crew members to contact, production people, rehearsals to consider, venues to book, promoters, and ticketing agencies and media to be informed. Indeed, Steve had only just finished his mammoth session on the *Rock In Rio* DVD and yet he was already determined to strap on the bass in aid of his old bandmate. Likewise, Clive's old pal Dave Murray, who now lives in Maui, Hawaii, never once considered the idea of doing any benefit show a trial.

"I got an email from Rod explaining the seriousness of the situation and, yeah, we were all in total agreement that something should be done," recalls Dave. "For me it was, 'Tell me when and where and I'll be there.' There was never any question of us not doing it once it was raised as a possibility; it's looking after one of your own and that's important."

"All the guys in the band were 100 per cent behind the idea of doing some shows for Clive," smiles Rod, "And the people who came – that was really inspiring. There were fans from all over the world as it was the only show that we were doing in 2002. We had fans from North America, South America, Japan and Australia."

Fans that were lucky enough to attend saw Maiden blast through the recent *Brave New World* live set, (complete with giant Wicker Man in surely the smallest venue that it had ever been shoehorned into!) and one or two surprise additions, not least of which was a resurrected 'Children Of The Damned' – surely a fitting tribute to Clive's contribution to the *Beast* album. With only three rehearsals in 12 months Maiden were slightly nervous of reintroducing such a classic song, but after the first night's performance it seemed as if 'Children' had never been dropped.

When Clive walked out at the end of each night he received nothing less than a thunderous applause from the audience, many of whom were wearing specially commissioned Clive Burr tribute T-shirts, the money from which went into the drummer's recovery fund (alongside profits from the rest of the Maiden merchandise sold that evening). The band re-released the classic 'Run To The Hills' as a single and all profits also went straight to Clive. The single, backed with previously unheard live recordings of 'Total Eclipse' and 'Children Of The Damned' from 1982 with Clive on drums, crashed into the Top Ten, thereby underlining its timeless popularity even 20 years on from the original release. 'Run To The Hills' was even backed up with a performance from the band on *Top Of The Pops*. This was recorded on one very hectic afternoon of the first Brixton show, making it the only time that the BBC's venerable music show has ever mobilised its studio and crew to fit around a band's schedule! For all concerned it was an emotionally intense but fun project.

"I remember being backstage before the first gig with Clive and we were just swapping memories like it was yesterday," laughs Dave Murray. "When he came out onto the stage at the end of the night it was incredibly emotional for both him and the audience and, really, for the band too. Clive is still loved by the fans – he played drums on the first three records so he's not going to ever be forgotten."

To outsiders, it seemed if there was one person in Maiden that might've had mixed feelings about doing the benefit shows it would be Nicko. After all he had taken Clive's place in the band and prior to his joining both he and Clive had been very close friends. "I've always valued Clive's friendship, even when we lost touch for a while," admits Nicko. "When the idea was first mooted that maybe we should do something for Clive I felt compelled. I'd have done ten shows in a row if it had been possible – anything to help improve his lifestyle or aid the MS charity wouldn't get a second's hesitation from me. I consider it a privilege and joy to do anything like that." According to Nicko the show still dredged up a mixture of intense emotions though. "The hardest thing for me was when we had our picture taken together onstage at the end of the first show. I had my arm around Clive and I knew deep down all he really wanted to do was get up and play some of the old songs. I knew in my heart that that was exactly what I'd be feeling too. I didn't mention it and he certainly didn't wanna bring it up," says a clearly emotional Nicko. "I mean we played 'Run To The Hills', 'Beast', 'Hallowed Be Thy Name' and even dusted off 'Children Of The Damned' especially for it – songs that Clive recorded. When he came out at the end he got such an applause. What can you say? He's still such a part of the Maiden family and it must've been terribly difficult for him, I think."

"I believe we raised something like a quarter of a million pounds over the whole thing thanks to everyone doing little bits for nothing or at a cost," says Rod proudly. "Everybody chipped in. When we re-released 'Run To The Hills' we agreed that the band's royalties would go to Clive but we were totally surprised when the song publishers and then EMI Records agreed to do the same. It's very unusual for record companies to do stuff like that these days, because they get asked so much about charity projects that are then hijacked for personal publicity requirements," scorns Rod. "If we had wanted to self serve, it would have been pretty obvious – this was different because it was for a mate. Unfortunately singles don't make a lot of royalties these days because single sales generally now are very low compared to what they used to be; I think it generated another 10 or 20 grand perhaps. But the principle was good. I think it was a great team effort and everybody was very proud of what we achieved."

20 2002 *Collections*

Given that 2002 was earmarked as a year off for the band there was still a remarkable amount of activity under the Maiden monicker. Not only was the *Rock In Rio* double live album and DVD released but, towards the end of the year, news started to circulate on the Iron Maiden fan sites that a new box set collection could be in the offing.

When Eddie's Archive did appear in December 2002 not even the most die-hard of hardcore fans could be disappointed with the exclusivity of material on offer. Presented in a large metallic box decorated with the band's undead mascot, Eddie's Archive consists of three double CD sets. The first CD is a collection of 31 of the band's B-sides recorded up to 2000's 'Out Of The Silent Planet'. The second is a ripping 19-track live album titled *Beast Over Hammersmith* recorded live at the Hammersmith Odeon in 1982 for a concert video of Beast On the Road world tour. (Sadly this never saw the light of day, as the band were not happy with the visual quality due to lighting problems.) But the real treat for fans has to be the third disc, *The BBC Archives*. This last set collects together all of Maiden's live sessions broadcast by the corporation during the 1980s, including their very first rock show session from 1979, which features the only recorded material by the Harris/Murray/Di'Anno/Tony Parsons (guitar)/Doug Sampson (drums) line-up. Even die-hard Maiden collectors would've been hard pressed to find an excellent quality copy of that one! Also included is Maiden's 1980 appearance at Reading festival with Clive Burr and Dennis Stratton, though the band's subsequent headline show at the same festival in 1982 – which is also on the CD – has to take pride of place, if only to hear the crowd roars at the end of 'The Number Of The

Beast'. *The BBC Archives* CD is rounded off by Maiden's spectacular show at Donington '88, where they performed their highly acclaimed Seventh Son set list to 107,000 mud-drenched punters. Incidentally, until (if ever?) a DVD or audio CD is re-issued of the *Maiden England* video, *The BBC Archives* CD remains the only official Maiden release where fans can hear a truly savage live version of the under-appreciated gem that is 'Moonchild' on CD.

To top off such a collection of rare tracks, Eddie's Archive also comes with a sculpted "Eddie-style" pewter shot glass (guess who's looking at you when you down that one last tequila too many at the end of the night) and a hugely complex-looking Maiden family tree carefully drawn by celebrated letterer Pete Frame on a lavish-looking scroll. For Maiden-ites Eddie's Archive was, and remains, a must-have collector's item.

A rather more controversial release simultaneous to Eddie's Archive was the *Edward The Great* Greatest Hits collection. Coming only six years and two studio albums after the previous greatest hits collection, *Edward The Great* was not welcomed by nearly as many hardcore fans, even though such a collection was clearly not being marketed at them. *Edward The Great* was aimed at the younger end of the then exploding nu metal market, who couldn't afford to rush out and buy each separate album but who were equally desperate to discover who Iron Maiden were, having seen them plastered all over the TV on T-shirts worn by the likes of Sum 41 *et al.*

"We did get a bit of flak for the *Edward The Great* album but it wasn't aimed at the hardcore fan, it was aimed at the peripheral people who've heard the name or seen the name on a T-shirt and wouldn't know which record to pick up," reasons Steve. "I understand that the collectors will feel like that they have to have everything, but really those guys do bring that responsibility onto themselves – they've got more bloody Maiden stuff than I have! We always say that you don't have to buy everything!

"Eddie's Archive was released for the real collector. We always try hard to keep the quality there for people. We would make a hell of a lot more money if we didn't package a release looking like that, but we do it because we're proud of the Iron Maiden legacy and want to treat the fans with respect."

The box sets and greatest hits also coincided with a more widespread relaxation of the Maiden attitude to the kitsch side of merchandising. For years Kiss and Ozzy Osbourne had issued countless collectible figurines and lunchboxes of their stage or album artwork images, and for just as long Iron Maiden had resisted the temptation to market their mascot in the same way. But with the release of the *Killers*-era Eddie figurine as part of the McFarlane 'Rock Legends' series, alongside Alice Cooper, Kiss, AC/DC and Rob Zombie, it seemed that the gates had finally fallen. A second *Trooper*-era figure was issued alongside a *Beast* lunchbox, then shot glasses and even a giant 12" *Beast*-era Eddie complete with dancing devil all came onto the market.

"We actually thought about doing lunchboxes and stuff like that years ago," admits Steve. "Kiss did it first, and we had Eddie, but it didn't feel right at the time. But now it's like a cool thing to own. I know it has brought a more kitsch side to Iron Maiden and before that just didn't feel acceptable to us. But times change and we are all comfortable with that side of Iron Maiden being there now.

"People do actually want to own that stuff these days, whereas if we'd done it 15 years ago I think people would have thought that we'd just done it for the money. The way I look at it is that years ago it wasn't acceptable to have sponsors on football shirts, whereas nowadays if you don't have a sponsor then something's wrong with your team – times change and so do attitudes," reasons the bassist.

"As soon as I saw the *Beast* lunchbox I wanted one!" proclaims Bruce. "There I am going to work flying airliners during the day and I want to take my *Number Of The Beast* lunchbox with me for my sandwiches. Things like that are valid and as long as we tread the right side of a fine line then I'm OK with it all."

As an aside, its worth noting that while such cool kitsch merchandising and well-timed greatest hits packages created several easy jumping-on points to the Maiden cause for younger rock fans, bizarre as it sounds it pales in comparison to the power of something as seemingly banal as a name check in a hit record. Literally thousands of youngsters heard Iron Maiden's name for the very first time when indie rockers Wheatus gave props to the band in their infectious chart-topping single 'Teenage Dirtbag' in 2000. Oddly enough it even led to a mainstream rediscovery of Maiden in their homeland!

"I think we've always maintained our credibility among our fanbase but, yeah, the Wheatus thing was just weird," laughs Steve. "When new young bands do stuff like that or when Slipknot talk up Iron Maiden then I'm all for it because fans of those bands will then check us out and nine out of ten of 'em will go home with a smile on their faces.

"Across Europe and South America we've constantly regenerated new fans on each album, but in the UK and USA it's definitely been harder to reach those younger fans and bands like Wheatus and Sum 41 talking about Maiden has definitely helped raise awareness. I don't know why that difference exists in those countries but it does."

Once again, as the latest musical trend fades and now even nu metal's one-time platinum leaders are consigned to the musical scrap heap, Iron Maiden can be seen marching ever strongly forwards.

"We are at a place now where I can sit back and go, 'Gosh, Iron Maiden is an icon' and we really are," believes Bruce. "Without having to sound big headed about it, it's a fact. When Wheatus had us in their song, that's when I first thought 'Wow. How many other people feel the same sort of phenomenon over this as I do?' In practical terms it means Maiden can go out live, as we have done this summer [2003], effectively without a new record to promote, and still do the best business we have ever done in our whole career."

"We've outlasted countless trends," laughs Steve. "We've survived disco, thrash, new wave, grunge, nu metal and we're still here. I don't know how it works, whether it's older brothers or maybe even fathers now passing stuff down to their kids, I'm just glad that it does happen. I see young fans in Maiden shirts who weren't born when we recorded that first album...or even *No Prayer For The Dying* – now that is scary!"

21 *Dance Of Death*

When Iron Maiden's 13th studio album, *Dance of Death*, appeared in September 2003 it crashed into the album charts the world over. It secured Number One positions in Italy, Sweden, Finland, Greece and the Czech Republic; Number Two in the UK, Germany, Switzerland and Slovenia; Three in Brazil, Argentina, France, Spain, Norway, Poland, Hungary and Austria; Four in Japan, Portugal, Belgium, Iceland and Chile; Five in Canada; Twelve in Australia; and a respectable Number Eighteen in a notoriously fickle US market. All these figures underline the idea that these days a new Iron Maiden album isn't simply another rock album by another rock band – rather, it is a worldwide event that people look forward to with active zeal!

Adding to the impressive array of sales is the fact that in just 28 shows Maiden performed in front of over 600,000 fans across Europe and a further 200,000 in the US. By the time the European leg of the Dance Of Death tour was completed in December 2003 it is estimated that Iron Maiden played in front of over one million people in Europe alone in just six months!

Once again produced by Kevin Shirley, who so ably handled the recording of *Brave New World*, *Dance Of Death* was actually one of the easiest and most straightforward albums that Iron Maiden have ever recorded. Over the course of its 11 tracks fans are treated to the full range of Iron Maiden's formidable songwriting repertoire. For the headbangers and air guitarists, lead single 'Wildest Dreams' (which entered the UK charts at a impressive Number Four), 'Gates Of Tomorrow', 'Face In The Sand' and 'New Frontier' provide the required adrenaline factor, while fans of the band's more progressive side are

treated to some of Iron Maiden's finest ever arrangements in the shape
of the album's atmospheric title track, the stirring 'Montsegur' and the
truly stunning 'Paschendale'. And even then, as the listener is gasping
for breath following a bruising 'Age of Innocence', Maiden still provide
a final curve ball with their first semi-acoustic number in 22 years in the
form of 'Journeyman'. For once both fans and critics were as one in
celebrating *Dance Of Death* as one of Maiden's very finest albums to
be ranked alongside all-time classics such as *Killers*, *Number Of The
Beast* and *Piece Of Mind*.

"I hope *Dance Of Death* really does surprise people," laughs Steve.
"And I also hope everyone who thought that we were gonna take the
money and bugger off after *Brave New World* are eating their own
words!" says the bassist, taking a much earned swipe at the overly
cynical UK media who had suggested that Bruce's return for the *Brave
New World* album and tour would be Maiden's lucrative retirement
plan. "Dance is a really strong album but it's also a very varied album.
It has the right balance of straight hard stuff and some great epic stuff."

Work really started on the album in October of 2002 when all the
band came together to complete writing in rehearsal studios before
moving on to record in London's Sarm studios from January to April
2003. However, as with all Maiden albums, the individual band
members had been busy for some months before that preparing their
ideas. The UK-based guys, Adrian, Bruce, Steve and Janick could all
take advantage of at least living in the same country and often drove
round to each other's houses to sound out new ideas. When Dave and
Nicko arrived in October their ideas were also thrown into the mixing
pot and the real business of sorting out which ideas could be made into
whole songs began.

"We never all end up in the same room together to write. It's
usually two or three of us, me round at Adrian's or Janick's, then
Steve might call and pop round to work with Janick on something he's
written," explains Bruce of Maiden's songwriting philosophy. "Very
often when someone has written something they run it past me and
ask whether it's the right sort of thing to be happening for my voice
in such a song so I'll come in and have a stab at the melody. That's
how it works."

Says Steve: "We always allow ourselves a maximum eight weeks writing and that's it. We used to be on a cycle of finish a tour, take a week or two off and then be straight back to work writing the next record – that's how we did four albums in four years, but you can't really keep that cycle up for long! When it comes to writing we learned the lesson of keeping to quite short, intensive periods and putting ourselves under pressure because we seem to come up with the goods like that. It keeps us on our toes."

Just as on *Brave New World*, Maiden also welcomed producer Kevin Shirley as an integral part of the album-making process. "I think with Kevin we have finally found someone to replace Martin Birch," considers Steve. "When Martin left we were at a bit of a loss really and I think that to replace someone that you've worked with on that many albums is very, very hard. But in Kevin I think we finally have found that person. The similarities between them are amazing – they both like to have a laugh and a joke as they work which is very important when working with us!" he jokes. "Hopefully it'll carry on like that for a few albums yet."

While Kevin has made a noticeable difference to the sound of the last two Maiden albums, especially in the dynamics being captured, Steve, who of course produced both the *X Factor* and *Virtual XI* albums, stresses that Kevin doesn't adopt a Mutt Lange-style producer's role to become an active songwriter for the band.

"Neither Martin or Kevin were ever backwards at coming forwards with any ideas, it's just that most of the time they don't need to," explains the bassist. "It's great to have an objective outside opinion though. Also it's good to have a strong personality capable of getting in among it if there are any disagreements within the band. It doesn't happen often but when it does you need that strong personality to put across what they think. It's a breath of fresh air working with people like that.

"We arrange all our own songs so when someone comes in to produce Iron Maiden its not 'producing' in the true sense of the word 'cause we prefer to have a hands-on engineer and not someone who's gonna sit there pointing the finger at someone else to work the desk. We want someone there doing that work at hand to capture whatever we've thought at the time."

Having worked with Led Zeppelin and Aerosmith Kevin is no stranger to the intense pressures of recording with huge artists, but now comfortable with Iron Maiden after a second album he has a unique insight on working with the band, particularly Steve.

"This is a band that has carved their name in the metal genre and they don't need to stray from that," observes the softly spoken producer. "Steve doesn't want to have the band play to any trends or satisfy any quirks of radio programmers or label A&R men, he wants the band to do what they do and be what it is. That being said, I don't think you can take the producer out of the equation as much as Steve suggests! Part of my job is to make sure that things run smoothly. Within every band there is a certain amount of tension that creates some of the magic that we like to hear. You have the Page and Plant, the Jagger and Richards, the Daltrey and Townsend type relationships. All those great combinations of people are fraught with antagonism, but they create great music. I think that Iron Maiden have got the same thing within their band, cohesive as they are, there are always opposing elements," says Shirley. "One of the things that I do well is to bring those differing views together and make a whole environment that gels for everyone. I think it is a matter of making sure that there are no antagonisms that come into the process of recording."

Like Steve, having heard the results, Rod Smallwood is also adamant that Kevin's role as the future producer of Iron Maiden is secure and has no small relief that the responsibilities and pressure that Steve had placed himself under in his producer's role for two albums has now been removed once and for all.

"I wasn't happy having Steve producing those two albums," says Rod. "My view has always been: you write the songs, you lead the band, so it might be good to have a bit of objectivity and a bit of help in there. I still believe X Factor is quite a remarkable record and it's a shame that people don't give it more of a chance. It's a hard record to get into, because there's so much going on and it's quite dark too, but it was a dark period for Steve at the time. It's different to our other records, but it's actually quite phenomenally brilliant too!" finishes Rod, matter of factly.

However, one of Kevin's main strengths in the studio can be found in his actual recording process. Aided by Pro Tools production a modern producer can literally set up a series of independent recording booths in the same room and capture every single "live" moment of music that a band make. Having the three guitarists record together, then the drums, bass and vocals each in separate booths facing one another enables Kevin to get the best of both worlds – a fired-up Iron Maiden high on playing together live in a room while never missing a single take. Aside from capturing such an exciting atmosphere it also enables the producer to select the very best individual takes from each musician and patch them all together to get the most exciting-sounding version. It beats asking a band to do the same song for the 100th time, in search of the mythical perfect take anyway! Having worked so well on *Brave New World*, with the rawer, looser material the band had written for *Dance Of Death*, Maiden were keen on repeating the process, with startling results.

Opening with 'Wildest Dreams', the listener is confronted with a barrage of sheer energy as Bruce's brazen vocals battle alongside the fiery guitar leads. To herald their comeback Maiden couldn't have picked a better song. 'Rainmaker' is also an up-tempo number designed to get the heads banging and the hands waving at gigs, but, even second song in, it is quite apparent that this is no *Brave New World* part II – it is a far more raw and relaxed-sounding Iron Maiden than fans have heard for years. 'No More Lies', the first of the album's great epic pieces, and the only solo Harris composition on the record, harks back to the grandiose strains of 'Revelations'. Indeed, the Biblical reference is no coincidence, as Steve explains: "'No More Lies' is about The Last Supper but if it were to happen again in the present day." Yet it isn't simply about one religious figure; like with most Maiden songs that Steve writes he is looking for a common thread that everyone can connect with. "Thinking about dying is something that crosses everyone's mind at certain points in life," reasons Steve. "I think that the idea of what comes afterwards, whether you believe in life after death or any of that, conjures up many different ideas and emotions," he says. "People are scared and intrigued by the unknown and that's a very potent thing."

Following a track as stirring as 'No More Lies' isn't easy, but with intricate textures and sheer violent indulgence of 'Montsegur' the band surely manage it. Though the music was largely written by Janick and developed by Steve, the song's lyrical concept undoubtedly captures the imagination. Written about the medieval religious cult of the Cathars, who barricaded themselves within their French mountaintop fortress of Montsegur, Bruce retells a highly dramatiscd tale of blood-soaked battle, betrayal, conspiracy and martyrdom. Legend has it that the Cathars protected the secret of Jesus' bloodline as well as the Holy Grail. They smuggled those treasures from Montsegur under cover of night before martyring themselves at the hands of the royal French army, who had been sent to destroy them in the name of the Pope for heresy.

"There is so much great stuff and so many great stories throughout history that you can make parallels with the modern day – particularly when history repeats itself as often as it does – that it makes for some very colourful subject matter," reckons Bruce. "The way I look at it is that if you're going to plunder something for the lyrical basis of a song then at least plunder something that has really happened rather than invent some crass, sword and dorkery epic, y'know?" And who would argue?

The album's impressive title track comes in at a weighty 8.26 minutes but, like every great storytelling song, it seems over as soon as it has begun. Though Steve wrote the lyrics it was in fact Janick that came up with the concept that ultimately led the direction of the album's title, and from that the cover art and tour besides.

The "dance of death" is the very final scene from an old 1950s Ingmar Bergman-directed film called the *Seventh Seal*. As Janick explains: "The film depicts a knight searching for reasons to live. What struck me was that he was looking around the world for something worth surviving and fighting for but when the 'Death' character finally came to claim him the knight still wanted to survive long enough to find some faith and humanity in this world of plague and wars.

"The knight begs Death to let him live long enough to find his faith and hope, but in order to make that bargain Death plays chess with him for his soul. In the end Death comes for the knight and his troops anyway. At the end Death walks off and these figures on the horizon start doing a little jig, which is the dance of death. It's an allegorical tale but it is fascinating.

"I explained all this to Steve and played him the music I'd written and he came up with all the melodies," continues Janick in his fine Geordie lilt. "He then went away and came back with the words, which were a departure from the theme in the film but incorporated all the ideas about the dance of death still, which is great 'cause it took us in an entirely different direction. He read me the lyrics and they made me shiver. It's that old sea dog telling horror tales back in the days when people didn't have computers or TV, when they would get together and tell stories to frighten each other," says Janick fondly.

"It's quite a surreal song title anyhow and it gave us the opportunity to use Eddie in a different way, as the death character. That's why I love the album cover, 'cause it is kind of unsettling," concludes the guitarist.

Another Gers-penned rocker 'Gates Of Tomorrow' follows the title track, but Bruce won't be drawn on the meaning behind his strange lyrics, commenting, "I do like to be mysterious with lyrics and I don't think that things should reveal themselves very easily. I think the sense of interest lasts longer if lyrics remain a bit more enigmatic."

Dance Of Death is also an album of many firsts for the Maiden troop, not least of which is 'New Frontier' – the very first song that drummer Nicko McBrain had brought to the band in 20 years! Again an up-tempo Maiden rocker, the song does maintain an unexpected but very welcome catchy chorus brimming with infectious hooks. Though massaged by Bruce, the lyrics express Nicko's concern with the impending possibility of human cloning. The line "Create a beast made a man without a soul, is it worth the risk a war of God and man?" basically sums up Nicko's feelings on the matter.

"I personally believe that God created man and it's only God's right to create a human being because only He can give you a soul. When man attempts to make man then it's a monster in a test tube. A genetically created human can't have a soul to my mind," says the drummer with conviction. "Funny thing was when I played it to Adrian and he asked what it was about. He said he'd had an idea for cloning song too. So I told him he could bugger off with his cloning idea 'cause this was my only song and he's had hundreds!" says Nick before letting rip with a patented McBrain belly laugh.

If any doubts remained about Maiden being just the Steve Harris show in the studio then surely the group dynamics and shared songwriting on offer throughout *Dance Of Death* and, particularly on 'New Frontier', ought to put a final nail in them.

"It was only really like that in the early days because we had so much stored material and then because the others didn't really want to write that much anyway!" recollects Steve. "Over the last few albums there's been a tremendous amount of teamwork and sharing of the load, and it's a major relief for me because it helps take Maiden in different directions. As for 'New Frontier', the bottom line is that it's a good song – if it wasn't then it wouldn't be on the album."

If *Dance Of Death* has a heart then it has to be the poignant strains of 'Paschendale'. Unlikely as it sounds, the song was written by Maiden's resident commercial songwriter Adrian Smith, who decided that he'd have ago writing "a traditional Maiden epic" as he terms it. However, there is nothing traditional about 'Paschendale', surely Maiden's most spellbinding and epic moment since *Powerslave*'s 'Rime Of The Ancient Mariner'. Set in trenches of World War I-era France, Adrian, with help from Steve's captivating lyrics and melodies, paints an ultra-vivid picture of the sheer tragic pointlessness of war, punctuated with moments of exemplary courage and the glow of camaraderie. As Bruce remarks, purely as an observer, "the beauty of 'Paschendale' isn't in the epic-ness of the song – although you have to admit it is a powerful and stirring body of music – but the detail". He continues: "It's got a little guitar riff at the beginning – not the big heavy one, but a little plaintive one. When I was in Army cadets at school we used to go out on night exercises and they'd fire these parachute flares and star shells that would go up into the sky emitting an eerie, ghostly light as they twinkled and illuminated before falling back down. That eerie, twinkling sound that the flares made is the exact same sound of that small riff at the beginning of the song. As soon as I heard it shivers shot down my spine."

'Face In The Sand' has yet another first for Nicko – it marks the first time he was asked to record with a double bass drum ("Its like being asked to write with your left hand when you've been right handed all your life – it's bloody difficult!" bemoans Nick.) A moody, dark and eastern melody builds up into a blazing chant of accusation as Bruce pours his scorn onto the world. Lyrically, the song allows Bruce to vent his frustrations and cynicism over the TV and media coverage of the second Gulf War, which was raging as the album was being recorded. "I remember thinking about the desert sands as an image and how it moves and shifts with time," he reveals. "Specifically what I was thinking was that whatever empires you attempt to build – whether they are British, American, Iraqi or whatever, they'll all crumble and fade away into something else. So, to my mind at least, the best thing you can ever hope for, if you were to leave anything behind, is just an imprint in the sand – and the image of a reverse face in the sand came to mind. And that's about the most permanence as you'll ever get."

'Age Of Innocence', the second track that guitarist Dave Murray brought in to make the album, is a harder but bluesier number, reminiscent of UFO's finest moments. Lyrically, though, it is Steve's turn to vent as he has a long overdue go at the British Judicial system, commonly believed to be little more than a joke among many a proud Englishman. "We're not into writing political songs but I've had one or two incidents myself that have left me steaming with the unfairness of the system," fumes Steve. "It's got to the point where as a Dad I don't feel my kids are safe these days sometimes. It's not just about a protective parent thing, it's that feeling that we've lost any sense of natural justice and I think a lot of people are thinking the same things as me too."

Finishing the album is 'Journeyman', perhaps Maiden's most contemplative song in two decades. Not since 'Prodigal Son' (from 1981's *Killers* album) have the band recorded a semi-acoustic track or 'ballad'. But as Steve maintains, "it felt right – so we went with it". The nay sayers and knockers of Iron Maiden would surely struggle to get their blinkered views around the subtle charms of Bruce's wistful tale of *carpe diem*. Like the song says, you either use it or lose it. "We did record a version with an electric backing," reveals Bruce. "I'm sure we'll end up using it as a B-side sometime but, in the end, after all the battering that we've given the listener over the last hour of music it just seemed right to play out with something totally unexpected and left field."

"When Steve said, 'why don't we do it acoustically?' you could have knocked me over with a fucking feather!" laughs Bruce, with obvious glee. "We even made Nicko play with little softy-type sticks that were halfway between a stick and a brush and suddenly there was just such a great vibe to the song. Everybody seems open to that sort of experimentation now which is fantastic! I know what this band is capable of because I can hear them noodling around in the dressing room. They play all these great soulful guitar things that no one ever hears. If we all got together and decided to play something like that people wouldn't believe it was Iron Maiden, I swear. Maybe in the past we had this sort of unconscious self-censorship going on, as in 'We can't play that, we're Iron Maiden,' I don't know. Whatever it was seems to have gone and it's really opened out which is very good news."

Out of the Gers/Bergman "dance of death" concept the album's artwork was developed to become the sinister and dark carnival that you see today. The gorgeous sleeve photos were shot by photographer Simon Fowler at Luton Hoo mansion, the exact same location in which the late, great Stanley Kubrick directed his final masterpiece of burlesque, *Eyes Wide Shut*, with Tom Cruise and Nicole Kidman.

"That place had a very odd vibe to it," says Janick of Luton Hoo. "We really wanted to capture the atmosphere of it, too, as there is an uneasiness to it. I actually went for a walk around the mansion and it was pretty unsettling. When you go into an old place like that you soak up the atmosphere and it was all very gothic and made me feel really quite uncomfortable."

The band hit the road in late May, taking the headline slot at Donington on the first night of its now weekend-long run under the "Download" monicker. The 45,000 Maiden fans there were among the very first to hear what the band had spent the last six months working on as 'Wildest Dreams' nestled comfortably in among the regular Maiden classics – alongside a long overdue return of 'Die With Your Boots On'.

Earlier in the day, selected members of the media had been invited to hear tracks from the album on a specially designed Maiden "battle" bus. The luxurious road liner was decorated with a huge Maiden logo down each side, while its interior was plastered with Maiden artwork from over the years. Having already completed mixing on the album by early May for a September release, both Sanctuary and EMI were keen that no one should get any advance copies of the record and leak it onto the Internet. Yet with the band about to play in front of so many people on a summer tour it would be a wasted opportunity not to take advantage of the time and satisfy all the local press and media requests in each country. To that end Maiden's listening bus made perfect sense as journalists could hear the new record and then interview the band. And for Maiden the idea was a winner.

Throughout the summer tour Maiden adopted a stage set that reflected the entire history of the band, as various album Eddies were draped over the vast, mainly outdoor, stadium venues around Europe. Indeed the "new" Eddie came in two variants – a walking Edward the Great (complete with royal robe and crown, who was ready to do a nightly battle with Janick on stage) and a second, much larger, silver Eddie "Head" straight from the cover of *Visions Of The Beast*, the double DVD set released in June 2003, which collected together the band's entire 28 promo videos from *Women In Uniform* onwards.

As an international act capable of headlining major events world wide, even while recording of *Dance Of Death* was still underway the band's touring agency, K2, had begun to line up concert dates across the globe in order to take advantage of the summer festival season. Yet instead of the usual album/promo/tour cycle that Maiden had grown used to over the years the band opted for a very different schedule involving two separate tours over a nine-month period. The first would be a Greatest Hits tour dubbed the Give Me Ed 'Til I'm Dead tour (only the band's second ever, following the Ed Hunter trek of 1999). This saw the band play a series of huge outdoor shows across Europe, including all the major rock festivals such as Rock Am Ring in Germany, Roskilde in Holland, Donington in the UK and on into France, Italy, Spain, eastern Europe and Scandinavia – where Maiden are front-page news in the daily papers alongside acts such as The Rolling Stones as well as the new pop acts.

But the Give Me Ed tour was only half of an ambitious plan, as Maiden hoped to not only knock the festival crowds dead with a set of back-to-back classics, but return only a matter of weeks later with a very different live set themed around the *Dance Of Death* album. To play the same markets twice in six months is a risk for any band that tours with a large (and expensive) production, but it was a challenge that the Maiden camp faced head on.

"We really wanted to do things differently," says Bruce adamantly. "We wanted to break the routine of recording an album, doing promo for it then doing the album tour, then going on to do it again on a bigger level. We found that every time we did what I'd term a 'best of'-type tour – festivals, shows or the Ed Hunter tour – then we'd do fantastic business. So we wondered whether we could do a Greatest Hits tour with say three or four new numbers in there. Of course, that means the visions between the two types of tour start to get a bit blurred. Since we were booked to do a summer tour in 2003 anyway we figured that we could do a greatest hits set and drop in a new song or two because the album had been recorded. Then while we were traversing the globe do the promo for it at the same time. That way people could hear us do a new song live instead of hearing us just talking about playing live."

The Give Me Ed Tour was then taken to the USA and Canada, where they teamed up with special guests Ronnie James Dio and Motorhead to tour coast to coast for six weeks. This part of the tour included sell-out shows at legendary venues such as New York's Madison Square Garden and a return to Long Beach Arena.

On returning to the UK the band only had a few weeks to turnaround an entirely new set and production, including all rehearsals, so preparations were quite intense. The band had recorded the album as live as possible, but with such operatic and intense arrangements as the title track, 'Dance Of Death', and 'Paschendale' in place, work needed to be done to get the songs to deliver live. By the second week of October the full production set was pieced together in secret at the Brighton Exhibition Centre. The new dramatic stage quickly took shape, together with Eddie's new incarnation – Death himself.

22 *Dancing With Death On Tour*

Iron Maiden kicked off the European leg of the Dance Of Death world tour on 19 October in Debrecen, Hungary and culminated it 34 shows later with a triumphant sold-out date at London's 18,000-seater Earl's Court arena. The 3-month trek wound its way through 17 different countries playing in front of some 350,000 people – by far the band's biggest tour since their supposed commercial "peak" in the late '80s. The stage set was built around a medieval castle design, possibly a reference to the gates of Montsegur, and featured two grim reaper-style Eddie statue's standing guard on the castle's walls. The show's 30-foot backdrops referenced every period of Maiden's history when the appropriate album and single sleeves were rolled on during each song, from old favourites such as *Beast* and *Run To The Hills*, the surprise additions of 'Can I Play With Madness' and the often overlooked *X Factor* classic 'Lord Of The Flies'. There were also newer, far more surreal, designs for 'Rainmaker' and 'No More Lies'.

What separated the Dance Of Death tour from previous Maiden outings was the sheer sense of drama, particularly during the twin set peaks of the title track, which saw Bruce don a flamboyant cape and Venetian mask for his storytelling role of night terrors and dancing demons, and the truly epic 'Paschendale'. Undoubtedly the evening's highlight, 'Paschendale' saw the stage bathed in blood reds and peppered with blinding white flashes to simulate the impact of artillery ordinance. The song built from its mournful, plaintive beginnings with a helmeted Bruce draped over hastily erected barbed wire barriers, his battered trench coat flapping in the wind, into a thunderous climax of passion and fury with the three guitarists battling out their respective solos. Not since 'Rime Of The Ancient Mariner' had Maiden demanded so much attention from their live audience and they in turn rewarded the faithful with a sweeping journey through the front lines of World War I.

As ever, there were still those with a differing view, as a vocal minority expressed discomfort with the band's decision to move their show into an overly theatrical realm. Bruce, in particular, attracted some criticism for his stage costumes, but the singer takes such comments in his stride: "I used to dress up before this – I had the Egyptian mask for 'Powerslave' on the World Slavery tour in 1984 and I had that glowing jacket for the Somewhere In Time tour too. So this isn't the first time I've taken to dressing up onstage as has been erroneously reported."

For Bruce the costumes are a small part of a more significant cultural change within the Maiden camp – in terms of how the band approached the live show for Dance Of Death. Both Steve and Bruce are in complete agreement that with an album as intricate as *Dance Of Death*, Maiden were committed to pushing their audience's perceptions of what the band could achieve as a live act.

"It is a tough set to get into in a lot of ways, in terms of how much is going on musically," admits Steve. "We now have a set that demands that you really listen to it, specifically songs like 'Paschendale', 'Rainmaker' and 'Journeyman'. I always prefer the songs that you can throw yourself around to like 'Dance Of Death' and I must admit I wasn't sure how 'Journeyman' was going to work live in a Maiden show. When the others started to sit down with their acoustic guitars – I thought, 'Fuck that! I'm not ready for my Val Doonican chair just yet!'" laughs the bassist with typical candour. "I love the unexpectedness of it though, because no one could have thought that Iron Maiden would attempt an acoustic song like 'Journeyman' on record let alone perform it live as a first encore."

"When we sat down to plan this tour we agreed that we were going to make a lot of changes to breathe new life into the Iron Maiden live show. We agreed that we would cut out the ranting, yelling and rabble rousing that I usually do, however enjoyable it is, and concentrate on showing people that we knew we had made a really great quality album. One thing I really wanted to get across was just how seriously we took that record and how proud of it we really are. The only way to do that, I believe anyway, is to make things as dramatic as possible," says the singer with a steely eyed look.

"If anyone has the view that all rock 'n' roll singers have to be thin, skinny waifs wearing the right clothes at all times then they obviously belong to that 'does my bum look big in this?' pretentious club and they're never gonna like it whatever we do. That's their loss. I read the postings on the Maiden message boards too, so I've seen all the opinions, both good and bad, and the costumes are there for those people who do like the drama. You can't please everyone all the time. I've read postings from people the day after a show saying that they thought 'Journeyman' was the high point and that it was amazing that Maiden were choosing to start an encore with such a different and emotional song. Then straight underneath it you get the negative one saying, 'Bollocks! I thought it was cringe worthy and I felt so uncomfortable I just didn't know what to do'. And you know what?" asks the singer rhetorically, "that's called opening up your mind, and yes, it can be uncomfortable, but its also necessary in order to grow!

"It would be very easy for a band like Iron Maiden to slip into predictability and churn out sound bites and songs that say nothing at all and have no reaction from anybody. But I'd rather have a reaction through provocation than have no reaction at all. Above all else I want people to walk away from an Iron Maiden show and say to themselves, 'Now what? Where are they going next?' I want to put a question mark over people's perceptions of what Iron Maiden can do!"

Having already made their controversial position about cutting back on the amounts of touring very clear prior to the tour, some 30 dates into the trek Steve Harris was relieved (and exhausted) enough to know that the band had made the right decision. "Without doubt I know we're making the right choice aiming for fewer, bigger shows," he sighed, having just spent an hour on the chiropractor's bench loosening for the two-hour show. "Every time we tour during the winter everyone gets bloody sick. Not just the band but the crew as well. This last tour I've had the flu, then Bruce got it which meant we had to cancel a couple of shows, and Nicko has it right now. I know we're making the right decision to focus on bigger gigs where we can deliver the right type of show."

One aspect of touring that is often overlooked is how band feelings can change when playing the newer material to crowds who may not yet have heard it. As a tour progresses it's inevitable that opinions can differ over what is working and what, if any, changes have to be made either to a set or to a specific song. For the first few dates of the Dance Of Death tour there was no 'Wrathchild' in the set and the band quickly realised that the early numbers needed another lift before they assaulted the crowd with a large section of newer and more progressive material. But, even several months after the initial rush of finishing the record, seeing it race up the charts and playing it on tour alongside the classics, Maiden were still royally chuffed with the album, which, for a band of "bloody minded perfectionists" is a minor miracle.

"I still think it's the best album we've done since *Seventh Son* for sure," said Bruce in December 2003. "The songs have really developed live and if anything now I've been out performing it the song 'Dance Of Death' itself has to be one of my favourite songs on the whole tour. At the start of it all I sensed that a few people around us and in the media were kind of embarrassed by the song ['Dance Of Death'] because they felt it was a bit Jethro Tull-like and that meant they looked down their noses at it. Basically, I think that they didn't know whether it was OK to like it or be professionally embarrassed by it, but all you've got to do is look at the audience reaction and they love it. I couldn't care less what these pretentious journalist-types think of it. That said, it's a close run thing between 'Dance Of Death' and 'Paschendale' when it comes to which is my favourite to play live. 'Paschendale' has lived up to all the expectations I had for it prior to the tour. When Nicko starts up the little hi-hat intro you can physically hear an awed hush from the crowd, 'Wow, they're actually gonna play it!'" says the gleeful singer.

Indeed, while *Brave New World* certainly benefited from Bruce's return, Maiden's phenomenal concert run across Europe in the latter half 2003 underlined the premise that, career wise, the band were enjoying a second coming to rival anything from the 1980s. Clearly there was a sense of momentum behind Iron Maiden that hadn't been felt for years. Ultimately *Dance Of Death* was benefiting not only from the goodwill but was also fulfilling its function by being a vital enough album that many lapsed older fans had rediscovered their love for the band while new, younger fans were switching on in their thousands. If, as Bruce suggests, Iron Maiden's intention while making *Dance...* had been to force people to reinterpret their perceptions of the band, then it was certainly mission accomplished.

"I know that there is this feeling among fans – and within the band to a degree – that *Dance Of Death* isn't just another Iron Maiden album, but I like to feel like that about all of them," says Steve candidly. "We've never consciously short-changed anyone with a record that wasn't the best we could do at that particular time and I'm proud of that."

It's long been known that Maiden's singer has enjoyed the odd flight in-between shows – during the US Give Me Ed summer trek Bruce was even operating an informal taxi service across the States for band members and their families whenever the occasion demanded. But during the autumn of 2002 Bruce fulfilled a lifelong dream when he was granted a commercial airline pilot's license after completing an intensive British Airway's training course. This in turn led Bruce to take up a job as a co-pilot for Greek-owned Astraeus airlines, which operates many flights out of the London airports. During Maiden's downtime none of this would present a problem and Bruce could easily fly quick shuttle jaunts around Europe one day and turn up to present his radio show on the digital-based BBC Radio 6 the next. But how could this possibly be done when Maiden were on tour? In the past Bruce had been accused by some factions of being more concerned with his activities outside of Maiden then his duties within it but, as the man himself readily admits, he has an extremely low boredom threshold.

"Look at the words to 'Journeyman' if you want explanations as to why I do the things I do," points out Captain Dickinson. "You can choose to lock yourself away in your own little world or you can choose to go and do something mad and glorious – it's all up to you. I've never wanted to be someone who looks back on my life and says, 'I wish I'd done that when I was still young enough'. If you want to do it work out a way and go do it!"

During the European leg of the Dance Of Death tour Bruce and Maiden took the piloting angle one stage further to cook up a once-in-a-lifetime experience for fans and media alike on what became known as Bruce Air...

"Bruce Air or Beast Airlines as it might end up being known as was something that Steve and I cooked up over the summer," reveals the beaming pilot. "I'm currently flying commercial airliners regularly now, so very feasibly we can sell plane tickets to fans wishing to travel to overseas Maiden gigs quite easily. We put together a short list of places like Paris, Copenhagen, Barcelona – Steve was quite hot on Wroclaw in Poland 'cause he figured it was such an unusual place to visit that loads of people would go to see us there, but once the bean counters got involved the red tape started to be too much so we canned that. But in the end our record company hijacked the idea for a Paris one for their own ends and we took out a plane-load of TV and journalists the day we played Bercy, and so we did a special fan-only flight to Dublin the week after. Nicko came along on both trips to do his air hostess bit and we both went up and down the aisles on the plane signing stuff."

The Paris trip proved to be a particularly exhausting affair for Bruce as it was the morning of England's historic Rugby World Cup victory and the nerve-wracking extra time play put serious pressure on the mid-morning take-off time as 200 hyped-up Brits refused to board until the final whistle blew! Upon landing in Paris there was an interminable round of pics and TV interviews to be conducted before Maiden's multi-skilled singer headed off to the venue to play in front of 16,000 rabid Frenchmen. That might have been enough for most front men but not SuperBruce who, along with Nicko, then turned out for the midnight after show party before getting up early next morning for yet another press conference. By 3pm Bruce was back in the pilot's seat for what turned out to be a hairy flight back to London's Gatwick airport! (Just don't mention the wind shear...)

As ever, the Maiden machine marches on. At the time of writing the band are scheduled to head off to South America and Japan for the Far Eastern leg of the Dance Of Death tour and the pumping 'No More Lies' has been chosen as a third single from the album. There may be fewer live dates in the future but clearly there's no slowing down to be seen.

"I'm really looking forward to what we come up with next, musically," enthuses Bruce. "There is so much more music left in the band, and whether millions of people are interested in it is really of no concern to me 'cause I am interested in it, and that's the most important thing. That's what keeps me going. Everybody seems to be really open minded at the moment, discussing things and bouncing ideas around and that is great.

"For example, in principle none of us are that opposed to doing something with an orchestra, but not the kind of things that other people have done. Nothing like Kiss or Metallica where you play your regular show with a big orchestra in the background. I love what the guy did when he took some of the themes from the Queen songs and turned them into a symphony. You can hardly recognise them, as it's a complete piece of classical music based around the themes of the songs. I like that. It's not heavy metal. It shows you just can't keep a good tune down."

Now at the very pinnacle of their careers it's both refreshing and reassuring to know that, far from becoming a touring icon band with little more validity than a cabaret act, Iron Maiden are still firing on all creative cylinders. Indeed, if Bruce has anything to do with it then the band will be making albums every year until they die.

"Yeah, I do get bored easily I know," admits the singer / fencer / novelist / airline pilot / BBC radio DJ. "There are lots of possibilities of things we could do in the future," he hints. "Steve and I even talked about writing two albums out of the material we came up with on this last lot of writing, so we'll see what happens."

Index